The Ethics of Leadership

JOANNE B. CIULLA, PH.D.

THOMSON

WADSWORTH

Australia • Canada • Mexico • Singapore • Spain
United Kingdom • United States

THOMSON

TM

WADSWORTH

Philosophy Editor: Steve Wainwright
Assistant Editor: Lee McCracken
Editorial Assistant: Anna Lustig
Marketing Manager: Worth Hawes
Marketing Assistant: Justine Ferguson
Project Manager, Editorial Production:
  Barrett Lackey
Print Buyer: Robert King

Permissions Editor: Bob Kauser
Production Service: Shepherd, Inc.
Copy Editor: Beth Baugh
Cover Designer: design by Yvo
Cover Printer: Webcom Limited
Compositor: Shepherd, Inc.
Printer: Webcom Limited

Printed in Canada
1 2 3 4 5 6 7 06 05 04 03 02

For more information about our products, contact us at:
Thomson Learning Academic Resource Center
1-800-423-0563
For permission to use material from this text,
contact us by: **Phone:** 1-800-730-2214
Fax: 1-800-730-2215
Web: http://www.thomsonrights.com

Library of Congress Control Number:
2002104099

ISBN: 0-15-506317-0

Wadsworth/Thomson Learning
10 Davis Drive
Belmont, CA 94002-3098
USA

Asia
Thomson Learning
5 Shenton Way #01-01
UIC Building
Singapore 068808

Australia
Nelson Thomson Learning
102 Dodds Street
South Melbourne, Victoria 3205
Australia

Canada
Nelson Thomson Learning
1120 Birchmount Road
Toronto, Ontario M1K 5G4
Canada

Europe/Middle East/Africa
Thomson Learning
High Holborn House
50/51 Bedford Row
London WC1R 4LR
United Kingdom

For my parents Andrew and Corrine Ciulla

Table of Contents

Chapter 6

Moral Leadership and Culture   227

Credits   275

Acknowledgments

This book is the result of an evolutionary process that took place over 10 years of teaching ethics to leadership majors at the Jepson School of Leadership Studies. I owe a debt of gratitude to my students for thinking out loud with me about the complexities of ethics and leadership, and helping me sort out what material does and doesn't work in the classroom. In addition I want to thank my colleague Dr. Terry L. Price for his input into the course and the readings in this text. I am also grateful to my friend Dr. Robert C. Solomon for encouraging me to write this text and for his insights into Nietzsche.

For many years, I have had the pleasure of teaching programs on ethics and leadership in a variety of organizations. The short case studies in the book come from real problems that people in these programs have faced. My thanks to all of those people who have shared their stories with me so that I could write these cases and students could learn from them.

Lastly, as always, I am grateful to my husband René for his love and support.

Introduction

ETHICS AND THE STUDY OF LEADERSHIP

The study of ethics is about what we should do and what we should be. It's about right, wrong, good, evil and the relationship of humans to each other and to other living things. Leadership is a particular type of relationship, the hallmarks of which are power and/or influence, obligation, and responsibility. By understanding ethics we gain a better understanding of the leader/follower relationship. The central issues in ethics are also the central issues of leadership. They include the problems of authenticity, self-interest, and self-discipline, and moral obligations of justice, duty, and the greatest good. In leadership we see morality magnified. The actions of leaders usually have a greater impact on a greater number of people than the actions of other individuals. We also look to leaders as role models. Hence, their moral failures and triumphs carry a greater weight and volume than those of nonleaders.

We often hear people say that leaders should be held to a "higher" ethical standard. The problem with this idea is that it assumes it is acceptable for everyone else to have a lower ethical standard. The ethical standards of followers are just as important as those of leaders. The morality of followers can have a strong influence on the morality their leaders. People often get the leaders they deserve.

Some leadership scholars don't like to use the word "followers" because they think it carries a negative connotation. They prefer to use words like "associate" or "constituent" instead. I have no problem with the word "follower." Its denotation is clear and in reality the leader/follower relationship is fluid—sometimes leaders are followers and sometimes followers are leaders. We all play both roles. Good followers have many of the same qualities as good leaders. As you will see in this text, the ethics of leadership is not about *higher* or *lower* standards, but about the distinctive moral challenges that come from the role of leaders and their relationship to followers.

THE DEFINITION PROBLEM

Leadership scholars are often concerned about the definition of leadership. Some believe that if they could agree on a common definition of leadership, they would be better able to understand it. The meaning of a word is not decided by scholars. It is determined by the way people in a culture use it and think about it. The denotation of the word "leadership" stays basically the same in English, with slight variations that tell us about the values and paradigms of leadership in a certain place and at a certain time. Joseph Rost collected 221 definitions of leadership, ranging from the 1920s to the 1990s.[1] All of these definitions generally say the same thing—leadership is about one person getting other people to do something. Where the definitions differ is in how leaders motivate their followers and who has a say in the goals of the group or organization. As you look at the following definitions from American sources, think about the famous leaders of that era. What were they like? What were their followers like? What events shaped the ideas behind these definitions?

1920s [Leadership is] the ability to impress the will of the leader on those led and induce obedience, respect loyalty and cooperation.

1930s Leadership is a process in which the activities of many are organized to move in a specific direction by one.

1940s Leadership is the result of an ability to persuade or direct men, apart from the prestige or power that comes from office or external circumstance.

1950s [Leadership is what leaders do in groups.] The leader's authority is spontaneously accorded him by his fellow group members.

1960s [Leadership is] acts by a person which influence other persons in a shared direction.

1970s Leadership is defined in terms of discretionary influence. Discretionary influence refers to those leader behaviors under control of the leader which he may vary from individual to individual.

1980s Regardless of the complexities involved in the study of leadership, its meaning is relatively simple. Leadership means to inspire others to undertake some form of purposeful action as determined by the leader.

1990s Leadership is an influence relationship between leaders and followers who intend real changes that reflect their mutual purposes.

---

[1]Rost, Joseph, *Leadership for the Twenty-First Century* (Praeger, 1991), see pp. 47–102.

Notice that in the 1920s leaders "impressed" their will on those they led. In the 1940s they "persuaded" followers, in the 1960s they "influenced" them, and in the 1990s leaders and followers influenced each other. Although these definitions are social and historical constructions, they are also personal. There are still people today who subscribe to the 1920 model of leadership. The difference between the definitions rests on a normative question: How should leaders treat followers and How should followers treat leaders? What is and what ought to be the nature of their relationship to each other?

Leadership scholars who worry about constructing the ultimate definition of leadership are asking the wrong question, but inadvertently trying to answer the right one. The ultimate question about leadership is not "What is the definition of leadership?" The whole point of studying leadership is, "What is good leadership?" The use of word good here has two senses: morally good and technically good or effective.

ETHICS AND EFFECTIVENESS

In the center of many public debates about leadership today is the question, "What constitutes a good leader?" We want our leaders to be effective and morally good. Nonetheless, we are often more likely to say leaders are good when they are effective but not moral, than they are good when they are moral, but not effective. Leaders face the same challenge found in all areas of professional ethics. They have to stay in business, produce results, or get reelected to be leaders. If they are not minimally effective at doing these things, their morality as leaders is usually irrelevant, because they are no longer in charge. Some people justify their ruthless climb to the top with the claim that when they get there they will do ethical things. In leadership, one is often tempted to put what is effective before what is ethical. We hope for leaders who know when ethics should and shouldn't take priority over effectiveness. For example, in business this may mean knowing when employee safety or protection of the environment are more important than profits. History tends to dismiss as irrelevant the morally good leaders who are unsuccessful. President Jimmy Carter was a man of great personal integrity, but during his presidency, he was ineffective and generally considered a poor leader. However, after he left the White House Carter took on other leadership roles in which he was very successful. He is now respected and admired as a leader.

The conflict between ethics and effectiveness and the definition problem are apparent in what I have called, "the Hitler problem."[2] The answer to the question "Was Hitler a good leader?" is yes if a leader is defined as someone

---

[2]Ciulla, Joanne B., "Leadership Ethics: Mapping the Territory," in *Ethics the Heart of Leadership*, ed. Joanne B. Ciulla (Praeger, 1998), pp. 3–26, and in *Business Ethics Quarterly*, January, 1995, pp. 5–28.

who is effective at getting people together to perform some task. The answer is no, if the leader gets the job done, but the job itself is immoral or is done using immoral means. In other words, leadership is about more than being effective at getting things done. The quality of leadership also depends on the ethics of the means and the ethics of the ends of a leader's actions. Robin Hood steals from the rich to give to the poor. He uses unethical means to achieve morally worthy ends. Most of us want leaders who do the right thing, the right way, and for the right reasons and are personally moral. It's a tall order, one that shows why ethics is so important for leadership development. As you read this text you will find this tension between ethics and effectiveness in a number of the readings.

THE DESIGN AND OVERVIEW OF THIS TEXT

This text is designed not only for a course on ethics and leadership, but also as a companion text in other courses in professional ethics, such as business, public administration, law, and education. The book consists of selections from major Eastern and Western philosophic texts. Because this is a text on applied ethics, each chapter includes an introduction that helps the reader frame how the ethical theories apply to leadership issues. Each philosophic reading is preceded by an introduction that helps those without philosophy backgrounds understand who the author is and the context of the selection.[3] After each philosophic reading there is a short case or story designed to help students apply the ethical concepts in the reading to practical problems. The cases in this book are not geared toward any particular business or profession. They are designed to illustrate particular types of moral situations. When students read these cases, they are encouraged to think about how the issues in the case apply to problems in their own profession or area of study. Instructors who use this as a companion text will probably want to supplement it with cases specific to the topic of their course. Last, the chapters in this text also contain readings from leadership studies, literature, management, and anthropology that further integrate the discussion of ethics with leadership.

Following this introduction is a short case called "The Parable of the Sadhu." The case raises a number of the ethical issues found in this text, such as questions about individual and group responsibility and leadership and cultural values.

---

[3]I use the convention of inserting a short biography of authors who are dead. Contemporary authors are identified by their field and university.

The first chapter starts with one of the most morally distinctive elements of leadership—how leaders use their power. Power is not inherently bad, but there are ethical and unethical uses of power. Leaders can use their power and authority for their own self-interest or the interest of others, or if they are lucky, they can use it for both. The readings in the first chapter present a set of challenging questions about the relationships among self-interest, power, and morality.

Chapters 2 though 4 look at leadership from the ethical frameworks of virtue, duty, and utility. Chapter 2 treats one of the most talked-about aspects of leadership today, the leader's moral character. The readings in this chapter discuss virtue and character development. They also explore the moral failures of leaders and make us reflect on how a leader's behavior in private life is related to his or her behavior as a leader. Chapter 3 focuses on the duties of leaders and followers. Hannah Arendt's description of Eichmann helps us examine the moral responsibilities of followers to object or resist following orders when they disagree with their leaders.

Leaders are obliged to promote the greatest good for their constituents and organizations. Chapter 4 helps us reflect on this obligation. However, it also looks at the fundamental conflict we face when their moral principles conflict with their obligation to serve their constituents. This kind of conflict highlights the need for leaders to develop a moral perspective and imagination that facilitates a deeper understanding of what really constitutes the greatest good.

In chapter 5 readings on charismatic leadership, servant leadership, and transformational leadership provide the reader with an opportunity to critically reflect on the moral implications of these leadership theories. The case study of Jim Jones and the People's Temple highlights the emotional nature of charismatic leaders and the potential dangers inherent in the relationship of charismatic leaders to their followers. Robert C. Solomon's provocative article on charismatic leadership and trust ties together the moral and emotional aspects of leadership.

Leadership and ethics vary across cultures in obvious ways, but they are fairly uniform across cultures in less obvious ways. Chapter 6 looks at the question of ethical relativism and leadership: Are there universal ethical values that should guide leaders of international organizations or leaders in cultures other than their own? In an increasingly interconnected world and diverse society, leaders are often forced to choose the values they think are best, regardless of the culture they live in or the culture of their followers. These choices are among the most difficult moral challenges leaders face today. The final article in the text is about Kofi Annan, a global leader who regularly makes these kinds of ethical choices on a global stage.

Case: The Parable of the Sadhu
Bowen H. McCoy

This case is a true story of what happened to Bowen McCoy when he went on a walking trip in the Himalayas. At the time of this story McCoy was a managing director of Morgan Stanley and president of Morgan Stanley Realty. The company had given him a six-month sabbatical leave. McCoy, who is also an ordained ruling elder of the United Presbyterian Church, said he wanted to use this time to travel and collect his thoughts. He spent the first three months walking 600 miles through 200 villages and climbing some 120,000 vertical feet. His only Western companion was an anthropologist who explained the culture to McCoy as they passed through the villages along the way.

The case sets the stage for a number of themes in this text. As you read the case, reflect on not only the ethics of the main characters, but the role of self-interest, influence, personal responsibility, cross-cultural ethics, and leadership in a group and between groups. Also think about the role a leader plays in setting and revising his or her goals and the goals of a group.

The Nepal experience was more rugged and adventuresome than I had anticipated. Most commercial treks last two or three weeks and cover a quarter of the distance we traveled.

My friend Stephen, the anthropologist, and I were halfway through the 60-day Himalayan part of the trip when we reached the high point, an 18,000-foot pass over a crest that we'd have to traverse to reach to the village of Muklinath, an ancient holy place for pilgrims.

Six years earlier I had suffered pulmonary edema, an acute form of altitude sickness, at 16,500 feet in the vicinity of Everest base camp, so we were understandably concerned about what would happen at 18,000 feet. Moreover, the Himalayas were having their wettest spring in 20 years; hip-deep powder and ice had already driven us off one ridge. If we failed to cross the pass, I feared that the last half of our "once in a lifetime" trip would be ruined.

The night before we would try the pass, we camped at a hut at 14,500 feet. In the photos taken at that camp, my face appears wan. The last village we'd passed through was a sturdy two-day walk below us, and I was tired.

During the late afternoon, four backpackers from New Zealand joined us, and we spent most of the night awake, anticipating the climb. Below we could see the fires of two other parties, which turned out to be two Swiss couples and a Japanese hiking club.

To get over the steep part of the climb before the sun melted the steps cut in the ice, we departed at 3:30 A.M. The New Zealanders left first, followed by Stephen and myself, our porters and Sherpas, and then the Swiss. The Japanese lingered in their camp. The sky was clear, and we were confident that no spring storm would erupt that day to close the pass.

At 15,500 feet, it looked to me as if Stephen were shuffling and staggering a bit, which are symptoms of altitude sickness. (The initial stage of altitude sickness brings a headache and nausea. As the condition worsens, a climber may encounter difficult breathing, disorientation, aphasia, and paralysis.) I felt strong, my adrenaline was flowing, but I was very concerned about my ultimate ability to get across. A couple of our porters were also suffering from the height, and Pasang, our Sherpa sirdar (leader), was worried.

Just after daybreak, while we rested at 15,500 feet, one of the New Zealanders, who had gone ahead, came staggering down toward us with a body slung across his shoulders. He dumped the almost naked, barefoot body of an Indian holy man—a sadhu—at my feet. He had found the pilgrim lying on the ice, shivering and suffering from hypothermia. I cradled the sadhu's head and laid him out on the rocks. The New Zealander was angry. He wanted to get across the pass before the bright sun melted the snow. He said, "Look, I've done what I can. You have porters and Sherpa guides. You care for him. We're going on!" He turned and went back up the mountain to join his friends.

I took a carotid pulse and found that the sadhu was still alive. We figured he had probably visited the holy shrines at Muklinath and was on his way home. It was fruitless to question why he had chosen this desperately high route instead of the safe, heavily traveled caravan route through the Kali Gandaki gorge. Or why he was almost naked and with no shoes, or how long he had been lying in the pass. The answers weren't going to solve our problem.

Stephen and the four Swiss began stripping off outer clothing and opening their packs. The sadhu was soon clothed from head to foot. He was not able to walk, but he was very much alive. I looked down the mountain and spotted below the Japanese climbers marching up with a horse.

Without a great deal of thought, I told Stephen and Pasang that I was concerned about withstanding the heights to come and wanted to get over the pass. I took off after several of out porters who had gone ahead.

On the steep part of the ascent where, if the ice steps had given way, I would have slid down about 3,000 feet, I felt vertigo. I stopped for a breather, allowing the Swiss to catch up with me. I inquired about the sadhu and Stephen. They said that the sadhu was fine and that Stephen was just behind. I set off again for the summit.

Case continued

Stephen arrived at the summit an hour after I did. Still exhilarated by victory, I ran down the snow slope to congratulate him. He was suffering from altitude sickness, walking 15 steps, then stopping, walking 15 steps, then stopping. Pasang accompanied him all the way up. When I reached them, Stephen glared at me and said: "How do you feel about contributing to the death of a fellow man?"

I did not fully comprehend what he meant.

"Is the sadhu dead?" I inquired.

"No," replied Stephen, "but he surely will be!"

After I had gone, and the Swiss had departed not long after, Stephen had remained with the sadhu. When the Japanese had arrived, Stephen had asked to use their horse to transport the sadhu down to the hut. They had refused. He had then asked Pasang to have a group of our porters carry the sadhu. Pasang had resisted the idea, saying that the porters would have to exert all their energy to get themselves over the pass. He had thought they could not carry a man down 1,000 feet to the hut, reclimb the slope, and get across safely before the snow melted. Pasang had pressed Stephen not to delay any longer.

The Sherpas had carried the sadhu down to a rock in the sun at about 15,000 feet and had pointed out the hut another 500 feet below. The Japanese had given him food and drink. When they had last seen him he was listlessly throwing rocks at the Japanese party's dog, which had frightened him.

We do not know if the sadhu lived or died.

Questions

1. Who is responsible for the well-being of the sadhu? What are the duties of the people involved in this case? What action would best serve the greatest good? What is the greatest good here?
2. Would the climbers have acted differently if the sadhu were a Western woman?
3. How are the problems in this case similar to problems that arise in organizations every day? What kinds of sadhus do people confront in everyday life?
4. Who were the leaders in this case? Were they "good" leaders? What do you think a good leader would do in this situation?

THE MORAL
CHALLENGES OF POWER
AND SELF-INTEREST

CHAPTER

1

INTRODUCTION

It might seem odd to begin an ethics text with an article on sources of power and influence. Power is one factor that makes the study of ethics and leadership different from other areas of applied ethics. One might even say that the ethics of a leader largely depends on how he or she gets, distributes, and exercises power and influence. We sometimes have a moral obligation to do something because we can do it or we have the resources to do it. Because leaders have power, they often have more and greater obligations and responsibilities. As you will see in Gary Yukl's article, leaders and followers may have many different kinds of power. We start with his article because these categories of power will come up again and again in some of the other readings in this text.

The reading from Plato's *Republic* helps us to think about justice, power, and self-interest. Thrasymachus, the protagonist in the dialogue, believes that for rulers, justice is whatever is in their own self-interest. Socrates argues that justice is in the interests of the followers, not the ruler, and because of this few people want to lead. The idea that just people are reluctant to lead explains why we are sometimes uncomfortable with those who seem too eager to take on leadership positions. We often feel better about giving leadership to individuals who are more circumspect and conscious of the responsibilities of power—in other words, the ones who know leadership is not necessarily in their best interest. Plato's "The Ring of Gyges" offers us a kind of moral experiment that helps us explore the temptations of power and self-interests when there is no accountability.

Our ideas about ethics and leadership come from the assumptions that we make about human nature. We all carry a theory of human nature around with us in our heads. This overview of "what people are like" determines how we treat people and how we think of our moral obligations to them. For example, the management theorist Douglas McGregor has described theory X and

1

theory Y perspectives on management. He said that theory X rests on the idea
that the average human being dislikes work and will avoid it if he or she can.
If people are really like this, leaders would have to coerce, control, direct, and
threaten people to get things done. This theory also implies that most people
are like sheep, that they don't want responsibility, and that they desire security
above all things.[1] In contrast to theory X, theory Y assumes that the average
human being does not dislike work and, under the right conditions, finds work
a source of satisfaction. It implies that people have the capacity to be creative
and to take and seek responsibility. If you believe theory Y, you will give people responsibility and try to help them find reward and meaning in their work.
If you believe theory X, you will have to use carrots and big sticks to get people to do what you want.

Thomas Hobbes paints a picture of human nature that many still subscribe to today. He believed that people are chiefly motivated by self-interest
and the desire for safety and self-preservation. As a result of this, in the
absence of a state, or in a state of nature, everyone is at war, because they are
all out to get what they want for themselves. This state of war is a state of fear,
which moves people to relinquish some of their liberty to a sovereign so they
can have security. This is not exactly theory X, but it's close.

We get a slightly different slant on leadership and morality from Niccoló
Machiavelli. He tells us that men are generally "simple and governed by their
present needs." Although Machiavelli says people want ethical leaders, he also
thinks it is very easy to fool them into believing a leader has good moral qualities when in fact he does not. (Today we call this "impression management.")
For Machiavelli, leaders should focus their attention on acquiring and maintaining their power. Like the character Thrasymachus in Plato's *Republic*,
Machiavelli argues that justice and morality must be used to serve the leader's
self-interest. The selections from the *Prince* clearly illustrate how the need to
get and hold on to power may conflict with moral leadership.

Machievelli and Hobbes start with the assumption that human nature is
such that all human action *is* based on self-interest. This position is called *psychological egoism*. The next reading in this chapter is from *Atlas Shrugged*, a
novel by Ayn Rand. In it, Rand argues that the problem with people is that
they should act according to their self-interest, but they don't because they are
misguided by conventional morality to make sacrifices for others who are not
worthy. She asserts that morality based on duty, the greatest good, and self-
sacrifice require people to relinquish their happiness for the happiness of others. Rand argues that ethics should be based on self-interest and that the other
moral theories in this text (especially Kant's) only make people weak and miserable. Rand's position, that one *ought* to act in one's self-interest is called *ethical egoism*.

---

[1]McGregor, Douglas, *The Human Side of Management* (New York: McGraw Hill, 1985), 33–34.

From Thrasymachus and Machiavelli to present-day writers, there have always been those who not only believe that leaders always act in their self-interest, but that they should do so. On the other extreme are those who argue that leadership is about serving the interests of others. This chapter raises a number of questions: *Is self-interest the only thing that motivates us? Should self-interest come before the interests of others or the greatest good? What are the legitimate ways for leaders to exercise power?* Perhaps the most provocative questions raised in this chapter are: *Can a moral leader be a successful leader? Does a leader have to be moral to be successful?*

Sources of Power and Influence

Gary Yukl

Gary Yukl is professor of organizational behavior at the State University of New York at Albany. The following essay is from his textbook, *Leadership in Organizations*, which is one of the standard texts for teaching the social science theories on leadership. In this essay Yukl provides an overview of the research on sources of power. Because leadership studies is by necessity an interdisciplinary field, it is useful to look at the descriptions of power that come from this area of leadership research and use them as a starting point for thinking about the moral implications of power that come up in the other readings in the chapter. For example, how leaders use their power to reward, punish, and distribute resources raise questions about justice and fairness. Referent power and the power that comes from a leader's personality and reputation, help us think about the moral character of leaders and their ability to model virtues and shape the moral environment of an organization. Last, it is particularly useful to reflect on a leader's ability to control information.

The essence of leadership is influence over followers. However, the influence process between a leader and followers is not unidirectional. Leaders influence followers, but followers also have some influence over leaders. Moreover, in large organizations, the effectiveness of middle-level and lower-level managers depends on their influence over superiors and peers as well as their influence over subordinates. Influence in one direction tends to enhance influence in other directions.

Power

Power generally refers to an agent's capacity to influence a target person, but the term has been used in different ways by different theorists (Dahl, 1957;

Grimes, 1978; House, 1988b; Jacobs, 1970; Kotter, 1985; Mintzberg, 1983; Pfeffer, 1981). Sometimes power means the agent's capacity to influence a target person's behavior, whereas at other times it means influence over the target person's attitudes as well as behavior. Sometimes power is defined in relative rather than absolute terms as the extent to which the agent has more influence over the target than the target has over the agent ("net power"). A variation of this definition is the target's capacity to influence the agent without fear of retaliation ("usable power"). Sometimes power refers to the agent's influence over a single target person, and sometimes power is measured in relation to multiple target persons. Sometimes power is used to mean potential influence over things as well as people. Finally, recognizing the difficulty of measuring potential influence, some people define power as the amount of influence actually exercised by the agent ("enacted power"). None of these definitions is inherently superior for all purposes, but for clarity of communication it is helpful to settle on one definition.

Power Types and Sources

Efforts to understand power usually involve distinctions among different types of power in organizations. French and Raven (1959) developed a taxonomy to classify different types of power according to their source (see Table 1-1). Some types of power correspond closely to some of Kelman's influence processes. Instrumental compliance is associated primarily with the use of reward and coercive power. Identification is associated primarily with use of referent power. Internalization is associated primarily with use of expert power.

Legitimate power cuts across all three types of influence processes and may involve elements of each of them (Kelman, 1974). The French and Raven taxonomy has influenced much of the research on power for the past three decades, but it does not include all of the power sources relevant to managers. For example, control over information is also a relevant power source for managers (Pettigrew, 1972; Yukl & Falbe, 1991).

TABLE 1-1   French and Raven Power Taxonomy

Reward	The target person complies in order to obtain rewards he or she believes are controlled by the agent.
Coercive power	The target person complies in order to avoid punishments he or she believes are controlled by the agent.
Legitimate power	The target person complies because he or she believes the agent has the right to make the request and the target person has the obligation to comply.
Expert power	The target person complies because he or she believes that the agent has special knowledge about the best way to do something.
Referent power	The target person complies because he or she admires or identifies with the agent and wants to gain the agent's approval.

Another conceptualization of power sources that is widely accepted is the dichotomy between "position power" and "personal power" (Bass, 1960; Etzioni, 1961). According to this two-factor conceptualization, power is derived in part from the opportunities inherent in a person's position in the organization, and in part from attributes of the agent and agent-target relationship. Research by Yukl and Falbe (1991) showed that these two types of power are relatively independent, and each includes several distinct but partially overlapping components. Position and personal determinants of power interact in complex ways, and sometimes it is difficult to distinguish between them.

Position Power

Position power includes potential influence derived from legitimate authority, control over resources and rewards, control over punishments, control over information, and control over the organization of the work and the physical work environment.

Formal Authority

Power stemming from formal authority is sometimes called legitimate power (French & Raven, 1959). Authority is based on perceptions about the prerogatives, obligations, and responsibilities associated with particular positions in an organization or social system. Authority includes the perceived right of one position occupant to influence specified aspects of the behavior of other position occupants. The agent has the right to make particular types of requests, and the target person has the duty to obey. For example, a manager usually has the legitimate right to establish work rules, give work assignments, and direct the task behavior of subordinates. The subordinates, in turn, usually have the legitimate right to request necessary information and assistance from the manager. Authority also involves the right of a person to exercise control over things, such as money, resources, equipment, and materials, and this control is another source of power.

As noted earlier, the influence processes associated with legitimate power are very complex, because compliance with authority may involve elements of internalization, identification, and instrumental compliance. People are more likely to obey legitimate rules and carry out legitimate requests if they have an internalized value that it is proper to obey authority figures, show respect for the law, and follow tradition. Moreover, people are more likely to comply with legitimate rules and requests if they identify with the organization (or social system) and are loyal to it, as compared to marginal or involuntary members who do not identify with it. Influence derived from legitimate power also has an instrumental aspect. Members agree to comply with rules and directions from leaders in return for the benefits of membership (March & Simon, 1958). The conditions for continued membership in an organization may be set forth in a formal, legal contract, but the agreement to comply with legitimate authority is usually an implicit mutual understanding. This implicit social contract is the ultimate basis for authority.

One prerequisite for acceptance of a person's authority is the perceived legitimacy of the person as an occupant of a leadership position in the organization. This aspect of legitimacy depends to a large extent on how the leader was selected. In earlier times, leaders were usually selected on the basis of bloodlines and rules of succession; for example, the eldest male child was first in line to succeed a ruler or inherit the family business. Now in most large organizations, leaders are usually appointed by superiors or elected by the membership. For example, the chief executive officer (CEO) of a corporation is appointed by the board of directors, and the president of a labor union is elected by the membership. The specific procedures for selecting a leader are usually based on tradition and the provisions of a legal charter or constitution. If a leader is selected in a way that deviates from the process considered legitimate by members, the authority of the leader is likely to be weakened. The importance of legitimate selection is evident in the concerted effort of most leaders to establish a recognized basis for their authority. Elected leaders are concerned about being able to claim a "mandate" by voters, and elaborate inauguration ceremonies are held by many kinds of leaders to formalize the transfer of power and enhance the legitimacy of their selection.

The perceived legitimacy of a request also depends on whether it falls within the agent's scope of authority. A person's scope of authority is the range of requests that can properly be made and the range of actions which can properly be taken. Scope of authority depends in large part on the influence needed to accomplish recognized role requirements and organizational objectives (Barnard, 1952). However, even when a leader's scope of authority is delineated by documents such as an organization charter, a written job description, or an employment contract, there usually remains considerable ambiguity (Davis, 1968). Reitz (1977, p. 468) provides some examples of the kinds of questions that may be raised about a leader's scope of authority:

> An executive can rightfully expect a supervisor to work hard and diligently; may he also influence the supervisor to spy on rivals, spend weekends away from home, join an encounter group? A coach can rightfully expect his players to execute specific plays; may he also direct their life styles outside the sport? A combat officer can rightfully expect his men to attack on order; may he also direct them to execute civilians whom he claims are spies? A doctor can rightfully order a nurse to attend a patient or observe an autopsy; may he order her to assist in an abortion against her will?

Questions about scope of authority are especially difficult in lateral relations. Even though a person has no direct authority over someone in a position outside of the chain of command, the person often has the legitimate right to make requests necessary to carry out job responsibilities, such as requests for information, supplies, support services, technical advice, and assistance in carrying out joint tasks.

A major reason for ambiguity about the legitimacy of a request is that people evaluate not only the agent's scope of formal authority, but also the extent to which the request is consistent with the basic values, principles, and traditions of the organization or social system. The legitimacy of a request may be questioned if it contradicts a basic value of the organization or the larger society to which members of the organization belong. For example, soldiers may disobey the order of an army general to shoot everyone in a village that has provided support to insurgents, because the soldiers perceive this to be use of excessive force and contrary to basic human rights.

Control over Resources and Rewards

Another source of power in organizations is control over resources and rewards. This control stems in part from formal authority. The higher a person's position in the authority hierarchy of the organization, the more control over scarce resources the person is likely to have. Executives have more control than middle managers, who in turn have more control than first-line managers. Executives have authority to make decisions about the allocation of resources to various subunits and activities, and in addition they have the right to review and modify resource allocation decisions made at lower levels.

Potential influence based on control over rewards is sometimes called reward power (French & Raven, 1959). Reward power depends not only on control over resources, but also on the perceptions of the target person that a request or assignment is feasible and, if carried out, will actually result in the promised reward. An attempt to use reward power will be unsuccessful if the agent lacks credibility or the requirements for obtaining the reward appear impossible.

One form of reward power is influence over compensation and career progress. Most managers are authorized to give pay increases, bonuses, or other economic incentives to deserving subordinates. Reward power is derived also from control over tangible benefits such as a promotion, a better job, a better work schedule, a larger operating budget, a larger expense account, more authority and responsibility, formal recognition of accomplishments (e.g., awards, commendations), and status symbols such as a larger office or a reserved parking space. The extent of a manager's authority and discretion to allocate rewards to subordinates varies greatly across organizations and from one type of management position to another within the same organization. Some managers have the opportunity to use all these rewards, whereas other managers are severely limited in their authority over rewards.

Reward power is also a source of influence over peers. Some organizations, especially those with a matrix structure (e.g., product managers, project managers), utilize the formal evaluations by a manager's peers in making decisions about pay increases or promotions. Another source of reward power in lateral relations is dependence on a peer for resources, information, assistance, or support that is not prescribed by the formal authority system. Trading of favors needed to accomplish task objectives is a common form of influence among peers in organizations, and research indicates that it is important for the success of middle managers (Cohen & Bradford, 1989; Kaplan, 1984; Kotter, 1982; Strauss, 1962).

Control over Punishments

Another source of power is control over punishments and the capacity to prevent someone from obtaining desired rewards. This form of power is sometimes called coercive power (French & Raven, 1959). The formal authority system of an organization and its traditions deal with the use of punishment as well as use of rewards. A leader's authority over punishments varies greatly across different types of organizations. The coercive power of military and political leaders is usually greater than that of corporate managers. Over the last two centuries, there has been a general decline in use of legitimate coercion by all types of leaders (Katz & Kahn, 1978). For example, managers once had the right to dismiss employees for any reason they thought was justified. The captain of a ship could flog sailors who were disobedient or who failed to perform their duties diligently. Military officers could execute a soldier for desertion or failure to obey an order during combat. Nowadays, these forms of coercive power are prohibited or sharply restricted in most nations.

Even though coercion has been one of the most common forms of leader influence throughout history, its frequent use may be due more to ignorance or to the psychological needs of some leaders than to demonstrated effectiveness. Even under extreme conditions where leaders have the power to torture and murder workers, coercion is often ineffective. Webber (1975) relates an example of the disastrous consequences resulting from reliance on coercion in a Nazi bomb factory using slave labor during World War II. The workers hindered production by persistently requesting detailed instructions and doing nothing constructive on their own initiative. They sabotaged production by improperly fitting the bomb fuses, and it was impossible for the guards to detect the sabotage and ensure minimal performance unless they watched each worker closely, which required nearly as many guards as slaves.

There are some situations in which coercion is appropriate, and historical accounts provide evidence of its effective use by political and military leaders in maintaining discipline and dealing with rebels and criminals. Nevertheless, coercion is effective only when applied to a small percentage of followers under conditions considered legitimate by a majority of them. When leaders are tempted to use coercion on a large scale against followers, it undermines their authority and creates a hostile opposition seeking to restrict their power or remove them from office (Blau, 1956).

Control over Information

Another important source of power is control over information. This type of power involves both the access to vital information and control over its distribution to others (Pettigrew, 1972). Some access to information results from a person's position in the organization's communication network. Managerial positions often provide opportunities to obtain information that is not directly available to subordinates or peers (Mintzberg, 1973, 1983). Boundary role positions (e.g., marketing, purchasing, public relations) provide access to important information about events in the external environment of an organization. However, it is not merely a matter of occupying a particular position and having information appear as if by magic; a person must be actively involved in cultivating a network of information sources and gathering information from them (Kotter, 1982).

A middle manager who is the only channel for downward communication of decisions made by superiors is in a position to interpret them selectively for subordinates and peers. In a similar manner, a leader who controls the flow of vital information about outside events has an opportunity to interpret these events for subordinates and influence their perception and attitudes (Kuhn, 1963). A manager may use deliberate distortion of information to persuade people that a particular course of action is desirable. Examples of information distortion include selective editing of reports and documents, biased interpretation of data, and presentation of false information. Some managers attempt to increase subordinate dependence on them by hoarding information necessary to solve task problems, plan operations, and make strategic decisions. In effect, control over information is used to enhance the manager's expertise and give the person more expert power than subordinates. If the leader is the only one who "knows what is going on," subordinates will lack evidence to dispute the leader's claim that an unpopular decision is justified by circumstances. Moreover, control of information makes it easier for a leader to cover up failures and mistakes that would otherwise undermine a carefully cultivated image of expertise (Pfeffer, 1977a).

Control over information is a source of upward influence as well as downward and lateral influence. When subordinates have exclusive access to information needed by superiors to make decisions, this advantage can be used as a source of influence over the superior's decisions. Some subordinates actively seek this type of influence by gradually assuming more and more responsibility for collecting, storing, analyzing, and reporting operating information. If a leader is completely dependent on a subordinate to interpret complex analyses of operating information, the subordinate may be invited to participate directly in making decisions based on these analyses (Korda, 1975). However, even without direct participation, a subordinate with information control will be able to influence a superior's decisions.

Personal Power

Personal power includes potential influence derived from task expertise, friendship and loyalty, and a leader's persuasive and charismatic qualities.

Expertise

A major source of personal power is expertise in solving problems and performing important tasks. This form of power is sometimes called expert power (French & Raven, 1959). Expertise is a source of power for a person only if others are dependent on the person for advice. The more important a problem is to the target person, the greater the power derived by the agent from possessing the necessary expertise to solve it. Dependency is increased when the target person cannot easily find another source of advice besides the agent (Hickson, Hinings, Lee, Schneck, & Pennings, 1971; Patchen, 1974).

It is not enough for the agent to possess expertise, the target person must recognize this expertise and perceive the leader to be a reliable source of information and advice. Sometimes a target person trusts the agent's expertise enough to carry out a request without receiving any explanation for it. A good example is the patient who takes medicine prescribed by a doctor without knowing what the medicine is or what effects it will have. However, it is rare to possess this much expert power. In most cases, the agent must support a proposal or request by making logical arguments and presenting evidence that appears credible.

In the short run, perceived expertise is more important than real expertise, and an agent may be able to fake it for a time by acting confident and pretending to be an expert. However, over time, as the agent's knowledge is put to the test, target perceptions of the agent's expertise are likely to become more accurate. Thus, it is essential for leaders to develop and maintain a reputation for technical expertise and strong credibility.

Reputation depends in part on actual expertise and in part on impression management. Actual expertise is maintained through a continual process of education and practical experience. For example, in many professions it is important to keep informed about new developments by reading technical publications and attending workshops and seminars. Evidence of expertise can be displayed in the forms of diplomas, licenses, and awards. At an opportune time, a person can refer casually to earlier accomplishments or positions of importance. However, the most convincing approach is to demonstrate expertise by solving important problems, making good decisions, providing sound advice, and successfully completing challenging but highly visible projects. An extreme tactic is to intentionally but covertly precipitate crises just to demonstrate the ability to deal with them (Goldner, 1970; Pfeffer, 1977a).

Specialized knowledge and technical skill will remain a source of power only as long as there is continued dependence on the person who possesses them. If a problem is permanently solved or others learn how to solve it by themselves, the agent's expertise is no longer valuable. Thus, people sometimes try to protect their expert power by keeping procedures and techniques shrouded in secrecy, by using technical jargon to make the task seem more complex and mysterious, and by destroying alternate sources of information about task procedures such as written manuals, diagrams, blueprints, and computer programs (Hickson et al., 1971).

Special expertise in dealing with critical problems is just as much a source of upward and lateral power as it is of downward power. A person's ability to perform a vital function that superiors or peers cannot do increases their dependence on him or her (Mechanic, 1962). Expert power is greatest for someone with rare skills who has high job mobility and cannot be replaced easily.

Friendship and Loyalty

Another important source of power is the desire of others to please a person toward whom they feel strong affection. This form of power is sometimes called referent power (French & Raven, 1959). People are usually willing to do special favors for a friend, and they are more likely to carry out requests made by someone they greatly admire. The strongest form of referent power for a leader involves the influence process called personal identification. People who identify with a leader want to be like the leader and to be accepted by him or her. As noted earlier, people tend to imitate the behavior of someone with whom they identify. Thus, a manager who is well liked and admired can have considerable influence over subordinates and peers by setting an example of proper and desirable behavior.

The referent power of a leader over subordinates depends on feelings of friendship and loyalty developed slowly over a long period of time. The referent power of a leader is increased by acting friendly and considerate, showing concern for the needs and feelings of others, demonstrating trust and respect, and treating people fairly. Referent power is diminished by acting in a hostile, rejecting, or arrogant manner. Over time, actions speak louder than words, and a leader who tries to appear friendly but manipulates and exploits people will lose referent power.

Subordinates are aware that a powerful boss has the potential to cause them great inconvenience or harm, and even the subordinates of a benevolent leader tend to be sensitive to subtle indications of approval and disapproval. Dependence on the whims of a powerful authority figure is especially disturbing for subordinates who have a strong need for independence. The potentially disturbing aspects of the status differential between leader and subordinate increase the importance of symbolic acts that downplay the differential. Whyte (1969) describes an effective production foreman who spent his time on the shop floor, wore the same kind of work clothes as subordinates, and was willing to pitch in and help subordinates when there was an equipment breakdown, even though it occasionally meant getting dirty. Whyte concludes that symbolic actions of this type demonstrate acceptance and respect for subordinates and build loyalty for a small expenditure in time and effort.

Another approach for increasing a leader's referent power is to select as subordinates people who are likely to identify with the leader. For example, the marketing vice president of a manufacturing company recruited other immigrants from his homeland for several years before he became vice president, and their loyalty and identification was so strong that he could get them to implement new marketing programs faster than any of the company's competitors. This strategy can be extended beyond a leader's immediate work unit by using political influence to select friends for sensitive positions in other parts of an organization.

Referent power is a major source of lateral influence over peers, and it is especially important for middle managers who depend on peers to provide necessary information, assistance, and resources (Kanter, 1982; Kaplan, 1984; Kotter, 1982). Lateral referent power is established by acting friendly and considerate, and by providing assistance, favors, and political support (Kaplan, 1984). Success in developing and maintaining referent power depends on interpersonal skills such as charm, tact, diploma, empathy, and humor.

Charisma

Charisma is a term used to describe a person who appears to have extraordinary ability and strong personal magnetism. Followers identify with a charismatic leader and experience an intense emotional attraction to him or her. The process of identification is usually faster and more intense for a charismatic leader than for a friendly but noncharismatic leader. The personal attributes of charismatic leaders are not well understood, but they appear to include qualities such as strong convictions, enthusiasm, and a dramatic, persuasive manner of speaking (Berlew, 1974; House, 1977). Charismatic leaders have insight into the needs, hopes, and values of followers and are able to motivate commitment to proposals and strategies for change. However, it is not clear yet whether charisma is best viewed as a distinct form of personal power, as a variation of referent power, or as merely an attribution by followers that sometimes occurs during the reciprocal influence process between a leader and followers.

REVIEW QUESTIONS

1. How has a leader's ability to control information changed in recent years?
2. What is the impact of increased access to information on the power and authority of leaders?
3. How do leaders' ethical values affect the kind of power they use to gain the support and cooperation of followers?
4. How might followers use these same sources of power to influence leaders?
5. What are the potential ethical strengths and weaknesses of each of these sources of power?

Justice and the Leader

Plato, 428 B.C.–348 B.C.

Plato's *Republic* was written around 380 B.C. An Athenian by birth, Plato witnessed the aftermath of Athens' defeat to Sparta in the Peleponnesian War, the demise of Athenian democracy, and the politically motivated imprisonment and death of Socrates. Plato puzzled over the question of how to best run the state in his writings. He was ambivalent about democracy, but he was also aware of how other forms of government such as oligarchy could be corrupt. The *Republic* is best known for Plato's depiction of the ideal state led by a philosopher king. The philosopher king was someone who was well-educated in what we today would call the liberal arts, and he or she (women were eligible) had to be virtuous. Plato believed that only the wisest should rule. By wisdom Plato meant more than just intelligence. He believed that wisdom was both intelligence and moral virtue. A smart evil person was not wise and a wise person could not be evil. One does wonder, would organizations and the world be better run if only the smartest and most ethical people were leaders?

For leadership scholars, the model of the philosopher king is not the most important part of the *Republic*. The first two books of the *Republic* are about the nature of justice, but they also discuss some of the most important moral aspects of leadership. The following selections consider not only justice, but the way power and self-interest might distort a ruler's notion of justice. As the dialogue begins, we find Socrates engaged in a conversation with his friends at the home of the elderly businessman Cephalus. Cephalus says justice is "speaking the truth and paying whatever debts one has incurred." Cephalus leaves the conversation and his son Polemarchus takes his father's place. Polemarchus asserts that the poet Simonides was correct when he said that it is just to give to each what is owed to him. As the dialogue develops we meet Thrasymachus who asserts that justice is what is in the interest of the strongest. The following selection begins with Socrates questioning this assertion.

But what about this? Should one also give one's enemies whatever is owed to them?

By all means, one should give them what is owed to them. And in my view what enemies owe to each other is appropriately and precisely—something bad.

It seems then that Simonides was speaking in riddles—just like a poet!—when he said what justice is, for he thought it just to give to each what is

c appropriate to him, and this is what he called giving him what is owed to him.

- What else did you think he meant?

Then what do you think he'd answer if someone asked him: "Simonides, which of the things that are owed or that are appropriate for someone or something to have does the craft[10] we call medicine give, and to whom or what does it give them?"

It's clear that it gives medicines, food, and drink to bodies.

And what owed or appropriate things does the craft we call cooking give, and to whom or what does it give them?

d It gives seasonings to food.

Good. Now, what does the craft we call justice give, and to whom or what does it give it?

If we are to follow the previous answers, Socrates, it gives benefits to friends and does harm to enemies.

Simonides means, then, that to treat friends well and enemies badly is justice?

I believe so.

And who is most capable of treating friends well and enemies badly in matters of disease and health?

A doctor.

e And who can do so best in a storm at sea?

A ship's captain.

What about the just person? In what actions and what work is he most capable of benefiting friends and harming enemies?

In wars and alliances, I suppose.

All right. Now, when people aren't sick, Polemarchus, a doctor is useless to them?

True.

And so is a ship's captain to those who aren't sailing?

Yes.

And then good people are their enemies and bad ones their friends?

---

[10]The Greek word translated as "craft" here is *technē*. It has the sort of connotation for Socrates and Plato that "science" has for us. Thus fifth-century doctors tried to show that medicine is a craft, much as contemporary psychoanalysts try to convince us that psychoanalysis is a science. For further discussion see Reeve, *Socrates in the Apology,* 37–45.

That's right.

And so it's just to benefit bad people and harm good ones? *d*

Apparently.

But good people are just and able to do no wrong?

True.

Then, according to your account, it's just to do bad things to those who do no injustice.

No, that's not just at all, Socrates; my account must be a bad one.

It's just, then, is it, to harm unjust people and benefit just ones?

That's obviously a more attractive view than the other one, anyway.

Then, it follows, Polemarchus, that it is just for the many, who are mistaken in their judgment, to harm their friends, who are bad, and benefit their *e* enemies, who are good. And so we arrive at a conclusion opposite to what we said Simonides meant.

That certainly follows. But let's change our definition, for it seems that we didn't define friends and enemies correctly.

How did we define them, Polemarchus?

We said that a friend is someone who is believed to be useful.

And how are we to change that now?

Someone who is both believed to be useful and is useful is a friend; someone who is believed to be useful but isn't, is believed to be a friend but isn't. 335 And the same for the enemy.

According to this account, then, a good person will be a friend and a bad one an enemy.

Yes.

So you want us to add something to what we said before about justice, when we said that it is just to treat friends well and enemies badly. You want us to add to this that it is just to treat well a friend who is good and to harm an enemy who is bad?

Right. That seems fine to me. *b*

Is it, then, the role of a just man to harm anyone?

Certainly, he must harm those who are both bad and enemies.

Do horses become better or worse when they are harmed?

Worse.

With respect to the virtue[12] that makes dogs good or the one that makes horses good?

---

[12]If something is a knife (say) or a man, its *aretē* or virtue as a knife or a man is that state or property of it that makes it a good knife or a good man. See *Charmides* 161a8–9; *Euthyphro* 6d9–e1; *Gorgias* 506d2–4; *Protagoras* 332b4–6; *Republic* 353d9–354a2. The *aretē* of a knife might include having a sharp blade; the *aretē* or a man might include being intelligent, well-born, just, or courageous. *Aretē* is thus broader than our notion of moral virtue. It applies to things (such as knives) which are not moral agents. And it applies to aspects of moral agents (such as intelligence or family status) which are not normally considered to be moral aspects of them. For these reasons it is sometimes more appropriate to render *aretē* as "excellence." But "virtue" remains the best overall translation, and once these few facts are borne in mind, it should seldom mislead.

The one that makes horses good.

And when dogs are harmed, they become worse in the virtue that makes dogs good, not horses?

Necessarily.

Then won't we say the same about human beings, too, that when they are

c harmed they become worse in human virtue?

Indeed.

But isn't justice human virtue?

Yes, certainly.

Then people who are harmed must become more unjust?

So it seems.

Can musicians make people unmusical through music?

They cannot.

Or horsemen make people unhorsemanlike through horsemanship?

No.

Well, then, can those who are just make people unjust through justice?

d In a word, can those who are good make people bad through virtue?

They cannot.

It isn't the function of heat to cool things but of its opposite?

Yes.

Nor the function of dryness to make things wet but of its opposite?

Indeed.

Nor the function of goodness to harm but of its opposite?

Apparently.

And a just person is good?

Indeed.

Then, Polemarchus, it isn't the function of a just person to harm a friend or anyone else, rather it is the function of his opposite, an unjust person?

In my view that's completely true, Socrates.

e   If anyone tells us, then, that it is just to give to each what he's owed and understands by this that a just man should harm his enemies and benefit his friends, he isn't wise to say it, since what he says isn't true, for it has become clear to us that it is never just to harm anyone?

I agree.

You and I shall fight as partners, then, against anyone who tells us that Simonides, Bias, Pittacus, or any of our other wise and blessedly happy men said this.[13]

I, at any rate, am willing to be your partner in the battle.

---

[13]Bias of Priene in Ionia (now the reign of Turkey bordering on the eastern shore of the Aegean) and Pittacus of Mytilene (on the island of Lesbos in the eastern Aegean), both sixth century B.C., were two of the legendary seven sagas of Greece.

Do you know to whom I think the saying belongs that it is just to benefit *336* friends and harm enemies?

Who?

I think it belongs to Periander, or Perdiccas, or Xerxes, or Ismenias of Corinth, or some other wealthy man who believed himself to have great power.[14]

That's absolutely true.

All right, since it has become apparent that justice and the just aren't what such people say they are, what else could they be?

While we were speaking, Thrasymachus had tried many times to take over *b* the discussion but was restrained by those sitting near him, who wanted to hear our argument to the end. When we paused after what I'd just said, however, he couldn't keep quiet any longer. He coiled himself up like a wild beast about to spring, and he hurled himself at us as if to tear us to pieces.

Listen, then. I say that justice is nothing other than the advantage of the stronger. Well, why don't you praise me? But then you'd do anything to avoid having to do that.

I must first understand you, for I don't yet know what you mean. The advantage of the stronger, you say, is just.

What do you mean, Thrasymachus? Surely you don't mean something like this: Polydamus, the pancratist,[16] is stronger than we are; it is to his advantage to eat beef to build up his physical strength; therefore, this food is also advantageous and just for us who are weaker than he is? *d*

You disgust me, Socrates. Your trick is to take hold of the argument at the point where you can do it the most harm.

Not at all, but tell us more clearly what you mean.

Don't you know that some cities are ruled by a tyranny, some by a democracy, and some by an aristocracy?

Of course.

And in each city this element is stronger, namely, the ruler?

Certainly.

And each makes laws to its own advantage. Democracy makes democratic laws, tyranny makes tyrannical laws, and so on with the others. And they *e* declare what they have made—what is to their own advantage—to be just for their subjects, and they punish anyone who goes against this as lawless and

---

[14]Periander was tyrant of the city of Corinth (650–570 B.C.). Perdiccas is probably Perdiccas II, King of Macedon (c. 450–413 B.C.), who is also mentioned in the *Gorgias* 471a–e. Xerxes was the king of Persia who invaded Greece in the second Persian war (begun in 480 B.C.). Ismenias is mentioned in the *Meno* 90a. All four are either notorious tyrants or men famous for their wealth.

[16]*Pancration* was a mixture of boxing and wrestling combined with kicking and strangling. Biting and gouging were forbidden, but pretty well everything else, includng breaking and dislocating limbs, was permitted.

unjust. This, then, is what I say justice is, the same in all cities, the advantage
339 of the established rule. Since the established rule is surely stronger, anyone
who reasons correctly will conclude that the just is the same everywhere,
namely, the advantage of the stronger.

Now I see what you mean. Whether it's true or not, I'll try to find out.
But you yourself have answered that the just is the advantageous, Thrasymachus, whereas you forbade that answer to me. True, you've added "of the
stronger" to it.

b   And I suppose you think that's an insignificant addition.

It isn't clear yet whether it's significant. But it is clear that we must investigate to see whether or not it's true. I agree that the just is some kind of advantage. But you add that it's *of the stronger.* I don't know about that. We'll have
to look into it.

Go ahead and look.

We will. Tell me, don't you also say that it is just to obey the rulers?

I do.

c   And are the rulers in all cities infallible, or are they liable to error?

No doubt they are liable to error.

When they undertake to make laws, therefore, they make some correctly,
others incorrectly?

I suppose so.

And a law is correct if it prescribes what is to the rulers' own advantage
and incorrect if it prescribes what is to their disadvantage? Is that what you
mean?

It is.

And whatever laws they make must be obeyed by their subjects, and this
is justice?

Of course.

d   Then, according to your account, it is just to do not only what is to the
advantage of the stronger, but also the opposite, what is not to their advantage.

What are you saying?

The same as you. But let's examine it more fully. Haven't we agreed that,
in giving orders to their subjects, the rulers are sometimes in error as to what
is best for themselves, and yet that it is just for their subjects to do whatever
their rulers order? Haven't we agreed to that much?

Tell me: Is a doctor in the precise sense, whom you mentioned before, a
money-maker or someone who treats the sick? Tell me about the one who is
really a doctor.

He's the one who treats the sick.

What about a ship's captain? Is a captain in the precise sense a ruler of
sailors or a sailor?

A ruler of sailors.

We shouldn't, I think, take into account the fact that he sails in a ship, and he shouldn't be called a sailor for that reason, for it isn't because of his sailing *d* that he is called a ship's captain, but because of his craft and his rule over sailors?

That's true.

And is there something advantageous to each of these, that is, to bodies and to sailors?

Certainly.

And aren't the respective crafts by nature set over them to seek and provide what is to their advantage?

They are.

And is there any advantage for each of the crafts themselves except to be as complete or perfect as possible?

What are you asking?   *e*

This: If you asked me whether our bodies are sufficient in themselves, or whether they need something else, I'd answer: "They certainly have needs. And because of this, because our bodies are deficient rather than self-sufficient, the craft of medicine has now been discovered. The craft of medicine was developed to provide what is advantageous for a body." Do you think that I'm right in saying this or not?

You are right.

Now, is medicine deficient? Does a craft need some further virtue, as the *342* eyes are in need of sight, and the ears of hearing, so that another craft is needed to seek and provide what is advantageous to them?[17] Does a craft itself have some similar deficiency, so that each craft needs another, to seek out what is to its advantage? And does the craft that does the seeking need still another, and so on without end? Or does each seek out what is to its own advantage by *b* itself? Or does it need neither itself nor another craft to seek out what is advantageous to it, because of its own deficiencies? Or is it that there is no deficiency or error in any craft? That it isn't appropriate for any craft to seek what is to the advantage of anything except that of which it is the craft? And that, since it is itself correct, it is without either fault or impurity, as long as it is wholly and precisely the craft that it is? Consider this with the preciseness of language you mentioned. Is it so or not?

It appears to be so.

Medicine doesn't seek its own advantage, then, but that of the body?   *c*

Yes.

---

[17]Sight is the virtue of excellence of the eyes (see 335b n. 12). Without it, the eyes cannot achieve what is advantageous to them, namely, sight. So eyes need some further virtue to seek and provide what is advantageous to them. But Socrates assumes throughout Book I that virtues are crafts. Hence he can conclude that the eyes need a further craft to achieve what is advantageous to them.

And horse-breeding doesn't seek its own advantage, but that of horses? Indeed, no other craft seeks its own advantage—for it has no further needs—but the advantage of that of which it is the craft?

Apparently so.

Now, surely, Thrasymachus, the crafts rule over and are stronger than the things of which they are the crafts?

Very reluctantly, he conceded this as well.

No kind of knowledge seeks or orders what is advantageous to itself, then, *d* but what is advantageous to the weaker, which is subject to it.

He tried to fight this conclusion, but he conceded it in the end. And after he had, I said: Surely, then, no doctor, insofar as he is a doctor, seeks or orders what is advantageous to himself, but what is advantageous to his patient? We agreed that a doctor in the precise sense is a ruler of bodies, not a money-maker. Wasn't that agreed?

Yes.

So a ship's captain in the precise sense is a ruler of sailors, not a sailor?
e That's what we agreed.

Doesn't it follow that a ship's captain or ruler won't seek and order what is advantageous to himself, but what is advantageous to a sailor?

He reluctantly agreed.

So, then, Thrasymachus, no one in any position of rule, insofar as he is a ruler, seeks or orders what is advantageous to himself, but what is advantageous to his subjects; the ones of whom he is himself the craftsman. It is to his subjects and what is advantageous and proper to them that he looks, and everything he says and does he says and does for them.

When we reached this point in the argument, and it was clear to all that *343* his account of justice had turned into its opposite, instead of answering, Thrasymachus said: Tell me, Socrates, do you still have a wet nurse?

What's this? Hadn't you better answer *my* questions rather than asking *me* such things?

Because she's letting you run around with a snotty nose, and doesn't wipe it when she needs to! Why, for all she cares, you don't even know about sheep and shepherds. Just what is it I don't know?

b You think that shepherds and cowherds seek the good of their sheep and cattle, and fatten them and take care of them, looking to something other than their master's good and their own. Moreover, you believe that rulers in cities—true rulers, that is—think about their subjects differently than one does about sheep, and that night and day they think of something besides *c* their own advantage. You are so far from understanding about justice and what's just, about injustice and what's unjust, that you don't realize that justice is really the good of another, the advantage of the stronger and the ruler, and harmful to the one who obeys and serves. Injustice is the opposite, it rules the truly simple and just, and those it rules do what is to the advantage of the other and stronger, and they make the one they serve happy, but themselves not at all. You must look at it as follows, my most simple Socrates: A just man always gets less than an unjust one. First, in their contracts with *d* one another, you'll never find, when the partnership ends, that a just partner has got more than an unjust one, but less. Second, in matters relating to the city, when taxes are to be paid, a just man pays more on the same property, an unjust one less, but when the city is giving out refunds, a just man gets nothing, while an unjust one makes a large profit. Finally, when each of them *e* holds a ruling position in some public office, a just person, even if he isn't penalized in other ways, finds that his private affairs deteriorate because he has to neglect them, that he gains no advantage from the public purse because of his justice, and that he's hated by his relatives and acquaintances when he's unwilling to do them an unjust favor. The opposite is true of an unjust man in every respect. Therefore, I repeat what I said before: A person of great power outdoes everyone else.[18] Consider him if you want to fig- *344* ure out how much more advantageous it is for the individual to be just rather than unjust. You'll understand this most easily if you turn your thoughts to the most complete injustice, the one that makes the doer of injustice happiest and the sufferers of it, who are unwilling to do injustice, most wretched. This is tyranny, which through stealth or force appropriates the property of others, whether sacred or profane, public or private, not little by little, but all at once. If someone commits only one part of injustice and is caught, he's *b* punished and greatly reproached—such partly unjust people are called temple-robbers,[19] kidnappers, housebreakers, robbers, and thieves when they commit these crimes. But when someone, in addition to appropriating their possessions, kidnaps and enslaves the citizens as well, instead of these shameful names he is called happy and blessed, not only by the citizens *c* themselves, but by all who learn that he has done the whole of injustice. Those who reproach injustice do so because they are afraid not of doing it but of suffering it. So, Socrates, injustice, if it is on a large enough scale, is stronger, freer, and more masterly than justice. And, as I said from the first, justice is what is advantageous to the stronger, while injustice is to one's own profit and advantage.

Having emptied this great flood of words into our ears all at once like a *d* bath attendant, Thrasymachus intended to leave. But those present didn't let him and made him stay to give an account of what he had said. I too begged

---

[18]Outdoing (*pleonektein*) is an important notion in the remainder of the *Republic*. It is connected to *pleonexia*, which is what one succumbs to when one always wants to outdo everyone else by getting and having more and more. *Pleonexia* is, or is the cause of, injustice, since always wanting to outdo others leads one to try to get what belongs to them, what isn't one's own. It is contrasted with *doing or having one's own*, which is, or is the cause of, justice.

[19]The temples acted as public treasuries, so that a temple robber is the equivalent of a present-day bank robber.

him to stay, and I said to him: After hurling such a speech at us, Thrasymachus, do you intend to leave before adequately instructing us or finding out whether
e you are right or not? Or do you think it a small matter to determine which whole way of life would make living most worthwhile for each of us?

Is *that* what I seem to you to think? Thrasymachus said.

Either that, or else you care nothing for us and aren't worried about whether we'll live better or worse lives because of our ignorance of what you say you know. So show some willingness to teach it to us. It wouldn't be a bad investment for you to be the benefactor of a group as large as ours. For my
345 own part, I'll tell you that I am not persuaded. I don't believe that injustice is more profitable than justice, not even if you give it full scope and put no obstacles in its way. Suppose that there *is* an unjust person, and suppose he *does* have the power to do injustice, whether by trickery or open warfare; nonetheless, he doesn't persuade me that injustice is more profitable than justice. Per-
b haps someone here, besides myself, feels the same as I do. So come now, and persuade us that we are wrong to esteem justice more highly than injustice in planning our lives.

And how am I to persuade you, if you aren't persuaded by what I said just now? What more can I do? Am I to take my argument and pour it into your very soul?

God forbid! Don't do that! But, first, stick to what you've said, and then, if you change your position, do it openly and don't deceive us. You see, Thrasymachus, that having defined the true doctor—to continue examining
c the things you said before—you didn't consider it necessary later to keep a precise guard on the true shepherd. You think that, insofar as he's a shepherd, he fattens sheep, not looking to what is best for the sheep but to a banquet, like a guest about to be entertained at a feast, or to a future sale, like a money-maker rather than a shepherd. Shepherding is concerned only to provide
d what is best for the things it is set over, and it is itself adequately provided with all it needs to be at its best when it doesn't fall short in any way of being the craft of shepherding. That's why I thought it necessary for us to agree before that every kind of rule, insofar as it rules, doesn't seek anything other than what is best for the things it rules and cares for, and this is true both of
e public and private kinds of rule. But do you think that those who rule cities, the true rulers, rule willingly?

I don't think it, by god, I know it.

But, Thrasymachus, don't you realize that in other kinds of rule no one wants to rule for its own sake, but they ask for pay, thinking that their ruling will benefit not themselves but their subjects? Tell me, doesn't every craft dif-
346 fer from every other in having a different function? Please don't answer contrary to what you believe, so that we can come to some definite conclusion.

Yes, that's what differentiates them.

And each craft benefits us in its own peculiar way, different from the others. For example, medicine gives us health, navigation gives us safety while sailing, and so on with the others?

Certainly.

And wage-earning gives us wages, for this is its function? Or would you call medicine the same as navigation? Indeed, if you want to define matters *b* precisely, as you proposed, even if someone who is a ship's captain becomes healthy because sailing is advantageous to his health, you wouldn't for that reason call his craft medicine?

Certainly not.

Nor would you call wage-earning medicine, even if someone becomes healthy while earning wages?

Certainly not.

Nor would you call medicine wage-earning, even if someone earns pay while healing?

No.   *c*

We are agreed, then, that each craft brings its own peculiar benefit?

It does.

Then whatever benefit all craftsmen receive in common must clearly result from their joint practice of some additional craft that benefits each of them?

So it seems.

And we say that the additional craft in question, which benefits the craftsmen by earning them wages, is the craft of wage-earning?

He reluctantly agreed.

Then this benefit, receiving wages, doesn't result from their own craft, but rather, if we're to examine this precisely, medicine provides health, and *d* wage-earning provides wages; house-building provides a house, and wage-earning, which accompanies it, provides a wage; and so on with the other crafts. Each of them does its own work and benefits the things it is set over. So, if wages aren't added, is there any benefit that the craftsman gets from his craft?

Apparently none.

But he still provides a benefit when he works for nothing?   *e*

Yes, I think he does.

Then, it is clear now, Thrasymachus, that no craft or rule provides for its own advantage, but, as we've been saying for some time, it provides and orders for its subject and aims at its advantage, that of the weaker, not of the stronger. That's why I said just now, Thrasymachus, that no one willingly chooses to rule and to take other people's troubles in hand and straighten them out, but each asks for wages; for anyone who intends to practice his craft well never does or 347 orders what is best for himself—at least not when he orders as his craft prescribes—but what is best for his subject. It is because of this, it seems, that

true leadership =
for other

wages must be provided to a person if he's to be willing to rule, whether in the form of money or honor or a penalty if he refuses.

What do you mean, Socrates? said Glaucon. I know the first two kinds of wages, but I don't understand what penalty you mean or how you can call it a wage.

Then you don't understand the best people's kind of wages, the kind that moves the most decent to rule, when they are willing to rule at all. *b* Don't you know that the love of honor and the love of money are despised, and rightly so?

I do.

Therefore good people won't be willing to rule for the sake of either money or honor. They don't want to be paid wages openly for ruling and get called hired hands, nor to take them in secret from their rule and be called thieves. And they won't rule for the sake of honor, because they aren't ambi- *c* tious honor-lovers. So, if they're to be willing to rule, some compulsion or punishment must be brought to bear on them—perhaps that's why it is thought shameful to seek to rule before one is compelled to. Now, the greatest punishment, if one isn't willing to rule, is to be ruled by someone worse than oneself. And I think that it's fear of this that makes decent people rule when they do. They approach ruling not as something good or something to be enjoyed, but as something necessary, since it can't be entrusted to anyone better than— *d* or even as good as—themselves. In a city of good men, if it came into being, the citizens would fight in order *not to rule,* just as they do now in order to rule. There it would be quite clear that anyone who is really a true ruler doesn't by nature seek his own advantage but that of his subjects. And everyone, knowing this, would rather be benefited by others than take the trouble to benefit them. So I can't at all agree with Thrasymachus that justice is the *e* advantage of the stronger—but we'll look further into that another time. What Thrasymachus is now saying—that the life of an unjust person is better than that of a just one—seems to be of far greater importance. Which life would you choose, Glaucon? And which of our views do you consider truer?

I certainly think that the life of a just person is more profitable.

348   Did you hear all of the good things Thrasymachus listed a moment ago for the unjust life?

I heard, but I wasn't persuaded.

351   I'll ask what I asked before, so that we may proceed with our argument about justice and injustice in an orderly fashion, for surely it was claimed that injustice is stronger and more powerful than justice. But, now, if justice is indeed wisdom and virtue, it will easily be shown to be stronger than injustice, since injustice is ignorance (no one could now be ignorant of that). However, I don't want to state the matter so unconditionally, Thrasymachus, but to look *b* into it in some such way as this. Would you say that it is unjust for a city to try

to enslave other cities unjustly and to hold them in subjection when it has enslaved many of them?

Of course, that's what the best city will especially do, the one that is most completely unjust.

I understand that's your position, but the point I want to examine is this: Will the city that becomes stronger than another achieve this power without justice, or will it need the help of justice?

If what you said a moment ago stands, and justice is cleverness or wisdom, *c* it will need the help of justice, but if things are as I stated, it will need the help of injustice.

I'm impressed, Thrasymachus, that you don't merely nod yes or no but give very fine answers.

That's because I'm trying to please you.

You're doing well at it, too. So please me some more by answering this question: Do you think that a city, an army, a band of robbers or thieves, or any other tribe with a common unjust purpose would be able to achieve it if they were unjust to each other?

No, indeed.   *d*

What if they weren't unjust to one another? Would they achieve more?

Certainly.

Injustice, Thrasymachus, causes civil war, hatred, and fighting among themselves, while justice brings friendship and a sense of common purpose. Isn't that so?

Let it be so, in order not to disagree with you.

You're still doing well on that front. So tell me this: If the effect of injustice is to produce hatred wherever it occurs, then, whenever it arises, whether among free men or slaves, won't it cause them to hate one another, engage in civil war, and prevent them from achieving any *e* common purpose?

Certainly.

What if it arises between two people? Won't they be at odds, hate each other, and be enemies to one another and to just people?

They will.

Does injustice lose its power to cause dissension when it arises within a single individual, or will it preserve it intact?

Let it preserve it intact.

Apparently, then, injustice has the power, first, to make whatever it arises in—whether it is a city, a family, an army, or anything else—incapable of *352* achieving anything as a unit, because of the civil wars and differences it creates, and, second, it makes that unit an enemy to itself and to what is in every way its opposite, namely, justice. Isn't that so?

Certainly.

And even in a single individual, it has by its nature the very same effect. First, it makes him incapable of achieving anything, because he is in a state of civil war and not of one mind; second, it makes him his own enemy, as well as the enemy of just people. Hasn't it that effect?

Yes.

And the gods too are just?

Let it be so.

b So an unjust person is also an enemy of the gods, Thrasymachus, while a just person is their friend?

Enjoy your banquet of words! Have no fear, I won't oppose you. That would make these people hate me.

Come, then, complete the banquet for me by continuing to answer as you've been doing. We have shown that just people are cleverer and more capable of doing things, while unjust ones aren't even able to act together, for

c when we speak of a powerful achievement by unjust men acting together, what we say isn't altogether true. They would never have been able to keep their hands off each other if they were completely unjust. But clearly there must have been some sort of justice in them that at least prevented them from doing injustice among themselves at the same time as they were doing it to others. And it was this that enabled them to achieve what they did. When they started doing unjust things, they were only halfway corrupted by their injustice (for those who are all bad and completely unjust are completely incapable of accomplishing anything). These are the things I understand to hold, not the ones you first maintained. We must now examine, as we proposed before,[23]

d whether just people also live better and are happier than unjust ones. I think it's clear already that this is so, but we must look into it further, since the argument concerns no ordinary topic but the way we ought to live.

Go ahead and look.

I will. Tell me, do you think there is such a thing as the function of a horse?

e I do.

And would you define the function of a horse or of anything else as that which one can do only with it or best with it?

I don't understand.

Let me put it this way: Is it possible to see with anything other than eyes?

Certainly not.

Or to hear with anything other than ears?

No.

Then, we are right to say that seeing and hearing are the functions of eyes and ears?

Of course.

[23]See 347e.

What about this? Could you use a dagger or a carving knife or lots of other   353
things in pruning a vine?

Of course.

But wouldn't you do a finer job with a pruning knife designed for the purpose than with anything else?

You would.

Then shall we take pruning to be its function?

Yes.

Now, I think you'll understand what I was asking earlier when I asked
whether the function of each thing is what it alone can do or what it does bet-   *function*
ter than anything else.

I understand, and I think that this is the function of each.   *b*

All right. Does each thing to which a particular function is assigned also
have a virtue? Let's go over the same ground again. We say that eyes have
some function?   *virtu*

They do.

So there is also a virtue of eyes?

There is.

And ears have a function?

Yes.

So there is also a virtue of ears?

There is.

And all other things are the same, aren't they?

They are.

And could eyes perform their function well if they lacked their peculiar   *c*
virtue and had the vice instead?

How could they, for don't you mean if they had blindness instead of sight?

Whatever their virtue is, for I'm not now asking about that but about
whether anything that has a function performs it well by means of its own
peculiar virtue and badly by means of its vice?

That's true, it does.

So ears, too, deprived of their own virtue, perform their function badly?   *via*

That's right.

And the same could be said about everything else?   *d*

So it seems.

Come, then, and let's consider this: Is there some function of a soul that
you couldn't perform with anything else, for example, taking care of things,
ruling, deliberating, and the like? Is there anything other than a soul to which
you could rightly assign these, and say that they are its peculiar function?

No, none of them.

What of living? Isn't that a function of a soul?

It certainly is.

And don't we also say that there is a virtue of a soul?

We do.

e   Then, will a soul ever perform its function well, Thrasymachus, if it is deprived of its own peculiar virtue, or is that impossible?

It's impossible.

Doesn't it follow, then, that a bad soul rules and takes care of things badly and that a good soul does all these things well?

It does.

Now, we agreed that justice is a soul's virtue, and injustice its vice?

We did.

Then, it follows that a just soul and a just man will live well, and an unjust one badly.

Apparently so, according to your argument.

And surely anyone who lives well is blessed and happy, and anyone who
354   doesn't is the opposite.

Of course.

Therefore, a just person is happy, and an unjust one wretched.

So be it.

It profits no one to be wretched but to be happy.

Of course.

And so, Thrasymachus, injustice is never more profitable than justice.

REVIEW QUESTIONS

1. What does a leader have to do to be just, according to Plato?
2. Why is justice more than simply giving people what we owe them?
3. Do you think justice is what is in the interests of the stronger?
4. Why are some people today reluctant to run for office or take on other leadership roles?

Case: "The Ring of Gyges"
Plato

"The Ring of Gyges" is also from Plato's Republic. Glaucon takes over where Thrasymachus left off. The story plunges us into the problem of power and accountability. It begins with the argument by Glaucon that people are not willingly just, but only behave justly because they are afraid of getting caught or because they don't have the power to act unjustly. As you read this case, think about how many people have the moral character and self-discipline to behave ethically when they have great power and there are no checks on their power. As we see in the next chapter, this is one of the great moral challenges of leadership.

They say that to do injustice is naturally good and to suffer injustice bad, but that the badness of suffering it so far exceeds the goodness of doing it that those who have done and suffered injustice and tasted both, but who lack the power to do it and avoid suffering it, decide that it is profitable to come to an agreement with each other neither to do injustice nor to suffer it. As a result, they begin to make laws and covenants, and what the law commands they call lawful and just. This, they say, is the origin and essence of justice. It is intermediate between the best and the worst. The best is to do injustice without paying the penalty; the worst is to suffer it without being able to take revenge. Justice is a mean between these two extremes. People value it not as a good but because they are too weak to do injustice with impunity. Someone who has the power to do this, however, and is a true man wouldn't make an agreement with anyone not to do injustice in order not to suffer it. For him that would be madness. This is the nature of justice, according to the argument, Socrates, and these are its natural origins.

We can see most clearly that those who practice justice do it unwillingly and because they lack the power to do injustice, if in our thoughts we grant to a just and an unjust person the freedom to do whatever they like. We can then follow both of them and see where their desires would lead. And we'll catch the just person red-handed travelling the same road as the unjust. The reason for this is the desire to outdo others and get more and more.[2] This is what anyone's nature naturally pursues as good, but nature is forced by law into the perversion of treating fairness with respect.

The freedom I mentioned would be most easily realized if both people had the power they say the ancestor of Gyges of Lydia possessed. The story goes that he was a shepherd in the service of the ruler of Lydia. There was a violent thunderstorm, and an earthquake broke open the ground and created a chasm at the place where he was tending his sheep. Seeing this, he was filled with amazement and went down into it. And there, in addition to many other wonders of which we're told, he saw a hollow bronze horse. There were window like openings in it, and, peeping in, he saw a corpse, which seemed to be of more than human size, wearing nothing but a gold ring on its finger. He took the ring and came out of the chasm. He wore the ring at the usual monthly meeting that reported to the king on the state of the flocks. And as he was sitting among the others, he happened to turn the setting of the ring towards himself to the inside of his hand. When he did this, he became

Case continued

invisible to those sitting near him, and they went on talking as if he had gone. He wondered at this, and, fingering the ring, he turned the setting outwards again and became visible. So he experimented with the ring to test whether it indeed had this power—and it did. If he turned the setting inward, he became invisible; if he turned it outward, he became visible again. When he realized this, he at once arranged to become one of the messengers sent to report to the king. And when he arrived there, he seduced the king's wife, attacked the king with her help, killed him, and took over the kingdom.

Let's suppose, then, that there were two such rings, one worn by a just and the other by an unjust person. Now, no one, it seems, would be so incorruptible that he would stay on the path of justice or stay away from other people's property, when he could take whatever he wanted from the marketplace with impunity, go into people's houses and have sex with anyone he wished, kill or release from prison anyone he wished, and do all the other things that would make him like a god among humans. Rather his actions would be in no way different from those of an unjust person, and both would follow the same path. This, some would say, is a great proof that one is never just willingly but only when compelled to be. No one believes justice to be a good when it is kept private, since, wherever either person thinks he can do injustice with impunity, he does it. Indeed, every man believes that injustice is far more profitable to himself than justice. And any exponent of this argument will say he's right, for someone who didn't want to do injustice, given this sort of opportunity, and who didn't touch other people's property would be thought wretched and stupid by everyone aware of the situation, though, of course, they'd praise him in public, deceiving each other for fear of suffering injustice. So much for my second topic.

Questions

1. What would you do if you found the ring?
2. What do you think most people would do if they had the ring?
3. What criteria would you use to determine ethical and unethical uses for the ring?
4. Do leaders today possess the power of the ring to hide information about what they do while in office?

Self-Interest and Human Nature

Thomas Hobbes, 1588–1679

Thomas Hobbes was an English philosopher born in Malmesbury. During his 91 years of life, he witnessed the civil war in England and the reigns of Charles I and Charles II. Hobbes used to tell friends that his twin was fear because he was born prematurely when his mother heard about the approach of the Spanish Armada. In this article, Hobbes argues that the driving motivation behind human behavior and society is fear of death and the need for security.

His book *The Leviathan* is a justification of the monarchy and the formation of the commonwealth. Hobbes thought democratic leadership would lead to anarchy because he believed that humans are self-interested and have a natural tendency to assert themselves and seek power. A state of nature, says Hobbes, is a state of war. It is only out of fear that people give up some of their liberty and submit to the state. All society, according to Hobbes, was formed for either gain or glory, not love for each other, but for love of ourselves. Hobbes shows us how self-interest is compatible with and the basic premise of the golden rule. He observes that because people are alike and self-interested, they should know how to "do unto others," because they know how they would like to be treated. Notice that when self-interest turns into empathy, people are able to care about the interests of others.

Men by nature equal.

NATURE hath made men so equal, in the faculties of the body, and mind; as that though there be found one man sometimes manifestly stronger in body, or of quicker mind than another; yet when all is reckoned together, the difference between man, and man, is not so considerable, as that one man can thereupon claim to himself any benefit, to which another may not pretend, as well as he. For as to the strength of body, the weakest has strength enough to kill the strongest, either by secret machination, or by confederacy with others, that are in the same danger with himself.

And as to the faculties of the mind, setting aside the arts grounded upon words, and especially that skill of proceeding upon general, and infallible rules, called science; which very few have, and but in few things; as being not a native faculty, born with us; nor attained, as prudence, while we look after somewhat else, I find yet a greater equality amongst men, than that of strength. For prudence, is but experience; which equal time, equally bestows on all men, in those things they equally apply themselves unto. That which may perhaps make such equality incredible, is but a vain conceit of one's own wisdom, which almost all men think they have in a greater degree, than the vulgar; that is, than all men but themselves, and a few others, whom by fame, or for concurring with themselves, they approve. For such is the nature of

From Hobbes, Thomas. *Leviathan*, 1651.

men, that howsoever they may acknowledge many others to be more witty, or more eloquent, or more learned; yet they will hardly believe there be many so wise as themselves; for they see their own wit at hand, and other men's at a distance. But this proveth rather that men are in that point equal, than unequal. For there is not ordinarily a greater sign of the equal distribution of any thing, than that every man is contented with his share.

From equality proceeds diffidence.
From this equality of ability, ariseth equality of hope in the attaining of our ends. And therefore if any two men desire the same thing, which nevertheless they cannot both enjoy, they become enemies; and in the way to their end, which is principally their own conservation, and sometimes their delectation only, endeavour to destroy, or subdue one another. And from hence it comes to pass, that where an invader hath no more to fear, than another man's single power; if one plant, sow, build, or possess a convenient seat, others may probably be expected to come prepared with forces united, to dispossess, and deprive him, not only of the fruit of his labour, but also of his life, or liberty. And the invader again is in the like danger of another.

From diffidence war.
And from this diffidence of one another, there is no way for any man to secure himself, so reasonable, as anticipation; that is, by force, or wiles, to master the persons of all men he can, so long, till he see no other power great enough to endanger him: and this is no more than his own conservation requireth, and is generally allowed. Also because there be some, that taking pleasure in contemplating their own power in the acts of conquest, which they pursue farther than their security requires; if others, that otherwise would be glad to be at ease within modest bounds, should not by invasion increase their power, they would not be able, long time, by standing only on their defense, to subsist. And by consequence, such augmentation of dominion over men being necessary to a man's conservation, it ought to be allowed him.

Again, men have no pleasure, but on the contrary a great deal of grief, in keeping company, where there is no power able to over-awe them all. For every man looketh that his companion should value him, at the same rate he sets upon himself: and upon all signs of contempt, or undervaluing, naturally endeavours, as far as he dares, (which amongst them that have no common power to keep them in quiet, is far enough to make them destroy each other), to extort a greater value from his contemners, by damage; and from others, by the example.

So that in the nature of man, we find three principal causes of quarrel. First, competition; secondly, diffidence; thirdly, glory.

The first, maketh men invade for gain; the second, for safety; and the third, for reputation. The first use violence, to make themselves masters of other men's persons, wives, children, and cattle; the second, to defend them; the third, for trifles, as a word, a smile, a different opinion, and any other sign of undervalue, either direct in their persons, or by reflection in their kindred, their friends, their nation, their profession, or their name.

Out of civil states, there is always war of every one against every one.
Hereby it is manifest, that during the time men live without a common power to keep them all in awe, they are in that condition which is called war; and such a war, as is of every man, against every man. For WAR, consisteth not in battle only, or the act of fighting; but in a tract of time, wherein the will to contend by battle is sufficiently known: and therefore the notion of *time,* is to be considered in the nature of war; as it is in the nature of weather. For as the nature of foul weather, lieth not in a shower or two of rain; but in an inclination thereto of many days together: so the nature of war, consisteth not in actual fighting; but in the known disposition thereto, during all the time there is no assurance to the contrary. All other time is PEACE.

The incommodities of such a war.
Whatsoever therefore is consequent to a time of war, where every man is enemy to every man, the same is consequent to the time, wherein men live without other security, than what their own strength, and their own invention shall furnish them withal. In such condition, there is no place for industry; because the fruit thereof is uncertain: and consequently no culture of the earth; no navigation, nor use of the commodities that may be imported by sea; no commodious building; no instruments of moving, and removing, such things as require much force; no knowledge of the face of the earth; no account of time; no arts; no letters; no society; and which is worst of all, continual fear, and danger of violent death; and the life of man, solitary, poor, nasty, brutish, and short.

It may seem strange to some man, that has not well weighed these things; that nature should thus dissociate, and render men apt to invade, and destroy one another: and he may therefore, not trusting to this inference, made from the passions, desire perhaps to have the same confirmed by experience. Let him therefore consider with himself, when taking a journey, he arms himself, and seeks to go well accompanied; when going to sleep, he locks his doors; when even in his house he locks his chests; and this when he knows there be laws, and public officers, armed, to revenge all injuries shall be done him; what opinion he has of his fellow-subjects, when he rides armed; of his fellow citizens, when he locks his doors; and of his children, and servants, when he locks his chests. Does he not there as much accuse mankind by his actions, as I do by my words? But neither of us accuse man's nature in it. The desires, and other passions of man, are in themselves no sin. No more are the actions, that proceed from those passions, till they know a law that forbids them: which till laws be made they cannot know: nor can any law be made, till they have agreed upon the person that shall make it.

It may peradventure be thought, there was never such a time, nor condition of war as this; and I believe it was never generally so, over all the world: but there are many places, where they live so now. For the savage people in many places of America, except the government of small families, the concord whereof dependeth on natural lust, have no government at all; and live at this day in that brutish manner, as I said before. Howsoever, it may be perceived what manner of life there would be, where there were no common power to fear, by the manner of life, which men that have formerly lived under a peaceful government, use to degenerate into, in a civil war.

But though there had never been any time, wherein particular men were in a condition of war one against another; yet in all times, kings, and persons of sovereign authority, because of their independency, are in continual jealousies, and in the state and posture of gladiators; having their weapons pointing, and their eyes fixed on one another; that is, their forts, garrisons, and guns upon the frontiers of their kingdoms; and continual spies upon their neighbours; which is a posture of war. But because they uphold thereby, the industry of their subjects; there does not follow from it, that misery, which accompanies the liberty of particular men.

In such a war nothing is unjust.
To this war of every man, against every man, this also is consequent; that nothing can be unjust. The notions of right and wrong, justice and injustice have there no place. Where there is no common power, there is no law: where no law, no injustice. Force, and fraud, are in war the two cardinal virtues. Justice, and injustice are none of the faculties neither of the body, nor mind. If they were, they might be in a man that were alone in the world, as well as his senses, and passions. They are qualities, that relate to men in society, not in solitude. It is consequent also to the same condition, that there be no propriety, no dominion, no *mine* and *thine* distinct; but only that to be every man's, that he can get: and for so long, as he can keep it. And thus much for the ill condition, which man by mere nature is actually placed in; though with a possibility to come out of it, consisting partly in the passions, partly in his reason.

The passions that incline men to peace.
The passions that incline men to peace, are fear of death; desire of such things as are necessary to commodious living; and a hope by their industry to obtain them. And reason suggesteth convenient articles of peace, upon which men may be drawn to agreement. These articles, are they, which otherwise are called the Laws of Nature: whereof I shall speak more particularly, in the two following chapters.

Chapter XIV
Of The First And Second Natural Laws, And Of Contracts

Right of nature what.

THE RIGHT OF NATURE, which writers commonly call *jus naturale*, is the liberty each man hath, to use his own power, as he will himself, for the preservation of his own nature; that is to say, of his own life; and consequently, of doing any thing, which in his own judgment, and reason, he shall conceive to be the aptest means thereunto.

Liberty what.

By LIBERTY, is understood, according to the proper signification of the word, the absence of external impediments: which impediments, may oft take away part of a man's power to do what he would; but cannot hinder him from using the power left him, according as his judgment, and reason shall dictate to him.

A law of nature what.
Difference of right and law.

A LAW OF NATURE, *lex naturalis*, is a precept or general rule, found out by reason, by which a man is forbidden to do that, which is destructive of his life, or taketh away the means of preserving the same; and to omit that, by which he thinketh it may be best preserved. For though they that speak of this subject, use to confound *jus*, and *lex, right* and *law:* yet they ought to be distinguished; because RIGHT, consisteth in liberty to do, or to forbear: whereas LAW, determineth, and bindeth to one of them: so that law, and right, differ as much, as obligation, and liberty; which in one and the same matter are inconsistent.

Naturally every man has right to every thing.
The fundamental law of nature.

And because the condition of man, as hath been declared in the precedent chapter, is a condition of war of every one against every one; in which case every one is governed by his own reason; and there is nothing he can make use of, that may not be a help unto him, in preserving his life against his enemies; it followeth, that in such a condition, every man has a right to every thing; even to one another's body. And therefore, as long as this natural right of every man to every thing endureth, there can be no security to any man, how strong or wise soever he be, of living out the time, which nature ordinarily alloweth men to live. And consequently it is a precept, or general rule of reason, *that every man, ought to endeavour peace, as far as he has hope of obtaining it; and when he cannot obtain it, that he may seek, and use, all helps, and advantages of war.* The first branch of which rule, containeth the first, and fundamental law of nature; which is, *to seek peace, and follow it.* The second, the sum of the right of nature; which is, *by all means we can, to defend ourselves.*

The second law of nature.
From this fundamental law of nature, by which men are commanded to
endeavour peace, is derived this second law; *that a man be willing, when oth-*
ers are so too, as far-forth, as for peace, and defense of himself he shall think it
necessary, to lay down this right to all things; and be contented with so much
liberty against other men, as he would allow other men against himself. For as
long as every man holdeth this right, of doing any thing he liketh; so long are
all men in the condition of war. But if other men will not lay down their right,
as well as he; then there is no reason for any one, to divest himself of his: for
that were to expose himself to prey, which no man is bound to, rather than to
dispose himself to peace. This is that law of the Gospel; *whatsoever you*
require that others should do to you, that do ye to them. And that law of all
men, *quod tibi fieri non vis, alteri ne feceris.*

What it is to lay down a right.
To *lay down* a man's *right* to any thing, is to *divest* himself of the *liberty,* of
hindering another of the benefit of his own right to the same. For he that
renounceth, or passeth away his right, giveth not to any other man a right
which he had not before; became there is nothing to which every man had not
right by nature: but only standeth out of his way, that he may enjoy his own
original right, without hindrance from him; not without hindrance from
another. So that the effect which redoundeth to one man, by another man's
defect of right, is but so much diminution of impediments to the use of his
own right original.

Renouncing a right, what it is.
Transferring right what. Obligation.
Right is laid aside, either by simply renouncing it; or by transferring it to
another. By *simply* RENOUNCING; when he cares not to whom the benefit
thereof redoundeth. By TRANSFERRING; when he intendeth the benefit thereof
to some certain person, or persons.

Duty.
Injustice.
And when a man hath in either manner abandoned, or granted away his right;
then he is said to be OBLIGED, or BOUND, not to hinder those, to whom such
right is granted, or abandoned, from the benefit of it: and that he *ought,* and
it is his DUTY, not to make void that voluntary act of his own: and that such hindrance is INJUSTICE, and INJURY, as being *sine jure;* the right being before
renounced, or transferred. So that *injury,* or *injustice,* in the controversies of
the world, is somewhat like to that, which in the disputations of scholars is
called *absurdity.* For as it is there called an absurdity, to contradict what one
maintained in the beginning: so in the world, it is called injustice, and injury,

voluntarily to undo that, which from the beginning he had voluntarily done. The way by which a man either simply renounceth, or transferreth his right, is a declaration, or signification, by some voluntary and sufficient sign, or signs, that he doth so renounce, or transfer; or hath so renounced, or transferred the same, to him that accepteth it. And these signs are either words only, or actions only; or, as it happeneth most often, both words, and actions. And the same are the BONDS, by which men are bound, and obliged: bonds, that have their strength, not from their own nature, for nothing is more easily broken than a man's word, but from fear of some evil consequence upon the rupture.

Not all rights are alienable.
Whensoever a man transferreth his right, or renounceth it; it is either in consideration of some right reciprocally transferred to himself; or for some other good he hopeth for thereby. For it is a voluntary act: and of the voluntary acts of every man, the object is some *good to himself.* And therefore there be some rights, which no man can be understood by any words, or other signs, to have abandoned, or transferred. As first a man cannot lay down the right of resisting them, that assault him by force, to take away his life; because he cannot be understood to aim thereby, at any good to himself. The same may be said of wounds, and chains, and imprisonment; both because there is no benefit consequent to such patience; as there is to the patience of suffering another to be wounded, or imprisoned: as also because a man cannot tell, when he seeth men proceed against him by violence, whether they intend his death or not. And lastly the motive, and end for which this renouncing, and transferring of right is introduced, is nothing else but the security of a man's person, in his life, and in the means of so preserving life, as not to be weary of it. And therefore if a man by words, or other signs, seem to despoil himself of the end, for which those signs were intended; he is not to be understood as if he meant it, or that it was his will; but that he was ignorant of how such words and actions were to be interpreted.

REVIEW QUESTIONS

1. Is Hobbes right about the origins of society?
2. Is all human action self-interested?
3. If so, what kinds of power and influence would be most effective for a leader in society?
4. What would be the strengths and limitations of leadership based on the assumption that self interest is the soul driving force of human action?

The Qualities of Princes

Niccolò Machiavelli 1469–1527

Niccolò Machiavelli was born in Florence, Italy. Throughout his life he worked for the government of the Florentine Republic. At the age of twenty-nine he was made head of the second chancery, which dealt with the internal affairs of Florentine government. He later became secretary of the executive council that supervised diplomatic and military affairs. Machiavelli undertook a number of diplomatic missions to France, Germany, and other regions of Italy. He was sent twice to meet with Cesare Borgia, son of Pope Alexander VI. Borgia was a strong and completely ruthless prince who had carved out a portion of central Italy for his domination. In Borgia Machiavelli confronted the problem of ethics and effectiveness. He admired the way Borgia operated, but did not care much for the man himself. But Machiavelli was a pragmatist who believed that the desperate ills of Italy could only be cured by a new kind of prince who possessed the leadership qualities and methods of a Borgia. Hence, Borgia became the model for Machiavelli's book, *The Prince*.

When the Medici family dissolved the Florentine Republic, Machiavelli lost his government position and was briefly imprisoned. When Machiavelli was released, he retired to a small farm outside of Florence. In 1532 he wrote *The Prince*. Machiavelli, ever the politician, dedicated *The Prince* to Lorenzo de' Medici in hopes of getting a job from the new ruler of Florence.

The Prince is about how to get and maintain political power. Some regard *The Prince* as a defense of tyrannical rulers like Borgia, while others read the book as a defense of the merits of a nation state. Like Hobbes, Machiavelli lived in tumultuous times. He saw need for authority to bring order and justice to Italy; he also understood the sources of authority in power.

The following selections from *The Prince* pit ethics against effectiveness or the ethics of the means against the ethics of the ends. Like Hobbes, Machiavelli does not have a high opinion of human nature. He tells us "man is a sorry breed" who tends to believe what he sees on the surface. Machiavelli believed that effective leaders are not governed by traditional moral norms, but only by the principles that lead to success. So, leaders only need to appear moral and religious. It is not necessary that they actually be moral and religious. As you read these selections, look closely at Machiavelli's advice, while not all of it is ethical, some of it is quite useful.

XV
Of The Qualities of Princes

It now remains for us to consider what ought to be the conduct and bearing of a Prince in relation to his subjects and friends. And since I know that many have written on this subject, I fear it may be thought presumptuous in me to write of it also; the more so, because in my treatment of it I depart from the views that others have taken.

But since it is my object to write what shall be useful to whosoever understands it, it seems to me better to follow the real truth of things than an imaginary view of them. For many Republics and Princedoms have been imagined that were never seen or known to exist in reality. And the manner in which we live, and that in which we ought to live, are things so wide asunder, that he who quits the one to betake himself to the other is more likely to destroy than to save himself; since any one who would act up to a perfect standard of goodness in everything, must be ruined among so many who are not good. It is essential, therefore, for a Prince who desires to maintain his position, to have learned how to be other than good, and to use or not to use his goodness as necessity requires.

Laying aside, therefore, all fanciful notions concerning a Prince, and considering those only that are true, I say that all men when they are spoken of, and Princes more than others from their being set so high, are characterized by some one of those qualities which attach either praise or blame. Thus one is accounted liberal, another miserly (which word I use, rather than *avaricious*, to denote the man who is too sparing of what is his own, *avarice* being the disposition to take wrongfully what is another's); one is generous, another greedy; one cruel, another tender-hearted; one is faithless, another true to his word; one effeminate and cowardly, another high-spirited and courageous; one is courteous, another haughty; one impure, another chaste; one simple, another crafty; one firm, another facile; one grave, another frivolous; one devout, another unbelieving; and the like. Every one, I know, will admit that it would be most laudable for a Prince to be endowed with all of the above qualities that are reckoned good; but since it is impossible for him to possess or constantly practise them all, the conditions of human nature not allowing it, he must be discreet enough to know how to avoid the infamy of those vices that would deprive him of his government, and, if possible, be on his guard also against those which might not deprive him of it; though if he cannot wholly restrain himself, he may with less scruple indulge in the latter. He need never hesitate, however, to incur the reproach of those vices without which his authority can hardly be preserved; for if he well consider the whole matter, he will find that there may be a line of conduct having the appearance of virtue, to follow which would be his ruin, and that there may be another course having the appearance of vice, by following which his safety and well-being are secured.

XVII
Of Cruelty and Clemency

Passing to the other qualities above referred to, I say that every Prince should desire to be accounted merciful and not cruel. Nevertheless, he should be on his guard against the abuse of this quality of mercy. Cesare Borgia was reputed cruel, yet his cruelty restored Romagna, united it, and brought it to order and obedience; so that if we look at things in their true light, it will be seen that he was in reality far more merciful than the people of Florence, who, to avoid the imputation of cruelty, suffered Pistoja to be torn to pieces by factions.

A Prince should therefore disregard the reproach of being thought cruel where it enables him to keep his subjects united and obedient. For he who quells disorder by a very few signal examples will in the end be more merciful than he who from too great leniency permits things to take their course and so to result in rapine and bloodshed; for these hurt the whole State, whereas the severities of the Prince injure individuals.

And for a new Prince, of all others, it is impossible to escape a name for cruelty, since new States are full of dangers. Wherefore Virgil, by the mouth of Dido, excuses the harshness of her reign on the plea that it was new, saying:—

"A fate unkind, and newness in my reign

Compel me thus to guard a wide domain."

Nevertheless, the new Prince should not be too ready of belief, nor too easily set in motion; nor should he himself be the first to raise alarms; but should so temper prudence with kindliness that too great confidence in others shall not throw him off his guard, nor groundless distrust render him insupportable.

And here comes in the question whether it is better to be loved rather than feared, or feared rather than loved. It might perhaps be answered that we should wish to be both; but since love and fear can hardly exist together, if we must choose between them, it is far safer to be feared than loved. For of men it may generally be affirmed that they are thankless, fickle, false, studious to avoid danger, greedy of gain, devoted to you while you are able to confer benefits upon them, and ready, as I said before, while danger is distant, to shed their blood, and sacrifice their property, their lives, and their children for you; but in the hour of need they turn against you. The Prince, therefore, who without otherwise securing himself builds wholly on their professions is undone. For the friendships which we buy with a price, and do not gain by greatness and nobility of character, though they be fairly earned are not made good, but fail us when we have occasion to use them.

Moreover, men are less careful how they offend him who makes himself loved than him who makes himself feared. For love is held by the tie of obligation, which, because men are a sorry breed, is broken on every whisper of private interest; but fear is bound by the apprehension of punishment which never relaxes.

Nevertheless a Prince should inspire fear in such a fashion that if he do not win love he may escape hate. For a man may very well be feared and yet not hated, and this will be the case so long as he does not meddle with the property or with the women of his citizens and subjects. And if constrained to put any to death, he should do so only when there is manifest cause or reasonable justification. But, above all, he must abstain from the property of others. For men will sooner forget the death of their father than the loss of their patrimony. Moreover, pretexts for confiscation are never to seek, and he who has once begun to live by rapine always finds reasons for taking what is not his; whereas reasons for shedding blood are fewer.

But when a Prince is with his army, and has many soldiers under his command, he must needs disregard the reproach of cruelty, for without such a reputation in its Captain, no army can be held together or kept under any kind of control. Among other things remarkable in Hannibal this has been noted, that having a very great army, made up of men of many different nations and brought to fight in a foreign country, no dissension ever arose among the soldiers themselves, nor any mutiny against their leader, either in his good or in his evil fortunes. This we can only ascribe to the transcendent cruelty, which, joined with numberless great qualities, rendered him at once venerable and terrible in the eyes of his soldiers; for without this reputation for cruelty these other virtues would not have produced the like results.

Unreflecting writers, indeed, while they praise his achievements, have condemned the chief cause of them; but that his other merits would not by themselves have been so efficacious we may see from the case of Scipio, one of the greatest Captains, not of his own time only but of all times of which we have record, whose armies rose against him in Spain from no other cause than his too great leniency in allowing them a freedom inconsistent with military strictness. With which weakness Fabius Maximus taxed him in the Senate House, calling him the corrupter of the Roman soldiery. Again, when the Locrians were shamefully outraged by one of his lieutenants, he neither avenged them, nor punished the insolence of his officer; and this from the natural easiness of his disposition. So that it was said in the Senate by one who sought to excuse him, that there were many who knew better how to refrain from doing wrong themselves than how to correct the wrong-doing of others. This temper, however, must in time have marred the name and fame even of Scipio, had he continued in it, and retained his command. But living as he did under the control of the Senate, this hurtful quality was not merely disguised, but came to be regarded as a glory.

Returning to the question of being loved or feared, I sum up by saying, that since his being loved depends upon his subjects, while his being feared depends upon himself, a wise Prince should build on what is his own, and not on what rests with others. Only, as I have said, he must do his utmost to escape hatred.

How Princes Should Keep Faith

Every one understands how praiseworthy it is in a Prince to keep faith, and to live uprightly and not craftily. Nevertheless, we see from what has taken place in our own days that Princes who have set little store by their word, but have known how to overreach men by their cunning, have accomplished great things, and in the end got the better of those who trusted to honest dealing.

Be it known, then, that there are two ways of contending, one in accordance with the laws, the other by force; the first of which is proper to men, the second to beasts. But since the first method is often ineffectual, it becomes necessary to resort to the second. A Prince should, therefore, understand how to use well both the man and the beast. And this lesson has been covertly taught by the ancient writers, who relate how Achilles and many others of these old Princes were given over to be brought up and trained by Chiron the Centaur; since the only meaning of their having for instructor one who was half man and half beast is, that it is necessary for a Prince to know how to use both natures, and that the one without the other has no stability.

But since a Prince should know how to use the beast's nature wisely, he ought of beasts to choose both the lion and the fox; for the lion cannot guard himself from the toils, nor the fox from wolves. He must therefore be a fox to discern toils, and a lion to drive off wolves.

To rely wholly on the lion is unwise; and for this reason a prudent Prince neither can nor ought to keep his word when to keep it is hurtful to him and the causes which led him to pledge it are removed. If all men were good, this would not be good advice, but since they are dishonest and do not keep faith with you, you, in return, need not keep faith with them; and no prince was ever at a loss for plausible reasons to cloak a breach of faith. Of this numberless recent instances could be given, and it might be shown how many solemn treaties and engagements have been rendered inoperative and idle through want of faith in Princes, and that he who was best known to play the fox has had the best success. It is necessary, indeed, to put a good colour on this nature, and to be skilful in simulating and dissembling.

But men remain so simple, and governed so absolutely by their present needs, that he who wishes to deceive will never fail in finding willing dupes. One recent example I will not omit. Pope Alexander VI had no care or thought but how to deceive, and always found material to work on. No man ever had a more effective manner of asseverating, or ever made promises with more solemn protestations, or observed them less. And yet, because he understood this side of human nature, his frauds always succeeded.

It is not essential then, that a Prince should have all the good qualities which I have enumerated above, but it is most essential that he should seem to have them; I will even venture to affirm that if he has and invariably practices them all, they are hurtful, whereas the appearance of having them is useful. Thus, it is well to seem merciful, faithful, humane, religious, and upright, and also to be so; but the mind should remain so balanced that were it needful not to be so, you should be able and know how to change to the contrary.

And you are to understand that a Prince, and most of all a new Prince, cannot observe all those rules of conduct in respect whereof men are accounted good, being often forced, in order to preserve his Princedom, to act in opposition to good faith, charity, humanity, and religion. He must therefore keep his mind ready to shift as the winds and tides of Fortune turn, and, as I have already said, he ought not to quit good courses if he can help it, but should know how to follow evil courses if he must.

A Prince should therefore be very careful that nothing ever escapes his lips which is not replete with the five qualities above named, so that to see and hear him, one would think him the embodiment of mercy, good faith, integrity, humanity, and religion. And there is no virtue which it is more necessary for him to seem to possess than this last; because men in general judge rather by the eye than by the hand, for every one can see but few can touch. Every one sees what you seem, but few know what you are, and these few dare not oppose themselves to the opinion of the many who have the majesty of the State to back them up.

Moreover, in the actions of all men, and most of all of Princes, where there is no tribunal to which we can appeal, we look to results. Wherefore if a Prince succeeds in establishing and maintaining his authority, the means will always be judged honourable and be approved by every one. For the vulgar are always taken by appearances and by results, and the world is made up of the vulgar, the few only finding room when the many have no longer ground to stand on.

A certain Prince of our own days, whose name it is as well not to mention, is always preaching peace and good faith, although the mortal enemy of both; and both, had he practised them as he preaches them, would, oftener than once, have lost him his kingdom and authority.

REVIEW QUESTIONS

1. How does Machiavelli's view of human nature color his description of an effective leader? *Naturally dishonest oo seem to be honest*
2. Are there useful strategies for leaders in this essay that are not immoral?
3. Does Machiavelli think leaders should have some moral qualities?
4. If so, what are the moral qualities? *depends on view*
5. In today's world can leaders be effective by simply appearing to be ethical? *U? K?*

Why Self-Interest Is Best

Ayn Rand, 1905–1982

Ayn Rand was born Alissa Zinovievna Rosenbaum in St. Petersburg, Russia. In 1925 she immigrated to the United States where she renamed herself Ayn, after a Finnish writer she had never read, and Rand after the brand name on her type-writer. She worked as a movie extra, screenwriter, and script reader in Hollywood, California. Eventually Rand began writing books and soon became a controversial figure in twentieth-century literary and philosophical debate. She believed that society would be better off if people pursued their own self-interests. Even after her death Rand's books and ideas still garner an enthusiastic following.

Rand argues that people should live for their own happiness and never sacrifice their own goals for someone else's. It's easy to see why her objectivist philosophy of self-interest continues to attract an enthusiastic following. Whereas conventional morality requires us to place restrictions on ourselves and our desires, Rand's philosophy releases us from moral constraints such as the golden rule. She has a particular distaste for Christian ethics and Immanuel Kant's ethics, which she calls the morality of sacrifice.

The following reading is from her best-selling novel *Atlas Shrugged*. In the novel, all artists, inventors, scientists, and creative people go on strike. The economy crumbles and society falls into shambles. In the end John Galt, the hero of the novel, emerges to rebuild society according to his principles of creativity, self-interest, and self-reliance. The following excerpt is a speech by Galt that articulates Rand's ideas about ethics.

As you read this essay, note what is seductive about Rand's argument. One might argue that some leaders become very successful in business, politics, and their professions using Rand's approach to morality.

Yes, this *is* an age of moral crisis. Yes, you *are* bearing punishment for your evil. But it is not man who is now on trial and it is not human nature that will take the blame. It is your moral code that's through, this time. Your moral code has reached its climax, the blind alley at the end of its course. And if you wish to go on living, what you now need is not to *return* to morality—you who have never known any—but to *discover* it.

"You have heard no concepts of morality but the mystical or the social. You have been taught that morality is a code of behavior imposed on you by whim, the whim of a supernatural power or the whim of society to serve God's purpose or your neighbor's welfare, to please an authority beyond the grave or else next door—but not to serve *your* life or pleasure. Your pleasure, you have been taught, is to be found in immorality, your interests would best be served by evil, and any moral code must be designed not *for* you, but *against* you, not to further your life, but to drain it.

"For centuries, the battle of morality was fought between those who claimed that your life belongs to God and those who claimed that it belongs to your neighbors—between those who preached that the good is self-sacrifice for the sake of ghosts in heaven and those who preached that the good is self-sacrifice for the sake of incompetents on earth. And no one came to say that your life belongs to you and that the good is to live it.

"Both sides agreed that morality demands the surrender of your self-interest and of your mind, that the moral and the practical are opposites, that morality is not the province of reason, but the province of faith and force. Both sides agreed that no rational morality is possible, that there is no right or wrong in reason—that in reason there's no reason to be moral.

"Whatever else they fought about, it was against man's mind that all your moralists have stood united. It was man's mind that all their schemes and systems were intended to despoil and destroy. Now choose to perish or to learn that the anti-mind is the anti-life.

"Man's mind is his basic tool of survival. Life is given to him, survival is not. His body is given to him, its sustenance is not. His mind is given to him, its content is not. To remain alive, he must act, and before he can act he must know the nature and purpose of his action. He cannot obtain his food without a knowledge of food and of the way to obtain it. He cannot dig a ditch—or build a cyclotron—without a knowledge of his aim and of the means to achieve it. To remain alive, he must think.

"But to think is an act of choice. The key to what you so recklessly call 'human nature,' the open secret you live with, yet dread to name, is the fact that *man is a being of volitional consciousness.* Reason does not work automatically; thinking is not a mechanical process; the connections of logic are not made by instinct. The function of your stomach, lungs or heart is automatic; the function of your mind is not. In any hour and issue of your life, you are free to think or to evade that effort. But you are not free to escape from your nature, from the fact that *reason* is your means of survival—so that for *you,* who are a human being, the question 'to be or not to be' is the question 'to think or not to think.'

"A being of volitional consciousness has no automatic course of behavior. He needs a code of values to guide his actions. 'Value' is that which one acts to gain and keep, 'virtue' is the action by which one gains and keeps it. 'Value' presupposes an answer to the question: of value to whom and for what? 'Value' presupposes a standard, a purpose and the necessity of action in the face of an alternative. Where there are no alternatives, no values are possible.

"There is only one fundamental alternative in the universe: existence or non-existence—and it pertains to a single class of entities: to living organisms. The existence of inanimate matter is unconditional, the existence of life is not: it depends on a specific course of action. Matter is indestructible, it changes its forms, but it cannot cease to exist. It is only a living organism that faces a constant alternative: the issue of life or death. Life is a process of self-sustaining and self-generating action. If an organism fails in that action, it dies; its chemical elements remain, but its life goes out of existence. It is only the concept of 'Life' that makes the concept of 'Value' possible. It is only to a living entity that things can be good or evil.

"A plant must feed itself in order to live; the sunlight, the water, the chemicals it needs are the values its nature has set it to pursue; its life is the standard of value directing its actions. But a plant has no choice of action; there are alternatives in the conditions it encounters, but there is no alternative in its function: it acts automatically to further its life, it cannot act for its own destruction.

"An animal is equipped for sustaining its life; its senses provide it with an automatic code of action, an automatic knowledge of what is good for it or evil. It has no power to extend its knowledge or to evade it. In conditions where its knowledge proves inadequate, it dies. But so long as it lives, it acts on its knowledge, with automatic safety and no power of choice, it is unable to ignore its own good, unable to decide to choose the evil and act as its own destroyer.

"Man has no automatic code of survival. His particular distinction from other living species is the necessity to act in the face of alternatives by means of *volitional choice*. He has no automatic knowledge of what good for him or evil, what values his life depends on, what course of action it requires. Are you prattling about an instinct of self-preservation? An *instinct* of self-preservation is precisely what man does not possess. An 'instinct' is an unerring and automatic form of knowledge. A desire is not an instinct. A desire to live does not give you the knowledge required for living. And even man's desire to live is not automatic: your secret evil today is that *that* is the desire you do not hold. Your fear of death is not a love for life and will not give you the knowledge needed to keep it. Man must obtain his knowledge and choose his actions by a process of thinking, which nature will not force him to perform. Man has the power to act as his own destroyer—and that is the way he has acted through most of his history.

"A living entity that regarded its means of survival as evil, would not survive. A plant that struggled to mangle its roots, a bird that fought to break its wings would not remain for long in the existence they affronted. But the history of man has been a struggle to deny and to destroy his mind.

"Man has been called a rational being, but rationality is a matter of choice—and the alternative his nature offers him is: rational being or suicidal animal. Man has to be man—by choice; he has to hold his life as a value—by choice; he has to learn to sustain it—by choice; he has to discover the values it requires and practice his virtues—by choice.

"A code of values accepted by choice, is a code of morality.

"Whoever you are, you who are hearing me now, I am speaking to whatever living remnant is left uncorrupted within you, to the remnant of the human, to your *mind*, and I say: There *is* a morality of reason, a morality proper to man, and *Man's Life* is its standard of value.

"All that which is proper to the life of a rational being is the good; all that which destroys it is the evil.

"Man's life, as required by his nature, is not the life of a mindless brute, of a looting thug or a mooching mystic, but the life of a thinking being—not life by means of force or fraud, but life by means of achievement—not survival at any price, since there's only one price that pays for man's survival: reason.

"Man's life is the *standard* of morality, but your own life is its *purpose*. If existence on earth is your goal, you must choose actions and values by the standard of that which is proper to man—for the purpose of preserving, fulfilling and enjoying the irreplaceable value which is your life.

"Since life requires a specific course of action, any other course will destroy it. A being who does not hold his own life as the motive and goal of his actions is acting on the motive and standard of *death*. Such a being is a metaphysical monstrosity, struggling to oppose, negate, and contradict the fact of his own existence, running blindly amuck on a trail of destruction, capable of nothing but pain.

"Happiness is the successful state of life; pain is an agent of death. Happiness is that state of unconsciousness which proceeds from the achievement of one's values. A morality that dares to tell you to find happiness in the renunciation of your happiness—to value the failure of your values—is an insolent negation of morality. A doctrine that gives you, as an ideal, the role of a sacrificial animal seeking slaughter on the altars of others, is giving you *death* as your standard. By the grace of reality and the nature of life, man—every man—is an end in himself, he exists for his own sake, and the achievement of his own happiness is his highest moral purpose.

"But neither life nor happiness can be achieved by the pursuit of irrational whims. Just as man is free to attempt to survive in any random manner, but will perish unless he lives as his nature requires, so he is free to seek his happiness in any mindless fraud, but the torture of frustration is all he will find, unless he seeks the happiness proper to man. The purpose of morality is to teach you, not to suffer and die, but to enjoy yourself and love.

"Sweep aside those parasites of subsidized classrooms, who live on the profits of the mind of others and proclaim that man needs no morality, no values, no code of behavior. They, who pose as scientists and claim that man is only an animal, do not grant him inclusion in the law of existence they have granted to the lowest of insects. They recognize that every living species has a way of survival demanded by its nature, they do not claim that a fish can live out of water or that a dog can live without its sense of smell—but man, they claim, the most complex of beings, man can survive in any way whatever, man has no identity, no nature, and there's no practical reason why he cannot live with his means of survival destroyed, with his mind throttled and placed at the disposal of any orders *they* might care to issue.

"Sweep aside those hatred-eaten mystics who pose as friends of humanity and preach that the highest virtue man can practice is to hold his own life as of no value. Do they tell you that the purpose of morality is to curb man's instinct of self-preservation? It is for the purpose of self-preservation that man needs a code of morality. The only man who desires to be moral is the man who desires to live.

"No, you do not have to live; it is your basic act of choice; but if you choose to live, you must live as a man—by the work and the judgment of your mind.

"No, you do not have to live as a man: it is an act of moral choice. But you cannot live as anything else—and the alternative is that state of living death which you now see within you and around you, the state of a thing unfit for existence, no longer human and less than animal, a thing that knows nothing but pain and drags itself through its span of years in the agony of unthinking self-destruction.

"No, you do not have to think; it is an act of moral choice. But someone had to think to keep you alive; if you choose to default, you default on existence and you pass the deficit to some moral man, expecting him to sacrifice his good for the sake of letting you survive by your evil. . . .

"This much is true: the most _selfish_ of all things is the independent mind that recognizes no authority higher than its own and no value higher than its judgment of truth. You are asked to sacrifice your intellectual integrity, your logic, your reason, your standard of truth—in favor of becoming a prostitute whose standard is the greatest good for the greatest number.

"If you search your code for guidance, for an answer to the question: 'What _is_ the good?'—the only answer you will find is '_The good of others._' The good is whatever others wish, whatever you feel they feel they wish, or whatever you feel they ought to feel. 'The good of others' is a magic formula that transforms anything into gold, a formula to be recited as a guarantee of moral glory and as a fumigator for any action, even the slaughter of a continent. Your standard of virtue is not an object, not an act, nor a principle, but an _intention._ You need no proof, no reasons, no success, you need not achieve _in fact_ the good of others—all you need to know is that your motive was the good of others, _not_ your own. Your only definition of the good is a negation: the good is the 'non-good for me.'

"Your code—which boasts that it upholds eternal, absolute, objective moral values and scorns the conditional, the relative and the subjective—your code hands out, as its version of the absolute, the following rule of moral conduct: If _you_ wish it, it's evil; if others wish it, it's good; if the motive of your action is _your_ welfare, don't do it; if the motive is the welfare of others, then anything goes.

"As this double-jointed, double-standard morality splits you in half, so it splits mankind into two enemy camps: one is _you_, the other is all the rest of humanity. _You_ are the only outcast who has no right to wish or live. _You_ are the only servant, the rest are the masters, _you_ are the only giver, the rest are the takers, _you_ are the eternal debtor, the rest are the creditors never to be paid off. You must not question their right to your sacrifice, or the nature of their wishes and their needs: their right is conferred upon them by a negative, by the fact that they are 'non-you.'

"For those of you who might ask questions, your code provides a consolation prize and booby-trap: it is for your own happiness, it says, that you must serve the happiness of others, the only way to achieve your joy is to give it up to others, the only way to achieve your prosperity is to surrender your wealth to others, the only way to protect your life is to protect all men except yourself—and if you find no joy in this procedure, it is your own fault and the proof of your evil; if you were good, you would find your happiness in providing a banquet for others, and your dignity in existing on such crumbs as *they* might care to toss you.

"You who have no standard of self-esteem, accept the guilt and dare not ask the questions. But you know the unadmitted answer, refusing to acknowledge what you see, what hidden premise moves your world. You know it, not in honest statement, but as a dark uneasiness within you, while you flounder between guiltily cheating and grudgingly practicing a principle too vicious to name.

"I, who do not accept the unearned, neither in values nor in guilt, am here to ask the questions you evaded. Why is it moral to serve the happiness of others, but not your own? If enjoyment is a value, why is it moral when experienced by others, but immoral when experienced by you? If the sensation of eating a cake is a value, why is it an immoral indulgence in your stomach, but a moral goal for you to achieve in the stomach of others? Why is it immoral for you to desire, but moral for others to do so? Why is it immoral to produce a value and keep it, but moral to give it away? And if it is not moral for you to keep a value, why is it moral for others to accept it? If you are selfless and virtuous when you give it, are they not selfish and vicious when they take it? Does virtue consist of serving vice? Is the moral purpose of those who are good, self-immolation for the sake of those who are evil? . . .

"Under a morality of sacrifice, the first value you sacrifice is morality; the next is self-esteem. When need is the standard, every man is both victim and parasite. As a victim, he must labor to fill the needs of others, leaving himself in the position of a parasite whose needs must be filled by others. He cannot approach his fellow men except in one of two disgraceful roles: he is both a beggar and a sucker.

"You fear the man who has a dollar less than you, that dollar is rightfully his, he makes you feel like a moral defrauder. You hate the man who has a dollar more than you, that dollar is rightfully yours, he makes you feel that you are morally defrauded. The man below is a source of your guilt, the man above is a source of your frustration. You do not know what to surrender or demand, when to give and when to grab, what pleasure in life is rightfully yours and what debt is still unpaid to others—you struggle to evade, as 'theory,' the knowledge that by the moral standard you've accepted you are guilty every moment of your life, there is no mouthful of food you swallow that is not *needed* by someone somewhere on earth—and you give up the problem in blind resentment, you conclude that moral perfection is not to be achieved *or desired,* that you will muddle through by snatching as snatch can and by avoiding the eyes of the young, of those who look at you as if self-esteem were possible and they expected you to have it. Guilt is all that you retain within your soul—and so does every other man, as he goes past, avoiding *your* eyes. Do you wonder why your morality has not achieved brotherhood on earth or the good will of man to man?

"The justification of sacrifice, that your morality propounds, is more corrupt than the corruption it purports to justify. The motive of your sacrifice, it tells you, should be *love*—the love you ought to feel for every man. A morality that professes the belief that the values of the spirit are more precious than matter, a morality that teaches you to scorn a whore who gives her body indiscriminately to all men—this same morality demands that you surrender your soul to promiscuous love for all comers.

"As there can be no causeless wealth, so there can be no causeless love or any sort of causeless emotion. An emotion is a response to a fact of reality, an estimate dictated by your standards. To love is to *value.* The man who tells you that it is possible to value without values, to love those whom you appraise as worthless, is the man who tells you that it is possible to grow rich by consuming without producing and that paper money is as valuable as gold.

"Observe that he does not expect you to feel a causeless fear. When his kind get into power, they are expert at contriving means of terror, at giving you ample cause to feel the fear by which they desire to rule you. But when it comes to love, the highest of emotions, you permit them to shriek at you accusingly that you are a moral delinquent if you're incapable of feeling causeless love. When a man feels fear without reason, you call him to the attention of a psychiatrist; you are not so careful to protect the meaning, the nature and the dignity of love.

"Love is the expression of one's values, the greatest reward you can earn for the moral qualities you have achieved in your character and person, the emotional price paid by one man for the joy he receives from the virtues of another. Your morality demands that you divorce your love from values and hand it down to any vagrant, not as response to his worth, but as response to his *need,* not as reward, but as alms, not as a payment for virtues, but as a blank check on vices. Your morality tells you that the purpose of love is to set you free of the bonds of morality, that love is superior to moral judgment, that true love transcends, forgives and survives every manner of evil in its object, and the greater the love the greater the depravity it permits to the loved. To love a man for his virtues is paltry and human, it tells you; to love him for his flaws is divine. To love those who are worthy of it is self-interest; to love the unworthy is sacrifice. You owe your love to those who don't deserve it, and the less they deserve it, the more love you owe them—the more loathsome the object, the nobler your love—the more unfastidious your love, the greater your virtue—and if you can bring your soul to the state of a dump heap that welcomes anything on equal terms, if you can cease to value moral values, you have achieved the state of moral perfection.

"Such is your morality of sacrifice and such are the twin ideals it offers: to refashion the life of your body in the image of a human stockyards, and the life of your spirit in the image of a dump. . . .

"Since childhood, you have been hiding the guilty secret that you feel no desire, to be moral, no desire to seek self-immolation, that you dread and hate your code, but dare not say it even to yourself, that you're devoid of those moral 'instincts' which others profess to feel. The less you felt, the louder you proclaimed your selfless love and servitude to others, in dread of ever letting them discover your own self, the self that you betrayed, the self that you kept in concealment, like a skeleton in the closet of your body. And they, who were at once your dupes and your deceivers, they listened and voiced their loud approval, in dread of ever letting you discover that they were harboring the same unspoken secret. Existence among you is a giant pretense, an act you all perform for one another, each feeling that he is the only guilty freak, each placing his moral authority in the unknowable known only to others, each faking the reality he feels they expect him to fake, none having the courage to break the vicious circle.

"No matter what dishonorable compromise you've made with your impracticable creed, no matter what miserable balance, half-cynicism, half-superstition, you now manage to maintain, you still preserve the root, the lethal tenet: the belief that the moral and the practical are opposites. Since childhood, you have been running from the terror of a choice you have never dared fully to identify: If the *practical,* whatever you must practice to exist, whatever works, succeeds, achieves your purpose, whatever brings you food and joy, whatever profits you is evil—and if the good, the moral is the *impractical,* whatever fails, destroys, frustrates, whatever injures you and brings you loss or pain—then your choice is to be moral or to live.

"The sole result of that murderous doctrine was to remove morality from life. You grew up to believe that moral laws bear no relation to the job of living, except as an impediment and threat, that man's existence is an amoral jungle where anything goes and anything works. And in that fog of switching definitions which descends upon a frozen mind, you have forgotten that the evils damned by your creed were the virtues required for living, and you have come to believe that actual evils are the *practical* means of existence. Forgetting that the impractical 'good' was self-sacrifice, you believe that self-esteem is impractical; forgetting that the practical 'evil' was production, you believe that robbery is practical. . . .

"Accept the fact that the achievement of your happiness is the only *moral* purpose of your life, and that *happiness*—not pain or mindless self-indulgence—is the proof of your moral integrity, since it is the proof and the result of your loyalty to the achievement of your values. Happiness was the responsibility you dreaded, it required the kind of rational discipline you did not value yourself enough to assume—and the anxious staleness of your days is the monument to your evasion of the knowledge that there is no moral substitute for happiness, that there is no more despicable coward than the man who deserted the battle for his joy, fearing to assert his right to existence, lacking the courage and the loyalty to life of a bird or a flower reaching for the sun. Discard the protective rags of that vice which you called a virtue: humility—learn to value yourself, which means: to fight for your happiness—and when you learn that *pride* is the sum of all virtues, you will learn to live like a man.

"As a basic step of self-esteem, learn to treat as the mark of a cannibal any man's *demand* for your help. To demand it is to claim that your life is *his* property—and loathsome as such claim might be, there's something still more loathsome: your agreement. Do you ask if it's ever proper to help another man? No—if he claims it as his right or as a moral duty that you owe him. Yes—if such is your own desire based on your own selfish pleasure in the value of his person and his struggle."

REVIEW QUESTIONS

1. What does it mean to be successful as a leader? As a human being?
2. Would leaders in today's political and organizational settings be effective if they rejected what Rand calls the morality of sacrifice?
3. Describe the strengths and weaknesses of a leader who only acts on his or her own self-interest.
4. How does Rand's advice compare and contrast with Machiavelli's?
5. Would Rand agree with Hobbes's assessment of human nature?

Virtue and the Public and Private Morality of Leaders

Introduction

Today we often find ourselves disappointed by the moral character of leaders. As humans, leaders are subject to the same flaws and weaknesses as everyone else. Yet we want our leaders to transcend them and live up to higher moral standards. Some people turn wistfully to the past and wonder where all the leaders and heroes have gone. But when you think about it, ordinary people did not know as much about the personal behavior of their leaders in the past as we do today. It is difficult to have heroes in the information age where every wart and wrinkle of a leader's life can and often is made public. Ironically, the increase in information that we have about leaders has also increased our concern about their ethics. The more defects our leaders have, the more we long for ethical leaders. We have demystified our leaders and we're not sure we like it. The readings in this chapter help us to reflect on the public and private morality of leaders.

This chapter looks at leadership from the perspective of virtue. Aristotle tells us that virtues are habits that form our character. When we select a leader for a political office or for an organization, we typically look at the person's track record and assume that if that person has been honest in the past, he or she will be honest in the future. Sometimes we make the opposite assumption, that if someone has deceived us in the past, he or she will do so in the future. For example, the American public subjected presidential candidate Gary Hart to such scorn when he was caught cheating on his wife that he was forced out of the primary race. Yet there have been other times when we were willing to give a leader the benefit of a doubt. In the first presidential campaign of Bill Clinton, Clinton admitted to having an extramarital affair and went on to win the election. However, when Clinton lied about his affair with an intern during his second term in office, citizens and political leaders were outraged. The Clinton case raised some fundamental issues about the ethics of leaders, some of which are discussed in this chapter.

We often assume that we can judge a person's future moral behavior by his or her past moral behavior. The case "Sleazy or Stupid" helps us think about this question in a commonplace situation in the workplace. Here a manager has to decide if a comment made by a job applicant after the interview is grounds for not giving him the job.

Because leaders are also imperfect humans, they have moral weakness too. Yet, unlike most people, the impact of leaders' moral weaknesses are multiplied in proportion to their visibility, power, and the size of their constituencies. Leaders are supposed to model the virtues of their society or organization. When they don't, they often lose credibility and legitimacy. Morality not only requires good habits, but it also requires self-discipline and self-knowledge. Buddha's "First Sermon" tells us that people suffer when they lose touch with who they are and they become enslaved by their wants and "cravings."

Aristotle and Buddha both believe that the morality of a person is one seamless whole. People cannot segment themselves into the work person and the home person. Yet today some believe that when it comes to practical questions of leadership, a leader's behavior at home is none of our business and that we should only judge leaders by their performance on the job. The case "Does Personal Morality Matter?" makes us see how difficult it sometimes is to judge a person only by what he or she does at work.

The pressures of leadership make leaders more vulnerable to their moral weaknesses and their desires than others. One of the greatest fears we have about leaders is that they will abuse power or that power will distort their sense of self, moral purpose, and accountability. The temptations of power are perhaps the greatest personal challenges faced by leaders. Both the Old Testament and the Torah tell the story of "David and Bathsheba." It's the tale of a good leader who falls prey to his own moral weakness. King David abuses his power to satisfy his desire and cover up his mistake. The article, "The Bathsheba Syndrome: The Ethical Failure of Successful Leaders," vividly illustrates how personal moral failings and loss of focus can lead to failure on the job.

The last reading in this chapter, "The Conscience of Huckleberry Finn" is about the role of moral sentiments such as empathy, sympathy, or what we sometimes call "gut feelings" in ethics. Leaders are subject to the mores and moral norms of their society, but there are times when doing what is "right" doesn't feel right. Sometimes their gut feelings correct their moral choices; sometimes they misguide them.

As you read this chapter, consider the following questions: *Is it fair to judge a leader's character by one or two "unfortunate" incidents? Can we predict a leader's future behavior from his or her behavior in the past? Should leaders be penalized on the job for what they do off the job? Can we separate the character of a person's leadership from his or her moral character? When should leaders follow their hearts?*

Virtue Ethics

Aristotle 384 B.C.–322 B.C.

Aristotle was born in Stagira in Macedonia. His father, Nicomachus, was the court physician to the king of Macedonia, who was the grandfather of Alexander the Great. The following selections are from Aristotle's *Nicomachean Ethics,* which Aristotle named after his father. Aristotle went to study at Plato's Academy when he was seventeen and remained there for twenty years. In 345 B.C. he returned to Macedonia to be tutor to Alexander the Great. When Alexander became king in 335 B.C., Aristotle returned to Athens and started his own school called the Lyceum.

Aristotle believed that the study of ethics is inseparable from the study of politics. Humans are political animals and because most people live in groups, the ethics of the individual has to be studied as part of the ethics of groups. Like Plato, Aristotle attempts to show that people are better off being ethical than unethical. Happiness is the highest good in life, but Aristotle's notion of happiness, *eudaimona,* is somewhat different from our own today. By happiness he meant that people fill their function, which is to live in conformity with reason and have virtues that will allow them to exert rational control over their desires. By this definition, a happy life is one where people flourish. They do the things they want to do well and they are virtuous in the things they seek and the things they do. You will notice that technical excellence, which Aristotle often speaks of as craft, and moral excellence are tied to each other. There is no split between ethics and effectiveness for him. Aristotle said that the rational part of people consists of theoretical knowledge and practical knowledge. Ethics and politics are parts of practical knowledge. That's why he says both subjects should not be taught to the very young, but to people with experience.

The following reading focuses on Aristotle's description of virtue. Notice that a virtue is something that you can only have if you practice it. Aristotle says that virtue is a habit, but not a mindless one. You act virtuously with the intent to do the right thing. People learn about virtue from role models and from society. (The same is true of vices.) On a daily basis we make judgments about people's character, whether we are choosing a president, a baby-sitter, or a new employee.

2. Virtues of Character in General

2.1 How a Virtue of Character Is Acquired

Virtue, then, is of two sorts, virtue of thought and virtue of character. Virtue of thought arises and grows mostly from teaching, and hence needs experience and time. Virtue of character [i.e., of *ēthos*] results from habit [*ethos*]; hence its name "ethical," slightly varied from "*ethos.*"

**Virtue Comes About, Not by a Process
of Nature, but by Habituation**

Hence it is also clear that none of the virtues of character arises in us naturally.

(1) What is natural cannot be changed by habituation

For if something is by nature [in one condition], habituation cannot
bring it into another condition. A stone, e.g., by nature moves
downwards, and habituation could not make it move upwards, not even
if you threw it up ten thousand times to habituate it; nor could
habituation make fire move downwards, or bring anything that is by
nature in one condition into another condition.

Thus the virtues arise in us neither by nature nor against nature, but
we are by nature able to acquire them, and reach our complete
perfection through habit.

(2) Natural capacities are not acquired by habituation

Further, if something arises in us by nature, we first have the capacity
for it, and later display the activity. This is clear in the case of the
senses; for we did not acquire them by frequent seeing or hearing, but
already had them when we exercised them, and did not get them by
exercising them.

Virtues, by contrast, we acquire, just as we acquire crafts, by having
previously activated them. For we learn a craft by producing the same
product that we must produce when we have learned it, becoming
builders, e.g., by building and harpists by playing the harp; so also, then,
we become just by doing just actions, temperate by doing temperate
actions, brave by doing brave actions.

(3) Legislators concentrate on habituation

What goes on in cities is evidence for this also. For the legislator makes
the citizens good by habituating them, and this is the wish of every
legislator; if he fails to do it well he misses his goal. [The right]
habituation is what makes the difference between a good political system
and a bad one.

(4) Virtue and vice are formed by good and bad actions

Further, just as in the case of a craft, the sources and means that develop
each virtue also ruin it. For playing the harp makes both good and bad
harpists, and it is analogous in the case of builders and all the rest; for
building well makes good builders, building badly, bad ones. If it were
not so, no teacher would be needed, but everyone would be born a good
or a bad craftsman.

It is the same, then, with the virtues. For actions in dealings with
[other] human beings make some people just, some unjust; actions in
terrifying situations and the acquired habit of fear or confidence make
some brave and others cowardly. The same is true of situations involving

appetites and anger; for one or another sort of conduct in these situations makes some people temperate and gentle, others intemperate and irascible.

Conclusion: The importance of habituation

To sum up, then, in a single account: A state [of character] arises from [the repetition of] similar activities. Hence we must display the right activities, since differences in these imply corresponding differences in the states. It is not unimportant, then, to acquire one sort of habit or another, right from our youth; rather, it is very important, indeed all-important.

2.12 What Is the Right Sort of Habituation?

This is an appropriate question, for the aim of ethical theory is practical

Our present inquiry does not aim, as our others do, at study; for the purpose of our examination is not to know what virtue is, but to become good, since otherwise the inquiry would be of no benefit to us. Hence we must examine the right way to act, since, as we have said, the actions also control the character of the states we acquire.

First, then, actions should express correct reason. That is a common [belief], and let us assume it; later we will say what correct reason is and how it is related to the other virtues.

But let us take it as agreed in advance that every account of the actions we must do has to be stated in outline, not exactly. As we also said at the start, the type of accounts we demand should reflect the subject-matter; and questions about actions and expediency, like questions about health, have no fixed [and invariable answers].

And when our general account is so inexact, the account of particular cases is all the more inexact. For these fall under no craft or profession, and the agents themselves must consider in each case what the opportune action is, as doctors and navigators do.

The account we offer, then, in our present inquiry is of this inexact sort; still, we must try to offer help.

The right sort of habituation must avoid excess and deficiency

First, then, we should observe that these sorts of states naturally tend to be ruined by excess and deficiency. We see this happen with strength and health, which we mention because we must use what is evident as a witness to what is not. For both excessive and deficient exercises ruin strength: and likewise, too much or too little eating or drinking ruins health, while the proportionate amount produces, increases and preserves it.

The same is true, then, of temperance, bravery and the other virtues. For if, e.g., someone avoids and is afraid of everything, standing firm against nothing, he becomes cowardly, but if he is afraid of nothing at all and goes to face everything, he becomes rash. Similarly, if he gratifies himself with every pleasure and refrains from none, he becomes intemperate, but if he avoids them all, as boors do, he become some sort of insensible person. Temperance and bravery then, are ruined by excess and deficiency but preserved by the mean.

The same actions, then, are the sources and causes both of the emergence and growth of virtues and of their ruin; but further, the activities of the virtues will be found in these same actions. For this is also true of more evident cases, e.g. strength, which arises from eating a lot and from withstanding much hard labour, and it is the strong person who is most able to do these very things. It is the same with the virtues. Refraining from pleasures make us become temperate, and when we have become temperate we are most able to refrain from pleasures. And it is similar with bravery; habituation in disdaining what is fearful and in standing firm against it makes us become brave, and when we have become brave we shall be most able to stand firm.

2.14 But Our Claims about Habituation Raise a Puzzle: How Can We Become Good Without Being Good Already?

However, someone might raise this puzzle: "What do you mean by saying that to become just we must first do just actions and to become temperate we must first do temperate actions? For if we do what is grammatical or musical, we must already be grammarians or musicians. In the same way, then, if we do what is just or temperate, we must already be just or temperate."

First reply: Conformity versus understanding
But surely this is not so even with the crafts, for it is possible to produce something grammatical by chance or by following someone else's instructions. To be a grammarian, then, we must both produce something grammatical and produce it in the way in which the grammarian produces it, i.e. expressing grammatical knowledge that is in us.

Second reply: Crafts versus virtues
Moreover, in any case what is true of crafts is not true of virtues. For the products of a craft determine by their own character whether they have been produced well; and so it suffices that they are in the right state when they have been produced. But for actions expressing virtue to be done temperately or justly [and hence well] it does not suffice that they are themselves in the right state. Rather, the agent must also be in the right state when he does them. First, he must know [that he is doing virtuous actions]; second, he must decide on them, and decide on them for themselves; and, third, he must also do them from a firm and unchanging state.

As conditions for having a craft these three do not count, except for the knowing itself. As a condition for having a virtue, however, the knowing counts for nothing, or [rather] for only a little, whereas the other two conditions are very important, indeed all-important. And these other two conditions are achieved by the frequent doing of just and temperate actions.

Hence actions are called just or temperate when they are the sort that a just or temperate person would do. But the just and temperate person is not the one who [merely] does these actions, but the one who also does them in the way in which just or temperate people do them.

It is right, then, to say that a person comes to be just from doing just actions and temperate from doing temperate actions; for no one has even a prospect of becoming good from failing to do them.

Virtue requires habituation, and therefore requires practice, not just theory

The many, however, do not do these actions but take refuge in arguments, thinking that they are doing philosophy, and that this is the way to become excellent people. In this they are like a sick person who listens attentively to the doctor, but acts on none of his instructions. Such a course of treatment will not improve the state of his body; any more than will the many's way of doing philosophy improve the state of their souls.

Virtue and the human function

It should be said, then, that every virtue causes its possessors to be in a good state and to perform their functions well; the virtue of eyes, e.g., makes the eyes and their functioning excellent, because it makes us see well; and similarly, the virtue of a horse makes the horse excellent, and thereby good at galloping, at carrying its rider and at standing steady in the face of the enemy. If this is true in every case, then the virtue of a human being will likewise be the state that makes a human being good and makes him perform his function well.

Virtue seeks the mean relative to us: Argument from craft to virtue

This, then, is how each science produces its product well, by focusing on what is intermediate and making the product conform to that. This, indeed, is why people regularly comment on well-made products that nothing could be added or subtracted, since they assume that excess or deficiency ruins a good [result] while the mean preserves it. Good craftsmen also, we say, focus on what is intermediate when they produce their product. And since virtue, like nature, is better and more exact than any craft, it will also aim at what is intermediate.

Arguments from the nature of virtue of character

By virtue I mean virtue of character; for this [pursues the mean because] it is concerned with feelings and actions, and these admit of excess, deficiency and an intermediate condition. We can be afraid, e.g., or be confident, or have appetites, or get angry, or feel pity, in general have pleasure or pain, both too much and too little, and in both ways not well; but [having these feelings] at the right times, about the right things, towards the right people, for the right end, and in the right way, is the intermediate and best condition, and this is proper to virtue. Similarly, actions also admit of excess, deficiency and the intermediate condition.

Now virtue is concerned with feelings and actions, in which excess and deficiency are in error and incur blame, while the intermediate condition is correct and wins praise, which are both proper features of virtue. Virtue, then, is a mean in so far as it aims at what is intermediate.

Moreover, there are many ways to be in error, since badness is proper to what is unlimited, as the Pythagoreans pictured it, and good to what is limited; but there is only one way to be correct. That is why error is easy and correctness hard, since it is easy to miss the target and hard to hit it. And so for this reason also excess and deficiency are proper to vice, the mean to virtue; "for we are noble in only one way, but bad in all sorts of ways."

2.23 Definition of Virtue

Virtue, then, is (a) a state that decides, (b) [consisting] in a mean, (c) the mean relative to us, (d) which is defined by reference to reason, (e) i.e., to the reason by reference to which the intelligent person would define it. It is a mean between two vices, one of excess and one of deficiency.

It is a mean for this reason also: Some vices miss what is right because they are excessive, in feelings or in actions, while virtue finds and chooses what is intermediate.

Hence, as far as its substance and the account stating its essence are concerned, virtue is a mean; but as far as the best [condition] and the good [result] are concerned, it is an extremity.

The definition must not be misapplied to cases in which there is no mean
But not every action or feeling admits of the mean. For the names of some automatically include baseness, e.g. spite, shamelessness, envy [among feelings], and adultery, theft, murder, among actions. All of these and similar things are called by these names because they themselves, not their excesses or deficiencies, are base.

Hence in doing these things we can never be correct, but must invariably be in error. We cannot do them well or not well—e.g. by committing adultery with the right woman at the right time in the right way; on the contrary, it is true unconditionally that to do any of them is to be in error.

[To think these admit of a mean], therefore, is like thinking that unjust or cowardly or intemperate action also admits of a mean, an excess and a deficiency. For then there would be a mean of excess, a mean of deficiency, an excess of excess and a deficiency of deficiency.

Rather, just as there is no excess or deficiency of temperance or of bravery, since the intermediate is a sort of extreme [in achieving the good], so also there is no mean of these [vicious actions] either, but whatever way anyone does them, he is in error. For in general there is no mean of excess or of deficiency, and no excess or deficiency of a mean.

2.3 The Definition of Virtue as a Mean Applies
to the Individual Virtues

chart

However, we must not only state this general account but also apply it to the particular cases. For among accounts concerning actions, though the general ones are common to more cases, the specific ones are truer, since actions are about particular cases, and our account must accord with these. Let us, then, find these from the chart.

2.31 Classification of Virtues of Character

Virtues concerned with feelings

(1) First, in feelings of fear and confidence the mean is bravery. The excessively fearless person is nameless (and in fact many cases are nameless), while the one who is excessively confident is rash; the one who is excessively afraid and deficient in confidence is cowardly.

(2) In pleasures and pains, though not in all types, and in pains less than in pleasures, the mean is temperance and the excess intemperance. People deficient in pleasure are not often found, which is why they also lack even a name; let us call them insensible.

Virtues concerned with external goods

(3) In giving and taking money the mean is generosity, the excess wastefulness and the deficiency ungenerosity. Here the vicious people have contrary excesses and defects; for the wasteful person spends to excess and is deficient in taking, whereas the ungenerous person takes to excess and is deficient in spending. At the moment we are speaking in outline and summary, and that suffices; later we shall define these things more exactly.

(4) In questions of money there are also other conditions. Another mean is magnificence; for the magnificent person differs from the generous by being concerned with large matters, while the generous person is concerned with small. The excess is ostentation and vulgarity, and the deficiency niggardliness, and these differ from the vices related to generosity in ways we shall describe later.

(5) In honour and dishonour the mean is magnanimity, the excess something called a sort of vanity, and the deficiency pusillanimity.

(6) And just as we said that generosity differs from magnificence in its concern with small matters, similarly there is a virtue concerned with small honours, differing in the same way from magnanimity, which is concerned with great honours. For honour can be desired either in the right way or more or less than is right. If someone desires it to excess, he

is called an honour-lover, and if his desire is deficient he is called indifferent to honour, but if he is intermediate he has no name. The corresponding conditions have no name either, except the condition of the honour-lover, which is called honour-loving.

This is why people at the extremes claim the intermediate area. Indeed, we also sometimes call the intermediate person an honour-lover, and sometimes call him indifferent to honour; and sometimes we praise the honour-lover, sometimes the person indifferent to honour. We will mention later the reason we do this; for the moment, let us speak of the other cases in the way we have laid down.

Virtues concerned with social life

(7) Anger also admits of an excess, deficiency and mean. These are all practically nameless; but since we call the intermediate person mild, let us call the mean mildness. Among the extreme people let the excessive person be irascible, and the vice be irascibility, and let the deficient person be a sort of inirascible person, and the deficiency be inirascibility.

There are three other means, somewhat similar to one another, but different. For they are all concerned with association in conversations and actions, but differ in so far as one is concerned with truth-telling in these areas, the other two with sources of pleasure, some of which are found in amusement, and the others in daily life in general. Hence we should also discuss these states, so that we can better observe that in every case the mean is praiseworthy, while the extremes are neither praiseworthy nor correct, but blameworthy. Most of these cases are also nameless, and we must try, as in the other cases also, to make names ourselves, to make things clear and easy to follow.

(8) In truth-telling, then, let us call the intermediate person truthful, and the mean truthfulness; pretence that overstates will be boastfulness, and the person who has it boastful; pretence that understates will be self-deprecation, and the person who has it self-deprecating.

(9) In sources of pleasure in amusements let us call the intermediate person witty, and the condition wit; the excess buffoonery and the person who has it a buffoon; and the deficient person a sort of boor and the state boorishness.

(10) In the other sources of pleasure, those in daily life, let us call the person who is pleasant in the right way friendly, and the mean state friendliness. If someone goes to excess with no [further] aim he will be ingratiating; if he does it for his own advantage, a flatterer. The deficient person, unpleasant in everything, will be a sort of quarrelsome and ill-tempered person.

Mean states that are not virtues

(11) There are also means in feelings and concerned with feelings: shame, e.g., is not a virtue, but the person prone to shame as well as the virtuous

person we have described receives praise. For here also one person is called intermediate, and another—the person excessively prone to shame, who is ashamed about everything—is called excessive; the person who is deficient in shame or never feels shame at all is said to have no sense of disgrace; and the intermediate one is called prone to shame.

(12) Proper indignation is the mean between envy and spite; these conditions are concerned with pleasure and pain at what happens to our neighbours. For the properly indignant person feels pain when someone does well undeservedly; the envious person exceeds him by feeling pain when anyone does well, while the spiteful person is so deficient in feeling pain that he actually enjoys [other people's misfortunes].

There will also be an opportunity elsewhere to speak of these [means that are not virtues].

REVIEW QUESTIONS

1. According to Aristotle, how do leaders cultivate virtue in their followers?
2. What is the role of good habits in organizations? In societies?
3. What are the practical implications of Aristotle's theory for the way leaders run organizations?
4. What are the virtues cultivated in the organizations and the society to which you belong?

role modeling - habit

Case: Sleazy or Stupid?
Joanne B. Ciulla

Imagine that you are a senior manager. For the past month your office has been interviewing candidates for the director of a new section of your operation. Your staff has narrowed down the applicant pool to three people. Out of three candidates you are most impressed with Ted Brown. Ted has an MBA from the prestigious Horton School of Business. He is thirty-six years old and he has worked in various parts of your industry for the past eight years. Ted is very personable and he possesses a quick mind and a good sense of humor. He also has excellent business contacts and should be able to bring a substantial amount of new business.

He is the last candidate that you will interview for the position. All of the finalists were good, but by the end of the interview you think that Ted is the man for the job. The interview went longer than scheduled so Ted has to

From Joanne B. Ciulla.

Case continued

hurry and catch his plane back to New York. Before he leaves your office he turns to you and says, "I'd better ask your girl to call a car for me or I'll miss my plane."

You show Ted out of your office. On the way out Ted stops at your assistant's desk. You overhear him say to her, "Honey, be a good girl and call me a car—and move it or I'll be late!" Your assistant turns beet red but says nothing and dials the number.

You walk back into your office and think about the scene that you just witnessed. You spent two hours with someone that seemed like a nice guy, but in the past two minutes you now wonder about Ted.

Questions

1. What do you think Aristotle would say about this situation?
2. What does this incident tell you about Ted?
3. Would it be fair to deny someone a job because of an incident like this one?
4. As someone in a leadership position, what other things do you have to consider in deciding whether to hire Ted? Why is this decision ethically important?

The First Sermon
and The Synopsis of Truth

Buddha, around 563 B.C.–483 B.C.

The Buddha was born on the border of present day India and Nepal called the Kingdom of the Sakyas. He was the son of a king. He family name was Gotama and his given name was Siddhartha, which means "one whose aim is accomplished." There are many different stories about the life of the Buddha. Most say that at the age of twenty-nine the Buddha traveled outside of his palace and was greatly moved by the sights of a feeble old man, a sick man, a dead man, and a peaceful monk. He saw human suffering and wondered how the monk could be so serene in the midst of such misery. As a result of this experience, Buddha decided to leave his home and family to search for the truth. One day after six years of travel, Buddha arrived in Uruvela (now called Bodh Gaya). There he sat down cross-legged under a banyan tree and vowed not to get up until he found enlightenment. After battling evil and temptation, Buddha spent the night in meditation and achieved enlightenment. Several weeks after his enlightenment, the Buddha preached his first sermon, which is printed here.

As a religious figure, Buddha is not a savior. He is a teacher and role model. The word "Buddha" means "enlightened one." The Buddha's teachings are about how to make us better human beings. The moral principles in the Eightfold Path are derived from the Four Noble Truths described in "The First Sermon." The Buddha tells us that we suffer because of our desires and we suffer when we cannot have the things we desire. People have to master their desires and themselves. The way out of human suffering is through the Eightfold Path, which leads to self-mastery, wisdom, and compassion.

2. The First Sermon

These two extremes, O monks, are not to be practised by one who has gone forth from the world. What are the two? That conjoined with the passions, low, vulgar, common, ignoble, and useless, and that conjoined with self-torture, painful, ignoble, and useless. Avoiding these two extremes the Tathāgata[2] has gained the knowledge of the Middle Way, which gives sight and knowledge, and tends to calm, to insight, enlightenment, *nirvāna*.

What, O monks, is the Middle Way, which gives sight. . . ? It is the noble Eightfold Path, namely, right views, right intention, right speech, right action, right livelihood, right effort, right mindfulness, right concentration. This, O monks, is the Middle Way. . . .

(1) Now this, O monks, is the noble truth of pain: birth is painful, old age is painful, sickness is painful, death is painful, sorrow, lamentation, dejection, and despair are painful. Contact with unpleasant things is painful, not getting what one wishes is painful. In short the five *khandhas* of grasping are painful.[3]

(2) Now this, O monks, is the noble truth of the cause of pain: that craving which leads to rebirth, combined with pleasure and lust, finding pleasure here and there, namely, the craving for passion, the craving for existence, the craving for non-existence.

(3) Now this, O monks, is the noble truth of the cessation of pain: the cessation without a remainder of that craving, abandonment, forsaking, release, non-attachment.

(4) Now this, O monks, is the noble truth of the way that leads to the cessation of pain: this is the noble Eightfold Path, namely, right views, right intention, right speech, right action, right livelihood, right effort, right mindfulness, right concentration. . . .

---

[2]"Tathāgata" is a name for the Buddha. Literally it means one who has "thus come."

[3]The five *khandhas* (groups or agregates) are form, feeling (or sensation), perception (volitional disposition), predispositions (or impressions), and consciousness.

As long as in these noble truths my threefold knowledge and insight duly with its twelve divisions was not well purified, even so long, O monks, in the world with its gods, Māra,[2] Brahmā,[3] with ascetics, *brāhmins,* gods, and men, I had not attained the highest complete enlightenment. Thus I knew.

But when in these noble truths my threefold knowledge and insight duly with its twelve divisions was well purified, then, O monks, in the world . . . I had attained the highest complete enlightenment. Thus I knew. Knowledge arose in me; insight arose that the release of my mind is unshakable; this is my last existence; now there is no rebirth.

3. The Synopsis of Truth

Thus have I heard. Once when the Lord was staying at Benares in the Isipatana deerpark, he addressed the almsmen as follows: It was here in this very deerpark at Benares that the Truth-finder, *Arahat [arhat]* all-enlightened, set a-rolling the supreme Wheel of the Doctrine—which shall not be turned back from its onward course by recluse or *brāhmin,* god or Māra or Brahmā or by anyone in the universe,—the announcement of the Four Noble Truths, the teaching, declaration, and establishment of those Four Truths, with their unfolding, exposition, and manifestation.

What are these four?—The announcement, teaching . . . and manifestation of the Noble Truth of suffering[5]—of the origin of suffering— of the cessation of suffering—of the path that leads to the cessation of suffering.

Follow, almsmen, Sāriputta and Moggallāna and be guided by them; they are wise helpers unto their fellows in the higher life. . . . Sāriputta is able to announce, teach . . . and manifest the Four Noble Truths in all their details.

Having thus spoken, the Blessed One arose and went into his own cell.

The Lord had not been gone long when the reverent Sāriputta proceeded to the exposition of the Truth-finder's Four Noble Truths, as follows:

What, reverend sirs, is the Noble Truth of suffering?—Birth is a suffering; decay is a suffering; death is a suffering; grief and lamentation, pain, misery and tribulation are sufferings; it is a suffering not to get what is desired;—in brief all the factors of the fivefold grip on existence are suffering.

Birth is, for living creatures of each several class, the being born or produced, the issue, the arising or the re-arising, the appearance of the impressions, the growth of faculties.

Decay, for living creatures of each several class, is the decay and decaying, loss of teeth, grey hair, wrinkles, a dwindling term of life, sere faculties.

---

[2]The goddess of temptation.

[3]God in the role of creator.

[5]"Suffering" has been substituted for the translator's "ill" in this selection. Other frequent translations are "misery" and "pain."

Death, for living creatures of each several class, is the passage and passing hence, the dissolution, disappearance, dying, death, decease, the dissolution of the impressions, the discarding of the dead body.

Grief is the grief, grieving, and grievousness, the inward grief and inward anguish of anyone who suffers under some misfortune or is in the grip of some type of suffering.

Lamentation is the lament and lamentation, the wailing and the lamenting of anyone who suffers under some misfortune or is in the grip of some type of suffering.

Pain is any bodily suffering or bodily evil, and suffering bred of bodily contact, any evil feeling.

Misery is mental suffering and evil, any evil feeling of the mind.

Tribulation is the tribulation of heart and mind, the state to which tribulation brings them, in anyone who suffers under some misfortune or is in the grip of some type of suffering.

There remains not to get what is desired. In creatures subject to birth—or decay—or death—or grief and lamentation, pain, misery, and tribulation—the desire arises not to be subject thereto but to escape them. But escape is not to be won merely by desiring it; and failure to win it is another suffering.

What are in brief all the factors of the fivefold grip on existence which are sufferings?—They are: the factors of form, feeling, perception, impressions, and consciousness.

The foregoing, sirs, constitutes the Noble Truth of suffering.

What now is the Noble Truth of the origin of suffering? It is any craving that makes for re-birth and is tied up with passion's delights and culls satisfaction now here now there—such as the craving for sensual pleasure, the craving for continuing existence, and the craving for annihilation.

Next, what is the Noble Truth of the cessation of suffering?—It is the utter and passionless cessation of this same craving,—the abandonment and rejection of craving, deliverance from craving, and aversion from craving.

Lastly, what is the Noble Truth of the Path that leads to the cessation of suffering?—It is just the Noble Eightfold Path, consisting of right outlook, right resolves, right speech, right acts, right livelihood, right endeavour, right mindfulness and right rapture of concentration.

Right outlook is to know suffering, the origin of suffering, the cessation of suffering, and the path that leads to the cessation of suffering.

Right resolves are the resolve to renounce the world and to do no hurt or harm.

Right speech is to abstain from lies and slander, from reviling, and from tattle.

Right acts are to abstain from taking life, from stealing, and from lechery.

Right livelihood is that by which the disciple of the Noble One supports himself, to the exclusion of wrong modes of livelihood.

Right endeavour is when an almsman brings his will to bear, puts forth endeavour and energy, struggles and strives with all his heart, to stop bad and wrong qualities which have not yet arisen from ever arising, to renounce those which have already arisen, to foster good qualities which have not yet arisen, and, finally, to establish, clarify, multiply, enlarge, develop, and perfect those good qualities which are there already.

Right mindfulness is when realizing what the body is—what feelings are—what the heart is—and what the mental states are—an almsman dwells ardent, alert, and mindful, in freedom from the wants and discontents attendant on any of these things.

Right rapture of concentration is when, divested of lusts and divested of wrong dispositions, an almsman develops, and dwells in, the first ecstasy with all its zest and satisfaction, a state bred of aloofness and not divorced from observation and reflection. By laying to rest observation and reflection, he develops and dwells in inward serenity, in [the] focussing of heart, in the zest and satisfaction of the second ecstasy, which is divorced from observation and reflection and is bred of concentration—passing thence to the third and fourth ecstasies.

This, sirs, constitutes the Noble Truth of the Path that leads to the cessation of suffering. . . .

REVIEW QUESTIONS

1. What is "right livelihood" and how does it apply to the way one thinks about leadership?
2. How is the notion of "mindfulness" useful for thinking about the way a leader leads?
3. In today's fast-paced world, would Buddhist ethics make it easier or harder for a leader to be effective?

Case: Does Personal Morality Matter?
Joanne B. Ciulla

Over the past month you and your colleagues have been reviewing applications for regional manager. The regional manager's job involves overseeing and coordinating the operations of a large portion of the western United States. On Friday afternoon your committee finally makes its selection and plans to announce its choice on Monday morning. Out of a number of talented managers, they selected John Deer. John's peers often

From Joanne B. Ciulla.

used the words "brilliant" and "genius" to describe him. He held a consistent record of excellence in every task that he accomplished for the company.

A quiet, polite man, John rarely attended social functions and when he did, he never brought his wife. When you arrive at your office on Monday morning, you are surprised to get a call from John's wife Edith, whom you've never met. Her voice sounds shaky and you can hardly hear her. She says:

> *I'm sorry to be a bother, but I needed to talk to you. My husband John has been tense lately because he really wants the regional manager's job. Anyway, last night John gave me a very bad beating. Our two children saw the whole thing and were terrified. I took the children and ran out of the house. We are now staying at the Chicago shelter for battered women. Over the years, John has hit me on numerous occasions, but never like this. He's basically a good man, but he's very high strung. Anyway, the reason why I am calling is to beg you to give the job to John. Maybe then he'll feel happier and things will be better for our family.*

The phone call is so bizarre that you decide to check out Mrs. Deer's story. You call the Chicago shelter to find out if she is indeed there. The shelter director says that it is against their policy to give out the identity of her clients or any information on them. Then in the background you hear some confusion as Mrs. Deer grabs the phone from the director. Mrs. Deer tells the director to get on the other line and demands that she answer your questions. The director protests that she is not allowed to do this, but does as she is asked. She reports confirms that Mrs. Deer and her two children, ages 2 and 6, were admitted to the shelter last night at midnight after being treated at City Hospital. Mrs. Deer had a broken rib and bruises on the face, arms, and neck that were apparently caused by a blunt object.

It is now 10:30 a.m. The formal announcement is scheduled for noon. At this point John may already know that he got the job. You are angry and disgusted, but you know that you will have to put your personal feelings aside and consider a number of issues before you make any decisions about John. Because Mrs. Deer has no plans to press charges against her husband, you put aside legal considerations and think about your ethical obligations in this situation.

Questions

1. What are your moral obligations to the company, Mrs. Deer and her children, John Deer, and yourself?
2. How would Buddha and Aristotle describe what is wrong with John Deer?
3. Why is this decision so important? What are the broader ramifications of this decision?
4. How does the judgment of character in this case differ from the one in "Sleazy or Stupid"?

The Bathsheba Syndrome: The Ethical Failure of Successful Leaders

Dean Ludwig and Clinton Longnecker

Dean C. Ludwig and Clinton O. Longnecker are professors of management at the University of Toledo. Their article on what they describe as "the Bathsheba Syndrome" offers insight into self-discipline and the temptations of power. One of the most interesting things about the story of David and Bathsheba is that it fits the a pattern we see repeated again and again in scandals involving leaders. When leaders use their power to do something unethical, they often engage in cover-ups that are worse than the deed itself. The other fascinating aspect of this case is that King David was God's chosen one and an excellent King before the Bathsheba affair.

Introduction

The story of David and Bathsheba is familiar in a variety of traditions. Accounts of King David's life are contained in both the Old Testament and the Torah. These accounts describe a leader with a humble past, a dramatic and rapid rise to power, strong organizational skills, a charismatic personality, an ecclecric approach to problem solving, a strategic vision for his people, and a man of high moral character. In his day, he was a man who had it all. He had power, influence, wealth, physical comforts, loyal servants, a strong army, and a growing prosperous country. He was a king. Yet despite both the quality of his life and his moral character, King David was a leader who got caught up in a downward spiral of unethical decisions that had grave consequences for both his personal life and the organization that he was called upon to lead and protect. David's failings as a leader were dramatic even by today's standards and included an affair, the corruption of other leaders, deception, drunkenness, murder, the loss of innocent lives, and a "we beat the system" attitude when he thought he had managed to cover-up his crimes. The good, bright, successful, popular, visionary king, David, was nearly destroyed because he could not control his desire to have something that he knew it was wrong for him to have—Bathsheba.

Was David a leader lacking in principle? All accounts indicate that David was a man of strong principle and discernment. Did David abandon principle in the face of tough competitive pressure? At the time of David's indiscretion, he had just finished a series of triumphant campaigns and was riding the crest of success and popularity. Was David's a poor choice in the face of subtle, competing goods? David clearly knew the gravity of the violation he was engaging in and clearly knew the penalty if exposed. How did David, a good, talented, and successful leader get entangled in this downward spiral of events? Could his fall have been prevented? Would our current ethics training have helped David?

David's story appears in our newspapers with increasing frequency. We read of good, respected, successful leaders, men and women of intelligence, talent, and vision who suddenly self-destruct as they reach the apex of their careers. Consider the following four all too familiar composites adapted from recent news accounts:

The CEO of a prominent southern savings & loan is indicted for conspiracy to defraud. In his youth he was a model student and an eagle scout. He has been a prominent member of his church, a spokesman against child abuse, and a man of integrity and conviction according to his friends.

The mayor of large midwestern city is driven from office under accusations of marital infidelity and influence peddling that have enraged his constituency. Of humble Hispanic background, he was considered a rising star, a man who fought for minority rights, a model for minority aspirations, and a person whose life up to that point was beyond reproach.

The hard-working division president of a west coast plastics company was recently dismissed from his job because of gross abuse of his expense account, an affair with his secretary, and rumors of a drug problem. The CEO who fired him stated, "He was one of the brightest and best people I've known, and I've never known him to do anything wrong in his life until just recently. Then he self-destructed."

A prominent religious leader is forced to resign from his national office after growing a small organization into a successful national one. He has worked as a missionary overseas in a third world country, set up soup kitchens for the poor, worked hard to help people deal with addictions, and he has fallen because of fraud and tax evasion.

These are stories of modern day Davids. These stories are currently found on the front pages of the *New York Times* and the *Wall Street Journal* several times each week. It may be that the transgressions of our leaders are simply more newsworthy than in the past. It may be that the likelihood of detection is greater than it ever has been. It is also possible that such transgressions by our leaders occur with greater frequency than in the past. Whatever the reason, this publicity has focused a great deal of attention on the need for ethics training in business, in government, and in the schools which are churning out our would-be Davids.

There seems, however, to be a gap between the violations of which we read and the corrective measures which we are taking. After nearly a decade of concern about professional ethics and professional ethics training, it is time to examine some of our assumptions and to ask if we are attacking the core or the periphery of the professional ethics problem.

The Current Focus of the Professional Ethics Discussion

The popular press and at times the academic literature has far too quickly suggested that today's organizational leadership either lacks ethical standards (Andrews, 1989; Cam, 1970; Longenecker, 1985; Molander, 1987; Pitt and Abratt, 1986) or is willing to abandon ethical standards in the face of economic/competitive pressures (Gellerman, 1986; Hosmer, 1987; Levinson, 1988). In ethics training programs and in business schools we have far too quickly assumed that lack of standards or abandonment of standards in the face of competitive pressure are the key issues that need to be addressed in changing the ethical climate of business.

While competitive pressure certainly, at times, leads some leaders to abandon principle and take questionable actions which they believe serve some sort of utilitarian "greater good," we believe this analysis is terribly overused. In fact, one of the major purposes of this paper is to de-bunk the notion that the ethical failure of our leaders is largely due to lack of principle and/or the tough competitive climate of the 80s and 90s. Rather, we would like to suggest that many of the violations we have witnessed in recent years are the result of success and lack of preparedness in dealing with personal and organizational success. While our society places a high priority on being successful, some strongly suggest that little if any attention is placed on preparing people to deal with the trials and dilemmas associated with success (LaBier, 1986). Do ethics training programs and business schools prepare individuals for success and its trappings?

The profile of business ethics has been raised considerably in recent years because of highly publicized indiscretions by some of our most respected and admired leaders in business and government. Business ethics training, consulting, and research has itself become big business because of this publicity. Courses proliferate. Training programs proliferate. Research and publications proliferate. But is the attention missing the mark? Much of our attention in this proliferation has focused on subtle ethical dilemmas—delicate situations in which careful deliberation is needed to untangle competing obligations and claims. Our focus has also been on helping managers to articulate and adhere to operational principles in the face of competitive or organizational pressures (Nielsen, 1987; Waters et al., 1986).

Yet, examine the list of improprieties which has stirred this activity: substance abuse, sexual impropriety, tax evasion, insider trading, fraud, conflict of interest, perjury, patronage, diversion of resources, influence peddling, conspiracy to defraud. The specifics of the cases that have come before us rarely involve subtlety. They are usually gross violations which the actors know are wrong while in the act of perpetration. They are obvious breaches which the actors know would be condemned if revealed.

Likewise, look at the list of men and women who have fallen victim to these violations. Very often they are not individuals sitting in the middle of a competitive pressure cooker, making miscalculations in the heat of battle. Nor are they necessarily "destructive achievers" (Kelly, 1988), individuals devoid of operational principles who have climbed to the top in brutal pursuit of personal achievement. Far too often the leaders who have been accused and convicted of violations are men and women of generally strong principle who have built careers based more on service than self-gratification.

In short, too many of the perpetrators of the violations we have recently witnessed are men and women of strong personal integrity and intelligence—men and women who have climbed the ladder through hard work and "keeping their noses clean." But just at the moment of seemingly "having it all," they have thrown it all away by engaging in an activity which is wrong, which they know is wrong, which they know would lead to their downfall if discovered, and which they mistakenly believe they have the power to conceal. This, in essence, is what we have labeled the "Bathsheba Syndrome." The syndrome is so named to recall one of its first recorded occurrences—when the good and successful King David of Israel, believing he could cover up his impropriety, took Bathsheba to his bed while her husband was off in battle.

In summary, three assumptions have penetrated much of our discussion of business and professional ethics during the past decade:

1. Today's professionals lack personal operational principles and standards of conduct We have addressed this lack through personal moral development and the development of professional and company codes of conduct.
2. In today's complex, fast-paced, high-tech world, professionals are faced with a variety of subtle ethical dilemmas in which they must carefully discern rights, obligations, and competing goods, We have to address this situation by providing professionals with tools and models of ethical decision making, most notably utilitarian models.
3. In the face of tough competitive, economic, or strategic pressure during the 1980s and 1990s, many managers have abandoned personal principles for organizational purposes. We have tried to address this through the development of the organization as a moral environment.

There is a certain rationality to the above assumptions, and while the above listed approaches are, to an extent, valuable, they are certainly incomplete and the assumptions are possibly flawed. The business community bristles at the assumption that they are generally of low moral character, and as was mentioned, many of those leaders accused of violations are people of fairly high principles. Few of the violations that have focused attention on professional ethics have involved subtlety, and few of the violations have occurred in the face of heavy competitive pressure.

We suggest instead that many of the ethics violations we have witnessed in recent years result from a ready willingness to abandon personal principle—

not so much a matter of ethics as of virtue and lack of fortitude and courage. Further, we suggest that principle is abandoned more often in the wake of success than it is in the face of competitive pressure. It seems vitally important that we ask how success and ethical failure are related. Lord Acton long ago gave us the quip about power corrupting, and Will and Ariel Durant more recently refined Acton's comments in their statement: "Power dements even more than it corrupts, lowering the guard of foresight and raising the haste of action." But we still must understand how success and/or power corrupt, and why they corrupt some but not others.

Going back to the story of King David, we will examine some of the dynamics of success which may lead to ethical failure. We will point to four potential by-products of success which may cause many leaders to fall into ethical violation. First, personal and organizational success often allows leaders to become complacent and lose strategic focus, diverting attention to things other than the management of their organization. Second, success often leads to privileged access to information, people, or objects. Third, success often leads to unrestrained control of organizational resources. Fourth, success can inflate a leader's belief in his or her personal ability to manipulate or control outcomes. Even individuals with a highly developed moral sense can be challenged (tempted?) by the "opportunities" resulting from the convergence of these four dynamics.

The Story of David and Bathsheba

Most individuals are at least vaguely familiar with the story of David and Bathsheba, but we would especially like to point out some of the details leading up to David's violation and point out how in many ways the story of David and Bathsheba is paradigmatic for many of the ethical failures of successful leaders which we witness today. How did David, a good, talented, and successful leader, get entangled in this downward spiral of events? The scriptural accounts provide some insight, and offer food for thought for today's leaders.

David loses strategic focus in success. The story of David and Bathsheba begins by noting that David is not where he is supposed to be, doing what he is supposed to be doing. His recent successes in battle have apparently left David complacent—complacent that his overall strategy did not need revision for the time being and complacent that his subordinates were capable of executing the current strategy on their own. Instead of leading his troops into battle as was his role as king, he stayed home, leaving the direction of his troops during critical battles to his right hand man, Joab. David was apparently comfortable that Joab would be able to handle things.

How often today we see executives lead their organizations to the top of the competitive heap, displaying exceptional courage, energy, and leadership, only then to put their organizations on autopilot, kick-back, and indulge themselves for all of the sacrifices they have made along the way. Their set-up for ethical failure begins by not being where they are supposed to be. Not only does this expose the *leader* to potential conflict, but by not being with the troops through a time of crisis and competition, it opens the door to questionable ethical behavior by subordinates.

David's failure of leadership is certainly not that he delegated (though the accounts indicate that it was a king's duty to be with his troops in battle). Rather, David delegated and then ignored what was happening. He did not give supervision to Joab. In addition, David seemed to be delegating not out of a sense of necessity but out of a sense of self-indulgence. That is, David was delegating not because he needed to free time for other duties, but because he wanted more time for leisure (the accounts indicate that David was just rising from bed as evening came). David may have felt he needed or deserved a break after his earlier conquests; it is interesting that he did not feel his troops also needed or deserved to share in this break.

David's success leads to privileged access. As was mentioned, David's leisure allowed him the opportunity literally, to look around. He was not focused on organizational decision making. Instead, his lack of pre-occupation allowed him to see things he otherwise wouldn't have noticed. Second, his privileged position, high atop the roof of the palace, allowed him to see things that were sheltered to those at lower levels. It would have been clear to someone at a lower level that violation of Bathsheba's privacy was wrong, for they would have somehow had to circumvent the wall that separated her bath from public view. It was easy, however, for David to forget that it was not his right to view this beautiful woman at bath. His privileged vantage point was designed to give him a perspective—a view—that would help him lead his people, not a view that would feed his self-indulgence. By this point, David's lack of involvement in the leadership combined with his privileged position, allowed him to shift his focus to the satisfaction of personal wants.

Many of the scandals we have witnessed in recent years have evolved from privileged access to information, people and objects and from leaders' apparent, inability to understand that their privileged position is supposed to give them a perspective from which they can more effectively lead—not from which they can more effectively satisfy personal wants.

David's success leads to control of resources and inflated belief in personal ability to control outcomes. The story of David and Bathsheba unfolds through a degenerative progression of indulgence and cover-up. As the story of David and Bathsheba develops, David sends servants to investigate who this beautiful woman was that he saw from his roof. When he found that she was not only married, but married to one of his officers, he knew it would be a grave offense to take her to his bed. Yet, her husband was off in battle, and the servants, knowing the consequences, could certainly be counted on for silence. David sends for Bathsheba, sleeps with her, and she becomes pregnant.

In the hopes of covering this violation, David brings Bathsheba's husband in from the battlefield under the false pretense of finding out the state of the battle. After months in the field, he hopes Uriah will sleep with his wife, but noble Uriah decides it would be inappropriate while his comrades are still in battle. David then gets Uriah drunk in the hope that he will sleep with his wife, but he doesn't. Finally, David gives Uriah a message to carry back to Joab, the commander of the battle. The message is Uriah's death sentence—it tells Joab to send Uriah to the front of the fiercest battle and then withdraw, leaving Uriah and other innocents to die. After Uriah's death, David sent word to Joab not to let what had just happened seem evil in his sight. Smug in his cover-up, David then took Bathsheba into his house as his wife. It was the prophet Nathan, an outsider to the events, who finally exposed David.

David, in short, chose to do something he knew was clearly wrong in the firm belief that through his personal power and control over resources he could cover up. David's inflated, self-confident belief in his own personal ability to manipulate the outcome of this story is probably representative of the attitude of many of today's professionally trained managers of business. Trained in attitude and technique to "get things done" and "make things happen," today's business school graduates often possess a dangerously inflated self-confidence. Reinforced by success, given increasing control of resources, and subjected to decreasing levels of supervision, these managers too often stumble as they move into leadership roles.

Success as an Antecedent to Ethical Failure

We have outlined four by-products of success—loss of strategic focus, privileged access, control of resources, and inflated belief in ability to manipulate outcomes—and we have looked at the dynamics of these by-products in the life of David. We have noted that privileged access and control of resources are, when kept within reason, positive, justified, strategic perquisites of success. Privileged access is essential for comprehensive strategic vision. Control of resources is necessary for the execution of strategy.

On the other hand, we have suggested that the other two by-products—loss of strategic focus and inflated belief in personal ability to control outcomes—are essentially negative. Further, we suggest that privileged access and inflated belief in personal ability are primarily personal issues, while control of resources and loss of strategic focus are primarily organizational issues.

We suggest that several explosive combinations can be found within this matrix. First, when loss of strategic focus is coupled with privileged access, the door is opened for real abuse of some of the personal perquisites associated with success. Position and status are suddenly used to promote non-strategic, non-organizational purposes. An even more explosive combination occurs when control of resources is coupled with an inflated belief in personal ability to manipulate outcomes.

The Dark Side of Success

Success is the goal of every leader—both personal success and organizational success. Very often the two are intimately intertwined. Paradoxically, embedded in success may be the very seeds that could lead to the downfall of both the leader and the organization.

On a *personal* level the *benefits* of success to a leader are obvious to even the casual observer. Greater power and influence, increased status, a heightened sense of personal achievement, greater rewards and perks, and more personal latitude on the job are all by-products that come to leaders who can make things happen in their organization. We have summed all of these under the heading "privileged access." When a leader has proven him or herself to the organization, a host of *organizational* benefits tend to accompany this status. Leaders are granted greater control of resources and decision processes; they have increased access to information, people, and things; they are permitted to set their own agendas and have every worker's dream come true— no direct supervision. The combination of personal and organizational benefits that accompany success are indeed the very reasons all of us want to be successful. In a nutshell, success leads to increasing levels of power, influence, rewards, status, and control. None of these should in and of themselves be seen as negative.

Less readily apparent is the personal "dark side" of success—a side that is only recently being addressed by executive psychologists and is still seldom talked about (Blotnick, 1987). When leaders climb the organizational ladder and appear to have it all, they are confronted with a host of negatives that affect them on a very personal level. These negatives come in a variety of shapes and forms and affect leaders differently. The negatives of success may not appear to be obvious to most of us, but they nonetheless come with the territory of successful leadership. Collectively, they might be labeled as factors that are associated with an unbalanced personal life and a loss of touch with reality (Berglas, 1986). In this paper we have focused on one of their major manifestations: an inflated sense of personal ability, (and sometimes desire) to manipulate outcomes.

Literature on executive psychology describes a variety of negative dynamics associated with success. Successful leaders can often become emotionally expansive, which is to say that their appetite for success, thrills, gratification, and control becomes insatiable (Blotnick, 1987). Thus they lose their ability to be satisfied with their current status and they desire more of everything. Secondly, they can experience personal isolation and a lack of intimacy in their lives. Inability to share their problems and long hours away from home can cause leaders to be isolated from their families and friends, losing a valuable source of personal balance (Berglas, 1986). In addition, leaders find themselves without peers at work and can find making friends at work difficult. Many of these leaders literally lose touch with reality (Kets de Vries, 1989).

Furthermore, the status can bring with it increased stress and, at times, the fear of failure which can cause a leader to experience extreme levels of anxiety. It is one thing to make it to the top, but many leaders are not prepared for what it takes to stay there (Kelly, 1988). At the same time leaders can experience the "emptiness syndrome"— after working hard for years and finally "making it," they take a step back and ask themselves "is this all there is to success?" (Berglas, 1986). They have success, but they don't experience it in a meaningful way on a personal level which can cause them to seek other ways to satisfy their needs (LaBier, 1986).

Many times all of this simply adds up to an inflated sense of ego. This egocentricity can cause the leader to become abrasive, close-minded, disrespectful, and prone to extreme displays of negative emotion, all of which are warning signs along the road to megalomania (or the "I am the center of the universe phenomenon") (Blotnick, 1987).

We are not suggesting that all successful leaders fall prey to these negatives that are frequently associated with success, but rather want to make the case that success can bring with it some very negative emotional baggage. When we couple these negatives that affect leaders on a very personal basis with the organizational benefits of success discussed earlier, they create a rather potent combination for unethical behavior on the part of the successful leader. When we combine extreme organizational autonomy and control with a personal emotional state that is possibly inflated, isolated, or emotionally expansive, it is not hard to see how successful leaders frequently make unethical choices which not only harm them personally but contain the potential to destroy or severely damage the organizations they are responsible for protecting (Gellerman, 1985).

In the case of King David, we see both of these propensities in operation. We see a leader with complete free rein and a man who was apparently more concerned with personal gratification (at this particular moment in time) than with the responsibilities of being an effective leader. David clearly believed in his own ability to cover-up his wrongdoing. And as was addressed at length earlier in this paper, we also saw in David the explosive combination of privileged access combined with a loss of focus. David's inability to handle the by-products of success left him extremely vulnerable to ethical failure.

This ethical failure cost David dearly: the death of the child he bore with Bathsheba; the loss of his commander, Joab, who would later betray him; internal strife and conflict in his household for years to come; the loss of respect in his kingdom that led to future leadership problems; the loss of valuable fighting men and morale among his troops; and extreme personal guilt that he was continually forced to live with. All of these dynamics created even less balance in David's life. David was finally confronted with his ethical failure by the prophet Nathan (who was in this case the equivalent of a modern day whistle-blower) who led David to realize that his cover-up had been a failure. Even kings who fail to provide ethical leadership are eventually found out.

Whenever a modern leader falls prey to the Bathsheba Syndrome they are knowingly setting themselves and their organizations up for a fall whether they believe it or not. The lessons from David's sad experience are obvious:

1. Leaders are in their positions to focus on doing what is right for their organization's short-term and long-term success. This can't happen if they aren't where they are supposed to be, doing what they are supposed to be doing.
2. There will always be temptations that come in a variety of shapes and forms that will tempt leaders to make decisions they know they shouldn't make. With success will come additional ethical trials.
3. Perpetrating an unethical act is a personal, conscious choice on the part of the leader that frequently places a greater emphasis on personal gratification rather than on the organization's needs.
4. It is difficult if not impossible to partake in unethical behavior without implicating and/or involving others in the organization.
5. Attempts to cover-up unethical practices can have dire organizational consequences including innocent people getting hurt, power being abused, trust being violated, other individuals being corrupted, and the diversion of needed resources.
6. Not getting caught initially can produce self-delusion and increase the likelihood of future unethical behavior.
7. Getting caught can destroy the leader, the organization, innocent people, and everything the leader has spent his/her life working for.

Conclusions

In closing, some advice to successful leaders is warranted. First, it could happen to you. David was an intelligent, principled individual. So, too, are many of your colleagues that you read about in the paper these days. It is not simply the unprincipled and those under competitive pressure who fall victim to ethical violation. Stand forewarned of David's painful experience and read the papers for constant reminders that the chances of being caught have never been greater. Second, realize that living a balanced life reduces the likelihood of the negatives of success causing you to lose touch with reality (Blotnick, 1987). Family, relationships, and interests other than work must all be cultivated for long-term success to be meaningful. Third, understand that your primary function is to provide strategic direction and leadership at all levels.

Avoid becoming complacent with strategic direction and current performance. Strategic direction is never "set," no matter how successful. The privilege and status that has been granted to you is designed to enhance your strategic vision. It is not simply reward for a job already accomplished. Likewise, control of organizational resources has been given to you so that you can execute strategy—not to feed personal gratification. Fourth, build an ethical team of managers around you who will inspire you to lead by example and who will challenge or comfort you when you need either (Nielsen, 1987). Finally, ethical leadership is simply part of good leadership and requires focus, the appropriate use of resources, trust, effective decision making, and provision of model behavior that is worth following. Once it is lost it is difficult if not impossible to regain.

Several observations are also in order for boards of directors and others responsible for overseeing organizational leaders. First, board involvement should include concern for the leader's personal/psychological balance. Support for the leader's psychological well-being can be displayed via forced vacations, outside activities, and periodic visits to counselors and/or psychologists to help the leader keep both feet firmly planted on the ground. Second, boards should erect guard-rails (Andrews, 1989). Detection is the primary factor that deters unethical behavior. Organizations should thus make prudent use of such devices as regularly scheduled audits of critical organizational decision processes and resources. Organizations should also consider the use of ombudsmen for employees who might be willing to uncover unethical acts. Third, boards must clearly establish and implement ethical codes of conduct for organizational leaders and take steps to regularly heighten both the awareness and compliance with such standards. Clearly even successful leaders need both the input, direction, and support of a governing body to be prevented from falling into the dark side of success.

Finally, for those engaged in business ethics training we suggest a broadened understanding of why leaders/managers sometimes abandon their own principles. Do we too quickly focus on the maintenance of ethical behavior in the face of competitive pressure? Should we also discuss the maintenance of ethical behavior in the face of success? Is adherence to principle in either the face of competitive pressure or the wake of success a matter of ethics or of virtue? If success leads to increased levels of power, then we must take steps to deal with the phenomenon that "power corrupts." Researchers and academicians must look for creative ways to prevent this from occurring while not limiting the ability of leaders to lead.

REVIEW QUESTIONS

1. If virtue or good character is, as Aristotle says, a good habit, what happened to King David?

2. When we select leaders, is it possible to tell which ones are likely to fall prey to the Bathsheba Syndrome?
3. What is the relationship between what Ludwig and Longnecker call "strategic focus" and the Buddhist notion of "mindfulness"?
4. What practical things can leaders and their followers do to keep leaders from falling prey to the Bathsheba Syndrome?
5. What leaders in recent business and political scandals seem to have fallen prey to the Bathsheba Syndrome?

The Conscience of Huckleberry Finn

Jonathan Bennett

Jonathan Bennett was born in New Zealand and has lived in Canada and the United States. He is a professor emeritus of philosophy at Syracuse University. In this article he gives us a very different angle on public and private morality. According to Bennett, public morality is sometimes "bad morality" and private morality, which includes our moral feelings, is good morality and vice versa. Using three disparate examples, one from the story of Huckleberry Finn, another from a speech by Heinrich Himmler, and a third from the sermons of Jonathan Edwards, Bennett examines the conflict between public morality and a person's moral feelings or sympathies.

In this paper, I shall present not just the conscience of Huckleberry Finn but two others as well. One of them is the conscience of Heinrich Himmler. He became a Nazi in 1923; he served drably and quietly, but well, and was rewarded with increasing responsibility and power. At the peak of his career he held many offices and commands, of which the most powerful was that of leader of the S.S.—the principal police force of the Nazi regime. In this capacity, Himmler commanded the whole concentration-camp system, and was responsible for the execution of the so-called "final solution of the Jewish problem." It is important for my purposes that this piece of social engineering should be thought of not abstractly but in concrete terms of Jewish families being marched to what they think are bath-houses, to the accompaniment of loud-speaker renditions of extracts from *The Merry Widow* and *Tales of Hoffman,* there to be choked to death by poisonous gases. Altogether, Himmler succeeded in murdering about four and a half million of them, as well as several million gentiles, mainly Poles and Russians.

The other conscience to be discussed is that of the Calvinist theologian and philosopher Jonathan Edwards. He lived in the first half of the eighteenth century, and has a good claim to be considered America's first serious and considerable philosophical thinker. He was for many years a widely-renowned preacher and Congregationalist minister in New England; in 1748 a dispute with his congregation led him to resign (he couldn't accept their view that unbelievers should be admitted to the Lord's Supper in the hope that it would convert them); for some years after that he worked as a missionary, preaching to Indians through an interpreter; then in 1758 he accepted the presidency of what is now Princeton University, and within two months died from a small-pox inoculation. Along the way he wrote some first-rate philosophy: his book attacking the notion of free will is still sometimes read. Why I should be interested in Edwards' *conscience* will be explained in due course.

I shall use Heinrich Himmler, Jonathan Edwards and Huckleberry Finn to illustrate different aspects of a single theme, namely the relationship between *sympathy* on the one hand and *bad morality* on the other.

* * *

All that I can mean by a "bad morality" is a morality whose principles I deeply disapprove of. When I call a morality bad, I cannot prove that mine is better; but when I here call any morality bad, I think you will agree with me that it is bad; and that is all I need.

There could be dispute as to whether the springs of someone's actions constitute a *morality*. I think, though, that we must admit that someone who acts in ways which conflict grossly with our morality may nevertheless have a morality of his own—a set of principles of action which he sincerely assents to, so that for him the problem of acting well or rightly or in obedience to conscience is the problem of conforming to *those* principles. The problem of conscientiousness can arise as acutely for a bad morality as for any other: rotten principles may be as difficult to keep as decent ones.

As for "sympathy": I use this term to cover every sort of fellow-feeling, as when one feels pity over someone's loneliness, or horrified compassion over his pain, or when one feels a shrinking reluctance to act in a way which will bring misfortune to someone else. These *feelings* must not be confused with *moral judgments*. My sympathy for someone in distress may lead me to help him, or even to think that I ought to help him; but in itself it is not a judgment about what I ought to do but just a *feeling* for him in his plight. We shall get some light on the difference between feelings and moral judgments when we consider Huckleberry Finn.

Obviously, feelings can impel one to action, and so can moral judgments; and in a particular case sympathy and morality may pull in opposite directions. This can happen not just with bad moralities, but also with good ones like yours and mine. For example, a small child, sick and miserable, clings tightly to his mother and screams in terror when she tries to pass him over to the doctor to be examined. If the mother gave way to her sympathy, that is to her feeling for the child's misery and fright, she would hold it close and not let the doctor come near; but don't we agree that it might be wrong for her to act on such a feeling? Quite generally, then, anyone's moral principles may apply to a particular situation in a way which runs contrary to the particular thrusts of fellow-feeling that he has in that situation. My immediate concern is with sympathy in relation to bad morality, but not because such conflicts occur only when the morality is bad.

Now, suppose that someone who accepts a bad morality is struggling to make himself act in accordance with it in a particular situation where his sympathies pull him another way. He sees the struggle as one between doing the right, conscientious thing, and acting wrongly and weakly, like the mother who won't let the doctor come near her sick, frightened baby. Since we don't accept this person's morality, we may see the situation very differently, thoroughly disapproving of the action he regards as the right one, and endorsing the action which from his point of view constitutes weakness and backsliding.

Conflicts between sympathy and bad morality won't always be like this, for we won't disagree with every single dictate of a bad morality. Still, it can happen in the way I have described, with the agent's right action being our wrong one, and vice versa. That is just what happens in a certain episode in chapter 16 of *The Adventures of Huckleberry Finn*, an episode which brilliantly illustrates how fiction can be instructive about real life.

* * *

Huck Finn has been helping his slave friend Jim to run away from Miss Watson, who is Jim's owner. In their raft-journey down the Mississippi river, they are near to the place at which Jim will become legally free. Now let Huck take over the story:

> Jim said it made him all over trembly and feverish to be so close to freedom. Well, I can tell you it made me all over trembly and feverish, too, to hear him, because I begun to get it through my head that he *was* most free—and who was to blame for it? Why, *me*. I couldn't get that out of my conscience, no how nor no way. . . . It hadn't ever come home to me, before, what this thing was that I was doing. But now it did; and it stayed with me, and scorched me more and more. I tried to make out to myself that *I* warn't to blame, because *I* didn't run Jim off from his rightful owner; but it warn't no use, conscience up and say, every time: "But you knowed he was running for his freedom, and you could a paddled ashore and told somebody." That was so—I couldn't get around that, no way. That was where it pinched. Conscience says to me: "What had poor Miss Watson done to you, that you could see her nigger go off right under your eyes and never say one single word? What did that poor old woman do to you, that you could treat her so mean? . . ." I got to feeling so mean and so miserable I most wished I was dead.

Jim speaks of his plan to save up to buy his wife, and then his children, out of slavery; and he adds that if the children cannot be bought he will arrange to steal them. Huck is horrified:

> Thinks I, this is what comes of my not thinking. Here was this nigger which I had as good as helped to run away, coming right out flat-footed and saying he would

steal his children—children that belonged to a man I didn't even know; a man that hadn't ever done me no harm.

    I was sorry to hear Jim say that, it was such a lowering of him. My conscience got to stirring me up hotter than ever, until at last I says to it: "Let up on me—it ain't too late, yet—I'll paddle ashore at first light, and tell." I felt easy, and happy, and light as a feather, right off. All my troubles was gone.

This is bad morality all right. In his earliest years Huck wasn't taught any principles, and the only ones he has encountered since then are those of rural Missouri, in which slave-owning is just one kind of ownership and is not subject to critical pressure. It hasn't occurred to Huck to question those principles. So the action, to us abhorrent, of turning Jim in to the authorities presents itself *clearly* to Huck as the right thing to do.

For us, morality and sympathy would both dictate helping Jim to escape. If we felt any conflict, it would have both these on one side and something else on the other—greed for a reward, or fear of punishment. But Huck's morality conflicts with his sympathy, that is, with his unargued, natural feeling for his friend. The conflict starts when Huck sets off in the canoe towards the shore, pretending that he is going to reconnoitre, but really planning to turn Jim in:

> As I shoved off, [Jim] says: "Pooty soon I'll be a-shout'n for joy, en I'll say, it's all on accounts o' Huck I's a free man . . . Jim won't ever forgit you, Huck; you's de bes' fren' Jim's ever had; en you's de *only* fren' old Jim's got now."
>   I was paddling off, all in a sweat to tell on him; but when he says this, it seemed to kind of take the tuck all out of me. I went along slow then, and I warn't right down certain whether I was glad I started or whether I warn't. When I was fifty yards off, Jim says:
>   "Dah you goes, de ole true Huck; de on'y white genlman dat ever kep' his promise to ole Jim." Well, I just felt sick. But I says, I *got* to do it—I can't get *out* of it.

In the upshot, sympathy wins over morality. Huck hasn't the strength of will to do what he sincerely thinks he ought to do. Two men hunting for runaway slaves ask him whether the man on his raft is black or white:

> I didn't answer up prompt. I tried to, but the words wouldn't come. I tried, for a second or two, to brace up and out with it, but I warn't man enough—hadn't the spunk of a rabbit. I see I was weakening; so I just give up trying, and up and says: "He's white."

So Huck enables Jim to escape, thus acting weakly and wickedly—he thinks. In this conflict between sympathy and morality, sympathy wins.

    One critic has cited this episode in support of the statement that Huck suffers "excruciating moments of wavering between honesty and respectability." That is hopelessly wrong, and I agree with the perceptive comment on it by another critic, who says:

> The conflict waged in Huck is much more serious: he scarcely cares for respectability and never hesitates to relinquish it, but he does care for honesty

and gratitude—and both honesty and gratitude require that he should give Jim up. It is not, in Huck, honesty at war with respectability but love and compassion for Jim struggling his conscience. His decision is for Jim and hell: a right decision made in the mental chains that Huck never breaks. His concern for Jim is and remains *irrational*. Huck finds many reasons for giving Jim up stud none for stealing him. To the end Huck sees his compassion for Jim as a weak, ignorant, and wicked felony.[1]

That is precisely correct—and it can have that virtue only because Mark Twain wrote the episode with such unerring precision. The crucial point concerns *reasons,* which all occur on one side of the conflict. On the side of conscience we have principles, arguments, considerations, ways of looking at things:

"It hadn't ever come home to me before what I was doing"
"I tried to make out that I warn't to blame"
"Conscience said 'But you knowed. . .'—I couldn't get around that"
"What had poor Miss Watson done to you?"
"This is what comes of my not thinking"
". . . children that belonged to a man I didn't even know."

On the other side, the side of feeling, we get nothing like that. When Jim rejoices in Huck, as his only friend, Huck doesn't consider the claims of friendship or have the situation "come home" to him in a different light. All that happens is: "When he says this, it seemed to kind of take the tuck all out of me. I went along slow then, and I warn't right down certain whether I was glad I started or whether I warn't." Again, Jim's words about Huck's "promise" to him don't give Huck any *reason* for changing his plan: in his morality promises to slaves probably don't count. Their effect on him is of a different kind: "Well, I just felt sick." And when the moment for final decision comes, Huck doesn't weigh up pros and cons: he simply *fails* to do what he believes to be right—he isn't strong enough, hasn't "the spunk of a rabbit." This passage in the novel is notable not just for its finely wrought irony, with Huck's weakness of will leading him to do the right thing, but also for its masterly handling of the difference between general moral principles and particular unreasoned emotional pulls.

* * *

Consider now another case of bad morality in conflict with human sympathy the case of the odious Himmler. Here, from a speech he made to some S.S. generals, is an indication of the content of his morality:

What happens to a Russian, to a Czech, does not interest me in the slightest. What the nations can offer in the way of good blood of our type, we will take, if necessary by kidnapping their children and raising them here with us. Whether nations live in prosperity or starve to death like cattle interests me only in so far as we need them as slaves to our *Kultur;* otherwise it is of no interest to me.

Whether 10,000 Russian females fall down from exhaustion while digging an anti-tank ditch interests me only in so far as the antitank ditch for Germany is finished.

But has this a moral basis at all? And if it has, was there in Himmler's own mind any conflict between morality and sympathy? Yes there was. Here is more from the same speech:

> I also want to talk to you quite frankly on a very grave matter . . . I mean . . . the extermination of the Jewish race. . . . Most of you must know what it means when 100 corpses are lying side by side, or 500, or 1,000. To have stuck it out and at the same time—apart from exceptions caused by human weakness—to have remained decent fellows, that is what has made us hard. This is a page of glory in our history which has never been written and is never to be written.

Himmler saw his policies as being hard to implement while still retaining one's human sympathies—while still remaining a "decent fellow." He is saying that only the weak take the easy way out and just squelch their sympathies, and is praising the stronger and more glorious course of retaining one's sympathies while acting in violation of them. In the same spirit, he ordered that when executions were carried out in concentration camps, those responsible "are to be influenced in such a way as to suffer no ill effect in their character and mental attitude." A year later he boasted that the S.S. had wiped out the Jews

> without our leaders and their men suffering any damage in their minds and souls. The danger was considerable, for there was only a narrow path between the Scylla of their becoming heartless ruffians unable any longer to treasure life, and the Charybdis of their becoming soft and suffering nervous breakdowns.

And there really can't be any doubt that the basis of Himmler's policies was a set of principles which constituted his morality—a sick, bad, wicked *morality*. He described himself as caught in "the old tragic conflict between will and obligation." And when his physician Kersten protested at the intention to destroy the Jews, saying that the suffering involved was "not to be contemplated," Kersten reports that Himmler replied:

> He knew that it would mean much suffering for the Jews. . . . "It is the curse of greatness that it must step over dead bodies to create new life. Yet we must . . . cleanse the soil or it will never bear fruit. It will be a great burden for me to bear."

This, I submit, is the language of morality.

So in this case, tragically, bad morality won out over sympathy. I am sure that many of Himmler's killers did extinguish their sympathies, becoming "heartless ruffians" rather than "decent fellows"; but not Himmler himself. Although his policies ran against the human grain to a horrible degree, he did not sandpaper down his emotional surfaces so that there was no grain there, allowing his actions to slide along smoothly and easily.

He did, after all, bear his hideous burden, and even paid a price for it. He suffered a variety of nervous and physical disabilities, including nausea and stomach-convulsions, and Kersten was doubtless right in saying that these were "the expression of a psychic division which extended over his whole life."

This same division must have been present in some of those officials of the Church who ordered heretics to be tortured so as to change their theological opinions. Along with the brutes and the cold careerists, there must have been some who cared, and who suffered from the conflict between their sympathies and their bad morality.

* * *

In the conflict between sympathy and bad morality, then, the victory may go to sympathy as in the case of Huck Finn, or to morality as in the case of Himmler.

Another possibility is that the conflict may be avoided by giving up, or not ever having, those sympathies which might interfere with one's principles. That seems to have been the case with Jonathan Edwards. I am afraid that I shall be doing an injustice to Edwards' many virtues, and to his great intellectual energy and inventiveness; for my concern is only with the worst thing about him—namely his morality, which was worse than Himmler's.

According to Edwards, God condemns some men to an eternity of unimaginably awful pain, though he arbitrarily spares others—"arbitrarily" because none deserve to be spared:

> Natural men are held in the hand of God over the pit of hell; they have deserved the fiery pit, and are already sentenced to it; and God is dreadfully provoked, his anger is as great towards them as to those that are actually suffering the executions of the fierceness of his wrath in hell; . . . the devil is waiting for them, hell is gaping for them, the flames gather and flash about them, and would fain lay hold on them; . . . and . . . there are no means within reach that can be any security to them. . . . All that preserves them is the mere arbitrary will, and uncovenanted unobliged forebearance of an incensed God.

Notice that he says "they have deserved the fiery pit." Edwards insists that men *ought* to be condemned to eternal pain; and his position isn't that this is right because God wants it, but rather that God wants it because it is right. For him, moral standards exist independently of God, and God can be assessed in the light of them (and of course found to be perfect). For example, he says:

> They deserve to be cast into hell; so that . . . justice never stands in the way, it makes no objection against God's using his power at any moment to destroy them. Yea, on the contrary, justice calls aloud for an infinite punishment of their sins.

Elsewhere, he gives elaborate arguments to show that God is acting justly in damning sinners. For example, he argues that a punishment should be exactly as bad as the crime being punished; God is infinitely excellent; so any crime against him is infinitely bad; and so eternal damnation is exactly right as a punishment—it is infinite, but, as Edwards is careful also to say, it is "no more than infinite."

Of course, Edwards himself didn't torment the damned; but the question still arises of whether his sympathies didn't conflict with his *approval* of eternal torment. Didn't he find it painful to contemplate any fellow-human's being tortured forever? Apparently not:

> The God that holds you over the pit of hell, much as one holds a spider or some loathsome insect over the fire, abhors you, and is dreadfully provoked; . . . he is of purer eyes than to bear to have you in his sight; you are ten thousand times so abominable in his eyes as the most hateful venomous serpent is in ours.

When God is presented as being as misanthropic as that, one suspects misanthropy in the theologian. This suspicion is increased when Edwards claims that "the saints in glory will . . . understand how terrible the sufferings of the damned are; yet . . . will not be sorry for [them]." He bases this partly on a view of human nature whose ugliness he seems not to notice:

> The seeing of the calamities of others tends to heighten the sense of our own enjoyments. When the saints in glory, therefore, shall see the doleful state of the damned, how will this heighten their sense of the blessedness of their own state. . . . When they shall see how miserable others of their fellow-creatures are; . . . when they shall see the smoke of their torment, . . . and hear their dolorous shrieks and cries, and consider that they in the mean time are in the most blissful state, and shall surely be in it to all eternity; how they will rejoice!

I hope this is less than the whole truth! His other main point about why the saints will rejoice to see the torments of the damned is that it is *right* that they should do so:

> The heavenly inhabitants . . . will have no love nor pity to the damned. . . . [This will not show] a want of a spirit of love in them; . . . for the heavenly inhabitants will know that it is not fit that they should love [the damned] because they will know then, that God has no love to them, nor pity for them.

The implication that *of course* one can adjust one's feelings of pity so that they conform to the dictates of some authority—doesn't this suggest that ordinary human sympathies played only a small part in Edwards' life?

° ° °

Huck Finn, whose sympathies are wide and deep, could never avoid the conflict in that way; but he is determined to avoid it, and so he opts for the only other alternative he can see—to give up morality altogether. After he has tricked the slave-hunters, he returns to the raft and undergoes a peculiar crisis:

> I got aboard the raft, feeling bad and low, because I knowed very well I had done wrong, and I see it warn't no use for me to try to learn to do right; a body that don't get *started* right when he's little, ain't got no show—when the pinch comes there ain't nothing to back him up and keep him to his work, and so he gets beat. Then I thought a minute, and says to myself, hold on—s'pose you'd a done right and give Jim up; would you feel better than what you do now? No, says I, I'd feel bad—I'd feel just the same way I do now. Well, then, says I, what's the use you learning to do right, when it's troublesome to do right and ain't no trouble to do

wrong, and the wages is just the same? I was stuck. I couldn't answer that. So I reckoned I wouldn't bother no more about it, but after this always do whichever come handiest at the time.

Huck clearly cannot conceive of having any morality except the one he has learned—too late, he thinks—from his society. He is not entirely a prisoner of that morality, because he does after all reject it; but for him that is a decision to relinquish morality as such; he cannot envisage revising his morality, altering its content in face of the various pressures to which it is subject, including pressures from his sympathies. For example, he does not begin to approach the thought that slavery should be rejected on moral grounds, or the thought that what he is doing is not theft because a person cannot be owned and therefore cannot be stolen.

The basic trouble is that he cannot or will not engage in abstract intellectual operations of any sort. In chapter 33 he finds himself "feeling to blame, somehow" for something he knows he had no hand in; he assumes that this feeling is a deliverance of conscience; and this confirms him in his belief that conscience shouldn't be listened to:

> It don't make no difference whether you do right or wrong, a person's conscience ain't got no sense, and just goes for him *anyway*. If I had a yaller dog that didn't know no more than a person's conscience does, I would poison him. It takes up more room than all the rest of a person's insides, and yet ain't no good, nohow.

That brisk, incurious dismissiveness fits well with the comprehensive rejection of morality back on the raft. But this is a digression.

On the raft, Huck decides not to live by principles, but just to do whatever "comes handiest at the time"—always acting according to the mood of the moment. Since the morality he is rejecting is narrow and cruel, and his sympathies are broad and kind, the results will be good. But moral principles are good to have, because they help to protect one from acting badly at moments when one's sympathies happen to be in abeyance. On the highest possible estimate of the role one's sympathies should have, one can still allow for principles as embodiments of one's best feelings, one's broadest and keenest sympathies. On that view, principles can help one across intervals when one's feelings are at less than their best, i.e. through periods of misanthropy or meanness or self-centredness or depression or anger.

What Huck didn't see is that one can live by principles and yet have ultimate control over their content. And one way such control can be exercised is by checking of one's principles in the light of one's sympathies. This is sometimes a pretty straightforward matter. It can happen that a certain moral principle becomes untenable—meaning literally that one cannot hold it any longer—because it conflicts intolerably with the pity or revulsion or whatever that one feels when one sees what the principle leads to. One's experience may play a large part here: experiences evoke feelings, and feelings force one to modify principles. Something like this happened to the English poet Wilfred Owen, whose experiences in the First World War transformed him from an enthusiastic soldier into a virtual pacifist. I can't document his change of conscience in detail; but I want to present something which he wrote about the way experience can put pressure on morality.

The Latin poet Horace wrote that it is sweet and fitting (or right) to die for one's country—*dulce et decorum est pro patria mori*—and Owen wrote a fine poem about how experience could lead one to relinquish that particular moral principle. He describes a man who is too slow donning his gas mask during a gas attack—"As under a green sea I saw him drowning," Owen says. The poem ends like this:

> In all my dreams before my helpless sight
> He plunges at me, guttering, choking, drowning.
> If in some smothering dreams, you too could pace
> Behind the wagon that we flung him in,
> And watch the white eyes writhing in his face,
> His hanging face, like a devil's sick of sin;
> If you could hear, at every jolt, the blood
> Come gargling from the froth-corrupted lungs,
> Bitter as the cud
> Of vile, incurable sores on innocent tongues,—
> My friend, you would not tell with such high zest
> To children ardent for some desperate glory,
> The old Lie: Duke et decorum est
> Pro patria mori.

✳ ✳ ✳

There is a difficulty about drawing from all this a moral for ourselves. I imagine that we agree in our rejection of slavery, eternal damnation, genocide, and uncritical patriotic self-abnegation; so we shall agree that Huck Finn, Jonathan Edwards, Heinrich Himmler, and the poet Horace would all have done well to bring certain of their principles under severe pressure from ordinary human sympathies. But then we can say this because we can say that all those are bad moralities, whereas we cannot look at our own moralities and declare them bad. This is not arrogance: it is obviously incoherent for someone to declare the system of moral principles that he *accepts* to be *bad,* just as one cannot coherently say of anything that one *believes* it but it is *false.*

Still, although I can't point to any of my beliefs and say "That is false," I don't doubt that some of my beliefs *are* false; and so I should try to remain open to correction. Similarly, I accept every single item in my morality— that is inevitable—but I am sure that my morality could be improved, which is to say that it could undergo changes which I should be glad of once I had made them. So I must try to keep my morality open to revision, exposing it to whatever valid pressures there are—including pressures from my sympathies.

I don't give my sympathies a blank cheque in advance. In a conflict between principle and sympathy, principles ought sometimes to win. For example, I think it was right to take part in the Second World War on the allied side; there were many ghastly individual incidents which might have led someone to doubt the rightness of his participation in that war; and I think it would have been right for such a person to keep his sympathies in a subordinate place on those occasions, not allowing them to modify his principles in such a way as to make a pacifist of him.

Still, one's sympathies should be kept as sharp and sensitive and aware as possible, and not only because they can sometimes affect one's principles or one's conduct or both. Owen, at any rate, says that feelings and sympathies are vital even when they can do nothing but bring pain and distress. In another poem he speaks of the blessings of being numb in one's feelings: "Happy are the men who yet before they are killed/Can let their veins run cold," he says. These are the ones who do not suffer from any compassion which, as Owen puts it, "makes their feet/Sore on the alleys cobbled with their brothers." He contrasts these "happy" ones, who "lose all imagination," with himself and others "who with a thought besmirch/Blood over all our soul." Yet the poem's verdict goes against the "happy" ones. Owen does not say that they will act worse than the others whose souls are besmirched with blood because of their keen awareness of human suffering. He merely says that they are the losers because they have cut themselves off from the human condition:

> By choice they made themselves immune
> To pity and whatever moans in man
> Before the last sea and the hapless stars;
> Whatever mourns when many leave these shores;
> Whatever shares
> The eternal reciprocity of tears.

REVIEW QUESTIONS

1. What does a leader do when he or she thinks society's notions of morality are wrong"?
2. How do leaders know when to trust their moral feelings over what the majority thinks is right?
3. What is the relationship between moral sympathies and moral principles, and what are the dangers of leaders who rely on one without the other?

DUTIES OF LEADERS AND FOLLOWERS

INTRODUCTION

The readings in this section are about duty. Duties are the things we are morally obliged to do. Some general duties include the duty to tell the truth or the duty to protect human life. The idea of duty can be found in most cultures and it is a fundamental element of morality.

One of the greatest exponents of the moral imperative of duty is the philosopher Immanuel Kant. Kant's ethical theory emphasizes the importance of acting on principle or doing something because it is the right thing to do, regardless of the consequences. This can be an especially difficult way of thinking about morality for people in leadership positions. Sometimes doing one's duty requires moral courage, because the outcome of the action will anger others and maybe harm the agent. A manager may get fired because he complains about the safety of the company products. A politician may lose an election because she thinks it's irresponsible to give tax cuts.

The best way to understand the moral dynamics of duties is to look at a variety of cases studies. The case study "Innocent or Guilty?" is about a manager's duties to various stakeholders. The case "On Women and Girls" is less dramatic than the first, but it helps us think about what it means to treat people with respect or as "ends in themselves." There is also a case study about the Nazi war criminal, Adolph Eichmann. Eichmann claimed that he was acting on his Kantian duty and when he followed Hitler's orders to deport and then exterminate the Jews. This short selection from Hannah Arendt's book *Eichmann in Jerusalem* not only illustrates a gross misinterpretation of Kant, it also shows how dangerous a mindless notion of duty can be. The Eichmann case raises provocative questions about the moral obligations of followers and their responsibility for the actions of their leaders.

The reading "Moral Luck" provides us with an interesting way to think about free will and our ability to determine the outcome of our actions.

Bernard Williams argues that morality is not immune from luck. The case study "Is A Lie Always a Lie?" makes us think about whether we have duty to tell the truth even when we think we will be lucky enough to make our lies come true. As we saw in the story of David and Bathsheba, leaders are often tempted to lie because they believe they either won't get caught, or they can cover up their lies.

The last reading in this section is from Confucius's *Analects*. Confucius's ethics, while different in approach from Kant's, are also based on duty. The primary duty that all people have is respect for and obedience to their parents. However, Confucius also talks about the duties we have in the various roles we play in life and the relationships we have to others in various contexts.

The readings in this section are not only about duties, but the fact that moral decisions are often made by fallible people with incomplete information and the inability to control all the variables that affect outcomes. As you read the following essays, reflect on the following questions: *Would leaders be ethical if they always did their duty as described by Kant? As described by Confucius? What makes doing one's duty different from following rules? Does it really matter if leaders do something good for their constituents or community, not because it is the right thing to do but because it will make them look good? Does morality in leadership really require a good will?*

Good Will, Duty and the Categorical Imperative

Immanuel Kant, 1724–1804

Immanuel Kant was born in Königsberg, Prussia. He taught at the University of Königsberg, where he was a popular teacher. As you will see in the following selections from *The Grounding for the Metaphysics of Morals*, Kant argues that the supreme principle of morality is based on reason, not religious revelation. This book, written in 1785, brought him in conflict with the religious views of the government of Prussia. In 1792 King Frederick William II barred Kant from teaching or writing on religious subjects. Kant obeyed, but began writing again five years after the death of the king.

Kant's work in ethics is important for a number of reasons. On a practical level, Kant recast the basic ethical principles found in the Judeo-Christian religions into a secular form. For example, you will notice that his categorical imperative is a more detailed rendering of the golden rule. By making ethics secular, Kant created a moral system that was open to everyone capable of reason, regardless of their religious beliefs. The bedrock of his system was respect for the dignity of all human beings.

Kant's theory offers a very strict view of morality, one that captures the idea of "acting on principle" or doing something simply because it is the right thing to do. In Kant we see the conflict between duty and self-interest. Hypothetical imperatives are those that say an act is good because it attains a particular end. However, Kant says the morality of an act depends on a person's intentions (a good will), not the result of the act. This is because we often don't know how things will turn out. A moral act is one that is done for the right reasons, even if it has bad consequences. Sometimes doing one's duty does not make you or other people happy. Unlike Aristotle, Kant doesn't believe that leading a morally good life will make you happy, because he doesn't think we can tell in advance what will make us happy. Kant's theory reminds us that taking moral action doesn't always have a happy ending. So, for Kant, being ethical often hurts.

Some aspects of Kant's theory are particularly useful to think about in relation to leadership. First, his theory emphasizes the fact that no one is an exception to moral laws. Second, his theory makes us think about situations in which leaders must act on strongly held beliefs or duty duties that are not in their own interest. (Not all choices are win-win.) Third, he says that we should never use people. And finally, he says that everyone, no matter who they are, should be both the legislator and the follower of moral laws in what Kant calls "the kingdom of ends."

First Section
The Only Unqualified Good Is a Good Will

There is no possibility of thinking of anything at all in the world, or even out of it, which can be regarded as good without qualification, except a *good will*. Intelligence, wit, judgment, and whatever talents of the mind one might want to name are doubtless in many respects good and desirable, as are such qualities of temperament as courage, resolution, perseverance. But they can also become extremely bad and harmful if the will, which is to make use of these gifts of nature and which in its special constitution is called character, is not good. The same holds with gifts of fortune; power, riches, honor, even health, and that complete well-being and contentment with one's condition which is called happiness make for pride and often hereby even arrogance, unless there is a good will to correct their influence on the mind and herewith also to rectify the whole principle of action and make it universally conformable to its end. The sight of a being who is not graced by any touch of a pure and good will but who yet enjoys an uninterrupted prosperity can never delight a rational and impartial spectator. Thus a good will seems to constitute the indispensable condition of being even worthy of happiness.

A good will is good not because of what it effects or accomplishes, nor because of its fitness to attain some proposed end; it is good only through its willing, i.e., it is good in itself. When it is considered in itself, then it is to be esteemed very much higher than anything which it might ever bring about merely in order to favor some inclination, or even the sum total of all inclinations. Even if, by some especially unfortunate fate or by the niggardly provision of stepmotherly nature, this will should be wholly lacking in the power to accomplish its purpose; if with the greatest effort it should yet achieve nothing, and only the good will should remain (not, to be sure, as a mere wish but as the summoning of all the means in our power), yet would it, like a jewel, still shine by its own light as something which has its full value in itself. Its usefulness or fruitlessness can neither augment nor diminish this value. Its usefulness would be, as it were, only the setting to enable us to handle it in ordinary dealings or to attract to it the attention of those who are not yet experts, but not to recommend it to real experts or to determine its value.

But there is something so strange in this idea of the absolute value of a mere will, in which no account is taken of any useful results, that in spite of all the agreement received even from ordinary reason, yet there must arise the suspicion that such an idea may perhaps have as its hidden basis merely some high-flown fancy, and that we may have misunderstood the purpose of nature in assigning to reason the governing of our will. Therefore, this idea will be examined from this point of view.

The Highest Function of Reason Is to Establish a Good Will, Not Happiness

In the natural constitution of an organized being, i.e., one suitably adapted to the purpose of life, let us take as a principle that in such a being no organ is to be found for any end unless it be the most fit and the best adapted for that end. Now if that being's preservation, welfare, or in a word its happiness, were the real end of nature in the case of a being having reason and will, then nature would have hit upon a very poor arrangement in having the reason of the creature carry out this purpose. For all the actions which such a creature has to perform with this purpose in view, and the whole rule of his conduct would have been prescribed much more exactly by instinct; and the purpose in question could have been attained much more certainly by instinct than it ever can be by reason. And if in addition reason had been imparted to this favored creature, then it would have had to serve him only to contemplate the happy constitution of his nature, to admire that nature, to rejoice in it, and to feel grateful to the cause that bestowed it; but reason would not have served him to subject his faculty of desire to its weak and delusive guidance nor would it have served him to meddle incompetently with the purpose of nature. In a word, nature would have taken care that reason did not strike out into a practical use nor presume, with its weak insight, to think out for itself a plan for happiness and the means for attaining it. Nature would have taken upon herself not only the choice of ends but also that of the means, and would with wise foresight have entrusted both to instinct alone.

And, in fact, we find that the more a cultivated reason devotes itself to the aim of enjoying life and happiness, the further does man get away from true contentment. Because of this there arises in many persons, if only they are candid enough to admit it, a certain degree of misology, i.e., hatred of reason. This is especially so in the case of those who are the most experienced in the use of reason, because after calculating all the advantages they derive, I say not from the invention of all the arts of common luxury, but even from the sciences (which in the end seem to them to be also a luxury of the understanding), they yet find that they have in fact only brought more trouble on their heads than they have gained in happiness. Therefore, they come to envy, rather than despise, the more common run of men who are closer to the guidance of mere natural instinct and who do not allow their reason much influence on their conduct. And we must admit that the judgment of those who would temper, or even reduce below zero, the boastful eulogies on behalf of the advantages which reason is supposed to provide as regards the happiness and contentment of life is by no means morose or ungrateful to the goodness with which the world is governed. There lies at the root of such judgments, rather, the idea that existence has another and much more worthy purpose, for which, and not for happiness, reason is quite properly intended, and which must, therefore, be regarded as the supreme condition to which the private purpose of men must, for the most part, defer.

Reason, however, is not competent enough to guide the will safely as regards its objects and the satisfaction of all our needs (which it in part even multiplies); to this end would an implanted natural instinct have led much more certainly. But inasmuch as reason has been imparted to us as a practical faculty, i.e., as one which is to have influence on the will, its true function must be to produce a will which is not merely good as a means to some further end, but is good in itself. To produce a will good in itself reason was absolutely necessary, inasmuch as nature in distributing her capacities has everywhere gone to work in a purposive manner. While such a will may not indeed be the sole and complete good, it must, nevertheless, be the highest good and the condition of all the rest, even of the desire for happiness. In this case there is nothing inconsistent with the wisdom of nature that the cultivation of reason, which is requisite for the first and unconditioned purpose, may in many ways restrict, at least in this life, the attainment of the second purpose, viz., happiness, which is always conditioned. Indeed happiness can even be reduced to less than nothing, without nature's failing thereby in her purpose; for reason recognizes as its highest practical function the establishment of a good will, whereby in the attainment of this end reason is capable only of its own kind of satisfaction, viz., that of fulfilling a purpose which is in turn determined only by reason, even though such fulfillment were often to interfere with the purposes of inclination.

First Proposition: Only an Act Done from Duty Has Moral Worth

The concept of a will estimable in itself and good without regard to any further end must now be developed. This concept already dwells in the natural sound understanding and needs not so much to be taught as merely to be elucidated. It always holds first place in estimating the total worth of our actions and constitutes the condition of all the rest. Therefore, we shall take up the concept of *duty*, which includes that of a good will, though with certain subjective restrictions and hindrances, which far from hiding a good will or rendering it unrecognizable, rather bring it out by contrast and make it shine forth more brightly.

I here omit all actions already recognized as contrary to duty, even though they may be useful for this or that end; for in the case of these the question does not arise at all as to whether they might be done from duty, since they even conflict with duty. I also set aside those actions which are really in accordance with duty, yet to which men have no immediate inclination, but perform them because they are impelled thereto by some other inclination. For in this [second] case to decide whether the action which is in accord with duty has been done from duty or from some selfish purpose is easy. This difference is far more difficult to note in the [third] case where the action accords with duty and the subject has in addition an immediate inclination to do the action. For example, that a dealer should not overcharge an inexperienced purchaser certainly accords with duty; and where there is much commerce, the prudent merchant does not overcharge but keeps to a fixed price for everyone in general, so that a child may buy from him just as well as everyone else may. Thus customers are honestly served, but this is not nearly enough for making us believe that the merchant has acted this way from duty and from principles of honesty; his own advantage required him to do it. He cannot, however, be assumed to have in addition [as in the third case] an immediate inclination toward his buyers, causing him, as it were, out of love to give no one as far as price is concerned any advantage over another. Hence the action was done neither from duty nor from immediate inclination, but merely for a selfish purpose.

On the other hand, to preserve one's life is a duty; and, furthermore, everyone has also an immediate inclination to do so. But on this account the often anxious care taken by most men for it has no intrinsic worth, and the maxim of their action has no moral content. They preserve their lives, to be sure, in accordance with duty, but not from duty. On the other hand, if adversity and hopeless sorrow have completely taken away the taste for life, if an unfortunate man, strong in soul and more indignant at his fate than despondent or dejected, wishes for death and yet preserves his life without loving it—not from inclination or fear, but from duty—then his maxim indeed has a moral content.

To be beneficent where one can is a duty; and besides this, there are many persons who are so sympathetically constituted that, without any further motive of vanity or self-interest, they find an inner pleasure in spreading joy around them and can rejoice in the satisfaction of others as their own work. But I maintain that in such a case an action of this kind, however dutiful and amiable it may be, has nevertheless no true moral worth. It is on a level with such actions as arise from other inclinations, e,g., the inclination for honor, which if fortunately directed to what is in fact beneficial and accords with duty and is thus honorable, deserves praise and encouragement, but not esteem; for its maxim lacks the moral content of an action done not from inclination but from duty. Suppose then the mind of this friend of mankind to be clouded over with his own sorrow so that all sympathy with the lot of others is extinguished, and suppose him still to have the power to benefit others in distress, even though he is not touched by their trouble because he is sufficiently absorbed with his own; and now suppose that, even though no inclination moves him any longer, he nevertheless tears himself from this deadly insensibility and performs the action without any inclination at all, but solely from duty—then for the first time his action has genuine moral worth. Further still, if nature has put little sympathy in this or that man's heart, if (while being an honest man in other respects) he is by temperament cold and indifferent to the sufferings of others, perhaps because as regards his own sufferings he is endowed with the special gift of patience and fortitude and expects or even requires that others should have the same; if such a man (who would truly not be nature's worst product) had not been exactly fashioned by her to be a philanthropist, would he not yet find in himself a source from which he might give himself a worth far higher than any that a good-natured temperament might have? By all means, because just here does the worth of the character come out; this worth is moral and incomparably the highest of all, viz., that he is beneficent, not from inclination, but from duty.

To secure one's own happiness is a duty (at least indirectly); for discontent with one's condition under many pressing cares and amid unsatisfied wants might easily become a great temptation to transgress one's duties. But here also do men of themselves already have, irrespective of duty, the strongest and deepest inclination toward happiness, because just in this idea are all inclinations combined into a sum total. But the precept of happiness is often so constituted as greatly to interfere with some inclinations, and yet men cannot form any definite and certain concept of the sum of satisfaction of all inclinations that is called happiness. Hence there is no wonder that a single inclination which is determinate both as to what it promises and as to the time within which it can be satisfied may outweigh a fluctuating idea; and there is no wonder that a man, e.g., a gouty patient, can choose to enjoy what he likes and to suffer what he may, since by his calculation he has here at least not sacrificed the enjoyment of the present moment to some possibly groundless expectations of the good fortune that is supposed to be found in health. But even in this case, if the universal inclination to happiness did not determine his will and if health, at least for him, did not figure as so necessary an element in his calculations; there still remains here, as in all other cases, a law, viz,, that he should promote his happiness not from inclination but from duty, and thereby for the first time does his conduct have real moral worth.

Undoubtedly in this way also are to be understood those passages of Scripture which command us to love our neighbor and even our enemy. For love as an inclination cannot be commanded; but beneficence from duty, when no inclination impels us and even when a natural and unconquerable aversion opposes such beneficence, is practical, and not pathological, love. Such love resides in the will and not in the propensities of feeling, in principles of action and not in tender sympathy; and only this practical love can be commanded.

Second Proposition: The Moral Worth of an Act Is Not Based on the Consequences of the Act

The second proposition is this: An action done from duty has its moral worth, not in the purpose that is to be attained by it, but in the maxim according to which the action is determined, The moral worth depends, therefore, not on the realization of the object of the action, but merely on the principle of volition according to which, without regard to any objects of the faculty of desire, the action has been done. From what has gone before it is clear that the purposes which we may have in our actions, as well as their effects regarded as ends and incentives of the will, cannot give to actions any unconditioned and moral worth. Where, then, can this worth lie if it is not to be found in the will's relation to the expected effect? Nowhere but in the principle of the will, with no regard to the ends that can be brought about through such action. For the will stands, as it were, at a crossroads between its a priori principle, which is formal, and its a posteriori incentive, which is material; and since it must be determined by something, it must be determined by the formal principle of volition, if the action is done from duty—and in that case every material principle is taken away from it.

Third Proposition: The Moral Worth of an Act Comes from the Agent's Respect for the Law

The third proposition, which follows from the other two, can be expressed thus: Duty is the necessity of an action done out of respect for the law. I can indeed have an inclination for an object as the effect of my proposed action; but I can never have respect for such an object, just because it is merely an effect and is not an activity of the will. Similarly, I can have no respect for inclination as such, whether my own or that of another. I can at most, if my own inclination, approve it; and, if that of another, even love it, i.e., consider it to be favorable to my own advantage. An object of respect can only be what is connected with my will solely as ground and never as effect—something that does not serve my inclination but, rather, outweighs it, or at least excludes it from consideration when some choice is made—in other words, only the law itself can be an object of respect and hence can be a command. Now an action done from duty must altogether exclude the influence of inclination and therewith every object of the will. Hence there is nothing left which can determine the will except objectively the law and subjectively pure respect for this practical law, i.e., the will can be subjectively determined by the maxim that I should follow such a law even if all my inclinations are thereby thwarted.

Thus the moral worth of an action does not lie in the effect expected from it nor in any principle of action that needs to borrow its motive from this expected effect. For all these effects (agreeableness of one's condition and even the furtherance of other people's happiness) could have been brought about also through other causes and would not have required the will of a rational being, in which the highest and unconditioned good can alone be found. Therefore, the pre-eminent good which is called moral can consist in nothing but the representation of the law in itself, and such a representation can admittedly be found only in a rational being insofar as this representation, and not some expected effect, is the determining ground of the will. This good is already present in the person who acts according to this representation, and such good need not be awaited merely from the effect.

Second Section
Hypothetical Imperatives: Acts Are Good for Some Actual or Possible Purpose

Every practical law represents a possible action as good and hence as necessary for a subject who is practically determinable by reason; therefore all imperatives are formulas for determining an action which is necessary according to the principle of a will that is good in some way. Now if the action would be good merely as a means to something else, so is the imperative hypothetical. But if the action is represented as good in itself, and hence as necessary in a will which of itself conforms to reason as the principle of the will, then the imperative is categorical.

An imperative thus says what action possible by me would be good, and it presents the practical rule in relation to a will which does not forthwith perform an action simply because it is good, partly because the subject does not always know that the action is good and partly because (even if he does know it is good) his maxims might yet be opposed to the objective principles of practical reason.

A hypothetical imperative thus says only that an action is good for some purpose, either possible or actual. In the first case it is a problematic practical principle; in the second case an assertoric one. A categorical imperative, which declares an action to be of itself objectively necessary without reference to any purpose, i.e., without any other end, holds as an apodeictic practical principle.

Whatever is possible only through the powers of some rational being can be thought of as a possible purpose of some will. Consequently, there are in fact infinitely many principles of action insofar as they are represented as necessary for attaining a possible purpose achievable by them. All sciences have a practical part consisting of problems saying that some end is possible for us and of imperatives telling us how it can be attained. These can, therefore, be called in general imperatives of skill. Here there is no question at all whether the end is reasonable and good, but there is only a question as to what must be done to attain it. The prescriptions needed by a doctor in order to make his patient thoroughly healthy and by a poisoner in order to make sure of killing his victim are of equal value so far as each serves to bring about its purpose perfectly. Since there cannot be known in early youth what ends may be presented to us in the course of life, parents especially seek to have their children learn many different kinds of things, and they provide for skill in the use of means to all sorts of arbitrary ends, among which they cannot determine whether any one of them could in the future become an actual purpose for their ward, though there is always the possibility that he might adopt it. Their concern is so great that they commonly neglect to form and correct their children's judgment regarding the worth of things which might be chosen as ends.

The Categorical Imperative or Universality of Law

If I think of a hypothetical imperative in general, I do not know beforehand what it will contain until its condition is given. But if I think of a categorical imperative, I know immediately what it contains. Since, besides the law, the imperative contains only the necessity that this maxim should accord with this law, while the law contains no condition to restrict it, there remains nothing but the universality of a law as such with which the maxim of the action should conform. This conformity alone is properly what is represented as necessary by the imperative.

Hence there is only one categorical imperative and it is this: Act only according to that maxim whereby you can at the same time will that it should become a universal law.

Now if all imperatives of duty can be derived from this one imperative as their principle, then there can at least be shown what is understood by the concept of duty and what it means, even though there is left undecided whether what is called duty may not be an empty concept.

The universality of law according to which effects are produced constitutes what is properly called nature in the most general sense (as to form), i.e., the existence of things as far as determined by universal laws. Accordingly, the universal imperative of duty may be expressed thus: Act as if the maxim of your action were to become through your will a universal law of nature.

We shall now enumerate some duties, following the usual division of them into duties to ourselves and to others and into perfect and imperfect duties.

1. A man reduced to despair by a series of misfortunes feels sick of life but is still so far in possession of his reason that he can ask himself whether taking his own life would not be contrary to his duty to himself. Now he asks whether the maxim of his action could become a universal law of nature. But his maxim is this: from self-love I make as my principle to shorten my life when its continued duration threatens more evil than it promises satisfaction. There only remains the question as to whether this principle of self-love can become a universal law of nature. One sees at once a contradiction in a system of nature whose law would destroy life by means of the very same feeling that acts so as to stimulate the furtherance of life, and hence there could be no existence as a system of nature. Therefore, such a maxim cannot possibly hold as a universal law of nature and is, consequently, wholly opposed to the supreme principle of all duty.

2. Another man in need finds himself forced to borrow money. He knows well that he won't be able to repay it, but he sees also that he will not get any loan unless he firmly promises to repay it within a fixed time. He wants to make such a promise, but he still has conscience enough to ask himself whether it is not permissible and is contrary to duty to get out of difficulty in this way. Suppose, however, that he decides to do so. The maxim of his action would then be expressed as follows: when I believe myself to be in need of money, I will borrow money and promise to pay it back, although I know that I can never do so. Now this principle of self-love or personal advantage may perhaps be quite compatible with one's entire future welfare, but the question is now whether it is right. I then transform the requirement of self-love into a universal law and put the question thus: how would things stand if my maxim were to become a universal law? He then sees at once that such a maxim could never hold as a universal law of nature and be consistent with itself, but must necessarily be self-contradictory. For the universality of a law which says that anyone believing himself to be in difficulty could promise whatever he pleases with the intention of not keeping it would make promising itself and the end to be attained thereby quite impossible, inasmuch as no one would believe what was promised him but would merely laugh at all such utterances as being vain pretenses.

3. A third finds in himself a talent whose cultivation could make him a man useful in many respects. But he finds himself in comfortable circumstances and prefers to indulge in pleasure rather than to bother

himself about broadening and improving his fortunate natural aptitudes. But he asks himself further whether his maxim of neglecting his natural gifts, besides agreeing of itself with his propensity to indulgence, might agree also with what is called duty. He then sees that a system of nature could indeed always subsist according to such a universal law, even though every man (like South Sea Islanders) should let his talents rust and resolve to devote his life entirely to idleness, indulgence, propagation, and, in a word, to enjoyment. But he cannot possibly will that this should become a universal law of nature or be implanted in us as such a law by a natural instinct. For as a rational being he necessarily wills that all his faculties should be developed, inasmuch as they are given him for all sort of possible purposes.

4. A fourth man finds things going well for himself but sees others (whom he could help) struggling with great hardships; and he thinks: what does it matter to me? Let everybody be as happy as Heaven wills or as he can make himself; I shall take nothing from him nor even envy him; but I have no desire to contribute anything to his well-being or to his assistance when in need. If such a way of thinking were to become a universal law of nature, the human race admittedly could very well subsist and doubtless could subsist even better than when everyone prates about sympathy and benevolence and even on occasion exerts himself to practice them but, on the other hand, also cheats when he can, betrays the rights of man, or otherwise violates them. But even though it is possible that a universal law of nature could subsist in accordance with that maxim, still it is impossible to will that such a principle should hold everywhere as a law of nature. For a will which resolved in this way would contradict itself, inasmuch as cases might often arise in which one would have need of the love and sympathy of others and in which he would deprive himself, by such a law of nature springing from his own will, of all hope of the aid he wants for himself.

These are some of the many actual duties, or at least what are taken to be such, whose derivation from the single principle cited above is clear. We must be able to will that a maxim of our action become a universal law; this is the canon for morally estimating any of our actions. Some actions are so constituted that their maxims cannot without contradiction even be thought as a universal law of nature, much less be willed as what should become one. In the case of others this internal impossibility is indeed not found, but there is still no possibility of willing that their maxim should be raised to the universality of a law of nature, because such a will would contradict itself. There is no difficulty in seeing that the former kind of action conflicts with strict or narrow [perfect] (irremissible) duty, while the second kind conflicts only with broad [imperfect] (meritorious) duty. By means of these examples there has thus been fully set forth how all duties depend as regards the kind of obligation (not the object of their action) upon the one principle.

If then there is to be a supreme practical principle and, as far as the human will is concerned, a categorical imperative, then it must be such that from the conception of what is necessarily an end for everyone because this end is an end in itself it constitutes an objective principle of the will and can hence serve as a practical law. The ground of such a principle is this: rational nature exists as an end in itself. In this way man necessarily thinks of his own existence; thus far is it a subjective principle of human actions. But in this way also does every other rational being think of his existence on the same rational ground that holds also for me; hence it is at the same time an objective principle, from which, as a supreme practical ground, all laws of the will must be able to be derived. The practical imperative will therefore be the following: Act in such a way that you treat humanity, whether in your own person or in the person of another, always at the same time as an end and never simply as a means. We now want to see whether this can be carried out in practice. Let us keep to our previous examples.

First, as regards the concept of necessary duty to oneself, the man who contemplates suicide will ask himself whether his action can be consistent with the idea of humanity as an end in itself. If he destroys himself in order to escape from a difficult situation, then he is making use of his person merely as a means so as to maintain a tolerable condition till the end of his life. Man, however, is not a thing and hence is not something to be used merely as a means; he must in all his actions always be regarded as an end in himself. Therefore, I cannot dispose of man in my own person by mutilating, damaging, or killing him. (A more exact determination of this principle so as to avoid all misunderstanding, e.g., regarding the amputation of limbs in order to save oneself, or the exposure of one's life to danger in order to save it, and so on, must here be omitted; such questions belong to morals proper.)

Second, as concerns necessary or strict duty to others, the man who intends to make a false promise will immediately see that he intends to make use of another man merely as a means to an end which the latter does not likewise hold. For the man whom I want to use for my own purposes by such a promise cannot possibly concur with my way of acting toward him and hence cannot himself hold the end of this action. This conflict with the principle of duty to others becomes even clearer when instances of attacks on the freedom and property of others are considered. For then it becomes clear that a transgressor of the rights of men intends to make use of the persons of others merely as a means, without taking into consideration that, as rational beings, they should always be esteemed at the same time as ends, i.e., be esteemed only as beings who must themselves be able to hold the very same action as an end.

Third, with regard to contingent (meritorious) duty to oneself, it is not enough that the action does not conflict with humanity in our own person as an end in itself; the action must also harmonize with this end. Now there are in humanity capacities for greater perfection which belong to the end that nature has in view as regards humanity in our own person. To neglect these capacities might perhaps be consistent with the maintenance of humanity as an end in itself, but would not be consistent with the advancement of this end.

Fourth, concerning meritorious duty to others, the natural end that all men have is their own happiness. Now humanity might indeed subsist if nobody contributed anything to the happiness of others, provided he did not intentionally impair their happiness. But this, after all, would harmonize only negatively and not positively with humanity as an end in itself, if everyone does not also strive, as much as he can, to further the ends of others. For the ends of any subject who is an end in himself must as far as possible be my ends also, if that conception of an end in itself is to have its full effect in me.

Treat People as Ends in Themselves

This principle of humanity and of every rational nature generally as an end in itself is the supreme limiting condition of every man's freedom of action. This principle is not borrowed from experience, first, because of its universality, inasmuch as it applies to all rational beings generally, and no experience is capable of determining anything about them; and, secondly, because in experience (subjectively) humanity is not thought of as the end of men, i.e., as an object that we of ourselves actually make our end which as a law ought to constitute the supreme limiting condition of all subjective ends (whatever they may be); and hence this principle must arise from pure reason [and not from experience]. That is to say that the ground of all practical legislation lies objectively in the rule and in the form of universality, which (according to the first principle) makes the rule capable of being a law (say, for example, a law of nature). Subjectively, however, the ground of all practical legislation lies in the end; but (according to the second principle) the subject of all ends is every rational being as an end in himself. From this there now follows the third practical principle of the will as the supreme condition of the will's conformity with universal practical reason, viz., the idea of the will of every rational being as a will that legislates universal law.

The Autonomous Will Legislates and Is Subject to Moral Law

According to this principle all maxims are rejected which are not consistent with the will's own legislation of universal law. The will is thus not merely subject to the law but is subject to the law in such a way that it must be regarded also as legislating for itself and only on this account as being subject to the law (of which it can regard itself as the author).

Thus the principle that every human will as a will that legislates universal law in all its maxims, provided it is otherwise correct, would be well suited to being a categorical imperative in the following respect: just because of the idea of legislating universal law such an imperative is not based on any interest, and therefore it alone of all possible imperatives can be unconditional. Or still better, the proposition being converted, if there is a categorical imperative (i.e., a law for the will of every rational being), then it can only command that everything be done from the maxim of such a will as could at the same time have as its object only itself regarded as legislating universal law. For only then are the practical principle and the imperative which the will obeys unconditional, inasmuch as the will can be based on no interest at all.

The Kingdom of Ends

The concept of every rational being as one who must regard himself as legislating universal law by all his will's maxims, so that he may judge himself and his actions from this point of view, leads to another very fruitful concept, which depends on the aforementioned one, viz., that of a kingdom of ends.

By "kingdom" I understand a systematic union of different rational beings through common laws. Now laws determine ends as regards their universal validity; therefore, if one abstracts from the personal differences of rational beings and also from all content of their private ends, then it will be possible to think of a whole of all ends in systematic connection (a whole both of rational beings as ends in themselves and also of the particular ends which each may set for himself); that is, one can think of a kingdom of ends that is possible on the aforesaid principles.

For all rational beings stand under the law that each of them should treat himself and all others never merely as means but always at the same time as an end in himself. Hereby arises a systematic union of rational beings through common objective laws, i.e., a kingdom that may be called a kingdom of ends (certainly only an ideal), inasmuch as these laws have in view the very relation of such beings to one another as ends and means.

A rational being belongs to the kingdom of ends as a member when he legislates in it universal laws while also being himself subject to these laws. He belongs to it as sovereign, when as legislator he is himself subject to the will of no other.

A rational being must always regard himself as legislator in a kingdom of ends rendered possible by freedom of the will, whether as member or as sovereign. The position of the latter can be maintained not merely through the maxims of his will but only if he is a completely independent being without needs and with unlimited power adequate to his will.

Hence morality consists in the relation of all action to that legislation whereby alone a kingdom of ends is possible. This legislation must be found in every rational being and must be able to arise from his will, whose principle then is never to act on any maxim except such as can also be a universal law and hence such as the will can thereby regard itself as at the same time the legislator of universal law. If now the maxims do not by their very nature already necessarily conform with this objective principle of rational beings as legislating universal laws, then the necessity of acting on that principle is called practical necessitation, i.e., duty. Duty does not apply to the sovereign in the kingdom of ends, but it does apply to every member and to each in the same degree.

The practical necessity of acting according to this principle, i.e., duty, does not rest at all on feelings, impulses, and inclinations, but only on the relation of rational beings to one another, a relation in which the will of a rational being must always be regarded at the same time as legislative, because otherwise he could not be thought of as an end in himself. Reason, therefore, relates every maxim of the will as legislating universal laws to every other will and also to every action toward oneself; it does so not on account of any other practical motive or future advantage but rather from the idea of the dignity of a rational being who obeys no law except what he at the same time enacts himself.

Dignity, Not Price, Is the Foundation of Morality

In the kingdom of ends everything has either a price or a dignity. Whatever has a price can be replaced by something else as its equivalent; on the other hand, whatever is above all price, and therefore admits of no equivalent, has a dignity.

Whatever has reference to general human inclinations and needs has a market price; whatever, without presupposing any need, accords with a certain taste, i.e., a delight in the mere unpurposive play of our mental powers, has an affective price; but that which constitutes the condition under which alone something can be an end in itself has not merely a relative worth, i.e., a price, but has an intrinsic worth, i.e., dignity.

Now morality is the condition under which alone a rational being can be an end in himself, for only thereby can he be a legislating member in the kingdom of ends. Hence morality and humanity, insofar as it is capable of morality, alone have dignity. Skill and diligence in work have a market price; wit, lively imagination, and humor have an affective price; but fidelity to promises and benevolence based on principles (not on instinct) have intrinsic worth. Neither nature nor art contain anything which in default of these could be put in their place; for their worth consists, not in the effects which arise from them, nor in the advantage and profit which they provide, but in mental dispositions, i.e., in the maxims of the will which are ready in this way to manifest themselves in action, even if they are not favored with success. Such actions also need no recommendation from any subjective disposition or taste so as to meet with immediate favor and delight; there is no need of any immediate propensity or feeling toward them. They exhibit the will performing them as an object of immediate respect; and nothing but reason is required to impose them upon the will, which is not to be cajoled into them, since in the case of duties such cajoling would be a contradiction. This estimation, therefore, lets the worth of such a disposition be recognized as dignity and puts it infinitely beyond all price, with which it cannot in the least be brought into competition or comparison without, as it were, violating its sanctity.

What then is it that entitles the morally good disposition, or virtue, to make such lofty claims? It is nothing less than the share which such a disposition affords the rational being of legislating universal laws, so that he is fit to be a member in a possible kingdom of ends, for which his own nature has already determined him as an end in himself and therefore as a legislator in the kingdom of ends. Thereby is he free as regards all laws of nature, and he obeys only those laws which he gives to himself. Accordingly, his maxims can belong to a universal legislation to which he at the same time subjects himself. For nothing can have any worth other than what the law determines. But the legislation itself which determines all worth must for that very reason have dignity, i.e., unconditional and incomparable worth; and the word "respect" alone provides a suitable expression for the esteem which a rational being must have for it. Hence autonomy is the ground of the dignity of human nature and of every rational nature.

REVIEW QUESTIONS

1. What are the positives and negatives of a leader acting on principle without regard for the consequences?
2. Because most leaders have people who work for them, what does it mean to treat people as ends in themselves in the workplace?
3. Kant says that when it comes to moral choice and principles, everyone is both a leader and a follower. What are the ramifications of this idea for leaders in modern organizations?

Case: Innocent or Guilty?
Joanne B. Ciulla

You manage a data processing department. Three years ago, you hired Fred Jones, a twenty-five-year-old computer programmer. He proved to be an excellent worker who consistently received high performance ratings. Jones was very quiet and rarely socialized with other employees; however, whenever anyone had a computer problem, you could count on him to solve it.

A few months ago, Jones did not show up for work or call to say why. The next day you received a call from his mother. She said that Jones had been arrested and charged with the murder of his girlfriend. Later that week you received a letter from Jones. He said that he was devastated by the loss of his girlfriend. He went on to explain that the reason he was a suspect is because he had argued in public with her the day before her death. When the police came to question Jones, he had no one to back up his alibi because he had taken a long run in the country at the time of the murder. Jones ended the letter by saying that he was now living a nightmare. He lost his loved one and is accused of a brutal crime that he did not commit. He asks for an unpaid leave of absence. The company grants his request.

Jones goes on trial and the jury finds him guilty. His lawyer appeals the case on a procedural technicality. Jones is given a new trial and he is found innocent. One month later, Jones calls and says that he is ready to work again. You are ambivalent, but you see no reason why he shouldn't come back. After all, he has not been convicted of crime and he is a valuable employee. You mention to a colleague that Jones will be returning to work.

When you arrive at work the next morning, a group of employees are waiting for you in front of your office. They are angry and tell you that they refuse to work with Jones because they are afraid he is dangerous. They demand that he be fired or moved to some other part of the company. What should you do?

Questions

1. What are your duties in this situation?
2. To whom do you have moral obligations, or what duties do you have to the various stakeholders in this case?
3. How would a Kantian decide this case?
4. Would your ethical obligations in this case be different if people were afraid to work with Jones because he had AIDS?

From Joanne B. Ciulla.

Case: On "Women" and "Girls"
Joanne B. Ciulla

*You just started your first job after college. George is your immediate
supervisor. He is in his sixties and so is his secretary, Hazel. Both of them
have worked for the company for more than thirty years. Since you began
working in the office, you've noticed that George refers to his secretary and
members of the clerical staff as "the girls." You have even heard him say, "my
girl will call you." Sometimes he'll come in the morning and say "hi
beautiful" to Hazel, or "how are you girls doing today?" to the clerical staff.*

*When you joined the company, you read in the Corporate Ethics and
Business Ethics Policy Statements that "continued abuse of familiarities or
diminutives" are a form of harassment that can create a hostile work
environment. You find it offensive to hear an older woman called a girl, but no
one else seems to notice it. Hazel usually responds to these comments with a
smile, so you wonder if it bothers her. You also consider the fact that George is
from another generation and that his comments may be just harmless old habits.*

*You make a casual comment about it to George: "Don't you think that its
silly to call a sixty-year-old woman a girl?" George laughs and tells you in a
conspiratorial tone, "Of course its silly, but old Hazel loves being called a
girl, it makes her feel young. Sometimes I call her beautiful to make her feel
good, because with a face like hers, no one else will." He goes on to say, "It's
okay to talk that way with the old gals, but don't worry, I know that the
young professional women like you don't like being called girl."*

*After your conversation with George you go and ask Hazel if she enjoys
being called "beautiful" and "girl" by George. Hazel sighs and says, "I've
worked here a long time. When I was younger they called me 'doll,' 'baby,' and
sometimes worse names. I don't even hear them anymore. It makes some men
feel powerful to call their secretaries by these names. The way I see it, with the
flick of a few computer keys I could turn George's entire operation into chaos.
When you get to be my age, you don't make a big deal about these things." Now
you are really confused. You know what the law says about such behavior, but
putting the law aside for now, you wonder about the ethics of the situation.*

Questions

1. What would Kant say was wrong with George's behavior ?
2. What are George's and Hazel's duties in this case, to themselves, each
   other, and other relevant stakeholders?
3. Is there anything ethically wrong with Hazel's position?
4. What can future leaders learn from this seemingly trivial situation?

From Joanne B. Ciulla.

Moral Luck

Bernard Williams

Bernard Williams is a British philosopher who has held academic positions at Oxford University and Cambridge University. He is currently a professor at the University of California, Berkley. In this article, Williams challenges Kant's notion that we should make moral decisions on the basis of duty and not on the merits of the consequence of our decision. In other words, because the outcome of an act is often out of control or subject to luck, morality is on firmer ground if we focus on doing things for the right reason. In this article Williams argues that Kant's attempt to save morality from luck is bound to be disappointing.

Leaders do their best to accomplish good things, but as we know, their well-intentioned acts do not always pan out. If a president orders a commando attack on an airplane held by hijackers, her actions are considered moral and courageous if the attack is successful and no hostages are hurt. If the hostages are killed, we might consider her reckless and immoral. In part, the outcome depends on what Williams calls "internal luck," or the skill her staff and the quality of her judgment in planning the operation. It also depends on what Williams calls "external luck" or a variety of variables outside of the president's control. For example, the terrorist might trip and fall out of the plane holding a live hand grenade, and so on. Luck can go either way. A poorly planned raid by a reckless overconfident leader may turn out well and a careful well-planned raid may fail.

Risk is a natural part of leadership, and as Williams shows us, it is also part of all decisions, including ethical ones. Highly moral but unlucky leaders are not listed among the great leaders in history books. Some leaders are not very ethical or brilliant, but they are lucky. Luck is yet another dimension to the question of ethics and effectiveness that we discussed earlier.

There has been a strain of philosophical thought which identifies the end of life as happiness, happiness as reflective tranquillity, and tranquillity as the product of self-sufficiency—what is not in the domain of the self is not in its control, and so is subject to luck and the contingent enemies of tranquillity. The most extreme versions of this outlook in the Western tradition are certain doctrines of classical antiquity, though it is a notable fact about them that while the good man, the sage, was immune to the impact of incident luck, it was a matter of what may be called constitutive luck that one was a sage, or capable of becoming one: for the many and vulgar this was not (on the prevailing view) an available course.

The idea that one's whole life can in some such way be rendered immune to luck has perhaps rarely prevailed since (it did not prevail, for instance, in mainstream Christianity), but its place has been taken by the still powerfully influential idea that there is one basic form of value, moral value, which is immune to luck and—in the crucial term of the idea's most rigorous exponent—"unconditioned." Both the disposition to correct moral judgment, and the objects of such judgment, are on this view free from external contingency, for both are, in their related ways, the product of the unconditioned will. Anything which is the product of happy or unhappy contingency is no proper object of moral assessment, and no proper determinant of it, either. Just as, in the realm of character, it is motive that counts, not style, or powers, or endowment, so in action it is not changes actually effected in the world, but intention. With these considerations there is supposed to disappear even that constitutive luck from which the ancient sages were happy to benefit. The capacity for moral agency is supposedly present to any rational agent whatsoever, to anyone for whom the question can even present itself. The successful moral life, removed from considerations of birth, lucky upbringing, or indeed of the incomprehensible Grace of a non-Pelagian God, is presented as a career open not merely to the talents, but to a talent which all rational beings necessarily possess in the same degree. Such a conception has an ultimate form of justice at its heart, and that is its allure. Kantianism is only superficially repulsive—despite appearances, it offers an inducement, solace to a sense of the world's unfairness.

It can offer that solace, however, only if something more is granted. Even if moral value were radically unconditioned by luck, that would not be very significant if moral value were merely one kind of value among others. Rather, moral value has to possess some special, indeed supreme, kind of dignity or importance. The thought that there is a kind of value which is, unlike others, accessible to all rational agents, offers little encouragement if that kind of value is merely a last resort, the doss-house of the spirit. Rather, it must have a claim on one's most fundamental concerns as a rational agent, and in one's recognition of that one is supposed to grasp, not only morality's immunity to luck, but one's own partial immunity to luck through morality.

Any conception of "moral luck," on this view, is radically incoherent. The phrase indeed sounds strange. This is because the Kantian conception embodies, in a very pure form, something which is basic to our ideas of morality. Yet the aim of making morality immune to luck is bound to be disappointed. The form of this point which is most familiar, from discussions of freewill, is that the dispositions of morality, however far back they are placed in the direction of motive and intention, are as "conditioned" as anything else. However, the bitter truth (I take it to be both) that morality is subject, after all, to constitutive luck is not what I am going to discuss. The Kantian conception links, and affects, a range of notions: morality, rationality, justification, and ultimate or supreme value. The linkage between those notions, under the Kantian conception, has a number of consequences for the agent's reflective assessment of his own actions—for instance, that, at the ultimate and most important level, it cannot be a matter of luck whether he was justified in doing what he did.

It is this area that I want to consider. I shall in fact say very little until the end about the moral, concentrating rather on ideas of rational justification. This is the right place to start, I believe, since almost everyone has some commitment to ideas of this kind about rationality and justification, while they may be disposed to think, so far as morality is concerned, that all that is in question is the pure Kantian conception, and that conception merely represents an obsessional exaggeration. But it is not merely that, nor is the Kantian attempt to escape luck an arbitrary enterprise. The attempt is so intimate to our notion of morality, in fact, that its failure may rather make us consider whether we should not give up that notion altogether.

I shall use the notion of "luck" generously, undefinedly, but, I think, comprehensibly. It will be clear that when I say of something that it is a matter of luck, this is not meant to carry any implication that it is uncaused. My procedure in general will be to invite reflection about how to think and feel about some rather less usual situations, in the light of an appeal to how we—many people—tend to think and feel about other more usual situations, not in terms of substantive moral opinions or "intuitions" but in terms of the experience of those kinds of situation. There is no suggestion that it is impossible for human beings to lack these feelings and experiences. In the case of the less usual there is only the claim that the thoughts and experiences I consider are possible, coherent, and intelligible, and that there is no ground for condemning them as irrational. In the case of the more usual, there are suggestions, with the outline of a reason for them, that unless we were to be merely confused or unreflective, life without these experiences would involve a much vaster reconstruction of our sentiments and our view of ourselves than may be supposed—supposed, in particular, by those philosophers who discuss these matters as though our experience of our own agency and the sense of our regrets not only could be tidied up to accord with a very simple image of rationality, but already had been.

Let us take first an outline example of the creative artist who turns away from definite and pressing human claims on him in order to live a life in which, as he supposes, he can pursue his art. Without feeling that we are limited by any historical facts, let us call him *Gauguin*. Gauguin might have been a man who was not at all interested in the claims on him, and simply preferred to live another life, and from that life, and perhaps from that preference, his best paintings came. That sort of case, in which the claims of others simply have no hold on the agent, is not what concerns me here, though it serves to remind us of something related to the present concerns, that while we are sometimes guided by the notion that it would be the best of world in which morality were universally respected and all men were of disposition to affirm it, we have in fact deep and persistent reasons to be grateful that that is not the world we have.

Let us take, rather, a Gauguin who is concerned about these claims and what is involved in their being neglected (we may suppose this to be grim), and that he nevertheless, in the face of that, opts for the other life. This other life he might perhaps not see very determinately under the category of realising his gifts as a painter, but, to make things simpler, let us add that he does see it determinately in that light—it is as a life which will enable him really to be a painter that he opted for it. It will then be clearer what will count for him as eventual success in his project—at least, some possible outcomes will be clear example of success (which does not have to be the same thing as recognition, however many others may be unclear.

Whether he will succeed cannot, in the nature of the case, be foreseen. We are not dealing here with the removal of an external obstacle to something which, once that is removed, will fairly predictably go through. Gauguin, in our story, is putting a great deal on a possibility which has not unequivocally declared itself. I want to explore and uphold the claim that in such a situation the only thing that will justify his choice will be success itself. If he fails—and we shall come shortly to what, more precisely, failure may be—then he did the wrong thing, not just in the sense in which that platitudinously follows, but in the sense that having done the wrong thing in those circumstances he has no basis for the thought that he was justified in acting as he did. If he succeeds, he does have a basis for that thought.

As I have already indicated, I will leave to the end the question of how such notions of justification fit in with distinctively moral ideas. One should be warned already, however, that, even if Gauguin can be ultimately justified, that need not provide him with any way of justifying himself to others, or at least to all others. Thus he may have no way of bringing it about that those who suffer from his decision will have no justified ground of reproach. Even if he succeeds, he will not acquire a right that they accept what he has to say; if he fails, he will not even have anything to say.

The justification, if there is to be one, will be essentially retrospective. Gauguin could not do something which is thought to be essential to rationality and to the notion of justification itself, which is that one should be in a position to apply the justifying considerations at the time of the choice and in advance of knowing whether one was right (in the sense of its coming out right). How this can be in general will form a major part of the discussion. I do not want, at this stage of the argument, to lay much weight on the notion of morality, but it may help to throw some light on the matter of prior justification if we bring in briefly the narrower question whether there could be a prior justification for Gauguin's choice in terms of moral rules.

A moral theorist, recognizing that some value attached to the success of Gauguin's project and hence possibly to his choice, might try to accommodate that choice within a framework of moral rules, by forming a subsidiary rule which could, before the outcome, justify that choice. What could that rule be? It could not be that one is morally justified in deciding to neglect other claims if one is a great creative artist: apart from doubts about its content, the saving clause begs the question which at the relevant time one is in no position to answer. On the other hand, "if one is convinced that one is a great creative artist" will serve to make obstinacy and fatuous self-delusion conditions of justification, while "if one is reasonably convinced that one is a great creative artist" is, if anything, worse. What is reasonable conviction supposed to be in such a case? Should Gauguin consult professors of art? The absurdity of such riders surely expresses an absurdity in the whole enterprise of trying to find a place for such cases within the rules.

Utilitarian formulations are not going to contribute any more to understanding these situations than do formulations in terms of rules. They can offer the thought "it is better (worse) that he did it," where the force of that is, approximately, "it is better (worse) that it happened," but this in itself does not help towards a characterization of the agent's decision or its possible justification, and Utilitarianism has no special materials of its own to help in that. It has its own well-known problems, too, in spelling out the content of the "better"—on standard doctrine, Gauguin's decision would seem to have been a better thing, the more popular a painter he eventually became. But there is something more interesting than that kind of difficulty. The Utilitarian perspective, not uniquely but clearly, will miss a very important dimension of such cases, the question of what "failure" may relevantly be. From the perspective of consequences, the goods or benefits for the sake of which Gauguin's choice was made either materialise in some degree, or do not materialise. But it matters considerably to the thoughts we are considering, in what way the project fails to come off, if it fails. If Gauguin sustains some injury on the way to Tahiti which prevents his ever painting again, that certainly means that his decision (supposing it now to be irreversible) was for nothing, and indeed there is nothing in the outcome to set against the other people's loss. But that train of events does not provoke the thought in question, that after all he was wrong and unjustified. He does not, and never will, know whether he was wrong. What would prove him wrong in his project would not just be that it failed, but that he failed.

This distinction shows that while Gauguin's justification is in some ways a matter of luck, it is not equally a matter of all kinds of luck. It matters how intrinsic the cause of failure is to the project itself. The occurrence of an injury is, relative to these undertakings at least, luck of the most external and incident kind. Irreducibly, luck of this kind affects whether he will be justified or not, since if it strikes, he will not be justified. But it is too external for it to unjustify him, something which only his failure as a painter can do; yet still that is, at another level, luck, the luck of being able to be as he hoped he might be, might be wondered whether that is *luck* at all, or, if so, whether it may not be luck of that constitutive kind which affects everything and which we have already left on one side. But it is more than that, is not merely luck that he is such a man, but luck relative to the deliberations that went into his decision, that he turns out to be such a man: he might (epistemically) not have been. That is what sets the problem.

In some cases, though perhaps not in Gauguin's, success in such decisions might be thought not to be a matter of epistemic luck relative to the decision. There might be grounds for saying that the person who was prepared to take the decision, and was in fact right, actually knew that he would succeed, however subjectively uncertain he may have been. But even if this is right for some cases, it does not help with the problems of retrospective justification. For the concept of knowledge here is itself applied retrospectively, and while there is nothing wrong with that, it does not enable the agent at the time of his decision to make any distinctions he could not already make. As one might say, even if it did turn out in such a case that the agent did know, it was still luck, relative to the considerations available to him at the time and at the level at which he made his decision, that he should turn out to have known.

Some luck, in a decision of Gauguin's kind, is extrinsic to his project, some intrinsic; both are necessary for success, and hence for actual justification, but only the latter relates to unjustification. If we now broaden the range of cases slightly, we shall be able to see more clearly the notion of intrinsic luck. In Gauguin's case the nature of the project is such that two distinctions do, roughly, coincide. One is a distinction between luck intrinsic to the project, and luck extrinsic to it; the other is a distinction between what is, and what is not, determined by him and by what he is. The intrinsic luck in Gauguin's case concentrates itself on virtually the one question of whether he is a genuinely gifted painter who can succeed in doing genuinely valuable work. Not all the conditions of the project's coming off lie in him, obviously, since others' actions and refrainings provide many necessary conditions of its coming off—and that is an important locus of extrinsic luck. But the conditions of its coming off which are relevant to unjustification, the locus of intrinsic luck, largely lie in him—which is not to say, of course, that they depend on his will, though some may. This rough coincidence of two distinctions is a feature of this case. But in others, the locus of intrinsic luck (intrinsic, that is to say, to the project) may lie partly outside the agent, and this is an important, and indeed the more typical, case.

REVIEW QUESTIONS

Carter

1. Which past and present leaders would not have been highly regarded if luck hadn't played a role in the outcome of key decisions they made?
2. Why do leaders take more risks than other people?
3. Do followers forgive leaders who fail because of bad luck? Should they?
4. Does bad luck excuse a leader from responsibility for his or her action?

Case: Is a Lie Always a Lie?
Joanne B. Ciulla

You are an administrative assistant. For the past two years you have worked for Ben Hill. Ben is a very creative, energetic person who tends to take on more work than he can do. Working with him is fun but, it's usually frantic. Things are frequently late and you always seem to be on a tight deadline.

The phones ring constantly in Ben's office. Often Ben tells his secretary to say that he is not in or that he will be out of town until the end of the week. Sometimes when people hear that Ben is not in, they call you. This puts you in the awkward position of not only having to back up the lie that the secretary was instructed to tell, but sometimes to make up new lies as to where Ben is and what he is doing. There are also times when Ben tells his manager that your group is working on a project that the group hasn't even heard of, let alone started. Usually, Ben will eventually get his team working on the project.

Today Ben is away with his family on vacation. You get a call from Ben's boss. He says, "Would you stop by my office today, I need to talk to you about the Franklin project—Ben told me your team has been making tremendous progress on it." You have no idea what the Franklin project is, so you lie and tell Ben's manager that you are tied up in meetings all day. You agree to stop by first thing tomorrow.

Your first instinct is to contact Ben. But he is on a camping trip with his family, and he makes a point of not checking his messages when he is communing with nature. *You are positive that no one in your office is working on a Franklin project because you coordinate all of the projects for Ben.*

Sooner or later Ben's luck will run out. One small lie seems to require ten more lies. Yet the thing about Ben is that he has a way of turning his lies into truths. Ben reminds you of the French writer Andre Malraux. Malraux believed that the way to lead an exciting life was to tell big lies and then live your life so as to make them come true. But this is not the time for philosophizing. What are you going to tell Ben's boss?

Questions

1. What are your duties to Ben, the company, and yourself in this situation?
2. What is worse, saying that you have done something and not do it, or saying that you have done something and then do it the next day?
3. We all know that it is wrong to lie, but when it doesn't harm anyone, why is lying wrong?
4. What would Kant, Aristotle, and Williams say about Ben's behavior? Is there a downside to being morally lucky?

From Joanne. B. Ciulla.

Case: "The Accused and Duties of a Law-Abiding Citizen"
Hannah Arendt, 1906–1975[1]

Hannah Arendt was born in Hannover, Germany. At the age of twenty-two she received her Ph.D. in philosophy from the University of Heidelberg. She later fled from Germany to France and then on to the United States to escape the Nazis. The following case is an excerpt from Arendt's account of Adolf Eichmann's trial in her book, Eichmann in Jerusalem A Report on the Banality of Evil. Eichmann was both a leader and a follower who played a key role in the logistics of moving people to the death camps and handling the "paperwork" of the of the Holocaust. The first part of the case gives some background on Eichmann. In the second part, Eichmann discusses his idea of duty. He was not well educated and Arendt doubts that he ever read Kant, but Eichmann uses his version of Kant to explain his behavior.

Otto Adolf, son of Karl Adolf Eichmann and Maria née Schefferling, caught in a suburb of Buenos Aires on the evening of May 11, 1960, flown to Israel nine days later, brought to trial in the District Court in Jerusalem on April 11, 1961, stood accused on fifteen counts: "together with others" he had committed crimes against the Jewish people, crimes against humanity, and war crimes during the whole period of the Nazi regime and especially during the period of the Second World War. The Nazis and Nazi Collaborators (Punishment) Law of 1950, under which he was tried, provides that "a person who has committed one of these . . . offenses . . . is liable to the death penalty." To each count Eichmann pleaded: "not guilty in the sense of the indictment."

In what sense then did he think he was guilty? In the long cross-examination of the accused, according to him "the longest ever known," neither the defense nor the prosecution nor, finally, any of the three judges ever bothered to ask him this obvious question. His lawyer, Robert Servatius of Cologne, hired by Eichmann and paid by the Israeli government (following the precedent set at the Nuremberg Trials, where all attorneys for the defense were paid by the Tribunal of the victorious powers), answered the question in a press interview: "Eichmann feels guilty before God, not

---

"The Accused," "Duties of Law-Abiding Citizen," from *Eichmann in Jerusalem* by Hannah Arendt, copyright © 1963, 1964 by Hannah Arendt. Used by permission of Viking Penguin, a division of Penguin Putnam Inc.
[1]Adolf Eichmann's entire trial was filmed. There is an excellent documentary of the trial and Eichmann's testimony on video called "The Trial of Adolf Eichmann," ABC News Productions and Great Projects Film Company, Inc. (Alexandria, VA): PBS Home Video, [1997].

Case continued

before the law," but this answer remained without confirmation from the accused himself. The defense would apparently have preferred him to plead not guilty on the grounds that under the then existing Nazi legal system he had not done anything wrong, that what he was accused of were not crimes but "acts of state," over which no other state has jurisdiction (par in parem imperium non habet), *that it had been his duty to obey and that, in Servatius' words, he had committed acts "for which you are decorated if you win and go to the gallows if you lose." (Thus Goebbels had declared in 1943: "We will go down in history as the greatest statesmen of all times or as their greatest criminals.") Outside Israel (at a meeting of the Catholic Academy in Bavaria, devoted to what the* Rheinischer Merkur *called "the ticklish problem" of the "possibilities and limits in the coping with historical and political guilt through criminal proceedings"), Servatius went a step farther, and declared that "the only legitimate criminal problem of the Eichmann trial lies in pronouncing judgment against his Israeli captors, which so far has not been done"—a statement, incidentally, that is somewhat difficult to reconcile with his repeated and widely publicized utterances in Israel, in which he called the conduct of the trial "a great spiritual achievement," comparing it favorably with the Nuremberg Trials.*

Eichmann's own attitude was different. First of all, the indictment for murder was wrong: "With the killing of Jews I had nothing to do. I never killed a Jew, or a non-Jew, for that matter—I never killed any human being. I never gave an order to kill either a Jew or a non-Jew; I just did not do it," *or, as he was later to qualify this statement, "It so happened . . . that I had not once to do it"—for he left no doubt that he would have killed his own father if he had received an order to that effect. Hence he repeated over and over (what he had already stated in the so-called Sassen documents, the interview that he had given in 1955 in Argentina to the Dutch journalist Sassen, a former S.S. man who was also a fugitive from justice, and that, after Eichmann's capture, had been published in part by* Life *in this country and by* Der Stern *in Germany) that he could be accused only of "aiding and abetting" the annihilation of the Jews, which he declared in Jerusalem to have been "one of the greatest crimes in the history of Humanity."*

So Eichmann's opportunities for feeling like Pontius Pilate were many, and as the months and the years went by, he lost the need to feel anything at all. This was the way things were, this was the new law of the land, based on the Führer's order; whatever he did he did, as far as he could see, as a law-abiding citizen. He did his duty, as he told the police and the court over and over again; he not only obeyed orders, he also obeyed the law. Eichmann had a muddled inkling that this could be an important distinction, but neither the defense nor the judges ever took him up on it. The well-worn coins of "superior orders" versus "acts of state" were handed back and forth; they had governed the whole discussion of these matters during the Nuremberg Trials,

*for no other reason than that they gave the illusion that the altogether
unprecedented could be judged according to precedents, and the standards
that went with them. Eichmann, with his rather modest mental gifts, was
certainly the last man in the courtroom to be expected to challenge these
notions and to strike out on his own. Since, in addition to performing what
he conceived to be the duties of a law-abiding citizen, he had also acted upon
orders—always so careful to be "covered"—he became completely muddled,
and ended by stressing alternately the virtues and the vices of blind
obedience, or the "obedience of corpses," Kadavergehorsam, as he himself
called it.*

*The first indication of Eichmann's vague notion that there was more
involved in this whole business than the question of the soldier's carrying out
orders that are clearly criminal in nature and intent appeared during the
police examination, when he suddenly declared with great emphasis that he
had lived his whole life according to Kant's moral precepts, and especially
according to a Kantian definition of duty. This was outrageous, on the face of
it, and also incomprehensible, since Kant's moral philosophy is so closely
bound up with man's faculty of judgment, which rules out blind obedience.
The examining officer did not press the point, but Judge Raveh, either out of
curiosity or out of indignation at Eichmann's having dared to invoke Kant's
name in connection with his crimes, decided to question the accused. And, to
the surprise of everybody, Eichmann came up with an approximately correct
definition of the categorical imperative: "I meant by my remark about Kant
that the principle of my will must always be such that it can become the
principle of general laws" (which is not the case with theft or murder, for
instance, because the thief or the murderer cannot conceivably wish to live
under a legal system that would give others the right to rob or murder him).
Upon further questioning, he added that he had read Kant's* Critique of
Practical Reason. *He then proceeded to explain that from the moment he was
charged with carrying out the Final Solution he had ceased to live according
to Kantian principles, that he had known it, and that he had consoled himself
with the thought that he no longer "was master of his own deeds," that he
was unable "to change anything." What he failed to point out in court was
that in this "period of crimes legalized by the state," as he himself now called
it, he had not simply dismissed the Kantian formula as no longer applicable,
he had distorted it to read: Act as if the principle of your actions were the
same as that of the legislator or of the law of the land—or, in Hans Frank's
formulation of "the categorical imperative in the Third Reich," which
Eichmann might have known: "Act in such a way that the Führer, if he knew
your action, would approve it" (*Die Technik des Staates, *1942, pp. 15–16).
Kant, to be sure, had never intended to say anything of the sort; on the
contrary, to him every man was a legislator the moment he started to act: by
using his "practical reason" man found the principles that could and should*

Case continued

be the principles of law. But it is true that Eichmann's unconscious distortion agrees with what he himself called the version of Kant "for the household use of the little man." In this household use, all that is left of Kant's spirit is the demand that a man do more than obey the law, that he go beyond the mere call of obedience and identify his own will with the principle behind the law—the source from which the law sprang. In Kant's philosophy, that source was practical reason; in Eichmann's household use of him, it was the will of the Führer. Much of the horribly painstaking thoroughness in the execution of the Final Solution—a thoroughness that usually strikes the observer as typically German, or else as characteristic of the perfect bureaucrat—can be traced to the odd notion, indeed very common in Germany, that to be law-abiding means not merely to obey the laws but to act as though one were the legislator of the laws that one obeys. Hence the conviction that nothing less than going beyond the call of duty will do.

Whatever Kant's role in the formation of "the little man's" mentality in Germany may have been, there is not the slightest doubt that in one respect Eichmann did indeed follow Kant's precepts: a law was a law, there could be no exceptions. In Jerusalem, he admitted only two such exceptions during the time when "eighty million Germans" had each had "his decent Jew": he had helped a half-Jewish cousin, and a Jewish couple in Vienna for whom his uncle had intervened. This inconsistency still made him feel somewhat uncomfortable, and when he was questioned about it during cross-examination, he became openly apologetic: he had "confessed his sins" to his superiors. This uncompromising attitude toward the performance of his murderous duties damned him in the eyes of the judges more than anything else, which was comprehensible, but in his own eyes it was precisely what justified him, as it had once silenced whatever conscience he might have had left. No exceptions—this was the proof that he had always acted against his "inclinations," whether they were sentimental or inspired by interest, that he had always done his "duty."

Doing his "duty" finally brought him into open conflict with orders from his superiors. During the last year of the war, more than two years after the Wannsee Conference, he experienced his last crisis of conscience. As the defeat approached, he was confronted by men from his own ranks—who fought more and more insistently for exceptions and, eventually, for the cessation of the Final Solution. That was the moment when his caution broke down and he began, once more, taking initiatives—for instance, he organized the foot marches of Jews from Budapest to the Austrian border after Allied bombing had knocked out the transportation system. It now was the fall of 1944, and Eichmann knew that Himmler had ordered the dismantling of the extermination facilities in Auschwitz and that the game was up. Around this time, Eichmann had one of his very few personal interviews with Himmler, in the course of which the latter allegedly shouted at him, "If up to now you have been busy liquidating Jews, you will from now on, since I order it, take good care of Jews, act as their nursemaid. I remind you that it was I—and neither Gruppenführer Müller nor you—who founded the R.S.H.A. in 1933; I am the one who gives orders here!" Sole witness to substantiate these words was the very dubious Mr. Kurt Becher; Eichmann denied that Himmler had shouted at him, but he did not deny that such an interview had taken place. Himmler cannot have spoken in precisely these words, he surely knew that the R.S.H.A. was founded in 1939, not in 1933, and not simply by himself but by Heydrich, with his endorsement. Still, something of the sort must have occurred, Himmler was then giving orders right and left that the Jews be treated well—they were his "soundest investment"—and it must have been a shattering experience for Eichmann.

Questions

1. What is wrong with Eichmann's interpretation of a Kantian duty?
2. Is there a moral difference between obeying orders and obeying the law?
3. Did Eichmann see any difference between his duties as a leader and his duties as a follower? Is there a difference between the duties (in Kant's sense of the word) of leaders and the duties of their followers?
4. Where does Eichmann's moral reasoning seem to break down in this case?

The Analects

Confucius, 551 B.C.–479 B.C.

Confucius is considered to be the most influential thinker in Chinese civilization. He was born in the state of Lu, which today is called Shandong Province. Confucius was well educated and in his twenties he took an interest in teaching and politics. As Confucius looked at the world around him, he saw a disorder and moral decay. He believed that the only way to reform his decadent society was to reinstate the moral teachings of ancient sages. He was one of the first Chinese to devote his life to educating people about morality. At the age of fifty-one, he became a magistrate and minister of justice. At fifty-six he left his post and traveled for thirteen years with some of his pupils. He then returned home to write and edit the classics. Confucius gathered around him a large group of gentlemen scholars who formed the institution of the literati that came to dominate Chinese history and society.

Confucius was a humanist. He believed that people could make themselves better through learning and self-cultivation. He believed that people create their own destiny. Confucius said it is people who make the way great; the way does not make people great. Like Kant, his moral system rests on duty, but duty is rigidly determined by tradition. Confucius also uses the golden rule as a moral principle, though his is stated in the negative (see 15.23). Confucius tells us that the ideal way to live is harmony between the moral person and the well-ordered society. This harmony comes about because people fill their obligations to each other and conform to the rules of society. These obligations are based on five kinds of relationships: the relation between ruler and minister, father and son, elder brother and younger brother, husband and wife, and friend and friend. The most important of these relationships is filial piety.

The Analects is a collection of short comments by Confucius and his pupils that were probably compiled by students. It is not systematically organized and jumps from topic to topic. This book is generally considered to be the most reliable source of Confucius's teachings. In *The Analects* Confucius talks about the "chün-tzu," which is translated as "the superior man." The word chün-tzu literally means "son of the ruler"; however, Confucius mostly uses it to mean the morally superior person. For him nobility is not a matter of blood but of a person's character. Confucius contrasts the morally superior man who lives according to duty and principle with the inferior man whose life is based on the standard of profit. Confucius particularly disdains people who were motivated by profit and self-interest. The moral lessons for leaders are clear in *The Analects,* because Confucius directly addresses morality and leadership. As a humanist he emphasizes the need for leaders to be kind. Confucius leaders should be good role models, but most important, they should rigorously perform their duties.

1:2. Yu Tzu[14] said, "Few of those who are filial sons and respectful brothers will show disrespect to superiors, and there has never been a man who is not disrespectful to superiors and yet creates disorder. A superior man is devoted to the fundamentals (the root). When the root is firmly established, the moral law (Tao) will grow. Filial piety and brotherly respect are the root of humanity (*jen*)."

1:3. Confucius said, "A man with clever words and an ingratiating appearance is seldom a man of humanity."

1:4. Tseng-Tzu said, "Every day I examine myself on three points: whether in counseling others I have not been loyal; whether in intercourse with my friends I have not been faithful; and whether I have not repeated again and again and practiced the instructions of my teacher."[17]

---

[14]Confucius' pupil whose private name was Jo (538–c.457 B.C.), thirteen years (some say thirty-three years) Confucius' junior. In the *Analects,* with minor exceptions, he and Tseng Ts'an are addressed as Tzu, an honorific for a scholar or gentleman, giving rise to the theory that the *Analects* was compiled by their pupils, who supplemented Confucius' sayings with theirs.

[17]Ho Yen's interpretation: Whether I have transmitted to others what I myself have not practiced. This interpretation has been accepted by many.

1:6. Young men should be filial when at home and respectful to their elders when away from home. They should be earnest and faithful. They should love all extensively and be intimate with men of humanity. When they have any energy to spare after the performance of moral duties, they should use it to study literature and the arts (*wen*).[18]

1:8. Confucius said, "If the superior man is not grave, he will not inspire awe, and his learning will not be on a firm foundation.[19] Hold loyalty and faithfulness to be fundamental. Have no friends who are not as good as yourself. When you have made mistakes, don't be afraid to correct them."

Comment. The teaching about friendship here is clearly inconsistent with *Analects,* 8:5, where Confucius exhorts us to learn from inferiors. It is difficult to believe that Confucius taught people to be selfish. According to Hsing Ping (932–1010), Confucius meant people who are not equal to oneself in loyalty and faithfulness, assuming that one is or should be loyal and faithful; according to Hsü Kan (171–218), Confucius simply wanted us to be careful in choosing friends.

1:11. Confucius said, "When a man's father is alive, look at the bent of his will. When his father is dead, look at his conduct. If for three years [of mourning] he does not change from the way of his father, he may be called filial."

Comment. Critics of Confucius have asserted that Confucian authoritarianism holds an oppressive weight on the son even after the father has passed away. Fan Tsu-yü (1041–1098) did understand the saying to mean that the son should observe the father's will and past conduct, but he was almost alone in this. All prominent commentators, from K'ung An-kuo to Cheng Hsüan (127–200), Chu Hsi, and Liu Pao-nan have interpreted the passage to mean that while one's father is alive, one's action is restricted, so that his *intention* should be the criterion by which his character is to be judged. After his father's death, however, when he is completely autonomous, he should be judged by his conduct. In this interpretation, the way of the father is of course the moral principle which has guided or should have guided the son's conduct.

1:12. Yu Tzu said, "Among the functions of propriety (*li*) the most valuable is that it establishes harmony. The excellence of the ways of ancient kings consists of this. It is the guiding principle of all things great and

---

[18]*Wen,* literally "patterns," is here extended to mean the embodiment of culture and the moral law (Tao)—that is, the Six Arts of ceremony, music, archery, carriage-driving, writing, and mathematics.

[19]To K'ung An-kuo (fl. 130 B.C.), quoted by Ho Yen, *ku* means "obscure," not "firm." The sentence would read, "If he studies, he will not be ignorant."

small. If things go amiss, and you, understanding harmony, try to achieve it without regulating it by the rules of propriety, they will still go amiss."

1:14. Confucius said, "The superior man does not seek fulfillment of his appetite nor comfort in his lodging. He is diligent in his duties and careful in his speech. He associates with men of moral principles and thereby realizes himself. Such a person may be said to love learning."

1:15. Tzu-kung said, "What do you think of a man who is poor and yet does not flatter, and the rich man who is not proud?" Confucius replied, "They will do. But they are not as good as the poor man who is happy and the rich man who loves the rules of propriety (*li*)." Tzu kung said, "*The Book of Odes* says:

> As a thing is cut and filed.
> As a thing is carved and polished. . . .[26]

Does that not mean what you have just said?" Confucius said, "Ah! Tz'u. Now I can begin to talk about the odes with you. When I have told you what has gone before, you know what is to follow."

1:16. Confucius said, "[A good man] does not worry about not being known by others but rather worries about not knowing them."

2:1. Confucius said, "A ruler who governs his state by virtue is like the north polar star, which remains in its place while all the other stars revolve around it."

Comment. Two important principles are involved here. One is government by virtue, in which Confucianists stand directly opposed to the Legalists, who prefer law and force. The other is government through inaction, i.e., government in such excellent order that all things operate by themselves. This is the interpretation shared by Han and Sung Confucianists alike. In both cases, Confucianism and Taoism are in agreement.

2:2. Confucius said, "All three hundred odes can be covered by one of their sentences, and that is, 'Have no depraved thoughts.'"

2:3. Confucius said, "Lead the people with governmental measures and regulate them by law and punishment, and they will avoid wrongdoing but will have no sense of honor and shame. Lead them with virtue and regulate them by the rules of propriety (*li*), and they will have a sense of shame and, moreover, set themselves right."

2:4. Confucius said, "At fifteen my mind was set on learning. At thirty my character had been formed. At forty I had no more perplexities. At fifty I knew the Mandate of Heaven (*T'ien-ming*). At sixty I was at

---

[26]Ode no. 55. Describing the eloquence of a lover, but here taken by Tzu-kung to mean moral effort.

ease with whatever I heard. At seventy I could follow my heart's desire without transgressing moral principles."

Comment. What *T'ien-ming* is depends upon one's own philosophy. In general, Confucianists before the T'ang dynasty (618–907) understood it to mean either the decree of God, which determines the course of one's life, or the rise and fall of the moral order, whereas Sung scholars, especially Chu Hsi, took it to mean "the operation of Nature which is endowed in things and makes things be as they are." This latter interpretation has prevailed. The concept of *T'ien-ming* which can mean Mandate of Heaven, decree of God, personal destiny, and course of order, is extremely important in the history of Chinese thought. In religion it generally means fate or personal order of God, but in philosophy it is practically always understood as moral destiny, natural endowment, or moral order.

2:5.   Meng I Tzu asked about filial piety. Confucius said: "Never disobey." [Later,] when Fan Ch'ih was driving him, Confucius told him, "Meng-sun asked me about filial piety, and I answered him, 'Never disobey.'" Fan Ch'ih said, "What does that mean?" Confucius said, "When parents are alive, serve them according to the rules of propriety. When they die, bury them according to the rules of propriety and sacrifice to them according to the rules of propriety."

2:6.   Meng Wu-po asked about filial piety. Confucius said, "Especially be anxious lest parents should be sick."

2:7.   Tzu-yu asked about filial piety. Confucius said, "Filial piety nowadays means to be able to support one's parents. But we support even . dogs and horses. If there is no feeling of reverence, wherein lies the difference?"

2:11. Confucius said, "A man who reviews the old so as to find out the new is qualified to teach others."

2:12. Confucius said, "The superior man is not an implement (*ch'i*)."

Comment. A good and educated man should not be like an implement, which is intended only for a narrow and specific purpose. Instead, he should have broad vision, wide interests, and sufficient ability to do many things.

2:13. Tzu-kung asked about the superior man. Confucius said, "He acts before he speaks and then speaks according to his action."

2:14. Confucius said, "The superior man is broadminded but not partisan; the inferior man is partisan but not broadminded."

2:15. Confucius said, "He who learns but does not think is lost; he who thinks but does not learn is in danger."

2:17. Confucius said, "Yu, shall I teach you [the way to acquire] knowledge?[45] To say that you know when you do know and say that you do not know when you do not know—that is [the way to acquire] knowledge."

2:18. Tzu-chang was learning with a view to official emolument. Confucius said, "Hear much and put aside what's doubtful while you speak cautiously of the rest. Then few will blame you. See much and put aside what seems perilous while you are cautious in carrying the rest into practice. Then you will have few occasions for regret. When one's words give few occasions for blame and his acts give few occasions for repentance—there lies his emolument."

Comment. The equal emphasis on words and deeds has been a strong tradition in Confucianism. Eventually Wang Yang-ming identified them as one.

2:24. Confucius said, "It is flattery to offer sacrifice to ancestral spirits other than one's own. To see what is right and not to do it is cowardice."

3:3. Confucius said, "If a man is not humane (*jen*), what has he to do with ceremonies (*li*)? If he is not humane, what has he to do with music?"

3:4. Lin Fang asked about the foundation of ceremonies. Confucius said, "An important question indeed! In rituals or ceremonies, be thrifty rather than extravagant, and in funerals, be deeply sorrowful rather than shallow in sentiment."

3:12. When Confucius offered sacrifice to his ancestors, he felt as if his ancestral spirits were actually present. When he offered sacrifice to other spiritual beings, he felt as if they were actually present. He said, "If I do not participate in the sacrifice, it is as if I did not sacrifice at all."

3:13. Wang-sun Chia asked, "What is meant by the common saying, 'It is better to be on good terms with the God of the Kitchen [who cooks our food] than with the spirits of the shrine (ancestors) at the southwest corner of the house'?" Confucius said, "It is not true. He who commits a sin against Heaven has no god to pray to."

3:17. Tzu-kung wanted to do away with the sacrificing of a lamb at the ceremony in which the beginning of each month is reported to ancestors. Confucius said, "Tz'u! You love the lamb but I love the ceremony."

3:19. Duke Ting asked how the ruler should employ his ministers and how the ministers should serve their ruler. Confucius said, "A ruler should employ his ministers according to the principle of propriety, and ministers should serve their ruler with loyalty."

[45]The sentence may also mean: "Do you know what I teach you?"

3:24. The guardian at I (a border post of the state of Wei) requested to be presented to Confucius, saying, "When gentlemen come here, have never been prevented from seeing them." Confucius' followers introduced him. When he came out from the interview, he said, "Sirs, why are you disheartened by your master's loss of office? The Way has not prevailed in the world for a long time. Heaven is going to use your master as a bell with a wooden tongue [to awaken the people]."

4:2. Confucius said, "One who is not a man of humanity cannot endure adversity for long, nor can he enjoy prosperity for long. The man of humanity is naturally at ease with humanity. The man of wisdom cultivates humanity for its advantage."

4:3. Confucius said, "Only the man of humanity knows how to love people and hate people."

4:4. Confucius said, "If you set your mind on humanity, you will be free from evil."

4:5. Confucius said, "Wealth and honor are what every man desires. But if they have been obtained in violation of moral principles, they must not be kept. Poverty and humble station are what every man dislikes. But if they can be avoided only in violation of moral principles, they must not be avoided. If a superior man departs from humanity, how can he fulfill that name? A superior man never abandons humanity even for the lapse of a single meal. In moments of haste, he acts according to it. In times of difficulty or confusion, he acts according to it."

4:6. Confucius said, "I have never seen one who really loves humanity or one who really hates inhumanity. One who really loves humanity will not place anything above it. One who really hates inhumanity will practice humanity in such a way that inhumanity will have no chance to get at him. Is there any one who has devoted his strength to humanity for as long as a single day? I have not seen any one without sufficient strength to do so. Perhaps there is such a case, but have never seen it."

4:8. Confucius said, "In the morning, hear the Way; in the evening, die content!"

4:10. Confucius said, "A superior man in dealing with the world is not for anything or against anything. He follows righteousness as the standard."

4:11. Confucius said, "The superior man thinks of virtue; the inferior man thinks of possessions. The superior man thinks of sanctions; the inferior man thinks of personal favors."

4:12. Confucius said, "If one's acts are motivated by profit, he will have many enemies."

4:15. Confucius said, "Shen, there is one thread that runs through my doctrines." Tseng Tzu said, "Yes." After Confucius had left, the disciples asked him, "What did he mean?" Tseng Tzu replied, "The Way of our Master is none other than conscientiousness (*chung*) and altruism (*shu*)."

Comment. Confucian teachings may be summed up in the phrase "one thread" (*i-kuan*), but Confucianists have not agreed on what it means. Generally, Confucianists of Han and T'ang times adhered to the basic meaning of "thread" and understood it in the sense of a system or a body of doctrines. Chu Hsi, true to the spirit of Neo-Confucian speculative philosophy, took it to mean that there is one mind to respond to all things. In the Ch'ing period, in revolt against speculation, scholars preferred to interpret *kuan* as action and affairs, that is, there is only one moral principle for all actions. All agree, however, on the meanings of *chung* and *shu*, which are best expressed by Chu Hsi, namely, *chung* means the full development of one's [originally good] mind and *shu* means the extension of that mind to others. As Ch'eng I (Ch'eng I-ch'uan, 1033–1107) put it, *chung* is the Way of Heaven, whereas *shu* is the way of man; the former is substance, while the latter is function. Liu Pao-nan is correct in equating *chung* with Confucius' saying, "Establish one's own character," and *shu* with "Also establish the character of others." Here is the positive version of the Confucian golden rule. The negative version is only one side of it.

4:16. Confucius said, "The superior man understands righteousness (*i*); the inferior man understands profit."

Comment. Confucius contrasted the superior man and the inferior in many ways, but this is the fundamental difference for Confucianism in general as well as for Confucius himself. Chu Hsi associated righteousness with the Principle of Nature (*T'ien-li*) and profit with the feelings of man, but later Neo-Confucianists strongly objected to his thus contrasting principle and feelings.

4:18. Confucius said, "In serving his parents, a son may gently remonstrate with them. When he sees that they are not inclined to listen to him, he should resume an attitude of reverence and not abandon his effort to serve them. He may feel worried, but does not complain."

4:19. Confucius said, "When his parents are alive, a son should not go far abroad; or if he does, he should let them know where he goes."

4:21. Confucius said, "A son should always keep in mind the age of his parents. It is an occasion for joy [that they are enjoying long life] and also an occasion for anxiety [that another year is gone]."

4:24. Confucius said, "The superior man wants to be slow in word but diligent in action."

5:11. Tzu-kung said, "What I do not want others to do to me, I do not want to do to them." Confucius said, "Ah Tz'u! That is beyond you."

5:12. Tzu-kung said, "We can hear our Master's [views] on culture and its manifestation, but we cannot hear his views on human nature and the Way of Heaven [because these subjects are beyond the comprehension of most people]."

5:25. Yen Yüan and Chi-lu were in attendance. Confucius said, "Why don't you each tell me your ambition in life?" Tzu-lu said, "I wish to have a horse, a carriage, and a light fur coat and share them with friends, and shall not regret if they are all worn out." Yen Yüan said, "I wish never to boast of my good qualities and never to brag about the trouble I have taken [for others]."[78] Tzu-lu said, "I wish to hear your ambition." Confucius said, "It is my ambition to comfort the old, to be faithful to friends, and to cherish the young."[79]

5:27. Confucius said, "In every hamlet of ten families, there are always some people as loyal and faithful as myself, but none who love learning as much as I do."

6:5. Confucius said, "About Hui (Yen Yüan), for three months there would be nothing in his mind contrary to humanity. The others could (or can) attain to this for a day or a month at the most."

Comment. On the basis of this saying alone, some philosophers have concluded that Yen Yüan was a mystic and that Confucius praised mysticism!

6:16. Confucius said, "When substance exceeds refinement (*wen*), one becomes rude. When refinement exceeds substance, one becomes urbane. It is only when one's substance and refinement are properly blended that he becomes a superior man."

6:17. Confucius said, "Man is born with uprightness. If one loses it he will be lucky if he escapes with his life."

6:18. Confucius said, "To know it [learning or the Way] is not as good as to love it, and to love it is not as good as to take delight in it."

6:19. Confucius said, "To those who are above average, one may talk of the higher things, but may not do so to those who are below average."

6:20. Fan Ch'ih asked about wisdom. Confucius said, "Devote yourself earnestly to the duties due to men, and respect spiritual beings[86] but keep them at a distance. This may be called wisdom." Fan Ch'ih asked about humanity. Confucius said, "The man of humanity first of

---

[78]Another interpretation: For his own moral effort.

[79]This is Chu Hsi's interpretation. According to Hsing Ping, it would mean this: The old should be satisfied with me, friends should trust me, and the young should come to me.

[86]Meaning especially ancestors.

all considers what is difficult in the task and then thinks of success. Such a man may be called humane."

Comment. Many people have been puzzled by this passage, some even doubting the sincerity of Confucius' religious attitude—all quite unnecessarily. The passage means either "do not become improperly informal with spiritual beings," or "emphasize the way of man rather than the way of spirits."

6:21. Confucius said, "The man of wisdom delights in water; the man of humanity delights in mountains. The man of wisdom is active; the man of humanity is tranquil. The man of wisdom enjoys happiness; the man of humanity enjoys long life."

Comment. In the Confucian ethical system, humanity and wisdom are like two wings, one supporting the other. One is substance, the other is function. The dual emphasis has been maintained throughout history, especially in Tung Chung-shu (c.179–c.104 B.C.) and in a certain sense in K'ang Yu-wei (1858–1927). Elsewhere, courage is added as the third virtue, and Mencius grouped them with righteousness and propriety as the Four Beginnings.

6:23. Confucius said, "When a cornered vessel no longer has any corner, should it be called a cornered vessel? Should it?"

Comment. Name must correspond to actuality.

6:25. Confucius said, "The superior man extensively studies literature (*wen*) and restrains himself with the rules of propriety. Thus he will not violate the Way."

6:26. When Confucius visited Nan-tzu (the wicked wife of Duke Ling of Wei, r. 533—490 B.C.) [in an attempt to influence her to persuade the duke to effect political reform], Tzu-lu was not pleased. Confucius swore an oath and said, "If I have said or done anything wrong, may Heaven forsake me! May Heaven forsake me!"

6:28. Tzu-kung said, "If a ruler extensively confers benefit on the people and can bring salvation to all, what do you think of him? Would you call him a man of humanity?" Confucius said, "Why only a man of humanity? He is without doubt a sage. Even (sage-emperors) Yao and Shun fell short of it. A man of humanity, wishing to establish his own character, also establishes the character of others, and wishing to be prominent himself, also helps others to be prominent. To be able to judge others by what is near to ourselves may be called the method of realizing humanity."

7:1. Confucius said, "I transmit but do not create. I believe in and love the ancients. I venture to compare myself to our old P'eng."

Comment. This is often cited to show that Confucius was not creative. We must not forget, however, that he "goes over the old so as to find out what is new." Nor must we overlook the fact that he was the first one to offer education to all. Moreover, his concepts of the superior man and of Heaven were at least partly new.

7:2.   Confucius said, "To remember silently [what I have learned], to learn untiringly, and to teach others without being wearied—that is just natural with me."

7:6.   Confucius said, "Set your will on the Way. Have a firm grasp on virtue. Rely on humanity. Find recreation in the arts."

7:7.   Confucius said, "There has never been anyone who came with as little a present as dried meat (for tuition) that I have refused to teach him something."

7:8.   Confucius said, "I do not enlighten those who are not eager to learn, nor arouse those who are not anxious to give an explanation themselves. If I have presented one corner of the square and they cannot come back to me with the other three, I should not go over the points again."

7:15. Confucius said, "With coarse rice to eat, with water to drink, and with a bent arm for a pillow, there is still joy. Wealth and honor obtained through unrighteousness are but floating clouds to me."

7:16. Confucius said, "Give me a few more years so that I can devote fifty years to study Change. I may be free from great mistakes."

7:17. These were the things Confucius often talked about— poetry, history, and the performance of the rules of propriety. All these were what he often talked about.

7:18. The Duke of She asked Tzu-lu about Confucius, and Tzu-lu did not answer. Confucius said, "Why didn't you say that I am a person who forgets his food when engaged in vigorous pursuit of something, is so happy as to forget his worries, and is not aware that old age is coming on?"

7:19. Confucius said, "I am not one who was born with knowledge; I love ancient [teaching] and earnestly seek it."

7:20. Confucius never discussed strange phenomena, physical exploits, disorder, or spiritual beings.

7:22. Confucius said, "Heaven produced the virtue that is in me; what can Huan T'ui do to me?"

7:24. Confucius taught four things: culture (*wen*), conduct, loyalty, and faithfulness.

7:26. Confucius fished with a line but not a net. While shooting he would not shoot a bird at rest.

7:27. Confucius said, "There are those who act without knowing [what is right]. But I am not one of them. To hear much and select gentlemen want to do." Confucius said, "What harm is there? After all, we want each to tell his ambition." Tseng Hsi said, "In the late spring, when the spring dress is ready, I would like to go with five or six grownups and six or seven young boys to bathe in the I River, enjoy the breeze on the Rain Dance Altar, and then return home singing." Confucius heaved a sigh and said, "I agree with Tien."

Comment. Why did Confucius agree with Tseng Hsi? The field is wide open for speculation, and most Confucianists have taken the best advantage of it. Thus it was variously explained that Tseng Hsi was enjoying the harmony of the universe (Wang Ch'ung), that he was following traditional cultural institutions (Liu Pao-nan), that he was wisely refraining from officialdom at the time of chaos (Huang K'an), that he was thinking of the "kingly way" whereas other pupils were thinking of the government of feudal states (Han Yü), that he was in the midst of the universal operation of the Principle of Nature (Chu Hsi), and that he was expressing freedom of the spirit (Wang Yang-ming, 1472–1529). It is to be noted that the last two interpretations reflect the different tendencies of the two wings of Neo-Confucianism, one emphasizing the objective operation of the Principle of Nature, the other emphasizing the state of mind.

12:1. Yen Yüan asked about humanity. Confucius said, "To master oneself and return to propriety is humanity.[129] If a man (the ruler) can for one day master himself and return to propriety, all under heaven will return to humanity.[130] To practice humanity depends on oneself. Does it depend on others?" Yen Yüan said, "May I ask for the detailed items?" Confucius said, "Do not look at what is contrary to propriety, do not listen to what is contrary to propriety, do not speak what is contrary to propriety, and do not make any movement which is contrary to propriety." Yen Yüan said, "Although I am not intelligent, may I put your saying into practice."

12:2. Chung-kung asked about humanity. Confucius said, "When you go abroad, behave to everyone as if you were receiving a great guest. Employ the people as if you were assisting at a great sacrifice. Do not do to others what you do not want them to do to you. Then there will be no complaint against you in the state or in the family (the ruling clan)." Chung-kung said, "Although I am not intelligent, may I put your saying into practice."

12:5. Ssu-ma Niu, worrying, said, "All people have brothers but I have none." Tzu-hsia said, "I have heard [from Confucius] this saying: 'Life and death are the decree of Heaven (*ming*); wealth and honor

---

[129]An old saying. Other interpretations: (1) To be able to return to propriety by oneself; (2) to discipline oneself and to act according to propriety.

[130]Other interpretations: (1) Ascribe humanity to him; (2) will follow him.

depend on Heaven. If a superior man is reverential (or serious) without fail, and is respectful in dealing with others and follows the rules of propriety, then all within the four seas (the world) are brothers.' What does the superior man have to worry about having no brothers?"

12:7. Tzu-kung asked about government. Confucius said, "Sufficient food, sufficient armament, and sufficient confidence of the people." Tzu-kung said, "Forced to give up one of these, which would you abandon first?" Confucius said, "I would abandon the armament." Tzu-kung said, "Forced to give up one of the remaining two, which would you abandon first?" Confucius said, "I would abandon food. There have been deaths from time immemorial, but no state can exist without the confidence of the people."

12.11. Duke Ching of Ch'i asked Confucius about government. Confucius replied, "Let the ruler *be* a ruler, the minister *be* a minister, the father *be* a father, and the son *be* a son." The duke said, "Excellent! Indeed when the ruler is not a ruler, the minister not a minister, the father not a father, and the son not a son, although I may have all the grain, shall I ever get to eat it?"

12:16. Confucius said, "The superior man brings the good things of others to completion and does not bring the bad things of others to completion. The inferior man does just the opposite."

12:17. Chi K'ang Tzu asked Confucius about government. Confucius replied, "To govern (*cheng*) is to rectify (*cheng*). If you lead the people by being rectified yourself, who will dare not be rectified?"

12:19. Chi K'ang Tzu asked Confucius about government, saying, "What do you think of killing the wicked and associating with the good?" Confucius replied, "In your government what is the need of killing? If you desire what is good, the people will be good. The character of a ruler is like wind and that of the people is like grass. In whatever direction the wind blows, the grass always bends."

12:22. Fan Ch'ih asked about humanity. Confucius said, "It is to love men." He asked about knowledge. Confucius said, "It is to know man."

Comment. As a general virtue, *jen* means humanity, that is, that which makes a man a moral being. As a particular virtue, it means love. This is the general interpretation during the Han and T'ang times. Later in Neo-Confucianism, it was modified to mean man and Nature forming one body. The doctrine that knowledge of men is power has been maintained throughout the history of Confucianism. This humanistic interest has to a large degree prevented China from developing the tradition of knowledge for its own sake.

13:3. Tzu-lu said, "The ruler of Wei is waiting for you to serve in his administration. What will be your first measure?" Confucius said, "It will certainly concern the rectification of names." Tzu-lu said, "Is that so? You are wide of the mark. Why should there be such a rectification?" Confucius said, "Yu! How uncultivated you are! With regard to what he does not know, the superior man should maintain an attitude of reserve. If names are not rectified, then language will not be accord with truth. If language is not in accord with truth, then things cannot be accomplished. If things cannot be accomplished, then ceremonies and music will not flourish. If ceremonies and music do not flourish, then punishment will not be just. If punishments are not just, then the people will not know how to move hand or foot. Therefore the superior man will give only names that can be described in speech and say only what can be carried out in practice. With regard to his speech, the superior man does not take it lightly. That is all."

Comment. Most ancient Chinese philosophical schools had a theory about names and actuality. In the Confucian school, however, it assumes special importance because its focus is not metaphysical as in Taoism, or logical as in the School of Logicians, or utilitarian as in the Legalist School, but ethical. This means not only that a name must correspond to its actuality, but also that rank, duties, and functions must be clearly defined and fully translated into action. Only then can a name be considered to be correct or rectified. With the ethical interest predominant, this is the nearest the ancient Confucianists came to a logical theory, except in the case of Hsün Tzu, who was the most logical of all ancient Confucianists.

13:6. Confucius said, "If a ruler sets himself right, he will be followed without his command. If he does not set himself right, even his commands will not be obeyed."

13:16. The Duke of She asked about government. Confucius said, "[There is good government] when those who are near are happy and those far away desire to come."

13:18. The Duke of She told Confucius, "In my country there is an upright man named Kung. When his father stole a sheep, he bore witness against him." Confucius said, "The upright men in my community are different from this. The father conceals the misconduct of the son and the son conceals the misconduct of the father. Uprightness is to be found in this."

13:19. Fan Ch'ih asked about humanity. Confucius said, "Be respectful in private life, be serious (*ching*) in handling affairs, and be loyal in dealing with others. Even if you are living amidst barbarians, these principles may never be forsaken."

13:23. Confucius said, "The superior man is conciliatory but does not identify himself with others; the inferior man identifies with others but is not conciliatory."

13:26. Confucius said, "The superior man is dignified but not proud; the inferior man is proud but not dignified."

13:27. Confucius said, "A man who is strong, resolute, simple, and slow to speak is near to humanity."

13:29. Confucius said, "When good men have instructed the people [in morals, agriculture, military tactics] for seven years, they may be allowed to bear arms."

13:30. Confucius said, "To allow people to go to war without first instructing them is to betray them."

14:2. [Yüan Hsien] said, "When one has avoided aggressiveness, pride, resentment, and greed, he may be called a man of humanity." Confucius said, "This may be considered as having done what is difficult, but I do not know that it is to be regarded as humanity."

14:24. Confucius said, "The superior man understands the higher things [moral principles]; the inferior man understands the lower things [profit]."

14:29. Confucius said, "The superior man is ashamed that his words exceed his deeds."

14:30. Confucius said, "The way of the superior man is threefold, but I have not been able to attain it. The man of wisdom has no perplexities; the man of humanity has no worry; the man of courage has no fear." Tzu-kung said, "You are talking about yourself."

14:33. Confucius said, "He who does not anticipate attempts to deceive him nor predict his being distrusted, and yet is the first to know [when these things occur], is a worthy man."

14:36. Someone said, "What do you think of repaying hatred with virtue?" Confucius said, "In that case what are you going to repay virtue with? Rather, repay hatred with uprightness and repay virtue with virtue."

15:23. Tzu-kung asked, "Is there one word which can serve as the guiding principle for conduct throughout life?" Confucius said, "It is the word altruism (*shu*). Do not do to others what you do not want them to do to you."

15:28. Confucius said, "It is man that can make the Way great, and not the Way that can make man great."

Comment. Humanism in the extreme! Commentators from Huang K'an to Chu Hsi said that the Way, because it is tranquil and quiet and lets things take their own course, does not make man great. A better explanation is found in the *Doctrine of the Mean,* where it is said, "Unless there is perfect virtue, the perfect Way cannot be materialized."

15:31. Confucius said, "The superior man seeks the Way and not a mere living. There may be starvation in farming, and there may be riches in the pursuit of studies. The superior man worries about the Way and not about poverty."

15:32. Confucius said, "When a man's knowledge is sufficient for him to attain [his position] but his humanity is not sufficient for him to hold it, he will lose it again. When his knowledge is sufficient for him to attain it and his humanity is sufficient for him to hold it, if he does not approach the people with dignity, the people will not respect him. If his knowledge is sufficient for him to attain it, his humanity sufficient for him to hold it, and he approaches the people with dignity, yet does not influence them with the principle of propriety, it is still not good."

15:35. Confucius said, "When it comes to the practice of humanity, one should not defer even to his teacher."

15:38. Confucius said, "In education there should be no class distinction."

Comment. Confucius was the first to pronounce this principle in Chinese history. Among his pupils there were commoners as well as nobles, and stupid people as well as intelligent ones.

15:40. Confucius said, "In words all that matters is to express the meaning."

16:1. Confucius said, ". . . I have heard that those who administer a state or a family do not worry about there being too few people, but worry about unequal distribution of wealth. They do not worry about poverty, but worry about the lack of security and peace on the part of the people. For when wealth is equally distributed, there will not be poverty; when there is harmony, there will be no problem of there being too few people; and when there are security and peace, there will be no danger to the state. . . ."

16:4. Confucius said, "There are three kinds of friendship which are beneficial and three kinds which are harmful. Friendship with the upright, with the truthful, and with the well-informed is beneficial. Friendship with those who flatter, with those who are meek and who compromise with principles, and with those who talk cleverly is harmful."

16:8. Confucius said, "The superior man stands in awe of three things. He stands in awe of the Mandate of Heaven; he stands in awe of great men; and he stands in awe of the words of the sages. The inferior man is ignorant of the Mandate of Heaven and does not stand in awe of it. He is disrespectful to great men and is contemptuous toward the words of the sages."

16:9. Confucius said, "Those who are born with knowledge are the highest type of people. Those who learn through study are the next. Those who learn through hard work are still the next. Those who work hard and still do not learn are really the lowest type."

16:10. Confucius said, "The superior man has nine wishes. In seeing, he wishes to see clearly. In hearing, he wishes to hear distinctly. In his expression, he wishes to be warm. In his appearance, he wishes to be respectful. In his speech, he wishes to be sincere. In handling affairs, he wishes to be serious. When in doubt, he wishes to ask. When he is angry, he wishes to think of the resultant difficulties. And when he sees an opportunity for a gain, he wishes to think of righteousness."

17:2. Confucius said, "By nature men are alike. Through practice they have become far apart."

Comment. This is the classical Confucian dictum on human nature. Neo-Confucianists like Chu Hsi and Ch'eng I strongly argued that Confucius meant physical nature, which involves elements of evil, for since every man's original nature is good, men must be the *same* and therefore cannot be *alike.* Others, however, think that the word *chin* (near or alike) here has the same meaning as in Mencius' saying, "All things of the same kind are similar to one another." However, on the surface this saying is indisputably neutral, but all of Confucius' teachings imply the goodness of human nature.

17:3. Confucius said, "Only the most intelligent and the most stupid do not change."

17:4. Confucius went to the city of Wu [where his disciple Tzu-yu was the magistrate] and heard the sound of stringed instruments and singing. With a gentle smile, the Master said, "Why use an ox-knife to kill a chicken [that is, why employ a serious measure like music to rule such a small town]?" Tzu-yu replied, "Formerly I heard you say, 'When the superior man has studied the Way, he loves men. When the inferior man has studied the Way, he is easy to employ.' " Confucius said, "My disciples, what I just said was only a joke."

17:6. Tzu-chang asked Confucius about humanity. Confucius said, "One who can practice five things wherever he may be is a man of humanity." Tzu-chang asked what the five are. Confucius said, "Earnestness, liberality, truthfulness, diligence, and generosity. If one is earnest, one will not be treated with disrespect. If one is liberal, one will win the hearts of all. If one is truthful, one will be trusted. If one is diligent, one will be successful. And if one is generous, one will be able to enjoy the service of others."

REVIEW QUESTIONS

1. What strengths and weaknesses would a Confucian leader bring to running an organization or country today?
2. Compare and contrast leadership under Confucian principles with leadership under Kantian ones. How would the Confucian leader/follower relationship differ from the Kantian one?
3. Is morality that comes from tradition is superior to other ways of thinking about morality?

CHAPTER 4

LEADERSHIP FOR THE GREATEST GOOD

INTRODUCTION

It is difficult to even think about leadership without thinking about the greatest good for the greatest number of people. We usually choose leaders who we believe will bring about the greatest good for an organization, a country, or a community. Utilitarianism is a very familiar moral theory for Westerners. It is the foundation of democracy and at least on the surface, it bears some resemblance to a major tenet of economics, the cost-benefit analysis. Utilitarianism is the flip side of Kant's theory of ethics. Ethical theories based on duty are called deontic theories (from the Greek word for duty, *deon*). They are concerned with the moral intent of an act. Utilitarian theory is teleological (from the Greek word *telos*, which means purpose of end). Kant's theory is based on human reason; utilitarianism is based on reason and experience. Unlike Kant, John Stuart Mill believes that we know enough about causation from experience to influence outcomes. Acting to bring about the greatest happiness or good is a rational and empirical calculation.

You may find yourself drawn more to Kant's or to Mill's theory of ethics. As you will discover when you discuss the case "Prejudice or Preference," both theories capture important elements of the way we go about solving moral problems. In some cases we have to choose between our idea of the greatest good and our duties to various stakeholders. In other situations, such as the one in "Corneas in the Congo," the immediate greatest good comes in direct conflict with other principles and duties. Problems like this are among the most difficult for leaders. Often when leaders make a decision based on the greatest good, they set precedents for future action. Hence, they need the wisdom and imagination to see the greatest good of a particular action in the context of the big picture. The greatest good often looks different in the short term than in the long term.

One problem with utilitarianism is that the greatest happiness for the majority might be secured at the cost of tremendous misery for a few. Philosopher John Rawls's work on justice is one of the most important of the twentieth century. Rawls takes what is best about Kant's theory of ethics and what is best about utilitarianism and fuses them together. His theory of distributive justice offers a way around the problem of self-interest, and it takes into account our duties to those who are least advantaged and the greatest good for society as a whole. Ursala Le Guin's haunting story, "The Ones Who Walk Away from Omelas," illustrates the kind of problem with utilitarian justice that Rawls' theory aims to rectify.

Friedrich Nietzsche offers a different critique of utilitarianism and egalitarianism. He says that utilitarianism promotes mediocrity and fails to encourage excellence. It makes people prefer to be happy and comfortable rather than exceptional. His "Zarathustra's Prologue" is very modern in its critique of a society of people who would rather be entertained than do anything creative. If it were written today his critique might have focused on our inclination to subject everything to a cost-benefit analysis and what that has done to us as persons. All leaders face philosophic questions about what constitutes the greatest good and what will make the most people happy. Nietzsche challenges us to think about whether what makes people happy also makes them better human beings. In other words, utilitarianism without consideration for virtue or character may not be adequate as a moral theory.

The reading by the Taoist philosopher Lao Tzu may seem out of place in a section on utilitarianism, but Lao Tzu addresses both happiness and character in his moral and metaphysical work the "Tao Te Ching." In this reading Lao Tzu offers advice to leaders, but he also gives us a picture of reality that determines what constitutes a happy life. His notion of a leader's virtues and the greatest good are both familiar and different from the way Westerners think about these ideas.

The readings in this chapter address one of the most fundamental moral problems leaders face. A large part of leadership is to promote the greatest good, but the nature of the good and how one promotes it raise a number of questions: *Is doing what promotes the greatest happiness for the greatest number of people always the right thing to do? Is it right for a leader to act in ways that make his or her followers happy, but are not good for them? What are the difficulties in constructing a notion of the greatest good? When do leaders need to consider other duties and virtues that come in conflict with utility?*

What Utilitarianism Is

John Stuart Mill, 1806–1873

John Stuart Mill was born in London, England. He was a philosopher and economist, who wrote on everything from science to women's rights. Mill also served in the British Parliament. The most repeated biographical note about Mill is that he was a prodigy who began the study of Greek at the age of three and had mastered subjects ranging from science to law by a the age of seventeen. Mill was a very strong advocate of personal liberty and the public welfare. He was ahead of his time in advocating women's rights, compulsory education, and birth control.

Utilitarianism is a fundamental way of thinking about ethics and leadership because it emphasizes multiplying happiness, or making life better for the majority of stakeholders in an organization, a community, or a country. The notion of the greatest good also helps settle debates between conflicting duties and it requires us to take into account the interests and well-being of others. Unlike Kant, Mill believes that our experience equips us with the knowledge we need to produce the desired outcomes of our actions. He thinks Kant's notion of acting only according to good will, regardless of the consequences is impractical and too difficult for most people.

Mill defends utilitarianism from the charge that the "greatest good" or greatest happiness principle is a matter of mere expedience, or as we would say today a cost-benefit analysis. Notice too that Mill offers a resolution to the ethics verses effectiveness question. He says the intention of an action tells you about the morality of the individual and the consequence of the act tells you about the morality of the act.

The creed which accepts as the foundation of morals, Utility, or the Greatest Happiness Principle, holds that actions are right in proportion as they tend to promote happiness, wrong as they tend to produce the reverse of happiness. By happiness is intended pleasure, and the absence of pain; by unhappiness, pain, and the privation of pleasure. To give a clear view of the moral standard set up by the theory, much more requires to be said; in particular, what things it includes in the ideas of pain and pleasure; and to what extent this is left an open question. But these supplementary explanations do not affect the theory of life on which this theory of morality is grounded—namely, that pleasure, and freedom from pain, are the only things desirable as ends; and that all desirable things (which are as numerous in the utilitarian as in any other scheme) are desirable either for the pleasure inherent in themselves, or as means to the promotion of pleasure and the prevention of pain.

Now, such a theory of life excites in many minds, and among them in some of the most estimable in feeling and purpose, inveterate dislike. To suppose that life has (as they express it) no higher end than pleasure—no better and nobler object of desire and pursuit—they designate as utterly mean and grovelling; as a doctrine worthy only of swine, to whom the followers of Epicurus were, at a very early period, contemptuously likened; and modern holders of the doctrine are occasionally made the subject of equally polite comparisons by its German, French and English assailants.

When thus attacked, the Epicureans have always answered, that it is not they, but their accusers, who represent human nature in a degrading light; since the accusation supposes human beings to be capable of no pleasures except those of which swine are capable. If this supposition were true, the charge could not be gainsaid, but would then be no longer an imputation; for if the sources of pleasure were precisely the same to human beings and to swine, the rule of life which is good enough for the one would be good enough for the other. The comparison of the Epicurean life to that of beasts is felt as degrading, precisely because a beast's pleasures do not satisfy a human being's conceptions of happiness. Human beings have faculties more elevated than the animal appetites, and when once made conscious of them, do not regard anything as happiness which does not include their gratification. I do not, indeed, consider the Epicureans to have been by any means faultless in drawing out their scheme of consequences from the utilitarian principle. To do this in any sufficient manner, many Stoic as well as Christian elements require to be included. But there is no known Epicurean theory of life which does not assign to the pleasures of the intellect, of the feelings and imagination, and of the moral sentiments, a much higher value as pleasures than to those of mere sensation. It must be admitted, however, that utilitarian writers in general have placed the superiority of mental over bodily pleasures chiefly in the greater permanency, safety, uncostliness, etc., of the former—that is, in their circumstantial advantages rather than in their intrinsic nature. And on all these points utilitarians have fully proved their case; but they might have taken the other, and, as it may be called, higher ground, with entire consistency. It is quite compatible with the principle of utility to recognize the fact, that some *kinds* of pleasure are more desirable and more valuable than others. It would be absurd that while, in estimating all other things, quality is considered as well as quantity, the estimation of pleasures should be supposed to depend on quantity alone.

If I am asked, what I mean by difference of quality in pleasures, or what makes one pleasure more valuable than another, merely as a pleasure, except its being greater in amount, there is but one possible answer. Of two pleasures, if there be one to which all or almost all who have experience of both give a decided preference, irrespective of any feeling of moral obligation to prefer it, that is the more desirable pleasure. If one of the two is, by those who are competently acquainted with both, placed so far above the other that they prefer it, even though knowing it to be attended with a greater amount of discontent, and would not resign it for any quantity of the other pleasure which their nature is capable of, we are justified in ascribing to the preferred enjoyment a superiority in quality, so far outweighing quantity as to render it, in comparison, of small account.

Now it is an unquestionable fact that those who are equally acquainted with, and equally capable of appreciating and enjoying, both, do give a most marked preference to the manner of existence which employs their higher faculties. Few human creatures would consent to be changed into any of the lower animals, for a promise of the fullest allowance of a beast's pleasures; no intelligent human being would consent to be a fool, no instructed person would be an ignoramus, no person of feeling and conscience would be selfish and base, even though they should be persuaded that the fool, the dunce, or the rascal is better satisfied with his lot than they are with theirs. They would not resign what they possess more than he, for the most complete satisfaction of all the desires which they have in common with him. If they ever fancy they would, it is only in cases of unhappiness so extreme, that to escape from it they would exchange their lot for almost any other, however undesirable in their own eyes. A being of higher faculties requires more to make him happy, is capable probably of more acute suffering, and is certainly accessible to it at more points, than one of an inferior type; but in spite of these liabilities, he can never really wish to sink into what he feels to be a lower grade of existence. We may give what explanation we please of this unwillingness; we may attribute it to pride, a name which is given indiscriminately to some of the most and to some of the least estimable feelings of which mankind are capable; we may refer it to the love of liberty and personal independence, an appeal to which was with the Stoics one of the most effective means for the inculcation of it; to the love of power, or to the love of excitement, both of which do really enter into and contribute to it: but its most appropriate appellation is a sense of dignity, which all human beings possess in one form or other, and in some, though by no means in exact, proportion to their higher faculties, and which is so essential a part of the happiness of those in whom it is strong, that nothing which conflicts with it could be, otherwise than momentarily, an object of desire to them. Whoever supposes that this preference takes place at a sacrifice of happiness—that the superior being, in anything like equal circumstances, is not happier than the inferior—confounds the two very different ideas, of happiness, and content. It is indisputable that the being whose capacities of enjoyment are low, has the greatest chance of having them fully satisfied; and a highly endowed being will always feel that any happiness which he can look for, as the world is constituted, is imperfect. But he can learn to bear its imperfections, if they are at all bearable; and they will not make him envy the being who is indeed unconscious of the imperfections, but only because he feels not at all the good which those imperfections qualify. It is better to be a human being dissatisfied than a pig satisfied; better to be Socrates dissatisfied than a fool satisfied. And if the fool, or the pig, is of a different opinion, it is because they only know their own side of the question. The other party to the comparison knows both sides.

It may be objected, that many who are capable of the higher pleasures, occasionally, under the influence of temptation, postpone them to the lower. But this is quite compatible with a full appreciation of the intrinsic superiority of the higher. Men often, from infirmity of character, make their election for the nearer good, though they know it to be the less valuable; and this no less when the choice is between two bodily pleasures, than when it is between bodily and mental. They pursue sensual indulgences to the injury of health, though perfectly aware that health is the greater good. It may be further objected, that many who begin with youthful enthusiasm for everything noble, as they advance in years sink into indolence and selfishness. But I do not believe that those who undergo this very common change, voluntarily choose the lower description of pleasures in preference to the higher. I believe that before they devote themselves exclusively to the one, they have already become incapable of the other. Capacity for the nobler feelings is in most natures a very tender plant, easily killed, not only by hostile influences, but by mere want of sustenance; and in the majority of young persons it speedily dies away if the occupations to which their position in life has devoted them, and the society into which it has thrown them, are not favourable to keeping that higher capacity in exercise. Men lose their high aspirations as they lose their intellectual tastes, because they have not time or opportunity for indulging them; and they addict themselves to inferior pleasures, not because they deliberately prefer them, but because they are either the only ones to which they have access, or the only ones which they are any longer capable of enjoying. It may be questioned whether any one who has remained equally susceptible to both classes of pleasures, ever knowingly and calmly preferred the lower; though many, in all ages, have broken down in an ineffectual attempt to combine both.

From this verdict of the only competent judges, I apprehend there can be no appeal. On a question which is the best worth having of two pleasures, or which of two modes of existence is the most grateful to the feelings, apart from its moral attributes and from its consequences, the judgement of those who are qualified by knowledge of both, or, if they differ, that of the majority among them, must be admitted as final. And there needs be the less hesitation to accept this judgement respecting the quality of pleasures, since there is no other tribunal to be referred to even on the question of quantity. What means are there of determining which is the acutest of two pains, or the intensest of two pleasurable sensations, except the general suffrage of those who are familiar with both? Neither pains nor pleasures are homogeneous, and pain is always heterogeneous with pleasure. What is there to decide whether a particular pleasure is worth purchasing at the cost of a particular pain, except the feelings and judgement of the experienced? When, therefore, those feelings and judgement declare the pleasures derived from the higher faculties to be preferable *in kind,* apart from the question of intensity, to those of which the animal nature, disjoined from the higher faculties, is susceptible, they are entitled on this subject to the same regard.

I have dwelt on this point, as being a necessary part of a perfectly just conception of Utility or Happiness, considered as the directive rule of human conduct. But it is by no means an indispensable condition to the acceptance of the utilitarian standard; for that standard is not the agent's own greatest happiness, but the greatest amount of happiness altogether; and if it may possibly be doubted whether a noble character is always the happier for its nobleness, there can be no doubt that it makes other people happier, and that the world in general is immensely a gainer by it. Utilitarianism, therefore, could only attain its end by the general cultivation of nobleness of character, even if each individual were only benefited by the nobleness of others, and his own, so far as happiness is concerned, were a sheer deduction from the benefit. But the bare enunciation of such an absurdity as this last, renders refutation superfluous.

According to the Greatest Happiness Principle, as above explained, the ultimate end, with reference to and for the sake of which all other things are desirable (whether we are considering our own good or that of other people), is an existence exempt as far as possible from pain, and as rich as possible in enjoyments, both in point of quantity and quality; the test of quality, and the rule for measuring it against quantity, being the preference felt by those who, in their opportunities of experience, to which must be added their habits of self-consciousness and self-observation, are best furnished with the means of comparison. This, being, according to the utilitarian opinion, the end of human action, is necessarily also the standard of morality; which may accordingly be defined, the rules and precepts for human conduct, by the observance of which an existence such as has been described might be, to the greatest extent possible, secured to all mankind; and not to them only, but, so far as the nature of things admits, to the whole sentient creation.

The objectors to utilitarianism cannot always be charged with representing it in a discreditable light. On the contrary, those among them who entertain anything like a just idea of its disinterested character, sometimes find fault with its standard as being too high for humanity. They say it is exacting too much to require that people shall always act from the inducement of promoting the general interests of society. But this is to mistake the very meaning of a standard of morals, and to confound the rule of action with the motive of it. It is the business of ethics to tell us what are our duties, or by what test we may know them; but no system of ethics requires that the sole motive of all we do shall be a feeling of duty; on the contrary, ninety-nine hundredths of all our actions are done from other motives, and rightly so done, if the rule of duty does not condemn them. It is the more unjust to utiliarianism that this particular misapprehension should be made a ground of objection to it, inasmuch as utilitarian moralists have gone beyond almost all others in affirming that the motive has nothing to do with the morality of the action, though much with the worth of the agent. He who saves a fellow creature from drowning does what is morally right, whether his motive be duty, or the hope of being paid for his trouble: he who betrays the friend that trusts him, is guilty of a crime, even if his object be to serve another friend to whom he is under greater obligations. But to speak only of actions done from the motive of duty, and in direct obedience to principle: it is a misapprehension of the utilitarian mode of thought, to conceive it as implying that people should fix their minds upon so wide a generality as the world, or society at large. The great majority of good actions are intended, not for the benefit of the world, but for that of individuals, of which the good of the world is made up; and the thoughts of the most virtuous man need not on these occasions travel beyond the particular persons concerned, except so far as is necessary to assure himself that in benefiting them he is not violating the rights—that is, the legitimate and authorized expectations—of any one else. The multiplication of happiness is, according to the utilitarian ethics, the object of virtue: the occasions on which any person (except one in a thousand) has it in his power to do this on an extended scale, in other words, to be a public benefactor, are but exceptional; and on these occasions alone is he called on to consider public utility; in every other case, private utility, the interest or happiness of some few persons, is all he has to attend to. Those alone the influence of whose actions extends to society in general, need concern themselves habitually about so large an object. In the case of abstinences indeed—of things which people forbear to do, from moral considerations, though the consequences in the particular case might be beneficial—it would be unworthy of an intelligent agent not to be consciously aware that the action is of a class which, if practised generally, would be generally injurious, and that this is the ground of the obligation to abstain from it. The amount of regard for the public interest implied in this recognition, is no greater than is demanded by every system of morals; for they all enjoin to abstain from whatever is manifestly pernicious to society.

The same considerations dispose of another reproach against the doctrine of utility, founded on a still grosser misconception of the purpose of a standard of morality, and of the very meaning of the words right and wrong. It is often affirmed that utilitarianism renders men cold and unsymphathizing; that it chills their moral feelings towards individuals; that it makes them regard only the dry and hard consideration of the consequences of actions, not taking into their moral estimate the qualities from which those actions emanate. If the assertion means that they do not allow their judgement respecting the rightness or wrongness of an action to be influenced by their opinion of the qualities of the person who does it, this is a complaint not against utilitarianism, but against having any standard of morality at all; for certainly no known ethical standard decides an action to be good or bad because it is done by a good or a bad man, still less because done by an amiable, a brave, or a benevolent man, or the contrary. These considerations are relevant, not to the estimation of actions, but of persons; and there is nothing in the utilitarian theory inconsistent with the fact that there are other things which interest us in persons besides the rightness and wrongness of their actions. The Stoics, indeed, with the paradoxical misuse of language which was part of their system, and by which they strove to raise themselves above all concern about anything but virtue, were fond of saying that he who has that has everything; that he, and only he, is rich, is beautiful, is a king. But no claim of this description is made for the virtuous man by the utilitarian doctrine. Utilitarians are quite aware that there are other desirable possessions and qualities besides virtue, and are perfectly willing to allow to all of them their full worth. They are also aware that a right action does not necessarily indicate a virtuous character, and that actions which are blameable often proceed from qualities entitled to praise. When this is apparent in any particular case, it modifies their estimation, not certainly of the act, but of the agent. I grant that they are, notwithstanding, of opinion, that in the long run the best proof of a good character is good actions; and resolutely refuse to consider any mental disposition as good, of which the predominant tendency is to produce bad conduct. This makes them unpopular with many people; but it is an unpopularity which they must share with every one who regards the distinction between right and wrong in a serious light; and the reproach is not one which a conscientious utilitarian need be anxious to repel.

Again, Utility is often summarily stigmatized as an immoral doctrine by giving it the name of Expediency, and taking advantage of the popular use of that term to contrast it with Principle. But the Expedient, in the sense in which it is opposed to the Right, generally means that which is expedient for the particular interest of the agent himself; as when a minister sacrifices the interest of his country to keep himself in place. When it means anything better than this, it means that which is expedient for some immediate object, some temporary purpose, but which violates a rule whose observance is expedient in a much higher degree. The Expedient, in this sense, instead of being the same thing with the useful, is a branch of the hurtful. Thus, it would often be expedient, for the purpose of getting over some momentary embarrassment, or attaining some object immediately useful to ourselves or others, to tell a lie. But inasmuch as the cultivation in ourselves of a sensitive feeling on the subject of veracity is one of the most useful, and the enfeeblement of that feeling one of the most hurtful, things to which our conduct can be instrumental; and inasmuch as any, even unintentional, deviation from truth does that much towards weakening the trustworthiness of human assertion, which is not only the principal support of all present social well-being, but the insufficiency of which does more than any one thing that can be named to keep back civilization, virtue, everything on which human happiness on the largest scale depends; we feel that the violation, for a present advantage, of a rule of such transcendent expediency, is not expedient, and that he who, for the sake of a convenience to himself or to some other individual, does what depends on him to deprive mankind of the good, and inflict upon them the evil, involved in the greater or less reliance which they can place in each other's word, acts the part of one of their worst enemies. Yet that even this rule, sacred as it is, admits of possible exceptions, is acknowledged by all moralists; the chief of which is when the withholding of some fact (as of information from a male-factor, or of bad news from a person dangerously ill) would preserve some one (especially a person other than oneself) from great and unmerited evil, and when the withholding can only be effected by denial. But in order that the exception may not extend itself beyond the need, and may have the least pos-sible effect in weakening reliance on veracity, it ought to be recognized, and, if possible, its limits defined; and if the principle of utility is good for anything, it must be good for weighing these conflicting utilities against one another, and marking out the region within which one or the other preponderates.

Again, defenders of utility often find themselves called upon to reply to such objections as this—that there is not time, previous to action, for calculat-ing and weighing the effects of any line of conduct on the general happiness. This is exactly as if any one were to say that it is impossible to guide our con-duct by Christianity, because there is not time, on every occasion on which anything has to be done, to read through the Old and New Testaments. The answer to the objection is, that there has been ample time, namely, the whole past duration of the human species. During all that time mankind have been learning by experience the tendencies of actions; on which experience all the prudence, as well as all the morality of life, is dependent. People talk as if the commencement of this course of experience had hitherto been put off, and as if, at the moment when some man feels tempted to meddle with the property or life of another, he had to begin considering for the first time whether mur-der and theft are injurious to human happiness. Even then I do not think that he would find the question very puzzling; but, at all events, the matter is now done to his hand. It is truly a whimsical supposition that if mankind were agreed in considering utility to be the test of morality, they would remain with-out any agreement as to what *is* useful, and would take no measures for hav-ing their notions on the subject taught to the young, and enforced by law and opinion. There is no difficulty in proving any ethical standard whatever to work ill, if we suppose universal idiocy to be conjoined with it; but on any hypothesis short of that, mankind must by this time have acquired positive beliefs as to the effects of some actions on their happiness; and the beliefs which have thus come down are the rules of morality for the multitude, and for the philosopher until he has succeeded in finding better. That philosophers might easily do this, even now, on many subjects; that the received code of ethics is by no means of divine right; and that mankind have still much to learn as to the effects of actions on the general happiness, I admit, or rather, earnestly maintain. The corollaries from the principle of utility, like the precepts of every practical art, admit of indefinite improvement, and, in a progressive state of human mind, their improvement is perpetually going on. But to consider the rules of morality as improvable, is one thing; to pass over the intermediate generalizations entirely, and endeavour to test each individual action directly by the first principle, is another. It is a strange notion that the acknowledgement of a first principle is inconsistent with the admission of secondary ones. To inform a traveller respecting the place of his ultimate destination, is not to forbid the use of landmarks and direction-posts on the way. The proposition that happiness is the end and aim of morality, does not mean that no road ought to be laid down to that goal, or that persons going thither should not be advised to take one direction rather than another. Men really ought to leave off talking a kind of nonsense on this subject, which they would neither talk nor listen to on other matters of practical concernment. Nobody argues that the art of navigation is not founded on astronomy, because sailors cannot wait to calculate the Nautical Almanack. Being rational creatures, they go to sea with it ready calculated; and all rational creatures go out upon the sea of life with their minds made up on the common questions of right and wrong, as well as on many of the far more difficult questions of wise and foolish. And this, as long as foresight is a human quality, it is to be presumed they will continue to do. Whatever we adopt as the fundamental principle of morality, we require subordinate principles to apply it by: the impossibility of doing without them, being common to all systems, can afford no argument against any one in particular: but gravely to argue as if no such secondary principles could be had, and as if mankind had remained till now, and always must remain, without drawing any general conclusions from the experience of human life, is as high a pitch, I think, as absurdity has ever reached in philosophical controversy.

REVIEW QUESTIONS

1. What are the potential problems for leaders who always use utility as a guide for moral action?
2. If the consequences of leaders' actions are what count the most, is their character or what they do in their personal life relevant to their leadership? In other words what do we say about an evil or personally decadent leader who does wonderful things for society or an organization?
3. What kinds of things should a leader consider when deciding what constitutes the greatest good?

Case: Prejudice or Preference?
Joanne B. Ciulla

Sam, one of your senior professionals, has resigned unexpectedly to join one of your competitors. He was responsible for transactions with Magnolia Corporation, where he had a close relationship with the CEO, J. W. Crawford. You know there is a good chance Magnolia might go with Sam if you don't put a knowledgeable and experienced person on the account. This is your largest account and you don't want to lose it. In the past both the company and Sam have made a lot of money from various deals with Magnolia.

You know from Sam's client notes, and from your previous visits to Magnolia, that J. W. belongs to the "old school" and is most comfortable dealing with "one of the boys." Last year when Sam was visiting Magnolia he went on a hunting trip with J. W. The final night of the trip, J. W. surprised them with a "special treat". He invited a stripper to entertain them after a long dinner and plenty of drinks. On another occasion when Sam was there with Elaine Jones, who is a senior person at your firm, J. W. paid little attention to what she had to say and kept referring to her as "honey." On the way out of his office, J. W. gave her a pat on her behind.

Elaine is really the only person who knows J. W.'s business and has the expertise and seniority to take Sam's place. Ordinarily there would be no question of her taking over this client because of her experience and track record. Elaine is not known to turn down potentially lucrative deals; however, knowing what you do about J. W., you wonder if she's the person for the job.

Questions

1. How do you think about the greatest good in this case? Who are the stakeholders and what are your duties to each of them? Do any of your duties conflict with the greatest good?
2. Who is responsible for making this decision? Who is responsible for its outcome?
3. Would it make a difference if J. W. expressed the same attitudes toward other groups, such as African-Americans, Hispanics, or homosexuals? What would you do if J. W. wanted to work with Elaine *because* he found her attractive?
4. What are the long-term ramifications of your decision in this case?

From Joanne B. Ciulla.

Case: Corneas in the Congo
Joanne B. Ciulla

You are the head of a small aid agency in the Congo. The mission of your agency is to provide health services for refugees who have fled the various civil wars in the region. In recent years you have worked with a number of nongovernmental organization agencies, such as C.A.R.E., Doctors Without Borders, and the Christian Children's Fund. Your agency focuses on giving intensive help to small communities. You are now working in a camp of fifty people. Because of a peculiar parasite in the water that destroys the cornea of the eye, ten people in the camp have gone blind; half of them are children. Except for their inability to see, their health is reasonably good, given the conditions of the camp.

You contact Doctors Without Borders and they tell you that they will have two ophthalmologists in the area next week, but that the only thing they can do for the people who have gone blind is to give them cornea transplants. They could do the operations, but they said it was impossible to get corneas for transplant in Africa.

A few days later, the area director of Doctors Without Borders calls and tells you that a Chinese aid agency has twenty corneas and would be willing to exchange them for a truck and ten cases of medical supplies. This strikes you as odd so you ask, "Where did they get the corneas?" She then tells you that the corneas were donated to the Chinese aid agency by a wealthy Hong Kong businessman. He bought them from a middle man who buys body parts for transplant from prisons. The prisons carefully execute criminals and then take out livers and corneas for resale. Evidently, corrupt prison wardens make huge profits from this practice. This makes them very liberal with executions, especially of political prisoners.

You tell the director that the origin of these Chinese corneas makes you uncomfortable. The director says, "We have no problem with using them. If you don't want them, I'll give them to someone else. There are too many people in need here." She says, "You have one day to decide. Tomorrow I have to radio the plane in Kinshasa and tell it where to go next."

Questions

1. What principles are important to you in this decision? How would you think about the greatest good in this case?
2. As a leader, what are your duties and who are the stakeholders in the case?
3. What are the long-term ramifications of your decision?
4. Does your "gut feeling" about this case differ from what you think is right? If so, which would be your guide?

From Joanne B. Ciulla.

Distributive Justice

John Rawls

The Harvard philosopher John Rawls offers us a profound and important refinement of the utilitarian notion of justice. Although he admits that the idea of the greatest good is an excellent principle of justice in a society, he says that the problem with it is that there are no provisions for how one distributes these goods over society. Rawls makes these provisions based on a redefined notion of equality, not based on giving everyone an equal part of the goods of society, but on a fair distribution. In this essay he offers two principles of justice that would help insure that the goods of society were distributed to all of its members, not just those who are in the majority. His first principle assures the right of each person to extensive liberty that is compatible with like liberty for all. His second principle says that the inequalities are only tolerated in an institution if it is reasonable to expect that those inequalities can be made to work out for everyone, including the least advantaged.

Rawl's work on justice is among the most important contributions of twentieth century Western philosophy. Its principles of the general welfare and its notion of equality are attractive to those living in democratic societies where the greatest good is an important social and moral value.

W e may think of a human society as a more or less self-sufficient association regulated by a common conception of justice and aimed at advancing the good of its members.[1] As a co-operative venture for mutual advantage, it is characterized by a conflict as well as an identity of interests. There is an identity of interests since social co-operation makes possible a better life for all than any would have if everyone were to try to live by his own efforts; yet at the same time men are not indifferent as to how the greater benefits produced by their joint labours are distributed, for in order to further their own aims each prefers a larger to a lesser share. A conception of justice is a set of principles for choosing between the social arrangements which determine this division and for underwriting a consensus as to the proper distributive shares.

Now at first sight the most rational conception of justice would seem to be utilitarian. For consider: each man in realizing his own good can certainly balance his own losses against his own gains. We can impose a sacrifice on ourselves now for the sake of a greater advantage later. A man quite properly acts, as long as others are not affected, to achieve his own greatest good, to advance his ends as far as possible. Now, why should not a society act on precisely the same principle? Why is not that which is rational in the case of one man right

From John Rawls, Ed. Peter Laslett and W. G. Runciman, "Distributive Justice," *Philosophy, Politics, and Society*, 3rd series, 1967, 58–82. Copyright © 1967 Barnes & Noble Books, Div. of Harper & Row.

in the case of a group of men? Surely the simplest and most direct conception of the right, and so of justice, is that of maximizing the good. This assumes a prior understanding of what is good, but we can think of the good as already given by the interests of rational individuals. Thus just as the principle of individual choice is to achieve one's greatest good, to advance so far as possible one's own system of rational desires, so the principle of social choice is to realize the greatest good (similarly defined) summed over all the members of society. We arrive at the principle of utility in a natural way: by this principle a society, is rightly ordered, and hence just, when its institutions are arranged so as to realize the greatest sum of satisfactions.

The striking feature of the principle of utility is that it does not matter, except indirectly, how this sum of satisfactions is distributed among individuals, any more than it matters, except indirectly, how one man distributes his satisfactions over time. Since certain ways of distributing things affect the total sum of satisfactions, this fact must be taken into account in arranging social institutions; but according to this principle the explanation of common-sense precepts of justice and their seemingly stringent character is that they are those rules which experience shows must be strictly respected and departed from only under exceptional circumstances if the sum of advantages is to be maximized. The precepts of justice are derivative from the one end of attaining the greatest net balance of satisfactions. There is no reason in principle why the greater gains of some should not compensate for the lesser losses of others; or why the violation of the liberty of a few might not be made right by a greater good shared by many. It simply happens, at least under most conditions, that the greatest sum of advantages is not generally achieved in this way. From the standpoint of utility the strictness of common-sense notions of justice has a certain usefulness, but as a philosophical doctrine it is irrational.

If, then, we believe that as a matter of principle each member of society has an inviolability founded on justice which even the welfare of everyone else cannot override, and that a loss of freedom for some is not made right by a greater sum of satisfactions enjoyed by many, we shall have to look for another account of the principles of justice. The principle of utility is incapable of explaining the fact that in a just society the liberties of equal citizenship are taken for granted, and the rights secured by justice are not subject to political bargaining nor to the calculus of social interests. Now, the most natural alternative to the principle of utility is its traditional rival, the theory of the social contract. The aim of the contract doctrine is precisely to account for the strictness of justice by supposing that its principles arise from an agreement among free and independent persons in an original position of equality and hence reflect the integrity and equal sovereignty of the rational persons who are the contractees. Instead of supposing that a conception of right, and so a conception of justice, is simply an extension of the principle of choice for one man to society as a whole, the contract doctrine assumes that the rational individuals who belong to society must choose together, in one joint act, what is to count among them as just and unjust. They are to decide among themselves once and for all what is to be their conception of justice. This decision is thought of as being made in a suitably defined initial situation one of the significant features of which is that no one knows his position in society, nor even his place in the distribution of natural talents and abilities. The principles of justice to which all are forever bound are chosen in the absence of this sort of specific information. A veil of ignorance prevents anyone from being advantaged or disadvantaged by the contingencies of social class and fortune; and hence the bargaining problems which arise in everyday life from the possession of this knowledge do not affect the choice of principles. On the contract doctrine, then, the theory of justice, and indeed ethics itself, is part of the general theory of rational choice, a fact perfectly clear in its Kantian formulation.

Once justice is thought of as arising from an original agreement of this kind, it is evident that the principle of utility is problematical. For why should rational individuals who have a system of ends they wish to advance agree to a violation of their liberty for the sake of a greater balance of satisfactions enjoyed by others? It seems more plausible to suppose that, when situated in an original position of equal right, they would insist upon institutions which returned compensating advantages for any sacrifices required. A rational man would not accept an institution merely because it maximized the sum of advantages irrespective of its effect on his own interests. It appears, then, that the principle of utility would be rejected as a principle of justice, although we shall not try to argue this important question here. Rather, our aim is to give a brief sketch of the conception of distributive shares implicit in the principles of justice which, it seems, would be chosen in the original position. The philosophical appeal of utilitarianism is that it seems to offer a single principle on the basis of which a consistent and complete conception of right can be developed. The problem is to work out a contractarian alternative in such a way that it has comparable if not all the same virtues.

In our discussion we shall make no attempt to derive the two principles of justice which we shall examine; that is, we shall not try to show that they would be chosen in the original position.[2] It must suffice that it is plausible that they would be, at least in preference to the standard forms of traditional theories. Instead we shall be mainly concerned with three questions: first, how to interpret these principles so that they define a consistent and complete conception of justice; second, whether it is possible to arrange the institutions of a constitutional democracy so that these principles are satisfied, at least approximately; and third, whether the conception of distributive shares which they define is compatible with common-sense notions of justice. The significance of these principles is that they allow for the strictness of the claims of justice; and if they can be understood so as to yield a consistent and complete conception, the contractarian alternative would seem all the more attractive.

The two principles of justice which we shall discuss may be formulated as follows: first, each person engaged in an institution or affected by it has an equal right to the most extensive liberty compatible with a like liberty for all; and second, inequalities as defined by the institutional structure or fostered by it are arbitrary unless it is reasonable to expect that they will work out to everyone's advantage and provided that the positions and offices to which they attach or from which they may be gained are open to all. These principles regulate the distributive aspects of institutions by controlling the assignment of rights and duties throughout the whole social structure, beginning with the adoption of a political constitution in accordance with which they are then to be applied to legislation. It is upon a correct choice of a basic structure of society, its fundamental system of rights and duties, that the justice of distributive shares depends.

The two principles of justice apply in the first instance to this basic structure, that is, to the main institutions of the social system and their arrangement, how they are combined together. Thus, this structure includes the political constitution and the principal economic and social institutions which together define a person's liberties and rights and affect his life-prospects, what he may expect to be and how well he may expect to fare. The intuitive idea here is that those born into the social system at different positions, say in different social classes, have varying life-prospects determined, in part, by the system of political liberties and personal rights, and by the economic and social opportunities which are made available to these positions. In this way the basic structure of society favours certain men over others, and these are the basic inequalities, the ones which affect their whole life-prospects. It is inequalities of this kind, presumably inevitable in any society, with which the two principles of justice are primarily designed to deal.

Now the second principle holds that an inequality is allowed only if there is reason to believe that the institution with the inequality, or permitting it, will work out for the advantage of every person engaged in it. In the case of the basic structure this means that all inequalities which affect life-prospects, say the inequalities of income and wealth which exist between social classes, must be to the advantage of everyone. Since the principle applies to institutions, we interpret this to mean that inequalities must be to the advantage of the representative man for each relevant social position; they should improve each such man's expectation. Here we assume that it is possible to attach to each position an expectation, and that this expectation is a function of the whole institutional structure: it can be raised and lowered by reassigning rights and duties throughout the system. Thus the expectation of any position depends upon the expectations of the others, and these in turn depend upon the pattern of rights and duties established by the basic structure. But it is not clear what is meant by saying that inequalities must be to the advantage of every representative man. . . . [One] . . . interpretation [of what is meant by saying that inequalities must be to the advantage of every representative man] . . . is to choose some social position by reference to which the pattern of expectations as a whole is to be judged, and then to maximize with respect to the expectations of this representative man consistent with the demands of equal liberty and equality of opportunity. Now, the one obvious candidate is the representative man of those who are least favoured by the system of institutional inequalities. Thus we arrive at the following idea: the basic structure of the social system affects the life-prospects of typical individuals according to their initial places in society, say the various income classes into which they are born, or depending upon certain natural attributes, as when institutions make discriminations between men and women or allow certain advantages to be gained by those with greater natural abilities. The fundamental problem of distributive justice concerns the differences in life-prospects which come about in this way. We interpret the second principle to hold that these differences are just if and only if the greater expectations of the more advantaged, when playing a part in the working of the whole social system, improve the expectations of the least advantaged. The basic structure is just throughout when the advantages of the more fortunate promote the well-being of the least fortunate, that is, when a decrease in their advantages would make the least fortunate even worse off than they are. The basic structure is perfectly just when the prospects of the least fortunate are as great as they can be.

In interpreting the second principle (or rather the first part of it which we may, for obvious reasons, refer to as the difference principle), we assume that the first principle requires a basic equal liberty for all, and that the resulting political system, when circumstances permit, is that of a constitutional democracy in some form. There must be liberty of the person and political equality as well as liberty of conscience and freedom of thought. There is one class of equal citizens which defines a common status for all. We also assume that there is equality of opportunity and a fair competition for the available positions on the basis of reasonable qualifications. Now, given this background, the differences to be justified are the various economic and social inequalities in the basic structure which must inevitably arise in such a scheme. These are the inequalities in the distribution of income and wealth and the distinctions in social prestige and status which attach to the various positions and classes. The difference principle says that these inequalities are just if and only if they are part of a larger system in which they work out to the advantage of the most unfortunate representative man. The just distributive shares determined by the basic structure are those specified by this constrained maximum principle.

Thus, consider the chief problem of distributive justice, that concerning the distribution of wealth as it affects the life-prospects of those starting out in the various income groups. These income classes define the relevant representative men from which the social system is to be judged. Now, a son of a member of the entrepreneurial class (in a capitalist society) has a better prospect than that of the son of an unskilled labourer. This will be true, it seems, even when the social injustices which presently exist are removed and the two men are of equal talent and ability; the inequality cannot be done away with as long as something like the family is maintained. What, then, can justify this inequality in life-prospects? According to the second principle it is justified only if it is to the advantage of the representative man who is worse off, in this case the representative unskilled labourer. The inequality is permissible because lowering it would, let's suppose, make the working man even worse off than he is. Presumably, given the principle of open offices (the second part of the second principle), the greater expectations allowed to entrepreneurs has the effect in the longer run of raising the life-prospects of the labouring class. The inequality in expectation provides an incentive so that the economy is more efficient, industrial advance proceeds at a quicker pace, and so on, the end result of which is that greater material and other benefits are distributed throughout the system. Of course, all of this is familiar, and whether true or not in particular cases, it is the sort of thing which must be argued if the inequality in income and wealth is to be acceptable by the difference principle.

We should now verify that this interpretation of the second principle gives a natural sense in which everyone may be said to be made better off. Let us suppose that inequalities are chain-connected: that is, if an inequality raises the expectations of the lowest position, it raises the expectations of all positions in between. For example, if the greater expectations of the representative entrepreneur raises that of the unskilled labourer, it also raises that of the semi-skilled. Let us further assume that inequalities are close-knit: that is, it is impossible to raise (or lower) the expectation of any representative man without raising (or lowering) the expectations of every other representative man, and in particular, without affecting one way or the other that of the least fortunate. There is no loose-jointedness, so to speak, in the way in which expectations depend upon one another. Now with these assumptions, everyone does benefit from an inequality which satisfies the difference principle, and the second principle as we have formulated it reads correctly. For the representative man who is better off in any pair-wise comparison gains by being allowed to have his advantage, and the man who is worse off benefits from the contribution which all inequalities make to each position below. Of course, chain-connection and close-knitness may not obtain; but in this case those who are better off should not have a veto over the advantages available for the least advantaged. The stricter interpretation of the difference principle should be followed, and all inequalities should be arranged for the advantage of the most unfortunate even if some inequalities are not to the advantage of those in middle positions. Should these conditions fail, then, the second principle would have to be stated in another way.

It may be observed that the difference principle represents, in effect, an original agreement to share in the benefits of the distribution of natural talents and abilities, whatever this distribution turns out to be, in order to alleviate as far as possible the arbitrary handicaps resulting from our initial starting places in society. Those who have been favoured by nature, whoever they are, may gain from their good fortune only on terms that improve the well-being of those who have lost out. The naturally advantaged are not to gain simply because they are more gifted, but only to cover the costs of training and cultivating their endowments and for putting them to use in a way which improves the position of the less fortunate. We are led to the difference principle if we wish to arrange the basic social structure so that no one gains (or loses) from his luck in the natural lottery of talent and ability, or from his initial place in society, without giving (or receiving) compensating advantages in return. (The parties in the original position are not said to be attracted by this idea and so agree to it; rather, given the symmetries of their situation, and particularly their lack of knowledge, and so on, they will find it to their interest to agree to a principle which can be understood in this way.) And we should note also that when the difference principle is perfectly satisfied, the basic structure is optimal by the efficiency principle. There is no way to make anyone better off without making someone worse off, namely, the least fortunate representative man. Thus the two principles of justice define distributive shares in a way compatible with efficiency, at least as long as we move on this highly abstract level. If we want to say (as we do, although it cannot be argued here) that the demands of justice have an absolute weight with respect to efficiency, this claim may seem less paradoxical when it is kept in mind that perfectly just institutions are also efficient.

Notes

1. In this essay I try to work out some of the implications of the two principles of justice discussed in "Justice as Fairness," which first appeared in the *Philosophical Review*, 1958, and which is reprinted in *Philosophy, Politics and Society*, Series II, pp. 132–57.

2. This question is discussed very briefly in "Justice as Fairness," see pp. 138–41. The intuitive idea is as follows. Given the circumstances of the original position, it is rational for a man to choose as if he were designing a society in which his enemy is to assign him his place. Thus, in particular, given the complete lack of knowledge (which makes the choice one uncertainty), the fact that the decision involves one's life-prospects as a whole and is constrained by obligations to third parties (e.g., one's descendants) and duties to certain values (e.g., to religious truth), it is rational to be conservative and so to choose in accordance with an analogue of the maximum principle. Viewing the situation in this way, the interpretation given to the principles of justice earlier is perhaps natural enough. Moreover, it seems clear how the principle of utility can be interpreted; it is the analogue of the Laplacean principle for choice

uncertainty. (For a discussion of these choice criteria, see R. D. Luce and H. Raiffa, *Games and Decisions* [1957]. pp. 275–98.)

REVIEW QUESTIONS

1. Do you think political leaders and institutions in your country operate on the principles discussed by Rawls?
2. What kind of commitments would leaders have to make to run an organization according to Rawls's principles of distributive justice?
3. Would a business be as profitable as one run on Mill's notion of utilitarianism?
4. In what contexts would the "veil of ignorance" be useful to a leader? What assumptions does the veil of ignorance make about human nature? Does it insure objectivity?

city of happiness

Case: The Ones Who Walk Away from Omelas
Ursula Le Guin

Ursula Le Guin is a well-known science fiction writer who lives in Portland, Oregon. Many of Le Guin's stories and books are social commentaries set in various kinds of utopias. In this short story, she confronts us with the paradox of utilitarianism and helps us understand why Rawl's refinements to utilitarianism are important for social justice. The title of her story also makes us reflect on the moral obligations of leaders and followers. When should one create conflict and engage in correcting a social wrong and when should one simply walk away?

With a clamor of bells that set the swallows soaring, the Festival of Summer came to the city Omelas, bright-towered by the sea. The rigging of the boats in harbor sparkled with flags. In the streets between houses with red roofs and painted walls, between old moss-grown gardens and under avenues of trees, past great parks and public buildings, processions moved. Some were decorous: old people in long stiff robes of mauve and grey, grave master workmen, quiet, merry women carrying their babies and chatting as they walked. In other streets the music beat faster, a shimmering of gong and

Case continued

*tambourine, and the people went dancing, the procession was a dance.
Children dodged in and out, their high calls rising like the swallows' crossing
flights over the music and the singing. All the processions wound towards the
north side of the city, where on the great water-meadow called the Green
Fields boys and girls, naked in the bright air, with mud-stained feet and
ankles and long, lithe arms, exercised their restive horses before the race. The
horses wore no gear at all but a halter without bit. Their manes were braided
with streamers of silver, gold, and green. They flared their nostrils and
pranced and boasted to one another; they were vastly excited, the horse being
the only animal who has adopted our ceremonies as his own. Far off to the
north and west the mountains stood up half encircling Omelas on her bay.
The air of morning was so clear that the snow still crowning the Eighteen
Peaks burned with white-gold fire across the miles of sunlit air, under the
dark blue of the sky. There was just enough wind to make the banners that
marked the racecourse snap and flutter now and then. In the silence of the
broad green meadows one could hear the music winding through the city
streets, farther and nearer and ever approaching, a cheerful faint sweetness
of the air that from time to time trembled and gathered together and broke
out into the great joyous clanging of the bells.*

*Joyous! How is one to tell about joy? How describe the citizens
of Omelas?*

*They were not simple folk, you see, though they were happy. But we do
not say the words of cheer much any more. All smiles have become archaic.
Given a description such as this one tends to make certain assumptions.
Given a description such as this one tends to look next for the King, mounted
on a splendid stallion and surrounded by his noble knights, or perhaps in a
golden litter borne by great-muscled slaves. But there was no king. They did
not use swords, or keep slaves. They were not barbarians. I do not know the
rules and laws of their society, but I suspect that they were singularly few. As
they did without monarchy and slavery, so they also got on without the stock
exchange, the advertisement, the secret police, and the bomb. Yet I repeat
that these were not simple folk, not dulcet shepherds, noble savages, bland
utopians. They were not less complex than us. The trouble is that we have a
bad habit, encouraged by pedants and sophisticates, of considering happiness
as something rather stupid. Only pain is intellectual, only evil interesting.
This is the treason of the artist: a refusal to admit the banality of evil and the
terrible boredom of pain. If you can't lick 'em, join 'em. If it hurts, repeat it.
But to praise despair is to condemn delight, to embrace violence is to lose
hold of everything else. We have almost lost hold; we can no longer describe
a happy man, nor make any celebration of joy. How can I tell you about the
people of Omelas? They were not naïve and happy children—though their
children were, in fact, happy. They were mature, intelligent, passionate
adults whose lives were not wretched. O miracle! but I wish I could describe*

it better. I wish I could convince you. Omelas sounds in my words like a city in a fairy tale, long ago and far away, once upon a time. Perhaps it would be best if you imagined it as your own fancy bids, assuming it will rise to the occasion, for certainly I cannot suit you all. For instance, how about technology? I think that there would be no cars or helicopters in and above the streets; this follows from the fact that the people of Omelas are happy people. Happiness is based on a just discrimination of what is necessary, what is neither necessary nor destructive, and what is destructive. In the middle category, however—that of the unnecessary but undestructive, that of comfort, luxury, exuberance, etc.—they could perfectly well have central heating, subway trains, washing machines, and all kinds of marvelous devices not yet invented here, floating light-sources, fuelless power, a cure for the common cold. Or they could have none of that: it doesn't matter. As you like it. I incline to think that people from towns up and down the coast have been coming in to Omelas during the last days before the Festival on very fast little trains and double-decked trams, and that the train station of Omelas is actually the handsomest building in town, though plainer than the magnificent Farmers' Market. But even granted trains, I fear that Omelas so far strikes some of you as goody-goody. Smiles, bells, parades, horses, bleh. If so, please add an orgy. If an orgy would help, don't hesitate. Let us not, however, have temples from which issue beautiful nude priests and priestesses already half in ecstasy and ready to copulate with any man or woman, lover or stranger, who desires union with the deep godhead of the blood, although that was my first idea. But really it would be better not to have any temples in Omelas—at least, not manned temples. Religion yes, clergy no. Surely the beautiful nudes can just wander about, offering themselves like divine soufflés to the hunger of the needy and the rapture of the flesh. Let them join the processions. Let tambourines be struck above the copulations, and the glory of desire be proclaimed upon the gongs, and (a not unimportant point) let the offspring of these delightful rituals be beloved and looked after by all. One thing I know there is none of in Omelas is guilt. But what else should there be? I thought at first there were no drugs, but that is puritanical. For those who like it, the faint insistent sweetness of drooz may perfume the ways of the city, drooz which first brings a great lightness and brilliance to the mind and limbs, and then after some hours a dreamy languor, and wonderful visions at last of the very arcana and inmost secrets of the Universe, as well as exciting the pleasure of sex beyond all belief; and it is not habit-forming. For more modest tastes I think there ought to be beer. What else, what else belongs in the joyous city? The sense of victory, surely, the celebration of courage. But as we did without clergy, let us do without soldiers. The joy built upon successful slaughter is not the right kind of joy; it will not do; it is fearful and it is trivial. A boundless and generous contentment, a magnanimous triumph felt not against some outer enemy but

Case continued

in communion with the finest and fairest in the souls of all men everywhere and the splendor of the world's summer: this is what swells the hearts of the people of Omelas, and the victory they celebrate is that of life. I really don't think many of them need to take drooz.

Most of the processions have reached the Green Fields by now. A marvelous smell of cooking goes forth from the red and blue tents of the provisioners. The faces of small children are amiably sticky; in the benign grey beard of a man a couple of crumbs of rich pastry are entangled. The youths and girls have mounted their horses and are beginning to group around the starting line of the course. An old woman, small, fat, and laughing, is passing out flowers from a basket, and tall young men wear her flowers in their shining hair. A child of nine or ten sits at the edge of the crowd, alone, playing on a wooden flute. People pause to listen, and they smile, but they do not speak to him, for he never ceases playing and never sees them, his dark eyes wholly rapt in the sweet, thin magic of the tune.

He finishes, and slowly lowers his hands holding the wooden flute.

As if that little private silence were the signal, all at once a trumpet sounds from the pavilion near the starting line: imperious, melancholy, piercing. The horses rear on their slender legs, and some of them neigh in answer. Sober-faced, the young riders stroke the horses' necks and soothe them, whispering, "Quiet, quiet, there my beauty, my hope. . . ." They begin to form in rank along the starting line. The crowds along the racecourse are like a field of grass and flowers in the wind. The Festival of Summer has begun.

Do you believe? Do you accept the festival, the city, the joy? No? Then let me describe one more thing.

In a basement under one of the beautiful public buildings of Omelas, or perhaps in the cellar of one of its spacious private homes, there is a room. It has one locked door, and no window. A little light seeps in dustily between cracks in the boards, secondhand from a cobwebbed window somewhere across the cellar. In one corner of the little room a couple of mops, with stiff, clotted, foul-smelling heads, stand near a rusty bucket. The floor is dirt, a little damp to the touch, as cellar dirt usually is. The room is about three paces long and two wide: a mere broom closet or disused tool room. In the room a child is sitting. It could be a boy or a girl. It looks about six, but actually is nearly ten. It is feeble-minded. Perhaps it was born defective, or perhaps it has become imbecile through fear, malnutrition, and neglect. It picks its nose and occasionally fumbles vaguely with its toes or genitals, as it sits hunched in the corner farthest from the bucket and the two mops. It is afraid of the mops. It finds them horrible. It shuts its eyes, but it knows the mops are still standing there; and the door is locked; and nobody will come. The door is always locked; and nobody ever comes, except that sometimes— the child has no understanding of time or interval—sometimes the door *rattles terribly and opens, and a person, or several people, are there. One of them may come in and kick the child to make it stand up. The others never come close, but peer in at it with frightened, disgusted eyes. The food bowl and the water jug are hastily filled, the door is locked, the eyes disappear. The people at the door never say anything, but the child, who has not always lived in the tool room, and can remember sunlight and its mother's voice, sometimes speaks. "I will be good," it says. "Please let me out. I will be good!" They never answer. The child used to scream for help at night, and cry a good deal, but now it only makes a kind of whining, "eh-haa, eh-haa," and it speaks less and less often. It is so thin there are no calves to its legs; its belly protrudes; it lives on a half-bowl of corn meal and grease a day. It is naked. Its buttocks and thighs are a mass of festered sores, as it sits in its own excrement continually.*

They all know it is there, all the people of Omelas. Some of them have come to see it, others are content merely to know it is there. They all know that it has to be there. Some of them understand why, and some do not, but they all understand that their happiness, the beauty of their city, the tenderness of their friendships, the health of their children, the wisdom of their scholars, the skill of their makers, even the abundance of their harvest and the kindly weathers of their skies, depend wholly on this child's abominable misery.

This is usually explained to children when they are between eight and twelve, whenever they seem capable of understanding; and most of those who come to see the child are young people, though often enough an adult comes, or comes back, to see the child. No matter how well the matter has been explained to them, these young spectators are always shocked and sickened at the sight. They feel disgust, which they had thought themselves superior to. They feel anger, outrage, impotence, despite all the explanations. They would like to do something for the child. But there is nothing they can do. If the child were brought up into the sunlight out of that vile place, if it were cleaned and fed and comforted, that would be a good thing, indeed; but if it were done, in that day and hour all the prosperity and beauty and delight of Omelas would wither and be destroyed. Those are the terms. To exchange all the goodness and grace of every life in Omelas for that single, small improvement: to throw away the happiness of thousands for the chance of the happiness of one: that would be to let guilt within the walls indeed.

The terms are strict and absolute; there may not even be a kind word spoken to the child.

Often the young people go home in tears, or in a tearless rage, when they have seen the child and faced this terrible paradox. They may brood over it for weeks or years. But as times goes on they begin to realize that even if the child could be released, it would not get much good of its freedom: a little vague pleasure of warmth and food, no doubt, but little more. It is too

Case continued

degraded and imbecile to know any real joy. It has been afraid too long ever to be free of fear. Its habits are too uncouth for it to respond to humane treatment. Indeed, after so long it would probably be wretched without walls about it to protect it, and darkness for its eyes, and its own excrement to sit in. Their tears at the bitter injustice dry when they begin to perceive the terrible justice of reality, and to accept it. Yet it is their tears and anger, the trying of their generosity and the acceptance of their helplessness, which are perhaps the true source of the splendor of their lives. Theirs is no vapid, irresponsible happiness. They know that they, like the child, are not free. They know compassion. It is the existence of the child, and their knowledge of its existence, that makes possible the nobility of their architecture, the poignancy of their music, the profundity of their science. It is because of the child that they are so gentle with children. They know that if the wretched one were not there snivelling in the dark, the other one, the flute-player, could make no joyful music as the young riders line up in their beauty for the race in the sunlight of the first morning of summer.

Now do you believe in them? Are they not more credible? But there is one more thing to tell, and this is quite incredible.

At times one of the adolescent girls or boys who go to see the child does not go home to weep or rage, does not, in fact, go home at all. Sometimes also a man or woman much older falls silent for a day or two, and then leaves home. These people go out into the street, and walk down the street alone. They keep walking, and walk straight out of the city of Omelas, through the beautiful gates. They keep walking across the farmlands of Omelas. Each one goes alone, youth or girl, man or woman. Night falls; the traveler must pass down village streets, between the houses with yellow-lit windows, and on out into the darkness of the fields. Each alone, they go west or north, towards the mountains. They go on. They leave Omelas, they walk ahead into the darkness, and they do not come back. The place they go towards is a place even less imaginable to most of us than the city of happiness. I cannot describe it at all. It is possible that it does not exist. But they seem to know where they are going, the ones who walk away from Omelas.

Questions

1. In terms of Rawls's theory of distributive justice, what is wrong with the social arrangements in Omelas?
2. Would the social arrangements in Omelas be acceptable under Mill's theory of utilitarianism?
3. Are the ones who walk away from Omelas more ethical than the ones who stay?
4. Why don't more people walk away? Why doesn't anyone help the child?

5. How great does the greatest good have to be to justify the sacrifice of one person's happiness?

Zarathustra's Prologue

Frederich Nietzsche, 1844–1900

Frederich Neitzsche was born in Röcken, Prussia. As a student he was considered so promising that the University of Leipzig gave him a doctorate without requiring him to take exams or write a dissertation. A philosopher and classical philologist, Neitzsche became a professor at the University of Basil at the tender age of twenty-four. Nietzsche is also known for his literary style. He pokes and prods us and seems to enjoy keeping the reader off balance. Just when you think you understand what he is saying, he takes you off in another direction. Because of this and some of his seemingly contradictory ideas, philosophers are divided on their opinion of Neitzsche. Some read him as a foe of morality, whereas others see him as a revolutionary moralist.

In the following essay Neitzsche delivers a different kind of critique of utilitarianism than we find in Le Guin's story. His story argues that the values of utilitarianism and egalitarianism create morally inferior people. Writing at the turn of the century, Neitzsche believed European morality was on the verge of collapse. The problem, as he saw it, was that the heroic values that had sustained civilization had been replaced with the values of equality and utilitarianism. Out of these principles there emerged a "slave morality," based on resentment of those who are more creative, talented, and a cut above the rest. Nietzsche believed that this morality, based on the golden rule, appealed to the weak and failed to inspire excellence in people. This morality had created a society that celebrates mediocrity and does not encourage the development of people who are brave, noble, visionary, and capable of standing alone. He calls his ideal person who possess these qualities the "übermensch" or superman.

Because Nietzsche's writings tend to be intertwined, there are a few things that you need to understand before reading this piece. First, Nietzsche believes that the creative force in human nature is the will to power. But for him the greatest power is found in self-control, art, and philosophy, not in the subjugation of others. The will to power moves people to create their world and not simply accept the one they are handed. Second, the superman is someone who has conquered his or her passions and is not purely motivated by self-interest. Nietzsche's superman approaches life with what he calls "exuberance" and cultivates the virtues of generosity, sympathy, honesty, and politeness. The superman is not necessarily someone who wants to rule the world, but rather someone who creates his world. He is Nietzsche's idea of a morally better human being.

In "Zarathustra's Prologue" Nietzsche uses the character of Zarathustra, an Iranian religious reformer and mystic from the sixth century B.C., to tell us a story

From Friedrich Nietzsche, *Thus Spake Zarathustra*, pp. 33–47, (Amherst, NY: Prometheus Books), published 1993. Reprinted by permission of the publisher.

about what the masses want out of life. Zarathustra tells the crowd about the qualities of the superman, but the crowd says give us the "the last man." The last man is the utilitarian ideal of a person who does everything to meet his needs and make life comfortable and pleasant. This reading is rich with insights about leaders and followers and the limitations of some of utilitarianism and egalitarianism.

2

Zarathustra went down the mountain alone, no one meeting him. When he entered the forest, however, there suddenly stood before him an old man, who had left his holy cot to seek roots. And thus spake the old man to Zarathustra:

"No stranger to me is this wanderer: many years ago passed he by. Zarathustra he was called; but he hath altered.

Then thou carriedst thine ashes into the mountains: wilt thou now carry thy fire into the valleys? Fearest thou not the incendiary's doom?

Yea, I recognize Zarathustra. Pure is his eye, and no loathing lurketh about his mouth. Goeth he not along like a dancer?

Altered is Zarathustra; a child hath Zarathustra become; an awakened one is Zarathustra: what wilt thou do in the land of the sleepers?

As in the sea hast thou lived in solitude, and it hath borne thee up. Alas, wilt thou now go ashore? Alas, wilt thou again drag thy body thyself?"

Zarathustra answered: "I love mankind."

"Why," said the saint, "did I go into the forest and the desert? Was it not because I loved men far too well?

Now I love God: men, I do not love. Man is a thing too imperfect for me. Love to man would be fatal to me."

Zarathustra answered: "What spake I of love! I am bringing gifts unto men."

"Give them nothing," said the saint. "Take rather part of their load, and carry it along with them—that will be most agreeable unto them: if only it be agreeable unto thee!

If, however, thou wilt give unto them, give them no more than an alms, and let them also beg for it!"

"No," replied Zarathustra, "I give no alms. I am not poor enough for that."

The saint laughed at Zarathustra, and spake thus: "Then see to it that they accept thy treasures! They are distrustful of anchorites, and do not believe that we come with gifts.

The fall of our footsteps ringeth too hollow through their streets. And just as at night, when they are in bed and hear a man abroad long before sunrise, so they ask themselves concerning us: Where goeth the thief?

Go not to men, but stay in the forest! Go rather to the animals! Why not be like me—a bear amongst bears, a bird amongst birds?"

"And what doeth the saint in the forest?" asked Zarathustra.

The saint answered: "I make hymns and sing them; and in making hymns I laugh and weep and mumble: thus do I praise God.

With singing, weeping, laughing, and mumbling do I praise the God who is my God. But what dost thou bring us as a gift?"

When Zarathustra had heard these words, he bowed to the saint and said: "What should I have to give thee! Let me rather hurry hence lest I take aught away from thee!"—And thus they parted from one another, the old man and Zarathustra, laughing like schoolboys.

When Zarathustra was alone, however, he said to his heart: "Could it be possible! This old saint in the forest hath not yet heard of it, that *God is dead!*"

3

When Zarathustra arrived at the nearest town which adjoineth the forest, he found many people assembled in the market-place; for it had been announced that a rope-dancer would give a performance. And Zarathustra spake thus unto the people:

I teach you the Superman. Man is something that is to be surpassed. What have ye done to surpass man?

All beings hitherto have created something beyond themselves: and ye want to be the ebb of that great tide, and would rather go back to the beast than surpass man?

What is the ape to man? A laughing-stock, a thing of shame. And just the same shall man be to the Superman: a laughing-stock, a thing of shame.

Ye have made your way from the worm to man, and much within you is still worm. Once were ye apes, and even yet man is more of an ape than any of the apes.

Even the wisest among you is only a disharmony and hybrid of plant and phantom. But do I bid you become phantoms or plants?

Lo, I teach you the Superman!

The Superman is the meaning of the earth. Let your will say: The Superman *shall be* the meaning of the earth!

I conjure you, my brethren, *remain true to the earth,* and believe not those who speak unto you of superearthly hopes! Poisoners are they, whether they know it or not.

Despisers of life are they, decaying ones and poisoned ones themselves, of whom the earth is weary: so away with them!

Once blasphemy against God was the greatest blasphemy; but God died, and therewith also those blasphemers. To blaspheme the earth is now the dreadfulest sin, and to rate the heart of the unknowable higher than the meaning of the earth!

Once the soul looked contemptuously on the body, and then that contempt was the supreme thing:—the soul wished the body meagre, ghastly, and famished. Thus it thought to escape from the body and the earth.

Oh, that soul was itself meagre, ghastly, and famished; and cruelty was the delight of that soul!

But ye, also, my brethren, tell me: What doth your body say about your soul? Is your soul not poverty and pollution and wretched self-complacency?

Verily, a polluted stream is man. One must be a sea, to receive a polluted stream without becoming impure.

Lo, I teach you the Superman: he is that sea; in him can your great contempt be submerged.

What is the greatest thing ye can experience? It is the hour of great contempt. The hour in which even your happiness becometh loathsome unto you, and so also your reason and virtue.

The hour when ye say: "What good is my happiness! It is poverty and pollution and wretched self-complacency. But my happiness should justify existence itself!"

The hour when ye say: "What good is my reason! Doth it long for knowledge as the lion for his food? It is poverty and pollution and wretched self-complacency!"

The hour when ye say: "What good is my virtue! As yet it hath not made me passionate. How weary I am of my good and my bad! It is all poverty and pollution and wretched self-complacency!"

The hour when ye say: "What good is my justice! I do not see that I am fervour and fuel. The just, however, are fervour and fuel!"

The hour when we say: "What good is my pity! Is not pity the cross on which he is nailed who loveth man? But my pity is not a crucifixion."

Have ye ever spoken thus? Have ye ever cried thus? Ah! would that I had heard you crying thus!

It is not your sin—it is your self-satisfaction that crieth unto heaven; your very sparingness in sin crieth unto heaven!

Where is the lightning to lick you with its tongue? Where is the frenzy with which ye should be inoculated?

Lo, I teach you the Superman: he is that lightning, he is that frenzy!—

When Zarathustra had thus spoken, one of the people called out: "We have now heard enough of the rope-dancer; it is time now for us to see him!" And all the people laughed at Zarathustra. But the rope-dancer, who thought the words applied to him, began his performance.

4

Zarathustra, however, looked at the people and wondered. Then he spake thus:

Man is a rope stretched between the animal and the Superman—a rope over an abyss.

A dangerous crossing, a dangerous wayfaring, a dangerous looking-back, a dangerous trembling and halting.

What is great in man is that he is a bridge and not a goal; what is lovable in man is that he is an *over-going* and a *downgoing*.

I love those that know not how to live except as down-goers, for they are the over-goers.

I love the great despisers, because they are the great adorers, and arrows of longing for the other shore.

I love those who do not first seek a reason beyond the stars for going down and being sacrifices, but sacrifice themselves to the earth, that the earth of the Superman may hereafter arrive.

I love him who liveth in order to know, and seeketh to know in order that the Superman may hereafter live. Thus seeketh he his own down-going.

I love him who laboureth and inventeth, that he may build the house for the Superman, and prepare for him earth, animal, and plant: for thus seeketh he his own down-going.

I love him who loveth his virtue: for virtue is the will to down-going, and an arrow of longing.

I love him who reserveth no share of spirit for himself, but wanteth to be wholly the spirit of his virtue: thus walketh he as spirit over the bridge.

I love him who maketh his virtue his inclination and destiny: thus, for the sake of his virtue, he is willing to live on, or live no more.

I love him who desireth not too many virtues. One virtue is more of a virtue than two, because it is more of a knot for one's destiny to cling to.

I love him whose soul is lavish, who wanteth no thanks and doth not give back: for he always bestoweth, and desireth not to keep for himself.

I love him who is ashamed when the dice fall in his favour, and who then asketh: "Am I a dishonest player?"—for he is willing to succumb.

I love him who scattereth golden words in advance of his deeds, and always doeth more than he promiseth: for he seeketh his own down-going.

I love him who justifieth the future ones, and redeemeth the past ones: for he is willing to succumb through the present ones.

I love him who chasteneth his God, because he loveth his God: for he must succumb through the wrath of his God.

I love him whose soul is deep even in the wounding, and may succumb through a small matter: thus goeth he willingly over the bridge.

I love him whose soul is so overfull that he forgetteth himself, and all things are in him: thus all things become his down-going.

I love him who is of a free spirit and a free heart: thus is his head only the bowels of his heart; his heart, however, causeth his down-going.

I love all who are like heavy drops falling one by one out of the dark cloud that lowereth over man: they herald the coming of the lightning, and succumb as heralds.

Lo, I am a herald of the lightning, and a heavy drop out of the cloud: the lightning, however, is the *Superman.*—

5

When Zarathustra had spoken these words, he again looked at the people, and was silent. "There they stand," said he to his heart; "there they laugh: they understand me not; I am not the mouth for these ears.

Must one first batter their ears, that they may learn to hear with their eyes? Must one clatter like kettledrums and penitential preachers? Or do they only believe the stammerer?

They have something whereof they are proud. What do they call it, that which maketh them proud? Culture, they call it; it distinguisheth them from the goatherds.

They dislike, therefore, to hear of "contempt" of themselves. So I will appeal to their pride.

I will speak unto them of the most contemptible thing: that, however, is *the last man!*

And thus spake Zarathustra unto the people:

It is time for man to fix his goal. It is time for man to plant the germ of his highest hope.

Still is his soil rich enough for it. But that soil will one day be poor and exhausted, and no lofty tree will any longer be able to grow thereon.

Alas! there cometh the time when man will no longer launch the arrow of his longing beyond man—and the string of his bow will have unlearned to whizz!

I tell you: one must still have chaos in one, to give birth to a dancing star. I tell you: ye have still chaos in you.

Alas! There cometh the time when man will no longer give birth to any star. Alas! There cometh the time of the most despicable man, who can no longer despise himself.

Lo! I show you *the last man*.

"What is love? What is creation? What is longing? What is a star?"—so asketh the last man and blinketh.

The earth hath then become small, and on it there hoppeth the last man who maketh everything small. His species is ineradicable like that of the ground-flea; the last man liveth longest.

"We have discovered happiness"—say the last men, and blink thereby.

They have left the regions where it is hard to live; for they need warmth. One still loveth one's neighbour and rubbeth against him; for one needeth warmth.

Turning ill and being distrustful, they consider sinful: they walk warily. He is a fool who still stumbleth over stones or men!

A little poison now and then: that maketh pleasant dreams. And much poison at last for a pleasant death.

One still worketh, for work is a pastime. But one is careful lest the pastime should hurt one.

One no longer becometh poor or rich; both are too burdensome. Who still wanteth to rule? Who still wanteth to obey? Both are too burdensome.

No shepherd, and one herd! Everyone wanteth the same; everyone is equal: he who hath other sentiments goeth voluntarily into the madhouse.

"Formerly all the world was insane,"—say the subtlest of them, and blink thereby.

They are clever and know all that hath happened: so there is no end to their raillery. People still fall out, but are soon reconciled—otherwise it spoileth their stomachs.

They have their little pleasures for the day, and their little pleasures for the night, but they have a regard for health.

"We have discovered happiness,"—say the last men, and blink thereby.—

And here ended the first discourse of Zarathustra, which is also called "The Prologue", for at this point the shouting and mirth of the multitude interrupted him. "Give us this last man, O Zarathustra,"—they called out—"make us into these last men! Then will we make thee a present of the Superman!" And all the people exulted and smacked their lips. Zarathustra, however, turned sad, and said to his heart:

"They understand me not: I am not the mouth for these ears.

Too long, perhaps, have I lived in the mountains; too much have I hearkened unto the brooks and trees: now do I speak unto them as unto the goatherds.

Calm is my soul, and clear, like the mountains in the morning. But they think me cold, and a mocker with terrible jests.

And now do they look at me and laugh: and while they laugh they hate me too. There is ice in their laughter."

6

Then, however, something happened which made every mouth mute and every eye fixed. In the meantime, of course, the rope-dancer had commenced his performance: he had come out at a little door, and was going along the rope which was stretched between two towers, so that it hung above the market-place and the people. When he was just midway across, the little door opened once more, and a gaudily-dressed fellow like a buffoon sprang out, and went rapidly after the first one. "Go on, halt-foot," cried his frightful voice, "go on, lazy-bones, interloper, sallow-face!—lest I tickle thee with my heel! What dost thou here between the towers? In the tower is the place for thee, thou shouldst be locked up; to one better than thyself thou blockest the way!"—And with every word he came nearer and nearer the first one. When, however, he was but a step behind, there happened the frightful thing which made every mouth mute and every eye fixed—he uttered a yell like a devil, and jumped over the other who was in his way. The latter, however, when he thus saw his rival triumph, lost at the same time his head and his footing on the rope; he threw his pole away, and shot downward faster than it, like an eddy of arms and legs, into the depth. The market-place and the people were like the sea when the storm cometh on: they all flew apart and in disorder, especially where the body was about to fall.

Zarathustra, however, remained standing, and just beside him fell the body, badly injured and disfigured, but not yet dead. After a while consciousness returned to the shattered man, and he saw Zarathustra kneeling beside him. "What art thou doing there?" said he at last, "I knew long ago that the devil would trip me up. Now he draggeth me to hell: wilt thou prevent him?"

"On mine honour, my friend," answered Zarathustra, "there is nothing of all that whereof thou speakest: there is no devil and no hell. Thy soul will be dead even sooner than thy body; fear, therefore, nothing any more!"

The man looked up distrustfully. "If thou speakest the truth," said he, "I lose nothing when I lose my life. I am not much more than an animal which hath been taught to dance by blows and scanty fare."

"Not at all," said Zarathustra, "thou hast made danger thy calling; therein there is nothing contemptible. Now thou perishest by thy calling: therefore will I bury thee with mine own hands."

When Zarathustra had said this the dying one did not reply further; but he moved his hand as if he sought the hand of Zarathustra in gratitude.

7

Meanwhile the evening came on, and the market-place veiled itself in gloom. Then the people dispersed, for even curiosity and terror become fatigued. Zarathustra, however, still sat beside the dead man on the ground, absorbed in thought: so he forgot the time. But at last it became night, and a cold wind blew upon the lonely one. Then arose Zarathustra and said to his heart:

> Verily, a fine catch of fish hath Zarathustra made to-day! It is not a man he hath caught, but a corpse.
>
> Sombre is human life, and as yet without meaning: a buffoon may be fateful to it.
>
> I want to teach men the sense of their existence, which is the Superman, the lightning out of the dark cloud—man.
>
> But still am I far from them, and my sense speaketh not unto their sense. To men I am still something between a fool and a corpse.
>
> Gloomy is the night, gloomy are the ways of Zarathustra. Come, thou cold and stiff companion! I carry thee to the place where I shall bury thee with mine own hands.

REVIEW QUESTIONS

1. Would most people today prefer to be "the last man" or the superman? Which one would you prefer to have as your leader?
2. What does Zarathustra tell us about the challenges of leading people who have become too comfortable and uncritical?
3. What are the practical problems with egalitarianism and utilitarianism for leaders of organizations?
4. Do you think there is a morality of resentment in our society? If so, how has it affected the relationship between leaders and followers?

The Lao Tzu (Tao Te Ching)

Lao Tzu, about 570 B.C.–490 B.C.

The dates of Lao Tzu's birth are somewhat unclear, but most scholars today believe that he was born between the sixth and the fifth century B.C. Lao Tzu was born in the province of Henan and was the archivist at the court of Chou court.

According to some historical accounts he was an older contemporary of Confucius and the two actually met each other. Lao Tzu is considered to be the founder
of Taoism. Taoism and Confucianism are the two most important philosophic/
religious systems in Chinese culture. Lao Tzu's *Tao Te Ching* or "The Classic of
the Way and Its Virtue" is one of the major Taoist texts. It was written as a kind
of handbook for rulers. More than half of this text is written in rhymes.

Taoism emphasizes the joyful, passive, carefree side of life. The permanent
Tao or "way" is nonbeing, which has neither a name or perceptible qualities. It
is a kind of void that holds all possibilities and gives efficacy to being. In Taoism
the universe is a hierarchically organized mechanism in which, like a fractal,
each part replicates the whole. All humans are microcosms of the universe;
hence, their good is inextricable from the good of the whole. This position
sounds a bit like utilitarianism and a bit like enlightened self-interest, but it is
actually very different. The greatest good is not a quantity, but a quality of the
whole order of the universe. According to the law of the Tao, the natural order
of things is to always return to where they began. These mystical ideas may
sound very odd to Westerners. However, the contradictions and paradoxes found
in the *Tao Te Ching* are there to help us examine how we think about ourselves
in relation to the rest of the world. For example, Lao Tzu says "the ultimate mas-
tery comes out of passivity and weakness is the greatest strength." Lao Tzu offers
a minimalist ideal of leadership. He tells us that the "best man is like water"—
he benefits things but does not compete with them.

2. When the people of the world all know beauty as beauty,
There arises the recognition of ugliness.
When they all know the good as good,
There arises the recognition of evil.
Therefore:
Being and non-being produce each other;
Difficult and easy complete each other;
Long and short contrast each other;
High and low distinguish each other;
Sound and voice harmonize with each other;
Front and back follow each other.
Therefore the sage manages affairs without action
    (*wu-wei*)
And spreads doctrines without words.
All things arise, and he does not turn away from them.
He produces them, but does not take possession of them.
He acts, but does not rely on his own ability.
He accomplishes his task, but does not claim credit for it.
It is precisely because he does not claim credit that his accomplish-
    ment remains with him.

3. Do not exalt the worthy, so that the people shall not compete
Do not value rare treasures, so that the people shall not steal.

Do not display objects of desire, so that the people's hearts shall not
be disturbed.
Therefore in the government of the sage,
He keeps their hearts vacuous (*hsü*),[21]
Fills their bellies,
Weakens their ambitions,
And strengthens their bones,
He always causes his people to be without knowledge (cunning) or
desire,
And the crafty to be afraid to act.
By acting without action, all things will be in order.

8. The best (man) is like water.
Water is good; it benefits all things and does not compete with them.
It dwells in (lowly) places that all disdain.
This is why it is so near to Tao.
[The best man] in his dwelling loves the earth.
In his heart, he loves what is profound.
In his associations, he loves humanity.
In his words, he loves faithfulness.
In government, he loves order.
In handling affairs, he loves competence.
In his activities, he loves timeliness.
It is because he does not compete that he is without reproach.

9. To hold and fill to overflowing
Is not as good as to stop in time.
Sharpen a sword-edge to its very sharpest,
And the (edge) will not last long.
When gold and jade fill your hall,
You will not be able to keep them.
To be proud with honor and wealth
Is to cause one's own downfall.
Withdraw as soon as your work is done.
Such is Heaven's Way.

Comment. Note that one should withdraw only *after* his work is done. The Taoist
way of life is not that of a hermit, although hermits have taken its name. The idea of withdrawal is not entirely absent even in Confucianism. Mencius said that it was the way of
Confucius "to withdraw quickly from office when it was proper to do so."

---

[21]Literally "empty" *hsü* means absolute peace and purity of mind, freedom from worry and selfish
desires.

10. Can you keep the spirit and embrace the One without departing
     from them?
Can you concentrate your vital force (*ch'i*) and achieve the highest
     degree of weakness like an infant?
Can you clean and purify your profound insight so it will be spotless?
Can you love the people and govern the state without knowledge
     (cunning)?
Can you play the role of the female in the opening and closing of the
     gates of Heaven?
Can you understand all and penetrate all without taking any action?
To produce things and to rear them,
To produce, but not to take possession of them,
To act, but not to rely on one's own ability,
To lead them, but not to master them—
This is called profound and secret virtue (*hsüan-te*).

15. Of Old those who were the best rulers were subtly mysterious
     and profoundly penetrating;
Too deep to comprehend.
And because they cannot be comprehend,
I can only describe them arbitrarily:
Cautious, like crossing a frozen stream in the winter,
Being at a loss, like one fearing danger on all sides,
Reserved, like one visiting,
Supple and pliant, like ice about to melt,
Genuine, like a piece of uncarved wood,
Open and broad, like a valley,
Merged and undifferentiated, like muddy water.
Who can make muddy water gradually clear through tranquillity?
Who can make the still gradually come to life through activity?
He who embraces this Tao does not want to fill himself to overflowing.
It is precisely because there is no overflowing that he is beyond
     wearing out and renewal.

17. The best (rulers) are those whose existence is (merely) known by
     the people.
The next best are those who are loved and praised.
The next are those who are feared.
And the next are those who are despised.
It is only when one does not have enough faith in others that others
     will have no faith in him.
[The great rulers] value their words highly.
They accomplish their task; they complete their work.

Nevertheless their people say that they simply follow Nature
(*Tzu-jan*).[52]

18. When the great Tao declined,
The doctrines of humanity (*jen*) and righteousness (*i*) arose.
When knowledge and wisdom appeared,
There emerged great hypocrisy.
When the six family relationships[53] are not in harmony,
There will be the advocacy of filial piety and deep love to children.
When a country is in disorder,
There will be praise of loyal ministers.

23. Nature says few words.
For the same reason a whirlwind does not last a whole morning,
Nor does a rainstorm last a whole day.
What causes them?
It is Heaven and Earth (Nature).
If even Heaven and Earth cannot make them last long,
How much less can man?
Therefore he who follows Tao is identified with Tao.
He who follows virtue is identified with virtue.
He who abandons (Tao) is identified with the abandonment (of Tao).
He who is identified with Tao—Tao is also happy to have him.
He who is identified with virtue—virtue is also happy to have him.
And he who is identified with the abandonment (of Tao)— the aban-
donment (of Tao) is also happy to abandon him.
It is only when one does not have enough faith in others that others
will have no faith in him.

24. He who stands on tiptoe is not steady.
He who strides forward does not go.
He who shows himself is not luminous.
He who justifies himself is not prominent.
He who boasts of himself is not given credit.
He who brags does not endure for long.
From the point of view of Tao, these are like remnants of food and
tumors of action,
Which all creatures detest.
Therefore those who possess Tao turn away from them.

---

[52]*Tzu-jan*, literally "self-so," means being natural or spontaneous.
[53]Father, son, elder brother, younger brother, husband, and wife.

29. When one desires to take over the empire and act on it (interfere with it),
I see that he will not succeed.
The empire is a spiritual thing, and should not be acted on.
He who acts on it harms it.
He who holds on to it loses it.
Among creatures some lead and some follow.
Some blow hot and some blow cold.
Some are strong and some are weak.
Some may break and some may fall.
Therefore the sage discards the extremes, the extravagant, and the excessive.

30. He who assists the ruler with Tao does not dominate the world with force.
The use of force usually brings requital.
Wherever armies are stationed, briers and thorns grow.
Great wars are always followed by famines.
A good (general) achieves his purpose and stops,
But dares not seek to dominate the world.
He achieves his purpose but does not brag about it.
He achieves his purpose but does not boast about it.
He achieves his purpose but is not proud of it.
He achieves his purpose but only as an unavoidable step.
He achieves his purpose but does not aim to dominate.
(For) after things reach their prime, they begin to grow old, Which means being contrary to Tao.
Whatever is contrary to Tao will soon perish.

31. Fine weapons are instruments of evil.
They are hated by men.
Therefore those who possess Tao turn away from them.
The good ruler when at home honors the left (symbolic of good omens).
When at war he honors the right (symbolic of evil omens).
Weapons are instruments of evil, not the instruments of a good ruler.
When he uses them unavoidably, he regards calm restraint as the best principle.
Even when he is victorious, he does not regard it as praiseworthy,
For to praise victory is to delight in the slaughter of men.
He who delights in the slaughter of men will not succeed in the empire.
In auspicious affairs, the left is honored.

In unauspicious affairs, the right is honored.
The lieutenant-general stands on the left.
The senior general stands on the right.
That is to say that the arrangement follows that of funeral ceremonies.
For the slaughter of the multitude, let us weep with sorrow and
    grief.
For a victory, let us observe the occasion with funeral ceremonies.

44. Which does one love more, fame or one's own life?
Which is more valuable, one's own life or wealth?
Which is worse, gain or loss?
Therefore he who has lavish desires will spend extravagantly.
He who hoards most will lose heavily.
He who is contended suffers no disgrace.
He who knows when to stop is free from danger.
Therefore he can long endure.

45. What is most perfect seems to be incomplete;
But its utility is unimpaired.
What is most full seems to be empty;
But its usefulness is inexhaustible.
What is most straight seems to be crooked.
The greatest skills seems to be clumsy.
The greatest eloquence seems to stutter.
Hasty movement overcomes cold,
(But) tranquility overcomes heat.
By being greatly tranquil,
One is qualified to be the ruler of the world.

49. The sage has no fixed (personal) ideas.
He regards the people's ideas as his own.
I treat those who are good with goodness,
And I also treat those who are not good with goodness.
Thus goodness is attained.
I am honest to those who are honest,
And I am also honest to those who are not honest.
Thus honesty is attained.
The sage, in the government of his empire, has no subjective viewpoint.
His mind forms a harmonious whole with that of his people. They all
    lend their eyes and ears, and he treats them all as infants.

53. If I had but little knowledge
I should, in walking on a broad way,

Fear getting off the road.
Broad ways are extremely even,
But people are fond of by-paths.
The courts are exceedingly splendid,
While the fields are exceedingly weedy,
And the granaries are exceedingly empty.
Elegant clothes are worn,
Sharp weapons are carried,
Foods and drinks are enjoyed beyond limit,
And wealth and treasures are accumulated in excess.
This is robbery and extravagance.
This is indeed not Tao (the way).

54. He who is well established (in Tao) cannot be pulled away.
He who has a firm grasp (of Tao) cannot be separated from it.
Thus from generation to generation his ancestral sacrifice will never
    be suspended.
When one cultivates virtue in his person, it becomes genuine virtue.
When one cultivates virtue in his family, it becomes over-flowing
    virtue.
When one cultivates virtue in his community, it becomes lasting
    virtue.
When one cultivates virtue in his country, it becomes abundant
    virtue.
When one cultivates virtue in the world, it becomes universal.
Therefore the person should be viewed as a person.
The family should be viewed as a family.
The community should be viewed as a community.
The country should be viewed as a country.
And the world should be viewed as the world.
How do I know this to be the case in the world?
Through this (from the cultivation of virtue in the person to that in
    the world).

57. Govern the state with correctness.
Operate the army with surprise tactics.
Administer the empire by engaging in no activity.
How do I know that this should be so?
Through this:
The more taboos and prohibitions there are in the world,
The poorer the people will be.
The more sharp weapons the people have,
The more troubled the state will be.

The more cunning and skill man possesses,
The more vicious things will appear.
The more laws and orders are made prominent,
The more thieves and robbers there will be.
Therefore the sage says:
I take no action and the people of themselves are transformed.
I love tranquility and the people of themselves become correct.
I engage in no activity and the people of themselves become
    prosperous.
I have no desires and the people of themselves become simple.

Comment. Laissez-faire government. Even Confucius shared this ideal.

58. When the government is non-discriminative and dull,
The people are contented and generous.
When the government is searching and discriminative,
The people are disappointed and contentious.
Calamity is that upon which happiness depends;
Happiness is that in which calamity is latent.
Who knows when the limit will be reached?
Is there no correctness (used to govern the world?)
Then the correct again becomes the perverse
And the good will again become evil.
The people have been deluded for a long time.
Therefore the sage is as pointed as a square but does not
    pierce.
He is as acute as a knife but does not cut.
He is as straight as an unbent line but does not extend.
He is as bright as light but does not dazzle.

59. To rule people and to serve Heaven there is nothing better than
    to be frugal.
Only by being frugal can one recover quickly.
To recover quickly means to accumulate virtue heavily.
By the heavy accumulation of virtue one can overcome everything.
If one can overcome everything, then he will acquire a capacity the
    limit of which is beyond anyone's knowledge.
When his capacity is beyond anyone's knowledge, he is fit to rule a
    state.
He who possesses the Mother (Tao) of the state will last long.
This means that the roots are deep and the stalks are firm, which is
    the way of long life and everlasting existence.

60. Ruling a big country is like cooking a small fish.[109]
If Tao is employed to rule the empire,
Spiritual beings will lose their supernatural power.
Not that they lose their spiritual power,
But their spiritual power can no longer harm people.
Not only will their supernatural power not harm people,
But the sage also will not harm people.
When both do not harm each other.
Virtue will be accumulated in both for the benefit [of the people].

61. A big country may be compared to the lower part of a river.
It is the converging point of the world;
It is the female of the world.
The female always overcomes the male by tranquillity,
And by tranquillity she is underneath.
A big state can take over a small state if it places itself below the
    small state;
And the small state can take over a big state if it places itself below
    the big state.
Thus some, by placing themselves below, take over (others),
And some, by being (naturally) low, take over (other states).
After all, what a big state wants is but to annex and herd others,
And what a small state wants is merely to join and serve others.
Since both big and small states get what they want,
The big state should place itself low.

65. In ancient times those who practiced Tao well
Did not seek to enlighten the people, but to make them ignorant.
People are difficult to govern because they have too much
    knowledge.
Therefore he who rules the state through knowledge is a robber of
    the state;
He who rules a state not through knowledge is a blessing to the
    state.
One who knows these two things also (knows) the standard.
Always to know the standard is called profound and secret virtue.
Virtue becomes deep and far-reaching,
And with it all things return to their original natural state.
Then complete harmony will be reached.

---

[109]Too much handling will spoil it.

66. The great rivers and seas are kings of all mountain streams
Because they skillfully stay below them.
That is why they can be their kings.
Therefore, in order to be the superior of the people,
One must, in the use of words, place himself below them.
And in order to be ahead of the people,
One must, in one's own person, follow them.
Therefore the sage places himself above the people and they do not
    feel his weight.
He places himself in front of them and the people do not harm him.
Therefore the world rejoices in praising him without getting tired
    of it.
It is precisely because he does not compete that the world cannot
    compete with him.

68. A skillful leader of troops is not oppressive with his military
    strength.
A skillful fighter does not become angry.
A skillful conqueror does not compete with people.
One who is skillful in using men puts himself below them.
This is called the virtue of not-competing.
This is called the strength to use men.
This is called matching Heaven, the highest principle of old.

75. The people starve because the ruler eats too much tax-grain.
Therefore they starve.
They are difficult to rule because their ruler does too many things.
Therefore they are difficult to rule.
The people take death lightly because their ruler strives for life too
    vigorously.
Therefore they take death lightly.
It is only those who do not seek after life that excel in making life
    valuable.

80. Let there be a small country with few people.
Let there be ten times and a hundred times as many utensils
But let them not be used.
Let the people value their lives highly and not migrate far.
Even if there are ships and carriages, none will ride in them.
Even if there are armor and weapons, none will display them.
Let the people again knot cords and use them (in place of writing).
Let them relish their food, beautify their clothing, be content with
    their homes, and delight in their customs.

Though neighboring communities overlook one another and the
  crowning of cocks and barking of dogs can be heard,
Yet the people there may grow old and die without ever visiting one
  another.

81. True words are not beautiful;
Beautiful words are not true.
A good man does not argue;
He who argues is not a good man.
A wise man has no extensive knowledge;
He who has extensive knowledge is not a wise man.
The sage does not accumulate for himself.
The more he uses for others, the more he has himself.
The more he gives to others, the more he possesses of his own.
The Way of Heaven is to benefit others and not to injure.
The Way of the sage is to act but not to compete.

REVIEW QUESTIONS

1. Are Taoist leaders possible in today's competitive world? What would a
   Taoist leader be like in an organization or political office?
2. How is Lao Tzu's notion of the good different from Mill's?
3. Would we be happier with leaders who served the greatest good, but
   stayed in the background?
4. How is character or personal virtue related to the greatest good in this
   reading?

THE MORAL AND EMOTIONAL RELATIONSHIP OF LEADERS AND FOLLOWERS

INTRODUCTION

In the first chapter we looked at power and the moral challenges of power. This chapter looks at the power of emotions in ethics and in the relationship of leaders and followers. For some people charisma is almost synonymous with leadership. Charismatic leaders are exciting. They make followers feel good, and inspired. People enthusiastically follow charismatic leaders, sometimes because their feelings override their reason. Hence, one moral hazard of charismatic leadership is that it can make for weak followers, who are unable to have and provide critical perspective to their leaders. Love is blind and sometimes so are the followers of charismatic leaders. This does not mean that charismatic leaders are evil, but rather that they can have an enormous amount of influence. Charismatic leaders carry an exceptionally large moral burden, because often their followers are or would be happy to be dependent on them. In history, charismatic leaders are among the most admired, such as Nelson Mandela, and the most reviled, such as Adolph Hitler.

As Max Weber points out in the first essay, charismatic authority is not routine, rational, or subject to rules. One finds charismatic leaders in all walks of life, but most noticeably in religion and politics. The study of Jim Jones and the People's Temple offers an example of Weber's charismatic leader. We see how charismatic leaders can bring out the best in their followers, but also lose perspective on themselves when they are shielded from or no longer subject to critical feedback from their followers. They run into problems when they fall prey to their own charisma.

Robert C. Solomon argues that charisma is not a single quality, emotion, or set of emotions. He says we often confuse charisma and leadership with celebrity. According to Solomon, the fundamental moral and emotional element of this relationship is trust, not charisma. His article explores the process of getting and giving trust.

The reading in the last chapter by Lao Tzu and the reading in this chapter by Robert Greenleaf offer a sharp contrast to charismatic leadership. Lao Tzu tells us that the best leaders are the ones who are not noticed. They work behind the scenes to serve people. Greenleaf's theory of servant leadership is a contemporary variation of Eastern writers like Lao Tzu. The major thrust of both theories is that the leader's job is to serve followers and to improve and empower followers.

The obligation of leaders to make followers better and more independent is a fundamental element of James MacGregor Burns's theory of transforming leadership. (He now prefers the term "transforming leadership" to transformational leadership, which is used in this essay and by other scholars.) Burns believes that the way leaders influence followers is by working with them to embrace common values. It is interesting to note that whereas Burns's theory of transforming leadership depends on rational discourse about shared values, other scholars such as Bernard Bass and Jay Conger argue that the transformational process is based on charisma and emotion. Bass and Conger believe that transformational leaders "inspire" followers to transcend narrow self-interest and embrace broader goals. So within the theory of transformational leadership itself there is a split between how scholars think about the rational and emotional elements of the leadership process. One thing to keep in mind when you study leadership theories is that leaders too are made of what Kant called, "the crooked timber of humanity." They may inspire, transform, empower, and serve their followers to be good and do good or to be horrible and do horrendous things. Some types of leadership may be more ethical than others, but the ethical bottom line still depends on the ethics of what leaders do, how they do it, and why they do it.

Machiavelli's question, "Is it better to be loved or feared?" really asks us to choose between two types of power and two types of emotions in the leader/follower relationship. Discussions of charismatic leadership raise similar questions. *Is it better for a leader to lead using emotion or reason? Which leader/follower relationship is morally better? Is it possible to lead with one but not the other? Do you have to be charismatic to be a transforming or transformational leader? How much influence should a leader have over a follower's values and feelings?*

Legitimate Authority and Charisma

Max Weber, 1864–1920

Max Weber was a German economist and social historian from Erfurt, Germany.
He was educated at the universities of Heidelberg, Berlin, and Göttingen.
Weber combined his interests in religion and economics in his best known book,
The Protestant Ethic and the Spirit of Capitalism. This book demonstrated how
religious ideas influenced the development of capitalism. In the following essay
Weber explores the kind of authority that comes with charisma. He describes
charisma as "a certain quality of an individual personality by virtue of which he
is set apart from ordinary men." Weber goes on to say that charisma elicits an
intense personal and emotional response from others. Charismatic leaders also
summon a strong sense of duty and devotion from their followers. The authority
of these leaders over followers is not rational; the institutions they run do not
operate by rational, routine rules. Weber tells us that the legitimacy of charismatic leaders comes only from recognition of and belief in charismatic inspiration by followers.

Charismatic Authority

The term "charisma" will be applied to a certain quality of an individual
personality by virtue of which he is set apart from ordinary men and
treated as endowed with supernatural, superhuman, or at least specifically exceptional powers or qualities. These are such as are not accessible to the
ordinary person, but are regarded as of divine origin or as exemplary, and on
the basis of them the individual concerned is treated as a leader. In primitive
circumstances this peculiar kind of deference is paid to prophets, to people
with a reputation for therapeutic or legal wisdom, to leaders in the hunt, and
heroes in war. It is very often thought of as resting on magical powers. How the
quality in question would be ultimately judged from any ethical, aesthetic, or
other such point of view is naturally entirely indifferent for purposes of definition. What is alone important is how the individual is actually regarded by those
subject to charismatic authority, by his "followers" or "disciples."

For present purposes it will be necessary to treat a variety of different
types as being endowed with charisma in this sense. It includes the state of a
"berserker" whose spells of maniac passion have, apparently wrongly, sometimes been attributed to the use of drugs. In Medieval Byzantium a group of

---

people endowed with this type of charismatic war-like passion were maintained as a kind of weapon. It includes the "shaman," the kind of magician who in the pure type is subject to epileptoid seizures as a means of falling into trances. Another type is that of Joseph Smith, the founder of Mormonism, who, however, cannot be classified in this way with absolute certainty since there is a possibility that he was a very sophisticated type of deliberate swindler. Finally it includes the type of intellectual, such as Kurt Eisner,[1] who is carried away with his own demagogic success. Sociological analysis, which must abstain from value judgments, will treat all these on the same level as the men who, according to conventional judgments are the "greatest" heroes, prophets and saviours.

It is recognition on the part of those subject to authority which is decisive for the validity of charisma. This is freely given and guaranteed by what is held to be a "sign" or proof, originally always a miracle, and consists in devotion to the corresponding revelation, hero worship, or absolute trust in the leader. But where charisma is genuine, it is not this which is the basis of the claim to legitimacy. This basis lies rather in the conception that it is the *duty* of those who have been called to a charismatic mission to recognize its quality and to act accordingly. Psychologically this "recognition" is a matter of complete personal devotion to the possessor of the quality, arising out of enthusiasm, or of despair and hope.

No prophet has ever regarded his quality as dependent on the attitudes of the masses toward him. No elective king or military leader has ever treated those who have resisted him or tried to ignore him otherwise than as delinquent in duty. Failure to take part in a military expedition under such leader, even though recruitment is formally voluntary, has universally been met with disdain.

If proof of his charismatic qualification fails him for long, the leader endowed with charisma tends to think his god or his magical or heroic powers have deserted him. If he is for long unsuccessful, above all if his leadership fails to benefit his followers, it is likely that his charismatic authority will disappear. This is the genuine charismatic meaning of the "gift of grace."

Even the old Germanic kings were sometimes rejected with scorn. Similar phenomena are very common among so-called "primitive" peoples. In China the charismatic quality of the monarch, which was transmitted unchanged by heredity, was upheld so rigidly that any misfortune whatever, not only defeats in war, but drought, floods, or astronomical phenomena which were considered unlucky, forced him to do public penance and might even force his abdication. If such things occurred, it was a sign that he did not possess the requisite charismatic virtue, he was thus not a legitimate "Son of Heaven."

The corporate group which is subject to charismatic authority is based on an emotional form of communal relationship. The administrative staff of a

---

[1] The leader of the communistic experiment in Bavaria in 1919.

charismatic leader does not consist of "officials"; at least its members are not technically trained. It is not chosen on the basis of social privilege nor from the point of view of domestic or personal dependency. It is rather chosen in terms of the charismatic qualities of its members. The prophet has his disciples; the warlord his selected henchmen; the leader, generally, his followers. There is no such thing as "appointment" or "dismissal," no career, no promotion. There is only a "call" at the instance of the leader on the basis of the charismatic qualification of those he summons. There is no hierarchy; the leader merely intervenes in general or in individual cases when he considers the members of his staff inadequate to a task with which they have been entrusted. There is no such thing as a definite sphere of authority and of competence, and no appropriation of official powers on the basis of social privileges. There may, however, be territorial or functional limits to charismatic powers and to the individual's "mission." There is no such thing as a salary or a benefice. Disciples or followers tend to live primarily in a communistic relationship with their leader on means which have been provided by voluntary gift. There are no established administrative organs. In their place are agents who have been provided with charismatic authority by their chief or who possess charisma of their own. There is no system of formal rules, of abstract legal principles, and hence no process of judicial decision oriented to them. But equally there is no legal wisdom oriented to judicial precedent. Formally concrete judgments are newly created from case to case and are originally regarded as divine judgments and revelations. From a substantive point of view, every charismatic authority would have to subscribe to the proposition, "It is written . . . , but I say unto you, . . ."[5] The genuine prophet, like the genuine military leader and every true leader in this sense, preaches, creates, or demands *new* obligations. In the pure type of charisma, these are imposed on the authority of revelation by oracles, or of the leader's own will, and are recognized by the members of the religious, military, or party group, because they come from such a source. Recognition is a duty. When such an authority comes into conflict with the competing authority of another who also claims charismatic sanction, the only recourse is to some kind of a contest, by magical means or even an actual physical battle of the leaders. In principle only one side can be in the right in such a conflict; the other must be guilty of a wrong which has to be expiated.

Charismatic authority is thus specifically outside the realm of every-day routine and the profane sphere.[6] In this respect, it is sharply opposed both to rational, and particularly bureaucratic, authority, and to traditional authority, whether in its patriarchal, patrimonial, or any other form. Both rational and

---

[5]Something contrary to what was written, as Jesus said in opposition to the Scribes and Pharisees.

[6]Weber used the antithesis of *Charisma and Alltag* in two senses. On the one hand, of the extraordinary and temporary as opposed to the every-day and routine; on the other hand, the sacred as opposed to the profane.

traditional authority are specifically forms of every-day routine control of action; while the charismatic type is the direct antithesis of this. Bureaucratic authority is specifically rational in the sense of being bound to intellectually analysable rules; while charismatic authority is specifically irrational in the sense of being foreign to all rules. Traditional authority is bound to the precedents·handed down from the past and to this extent is also oriented to rules. Within the sphere of its claims, charismatic authority repudiates the past, and is in this sense a specifically revolutionary force. It recognizes no appropriation of positions of power by virtue of the possession of property, either on the part of a chief or of socially privileged groups. The only basis of legitimacy for it is personal charisma, so long as it is proved; that is, as long as it receives recognition and is able to satisfy the followers or disciples. But this lasts only so long as the belief in its charismatic inspiration remains.

The above is scarcely in need of further discussion. What has been said applies to the position of authority of such elected monarchs as Napoleon, with his use of the plebiscite. It applies to the "rule of genius," which has elevated people of humble origin to thrones and high military commands, just as much as it applies to religious prophets or war heroes.

REVIEW QUESTIONS

1. Is there something about a culture, particular historical conditions, or human nature that makes people more prone to desire and follow charismatic leaders?
2. Do charismatic leaders have an obligation to temper the feelings of their followers?
3. What is dangerous about charismatic leadership in an organization and in a society?

Case: "The Only God You'll Ever See": Jim Jones and the Peoples Temple
Charles Lindholm

Charles Lindholm is an anthropology professor at Harvard University. In his book Charisma, Lindholm analyzes notorious charismatic leaders, including Charles Manson, Adolph Hitler, and the following case study on Jim Jones. This

From Charles Lindholm, "The Only God You'll Ever See: Jim Jones and the Peoples Temple," *Charisma*, 1990, 7–14. Copyright © 1990 Basic Blackwell.

case study shows us why morality, self-knowledge, self-discipline, and critical followers are the crucial checks and balances that keep charismatic leaders from becoming bad or dangerous leaders.

Jim Jones was a religious leader who developed his Disciples of Christ Church into a cult. Jones opened his Peoples Temples in San Francisco and Los Angeles. He later moved his Temple to Jonestown, Guyana. In 1978, facing defections by members of his Temple and an investigation by Congressman Leo Ryan of California, Jones oversaw the mass suicide of 909 followers in Jonestown. Jones died that same day from a gunshot wound in the head.

We have seen his pattern of a charismatic cult leader and mass suicide more recently in the case of David Koresh's Branch Dividians in 1993, where eighty of his followers were killed after a fifty-one-day standoff with officers from the Bureau of Alcohol, Tobacco, and Firearms. This case takes us to the dark side of charismatic leadership, but it also provides insight into the leader/follower relationship of charismatic leaders.

To understand the tragedy of Jonestown, we first need to look at what it offered to those who participated. Unlike the Manson Family, the Peoples Temple (it was always written without an apostrophe) was not based on an antinomian belief system that repudiated the reality of the world. Instead, the Temple combined Pentecostal faith-healing with left-wing political activism. It opposed the divisions of modern society, and the invidious distinctions of racism, and favored instead a new communal ideology in which everyone would be treated equally and share in the common good, welded together in a loving community of healing and mutual caring under the leadership of Jim Jones.

The group itself was a much more complex and powerful organization than any of the other communes that thrived in the California atmosphere, involving about 5,000 followers at its largest. In attempting to implement his political program, Jones could mobilize his supporters in letter-writing campaigns and picket lines, giving the impression that his support base was even wider than it really was; he therefore was courted by a number of politicians, and was appointed to a city commissioner's job in San Francisco. The Temple in its prime was not a group that withdrew from the world; it was active, visible, and powerful; operating within the system to change the system.

Much of the early success of the Peoples Temple came because of the tremendous appeal Jones had for the black community, and this also differentiates the Temple sharply from most countercultural organizations, whose membership consisted of young, white, middle-class ex-students. While Jones did draw in a middle-class base of ex-political radicals and activists, as well as a cadre of white fundamentalist believers from his early evangelizing in the midwest, he was most successful at proselytizing impoverished and culturally oppressed blacks, who were impressed by the fact that the Temple was an encompassing, interracial community where people worked and lived together in harmony, without fear of hunger, loneliness, prejudice, or poverty.

Case continued

Of the membership in the fully formed Peoples Temple, 80 percent were black, two-thirds of them women, many elderly, many from extremely impoverished backgrounds, many ex-drug addicts or ex-criminals. Even in his early days in Indianapolis, when his church was mostly white, Jones had had a special capacity to appeal to the outsiders and the stigmatized. As one of his followers from that era says, Jones attracted "the kind of people most folks don't want to have nothing to do with. Fat, ugly old ladies who didn't have nobody in the world. He'd pass around hugs and kisses like he really did love them, and you could see it on their faces what he meant to them" (quoted in Feinsod 1981: 17). Within the Temple the deprived, the downtrodden, the unloved found a better world, working together and united by Jim Jones's love and caring, which apparently went beyond all social boundaries. He loved them all, he would take care of them all, he would struggle tirelessly for them, he would sacrifice himself for them without any concern for material rewards. "Here's a man who says as long as I have a home, you have a home. Here's a man with only one pair of shoes and no car, one suit of clothing—I think the suit he's got on tonight was borrowed. Here's a man who works over twenty hours a day. Here's JIM JONES" (Jones's introduction at a revival meeting, quoted in Reiterman and Jacobs 1982:307).

Indeed, this portrait was a true one as far as it went. Even though the Temple took in enormous sums of donations, and had a bankroll of about twenty million dollars in its final days, Jones, as a true charismatic in the Weberian mold, had little interest in wealth. According to one convert, "It [the money] became almost a joke with Jim. . . . We used to wonder what to do with it all. But we never spent it on much" (quoted in Kilduff and Layers 1979:82). And Jones did devote himself completely to the church, and to his congregation, working almost around the clock to achieve his dream of an interracial socialist community.

Another appeal of the Temple, aside from its mixture of classes and races, and the loving commitment of the leader, was the fact that many whole families participated, including, in some cases, three generations. This again is very unlike other cultic groups, which generally appealed to a narrow age range of converts. In the Temple, on the other hand, one did not have to give up attachments to one's closest relatives.

Being in the Peoples Temple was therefore a far cry from membership in an isolated, powerless group living on fantasies. It was a large community with a strong socialistic ideology of sharing and activism. It had achieved real successes and had real power. Many members testified that they had faith in Jones and in his vision precisely because, as one ex-temple member recalls, it seemed that "Jim has the knowledge and ability to make this world a better place."

As his congregation grew, Jones made increased claims for charismatic elevation. His exaggerated self-presentation was modeled on Father Divine, the black leader from Harlem who called himself God, and who controlled a large and active following. Jones presented himself to his black congregation as the spiritual successor to the recently deceased Father Divine, imitating a number of Divine's practices, including interrogation and public confession. These helped create a strong sense of merger in the group, and served to ratify Jones's position as communal center, orchestrating emotional outbursts, collective purges, and group catharsis.

Transgressors were encouraged to come forward and kneel before Jimmy and confess not their sins but their ill feelings toward others. Jimmy would direct the supplicants to make peace with their adversaries by verbalizing their animosities. Once stated, the ill feelings would vanish in a tearful outpouring, to be replaced by gusty emotions of unity, brotherhood, and Christian fellowship. (a convert to the Indiana Temple, quoted in Weightman 1983:20).

Jones now argued that since God is the force of love, the most loving person therefore is God incarnate. And this person had to be Jones himself. At the same time, Jones told his inner circle, "of course I'm not God, of course I'm not Jesus. But these people are so religious that in order to bring them around to socialism I have to tell them these things" (Jim Jones quoted in Yee and Layton 1981:158).

Yet even as he claimed to be both God and the leader of a secular socialist revolution, Jones became more and more fearful; his old nightmares returned, but in concrete form, as he saw plots against him, prophesied nuclear destruction, and claimed that extraterrestrial voices warned him to relocate the church. Threats and even shootings occurred; incidents which Jones probably fabricated himself. The manufacture of episodes of attack set a pattern that was repeated throughout Jones's life, and served to unite the congregation behind him in opposition to the unseen, but dangerous, "others." But his manufacture of enemies had another, psychological purpose, since in arranging dramatic menaces he brought his inner terrors into the world of the Temple, where the community could help him to fend off personal disintegration.

But despite community support, during this fevered period Jones had a mental breakdown that led him to retreat to Brazil for two years. In Brazil he, his wife, his son, and his interracial family of adopted children lived a very marginal life. His own conventional moral values, never held very deeply, were challenged by the Brazilian atmosphere of sexual freedom and emotionally charged cultic activity. In response, he continued his transformation, shedding his middle-class inhibitions and constructing a theory of self-sacrifice and millennial social change. When he returned to Indiana, Jones claimed himself to be "the only God you'll ever see." He now was prepared to initiate the final phase of the Temple, leading it first to California, where he won many more converts with his message and style, and then to Guyana, where his grandiose vision ended in the convulsions of cyanide.

Case continued

"Jim Loves You": Living in the Temple

The modes in which membership in the Temple was solidified developed over time, ending finally in the complete self-loss of the disciples in the group, and ultimately in the grave. We can see this process occurring quite clearly among the elite PC (Planning Commission), which began pragmatically in Indianapolis as an administrative staff, but quickly evolved into a confrontational encounter-group where hostilities were aired and all aspects of personal and group life were debated. Jones served as arbiter and focus of the meetings, offering final words and resolution of conflicts.

After he returned from Brazil the meeting came to focus on "antisocial" aspects of behavior, in particular sexual practices. People were obliged to take turns accusing each other of selfishness, sexual misconduct, and other crimes against the community, with one's closest relatives and loved ones called upon to lead the attack. "Sessions started with verbal sniping, slipped into verbal brutality that brought people to tears, and gradually plunged into the sphere of physical violence" (Reiterman and Jacobs 1982:161).

In these meetings, personal identity and trust of others was undermined while simultaneously Jones's centrality and the dominance of the group over the individual were reinforced. All the PC members were crowded together in a small, hot room, nearly immobilized, with little to eat or drink, for up to 20 hours, while continual confrontation and occasional violence occurred under their leader's expert orchestration. Lounging on a couch above the fray, Jones would intersperse the attacks with long passionate harangues, often telling of his sacrifices and sicknesses, which he suffered for the sake of the Temple, of his sexual prowess and his selfless willingness to satisfy PC members whose own sexuality was distorted, of his struggles to achieve an absolute community, struggles thwarted by the weaknesses of the PC members, of his undying love and his great dream.

Not only the elite, but all the followers, were told again and again that the only true love was Jim Jones's love: it was a love that could never be reciprocated because it was so all-encompassing, so draining of him, so selfless, so absolute.

The husband and wife tie was also attacked. Jones assigned new partners to married couples, and demanded pledges of celibacy from his following, arguing that "the only reason sex would ever become necessary would be to produce children, and of course at this time in history, when we are concerned about an impending nuclear disaster, we don't need any babies in our group" (Jim Jones quoted in Mills 1979:228). Only he, the leader who embodied them all, should produce children.

The actual intensity of Jones's sexual appetite is hard to judge, but certainly there was a general attempt by everyone to portray his sexuality as overwhelming. As one apostate says:

We all knew what we were supposed to say because we had seen it all before. We were supposed to say that we had approached him; that he had helped us psy-chologically; that he had the biggest penis we had ever seen; that he could screw longer than anybody and that we had never had an orgasm until we had sex with him. Until that moment I had always believed that what all the others previous to me had said was true; now I knew differently. (Debbie Layton quoted in Yee and Layton 1981:177)

This anecdote illustrates one of the most striking aspects of the Peoples Temple, namely the degree that the members, especially the elite inner cadre, colluded together to maintain the myth of Jim Jones's omnipotence, in both the figurative and literal sense. The PC were, in fact, privy to many of his weaknesses. They knew of his drug addiction, his ill health, his sexual predilections. They even knew that the "miracles" he used to draw in his religiously fundamentalist black followers were fraudulent. But the PC membership consciously agreed that these failings and lies should be overlooked because of the need to bolster Jones's posture of infallibility for the good of the group. As one member of the PC said, "a leader must maintain an image in order to command the respect of his followers" (Mills 1979:140). Therefore, Jones should be treated and portrayed as if he were the Messiah.

This argument was openly made by Jones himself, who, like Hitler, was very aware of the necessity of playing his part without any faults or breaks in the facade. In PC meetings, for instance, he was immune from attack during the heated encounters. "I would love to be able to accept your criticisms," he told the PC members. "Believe me, everything you say about everyone else, I do look to in myself. But brothers and sisters, we need a strong leader here, and it would not be wise" (Jim Jones quoted in Yee and Layton 1981:150). The converts thus connived in their own subordination; they "did not obey him because he disciplined them; they accepted his discipline because they had made him their leader" (Weightman 1983:160).

Yet, despite this self-conscious awareness in the elite members of the way in which Jones's image was built and the ways in which commitment was manufactured, the experience of the community, and of Jones's leadership, acted to estrange them from themselves, breaking own each individual's personal separateness to the extent that "like an unstable chemical radical he hunger[ed] to combine with whatever [came] within his reach" (Hoffer 1951:83). What they combined with was Jones, whose fantasies brought them all together. As in Tarde's metaphor of the photographic plate, knowledge of the process did not prevent it from occurring. But where Tarde and the crowd psychologists thought that the cognitive ego would naturally, but futilely, resist self-loss in the group, the Temple members instead consciously sought and helped to engender group immersion.

Case continued

Consequently, as in the Hitler cult, the elite cadre not only promoted, but also actually believed strongly in their leader's charisma. They had faith that Jones did have a magical power to heal, but that using this power exhausted him unduly, so that fakery was necessary to keep him alive. They believed in his Godlike qualities, and "were convinced that Jones could foresee the future, that he had information that no one else was aware of. These members also believed that the Temple was the only antidote to all the ills of the world" (Yee and Layton 1981:165).

This process of destabilization of the individual personality and recombination into the charismatic group was accomplished incrementally through a number of methods we have already noted: constant confrontations and public confessions which revealed each person's weaknesses and sexual inadequacies, as well as the untrustworthiness of friends and family; the denial of all emotional bonds between individuals and a focusing of affect on Jones; obligatory participation in group rituals of emotional intensification; propaganda that played upon the corruption and evil of the outer world; forced, self-incriminating confessions of homosexuality, and so on.

Their shared deceptions about Jones's ability to heal, about his sexuality, about his omnipotence, which were originally engaged in for the sake of group solidarity, also increased commitment among the elite by eroding their own ability to distinguish between truth and falsehood. Lies constantly repeated have a transforming effect, redefining reality not only for the listener, but for the speaker as well, who sees that the delusions become reality, and that assertions of transcendent power are associated with the actual inner experience of transcendence.

Commitment was further solidified by the requirements Jones made of his disciples. All worldly goods had to be invested in the Temple; children had to be given up into the Temple. Jones continually demanded that his followers cut their ties with the past completely and move from place to place, first from Indiana to California, then to the even greater isolation of Guyana. There solidarity reached its maximum, stimulated by Jones's absolute control of information, by the near continuous group meetings, by the fatigue and hunger of the members, by the blaring of loudspeakers bringing Jones's message to the people at any hour of the day, and by the atmosphere of paranoia that Jones emanated and cultivated.

This process of amalgamation into the group took place within a typically charismatic command structure in which rules were strict, rigid and highly elaborated, as the community reflected the leader's struggle to construct a world that would contain and channel his rage and fear. At the same time, the rules could change instantaneously, according to the leader's whim. As a result, "well-intentioned people, trying to obey the rules and regulations, often committed . . . crimes without realizing it" (Mills

1979:288). The followers had to learn to live in a total universe where complete arbitrariness was combined paradoxically with obsessional regimentation. The anxieties aroused by this situation pressed the disciples to greater identification with Jones as the sole point of orientation and guidance.

Jones's charisma was also maintained by the distance he kept from actual policy implementation. The community was run on a daily basis by an administrative core of eight to ten young white women. They stood above the PC and were Jones's closest and most loyal associates and confidants. They served to deflect any hostility felt by the rank and file for the direction of the commune. When things went wrong, they were to blame, not Jones; like Hitler, he kept his pronouncements on a transcendental plane.

Revolutionary Suicide

His techniques, coupled with the intensity of his charismatic personality and the desires of the followers for community, did indeed increase members' ties to the Temple. It was, as we have seen, a highly successful enterprise, both economically and politically. But there was a time bomb within it, since the communal dynamic demanded continued expansion; yet as the group grew, it reached its outer limits. Jones could no longer interact with everyone and fuel them with his fire; the necessities of bureaucratic planning and group maintenance meant that work was harder and less rewarding; the expansion of the group became more difficult. But most threatening were defections. In fact, withdrawal from the group paradoxically reflected the Temple's very success at giving its members improved senses of self-worth and empowerment. Some of them now felt they could deal with the world on their own terms.

But Jones and the Temple could not accept anyone growing beyond them. For Jones and the committed members, the community was everything; it provided the structure that kept them from falling into the void. Jones had spent his entire life creating relations of dependency, warding off emptiness by placing himself in the center of the worlds of others, absorbing them into his expansive fantasy. He, who had not had love, would give love completely; he, who never trusted, would command absolute trust; he, who was torn by ambivalence, would be a rock; he, who had a damaged family, would manufacture the perfect family—but it was a family no one could ever leave; it had to be eternal, and it had to engulf the world.

The community was caught in a downward spiral as Jones's paranoia and desire to maintain control created tensions that led some members to reconsider their ties to the Temple. The last straw for Jones was the effort by one apostate couple to gain custody of their child, whom Jones claimed as his heir. In response, Jones sent many of his followers to Guyana to build a refuge in the

Case continued

jungle which would form a nexus for a new, millennial society, and provide as well a safe place where his enemies could no longer threaten him. Of course, the demons could not be warded off; they were too deep in Jones's soul.

Furthermore, the truly heroic struggle by the emigrants to build Jonestown undercut community solidarity. Productive work in common gave many who participated an increased belief in themselves, a feeling that they were active and creative individuals. As Eric Hoffer writes, "the taste of continuous successful action is fatal to the spirit of the collectivity" (1951: 120). Jones could not countenance this challenge to the group and to his dominance. Therefore, when he arrived in Jonestown he immediately acted to erode the achievements of the pioneers who had preceded him and who had almost unbelievably managed to construct a viable enterprise in the middle of the jungle. He began to implement increasingly irrational procedures and focused on ideological indoctrination instead of farm production. And he soon talked of abandoning the commune in favor of migration to the Soviet Union. This led to resentment, to further defections, and more paranoia, in a fateful movement toward the eventual mass suicide.

When Congressman William Ryan's investigating team arrived in Jonestown from the United States to see if members were being held agains their wills, Jones felt his paranoid vision was coming true. At first, he managed to keep himself under control, and even provided hospitality and entertainment for his guests. The breaking point came when a few Temple members asked to leave Jonestown with the congressional party. This meant that even in Guyana, betrayal and disintegration were possible. The social world of the Temple no longer was solid; it was being torn apart by the blandishments of Satan.

For some weeks Jones had been preparing for this moment, claiming that CIA troops were already in the jungle, and manufacturing fake attacks on the compound—just as he had manufactured attacks on his early church in Indiana. This time, however, there was no place to run. Jones burned his bridges by having the congressional party attacked. He thus took revenge on America and on those who had betrayed him. Then he told his followers that instead of succumbing to the inexorable power of the state, the Peoples Temple would destroy itself in an act of defiance.

Suicide was proclaimed a revolutionary victory, an escape from inevitable corruption, an entrance into history, and a claim for the power of the love of Jim Jones, a love that would carry the followers to their ultimate merger with him in the unity of death, which Jones typically sexualized as "the orgasm of the grave" (Jim Jones quoted in Reston 1981:265). Jones could see this as a triumph because it matched his grandiose vision and permitted him the positive expression of his self-hatred. The fates of his individual followers were of no concern to Jones; they were nothing more than

*extensions of himself, poor weak beings whom he could not leave behind on
his journey to death: "I did not bring you to this point to leave you without a
future, without someone who loves you, who will plan and care for you" (Jim
Jones quoted in Reiterman and Jacobs 1982:451).*

*The only thing that could save him would be if he could have faith in
something outside himself: "If I had a leader — oh, how I would love to have
a leader. . . . If I had a God—and oh how I wish I had a God like you . . .
because I'm the only one there is as far as I could see. And I have searched
all over heaven and earth and I certainly looked through the belly of hell"
(Jim Jones quoted in Reiterman and Jacobs 1982:226).*

*But Jim Jones found no escape, no matter where he looked, neither in the
world, where he saw himself rejected and persecuted, nor in his heart, where
the love of the Temple could no longer ward off rage and fear. Meanwhile,
the community had been practicing for mass suicide for some time. The
notion of death had lost its terror for them. Like their leader, they believed
themselves besieged by a hostile world; the defections of their fellows
solidified them all the more, and they were ready to share the ultimate
emptiness with the man who had brought them together for eternity. It was
not Jim Jones, but the world, that was driving them to self-destruction:*

> Jim was the most honest, loving, caring concerned person whom I ever met and
> knew. . . . He knew how mean the world was and he took any and every stray
> animal and took care of each one. His love for humans was insurmount-
> able. . . . Jim Jones showed us all this — that we could live together with our
> differences, that we are all the same human beings. . . . We died because you
> would not let us live in peace. (Anne Moore's last testament quoted in Moore
> 1986:285–6)

*Because Jim Jones had brought them together, because they had lost
themselves and been reborn in the Temple, because they could not imagine
any alternative to their unity, because they believed themselves to be under
attack, the members were ready and willing to give up their lives rather than
lose their community or the leader who crystallized it. As one of them said,
"any life outside of this collective is shit. . . . All I want is to die a
revolutionary death" (quoted in Reston 1981:265–6). And so they killed
themselves just as they killed Congressman Ryan and his party; quite
willingly, and without compunction. Far from being inhuman, the suicide
was a quintessentially human act; one derived from the power of the group,
and the dream of transcendence.*

Questions

1. What were the positive aspects of Jones's leadership?
2. What was it about his leadership that inspired so much devotion?

3. Why did his close associates cover up for him and back up his lies? Compare and contrast this case with the "Bathsheba Syndrome."
4. Were there any points in this case where Jones might have looked more like a transformational leader?

The Myth of Charisma

Robert C. Solomon

Robert C. Solomon is a philosopher who teaches at the University of Texas at Austin. In his article Solomon argues that the focus on charisma distorts our understanding of the relationship between leaders and followers. Today people use the quality of charisma to mean a number of things; all of those things do not add up to a particular trait or quality that makes a person a dynamic leader. Solomon argues that the real issue we should be studying is how leaders and followers get and give trust to each other. Trust, according to Solomon, is at the intersection of the emotional and rational part of the leader/follower relationship. The process of giving and getting trust is fundamental to making this relationship work.

Charisma" is shorthand for the emotional power of a certain (rare) leaders, but it is, unfortunately, without ethical value and, I argue, without much explanatory value either. It is one of the most frequently recurrent terms in discussions of leadership. Derived in its current usage from the German sociologist Max Weber, it is, perhaps, the only such term that so explicitly refers to the emotional quality of leadership, albeit at considerable cost to clarity, imbued as the term is with mystery and magic. It is also used at great cost to an adequate understanding of emotions, because the very notion of charisma connotes an irrational as opposed to a rational influence. Although Weber is noted for his analysis of institutions and bureaucracy in terms of "rationality," he himself was an ethical noncognitivist and viewed rationality and rationalization as a costly "disenchantment" with the world. At the end of his famous book, *The Protestant Ethic and the Spirit of Capitalism,* he argued that rationalism is destructive of value, an "iron cage" in which both freedom and meaning are sacrificed to efficiency. One should not be surprised, therefore, that for him charisma offered a significantly religious promise.

The Weberian term is defined by the *American Heritage Dictionary* as follows: "1.a. A rare personal quality attributed to leaders who arouse fervent popular devotion and enthusiasm. b. Personal magnetism or charm. 2. Theology. An extraordinary power, such as the ability to perform miracles, granted to a Christian by the Holy Spirit."

The theological dimension of the term is to be noted, especially in Weber's classic use of the concept, as is the idea that charisma is by its very nature "rare." Its nature does not invite analysis; in fact, it discourages it. Even careful analytic writers like Robert Nozick are reduced to such impoverished New Age metaphors as an "aura." It will not do to take the nature of charisma as given, trying only to understand its use and effects. The fact that it is rare (and "blessed") encourages gratitude and reverence rather than critical analysis, and its kinship to "magnetism and charm" tends to foreclose any meaningful investigation. Indeed, James MacGregor Burns warns that the "term is so over-used it threatens to collapse under close analysis."

Bernard Bass describes charisma as displayed by leaders "to whom followers form deep emotional attachments and who in turn inspire their followers to transcend their own interests for superordinate goals." This is true, perhaps, but what are these emotional attachments? How do they work? What are their vicissitudes? The mysterious origins of charisma also invite a serious worry: What happens when this "blessing" turns into a curse and serves evil rather than good (the "Hitler Problem" again)? How do we know that the gift is from God rather than from Satan, except by the results? Thus C. Hodgkinson warns, "Beware charisma," and Michael Keeley, in a powerful essay, attacks "transformational leadership" precisely on the grounds that it gives too much credence to charisma and too little to the Madisonian "checks and balances" that control or contain charisma. Charisma, according to such authors, is a dangerous genie to let out of the bottle. But few of them pay much if any attention to what charisma actually is, leaving unanalyzed charisma's enviable status as "an extraordinary power" (if not exactly "the ability to perform miracles"), "a rare personal quality" of leaders "who arouse fervent popular devotion and enthusiasm."

I want to argue that charisma is not anything in particular. It is not a distinctive quality of personality or character, and it is not an essential implement of leadership. Rather, it is a misleading even if exciting concept that deflects us from the emotional complexity of leadership, which might better occupy our attention. Charisma is not a single quality, nor is it a single emotion or set of emotions. It is a generalized way of pointing to and emptily explaining an emotional relationship that is too readily characterized as fascination but should more fundamentally be analyzed in terms of trust. Within the range of what is usually identified as "charisma," I would want to make some distinctions.

What the leader is saying. Is it the message itself that is fascinating? Steve Forbes smartly suggested a simplified "flat tax" at precisely the time that most American taxpayers were brooding over, struggling with, and hating the brain-twisting annual exercise called "filling out your 1040." It is not surprising that people were fascinated, and other candidates quickly adopted the idea. The attention Forbes received had nothing to do with charisma. Often a good idea—even sound common sense—will evoke sufficient emotion that the praise goes to the speaker when it is the idea that is really being endorsed. (Ross Perot's appearance in 1992 is probably a case in point.)

The rhetorical persuasiveness of how he or she says it. Martin Luther King Jr. was a brilliant orator, although that by itself is not what made him a great leader. More recently, Pat Buchanan, though more of a curmudgeonly televangelical than a voice of hope, has obviously found the "hot buttons" of a substantial portion of the American public. Rhetorical skills alone do not count as charisma, or many English professors would be leaders. Nevertheless, rhetorical skills certainly play a considerable role in what is called charisma. Such skills may make a mediocre message—and the speaker—much more memorable than the ideas themselves deserve.

The hopes, wishes, fears of the audience. Obviously, what gets said is fascinating not just for its own sake; it speaks to powerful emotions on the part of the audience. But this by itself says more about the receptivity of the audience than the character of the speaker—riling people up is not yet leading them. Yet, insofar as leadership is an emotional relationship that concerns the future, responding to hopes, wishes, and fears may well be interpreted as charisma by an appreciative audience. Paranoia, notably, produces some of the most "charismatic" leaders.

His or her degree of enthusiasm, "infectiousness." What is obviously an aspect of the personality of a leader is his or her ability to excite and transmit emotion, even against the initial resistance or opposition of others. A recent analysis of Franklin Roosevelt suggests "his remarkable capacity to transmit his internal strength to others." Enthusiasm is certainly high up on the list of ingredients of charisma, and enthusiasm plus infectiousness takes us a long way to understanding what is meant by the term. Motivational speakers are often called "charismatic," but we should note again that this does not imply leadership.

Such personality traits as charm, intelligence, sincerity. Much of what passes for charisma is in fact some combination of much more easily understood character traits. "Charm" may be difficult to define (although literature abounds with some excellent witticisms, such as

"charm is getting what you want without asking"). Much of John
   Kennedy's famous charisma was, no doubt, a combination of his
   straightforward charm and his good looks. Inevitably, a fascinating
   or comforting leader is characterized as "attractive," "sexy,"
   "fatherly," or "motherly." (A concept that deserves some rigorous
   analysis is "presence." Although this term shares many of the
   problems of "charisma," at least it is rarely confused with magic.
   It is, for example, highly correlated with such mundane features
   as height.)

"Celebrity." These days celebrity is often confused with leadership, and
   it is celebrity, not leadership, that attracts the attribution of
   "charisma." But celebrity clearly requires no particular virtues or
   characteristics other than merely being much in the news, often on
   television, the butt of popular jokes and late-night humor, or being
   readily recognized. (Indeed, the talking heads who do nothing but
   read the news headlines on television are typically viewed as
   celebrities.) This is what Jay Conger calls "attribution." What does this
   have to do with leadership?

The nature of the situation or "context." Sometimes an individual who
   stands up or comes through in terrifying, dangerous, promising, or
   hate-filled circumstances may thereby get accepted as a leader (Boris
   Yeltsin facing the tanks is an apt example). This is not charisma; the
   circumstances, rather than any particular quality of the character in
   question, supply the aura of seeming greatness, at least for a while.

Change. Many leadership theorists (for example, Burns, Rost) note
   presiding over change as an essential ingredient in leadership.
   Whether this is so, being visibly "in charge" of change is itself often
   conflated with the dynamism of charisma. But, as in Tolstoy, there is
   always the question of where the action really is, in the leader or in
   the change itself. True, there is much to be said about managing
   change, and much to be debated about the ability of any leader to
   bring about change without the forces of society already mustered.
   But my point here is that the dynamics of change itself may be readily
   confused with the dynamic character of the leader.

Resemblance/continuity. On the other hand, sometimes charisma may be
   little more than continuity, a carryover, an echo of previous leadership or,
   perhaps, the result of an enduring myth or faulty memory. George H.
   Bush had enough seeming charisma to carry him through one
   presidential election, but it quickly became apparent that this was merely
   the fading continuation of the Reagan "magic." Harry Truman, by
   contrast, suffered from comparison with his great predecessor.
   Regardless of whether he had his own degree of charisma, he had to

establish his reputation for leadership from a decidedly disadvantaged position.

What is called charisma may be some blend or mixture of all these different ingredients, and no doubt more besides, but that is not the point of this crude dissection. I suggest that charisma doesn't refer to any character trait or "quality" in particular, but is rather a general way of referring to a person who seems to be a dynamic and effective leader. And as a term of analysis in leadership studies, I think that it is more of a distraction than a point of understanding.

The Emotional Core of Leadership: Trust

Charisma distracts us from looking at the relationship between the leader and the led, and, in particular, the relationship of trust. The mistake is not so much that charisma is dangerous in the "wrong" leaders, but rather that it is a distorted perspective on leadership. The word "trust" appears in virtually every current book on leadership, and it is taken as a commonplace that without trust, leadership is impossible. This has not always been the case. Machiavelli, for example, suggests that leaders should strive to be feared, not loved. But trust is hard to analyze, and it is hard to say anything very useful about it. Francis Fukuyama has recently published a four-hundred-page book simply entitled *Trust,* but one is hard put to find any discussion of the subject in those many pages. Fukuyama utterly ignores the dynamics of trust, the ways in which trust is created and cultivated, particularly between cultures and rival subcultural groups. Nevertheless, many of the examples of what Fukuyama calls "spontaneous sociability" are revealing.

Several standard definitions of trust (for example, N. Luhmann and B. Barber) characterize it primarily in terms of *expectations,* but this is only half the story. It also involves decisions and the dynamics of a relationship. Trust, in other words, is an emotional relationship, as is leadership. Putting it more succinctly, leadership is an emotional relationship of trust.

Niklas Luhmann distinguishes trust from confidence, noting that we trust (or don't trust) people but have (or do not have) confidence in institutions. This points to an important distinction, but it does not yet reach it. The distinction between persons and organizations is convenient and obvious but often, especially in business and organizational ethics, misleading or counterproductive. Organizations and institutions have many features of persons (not least, that in the eye of the law they are persons, with fiduciary obligations, rights and responsibilities). As such, we trust them (or not) much as we would trust a person who had made us a promise or with whom we had agreed upon a contract. On the other hand, we sometimes have confidence in people we do not or would not trust; for example, bureaucrats who are known for their fairness and efficiency but are personally unknown to us. We may also have confidence in someone precisely because we do not trust him or her; for instance, when we place our confidence in the double-dealing habits of an old enemy, or "have confidence" that our friend M will fail to quit smoking this time as he has failed in every one of the last thirty-one attempts to do so. (This use of "have confidence" is not wholly ironic.)

The distinction that Luhmann is after has been stated by Laurence Thomas, among others, who distinguishes between trust and prediction. We predict that something will happen. We trust that someone will do something. The distinction is between mechanism and agency, nature and persons. Trust, in other words, is not predicting that something will be the case. This, it seems to me, is fairly obvious, yet it has taken up a substantial portion of the literature (perhaps just because it is so seemingly straightforward). Here, I think, is where Luhmann is aiming us as well, although he mislocates the cleavage. Organizations and institutions are not mechanisms, no matter how efficiently (that is, "mechanically") they may be constructed. Organizations and institutions are people, working together. Those people, and consequently the organizations and institutions they create, are agents. Thus they have obligations, rights, and responsibilities. What they will do is not simply a matter of probabilities. It is a matter of trust. This is why the common-sensical notion (advocated by Luhmann and adopted by Barber) that trust is first of all a set of expectations is misleading. It is this, of course but it is much more than this. Trust, as opposed to prediction or confidence, presupposes a relationship. And relationships by their nature involve much more than a calculation of probabilities and outcomes. They involve values and emotions, responsibilities and the possibility of not only disappointment but betrayal.

Trust is an umbrella term. It is not an emotion as such, although in certain situations it can manifest itself as a very powerful emotion, notably and most dramatically in the case of betrayal, but also in its positive display. One way of describing this feature of trust is to say that, by its very nature, it is part of the "background" of our social activities. To say that trust is not as such an emotion is not, however, to remove it from the realm of emotion. Quite the contrary. Trust is the framework within which emotions appear, their precondition, the structure of the world in which they operate. Without trust, there can be no betrayal, but, more generally, without trust, there can be no cooperation, no community, no commerce, no conversation. And in a context without trust, of course, all sorts of emotions readily surface, starting with suspicion, quickly escalating to contempt, resentment, hatred, and worse. Thus "trust" serves to characterize an entire network of emotions and emotional attitudes, both between individuals and within groups and by way of a psychodynamic profile of entire societies. (This is Fukuyama's theme in *Trust*.) In such large contexts, one might even say that trust is something of an "atmosphere," a shared emotional understanding about who is or who is not to be included, contracted, "trusted."

One reason to argue that trust is not as such an emotion is to get rid of the uncritical picture of trust as a "warm fuzzy feeling" of the sort so disdained by hard-headed ethicists and leaders of all sorts. Thus I would disagree with John Dunn when he argues that trust is a human passion or sentiment. It is not, say, like compassion. It is not even an attitude. Not that I object to warm, fuzzy feelings. On the contrary, sentimentality can be a powerful (although easily exploited) quality of leadership and one that is often neglected in the more "macho" emphasis on charisma. But to think of trust as a particular feeling—not to mention a mawkish feeling—is to demean it and to give a misleading characterization of what trust entails. Trusting does not indicate a "softness," a gullibility, or a weakness. It is a strength, a precondition of any alliance or mutual understanding. It is not a vulnerability, except insofar as, by the very nature of the case, someone who is trusted is thereby in a position to betray that trust. And trust is, I would argue, necessarily a reciprocal relation. This is not to say that Franklin can only trust Benito if Benito trusts Franklin as well, but it is to say that trust is a relationship and not merely an attitude. If Franklin "trusts" Benito but Benito has no relation to Franklin, I am tempted to say that this cannot be a matter of trust at all, but rather predictability or confidence.

One might think of trust in negative terms, as, for example, a suspension of fear or a suspension of certain thoughts. However, although this notion captures an important insight (namely, that trust as such doesn't feel like anything in particular), it fails to capture the important positive dimensions of trust, because it fails to appreciate the nature and character of emotion. Put one way, perhaps too starkly, emotions are not feelings, except in the most generic and, for the most part, vacuous sense of that term (as any felt mental state or experience). Even anger, which would seem to be as profoundly "felt" as any emotion, is not just a feeling or even primarily a feeling. It is an attitude toward the world, specifically directed at a person, action, situation, or state of affairs. More accurately, anger is a systematic set of judgments—judgments of blame, especially—that cast their target in a particular role, put him or her on trial, consider him or her for punishment. Trust, by way of this perspective, is a certain conception of the world and other people. It is a way of seeing, a way of estimating and valuing. Thus it establishes a framework of expectations and agreements (explicit or not) in which actions conform or fail to conform. A leader, one might surmise, is one who succeeds in establishing or sustaining a framework of trust. Indeed, perhaps the increasingly evasive distinction between attentive leaders and actively participating followers has not to do with the recommendation or initiation of actions but rather with the primary responsibility for such a framework.

Trust can also be a decision. To talk about trust as background brings it dangerously close to something that is taken for granted, something that is either there or not there (Fukuyama's general assumption about "high trust" and "low trust" societies). But as we all know from our own experience, trust can be a very conscientious, extremely difficult, and deliberative decision. We meet someone new, or we find ourselves in a new situation with someone we do not know very well. Something comes up. Something must be done. We have to decide: Do we trust this person? In such cases, we establish a framework that was not in place before. Of course, there will be a more general framework within which this relationship and this situation takes place, and that general framework will influence and may well define the boundaries of the decision. One does not want to be too deterministic about this. Some of the most important trust decisions—in particular, decisions to trust a new leader—are made in defiance of an existing trust or distrust situation. But trust is not always in the background. Sometimes, such as when we have to decide whether or not to trust someone, it may be very much in the foreground. Indeed, it may be the definitive aspect of the situation. In leadership, the establishment of trust by a new president just taking office, for example, may be the most important factor in his or her success or failure.

But then, trust is also dynamic. As such, it can clearly be talked about in terms of emotion, but I think upon examination it turns out to be something more than an emotion. It is more of a family of emotions, negotiations, deliberations, and decisions. For example, a woman has all of the evidence imaginable that her husband has been and is still being unfaithful. She refuses to accept that evidence, or, rather, she refuses to accept it as evidence and thus refuses to accept the obvious conclusion. One might glibly say that this is self-deception, a blatant attempt to refuse to recognize what she in fact clearly knows. But I would argue that it can also be a conscious decision and not deception at all. It is not that the woman refuses to acknowledge (if only to herself) what she knows. It is rather that she has decided to trust her husband, regardless of his behavior (which can then be conveniently ignored or pushed to the side). So, too, I want to argue, whereas leaders may be said to earn the trust of their followers, it is the followers who have the capacity to give that trust. Trust thus becomes a part of the dynamics of the relationship between those who would be leaders and their followers, even when the leadership position is independently determined, as it usually is. (CEOs, supervisors, officers, deans, and college presidents—at least in Texas—are placed in their positions by such higher authorities as boards of directors and generals, not by those whom they are to lead.)

One problem in analyzing trust is a certain ambiguity, much of it due to the background-foreground contrast. But because trust covers so many situations, one is tempted to try to sharpen the edges and define trust in terms of its context or content. Thus Benjamin Barber distinguishes three different meanings of "trust" by virtue of the object or content of that trust: first, a general meaning regarding social expectations; second, a "competence" sense of trust, that one has the skills and knowledge to carry out one's responsibilities (for example, a doctor, an explosives expert, a White House economist); and third, a "partnership" or "fiduciary" sense, in which one is trusted to carry out certain duties or obligations, as a result of a certain relationship, usually by virtue of some commitment, contract, or agreement. I find such distinctions troubling, mainly because I think that it is a problem to distinguish kinds of trust on the basis of trust's object or content, but also because one's obligations and one's expected competencies are usually correlated in a logical way ("ought implies can," says Kant in a phrase of admirable brevity). Furthermore, it is not clear in what sense the two "specialized" senses of trust are not just that—not different meanings or senses of trust but only more specific instances of trust in general. And, as if to underscore the problem of multiplying senses needlessly, much of Barber's book is spent criticizing alternative accounts of trust on the grounds that they conflate the latter two senses of "trust," which gets in the way of some of his genuinely interesting observations about trust in practice, in the family, in politics, and (in a less obvious sense) in business. What he does not discuss, unfortunately, is the central role of trust in leadership (as opposed to politics) as such.

What I am suggesting is that different dimensions (not "senses") of trust be distinguished not on the basis of the object or content of trust, but on its social role, its role as an emotion, and its role as background. In many situations, paradigmatically in the primordial situation in which as infants we trust our parents, trust might best be considered part of the "background." It is present and taken for granted throughout in every transaction. It is not "at issue" and not in question. Often, such trust relationships are unrecognized as such, until, that is, the trust is breached. For example, banks have been the target of distrust and abuse by American populists and political activists since the last century. President Andrew Jackson even sought to outlaw them. And yet, the amount of trust taken for granted by anyone who has any business with banking at all is astounding. We trust that the money we deposit will be returned to us as promised. We trust that the bills and most checks we receive are valid and genuine. The fact that we ask for a "bank check" or "cashier's check" for absolute security is further evidence of our trust in banks, however great our distrust may be on some more abstract level. And yet, we all have seen the consequences of even a minor bank scare. Not just that bank, but all banks, are suddenly under scrutiny, under suspicion. Banking depends on trust—not as an issue, but as background. Trust has already been compromised once it has become an issue, once the question has come up, Is my money really safe in that bank? So, too, once a leader comes under suspicion, no matter that the charges against him may be malevolent and/or political, trust in him as a leader is already compromised. Thus the political effectiveness of raising the Whitewater issue, which proclaims itself to be a question of Clinton's character but in fact is intended to be and obviously has succeeded in casting doubt on his trustworthiness as a leader.

The emotional dimension of trust is more explicit, more dynamic. Here trust is an active relationship and transaction rather than the background of relationships and transactions. This is most evident when it is most in question; for example, at the negotiating table between two bitter and mutually distrustful enemies (the Bosnians and the Serbs, the Israelis and the Syrians). Trust here involves decisions. One decides to trust the other, however tentatively. It is here that the dynamic of trust gets really interesting, for even the slightest hint of betrayal can be met by the most awesome response. We can also witness the evolution or growth of trust, typically not in a single all-or-nothing decision but rather in incremental increases, although it may be generations before trust is sufficiently established to blend into the background. Sometimes, miraculously, mutual trust can just become a fact. Indeed, what I find most fascinating about trust is the human tendency to trust, despite all of the cynicism and suspicion to the contrary. Most people, in the absence of any clear warning or traumatic past experience, tend to be trusting. Trust in general is not so much an achievement as an assumption. It is the initial state rather than a result. People would rather trust than not (and, obviously, would rather be trusted than not). If this is so, it lends an interesting twist to all the current questions about a "crisis of trust" in American leadership. In a recent column, Alexander Cockburn sagely suggests that this "crisis" in fact reflects people's resentment and distrust of pollsters and professors rather than of one another. He also adds that the American people have always distrusted their leaders. Based upon my own reading, I believe this to be false, and so one is moved to ask what particular and obviously effective obstacles to trust are operative in the current political environment. Watergate and Vietnam have obviously worn out their explanatory power.

We talk a great deal about earning trust, but I would suggest that *giving* trust is a more promising avenue of pursuit. Earning trust is, ultimately, encouraging trust to slip into the background. Giving trust is a dynamic decision, the transformation of a relationship of the most basic and sometimes most difficult kind. This, I would suggest, is central to any conception of "transforming" or "transformational leadership," indeed, to any leadership at all. But this places an enormous burden on the led. Their decision to trust or not to trust makes leadership possible, and I believe much of the traditional talk about charisma as "a special quality" might better be viewed as the endowment or the projection of such a quality, by way of the people who then "find" that property worthy of following. When it is not part of the background, trust is something that has to be given. But for most leaders in most situations, certainly today, trust cannot be presumed to be part of the background. Thus they must make considerable effort in the name of earning people's trust, but earning usually entails desert, and the history of politics makes all too clear that life in politics is not fair. Ultimately, perhaps, in politics there is no such thing as deserving the people's trust. One is trustworthy, or one is not. One is trusted, or one is not. But whether or not trust can be earned, it can be wisely or foolishly given. Thus it is those who would follow, not those who would lead, who are the ultimate power in any leadership relationship.

Conclusion: Whether 'Tis Better to Be Loved or Feared

Whether it is "better to be loved or feared" is, of course, one of the more famous questions raised by Machiavelli in *The Prince*, and his answer was unambiguous. Better to be feared, he said, but what should be obvious, even within that grim framework, is that the emotional choices are woefully incomplete. One need not fear a leader to obey, nor need one love a leader to trust. Indeed, the extremes of emotion all too often tend to provoke the extremes of reaction, which Machiavelli clearly sees, and neither provides a very promising guide to leadership, much less ethical leadership. Charisma is designed to solve the problem by providing an emotional intermediary that salvages the power of fear and love but dispenses with the liabilities of both: the hatred generated by fear; the fickleness invited by love. But charisma serves this purpose only by introducing opacities and misunderstandings of its own. Thus I have suggested, albeit briefly, that trust would be a much better emotional vehicle for the discussion of leadership than charisma.

REVIEW QUESTIONS

1. What is the difference between charisma and celebrity?
2. A baseball player may "lead" the league in home runs, a movie star may win an Oscar, but does their fame make them leaders?
3. How have the leaders you have known gained your trust? What do you think and feel when you give trust to someone?

The Servant as Leader
Robert Greenleaf, 1904–1990

Robert K. Greenleaf worked for AT&T in America for many years doing management research and employee education. After he retired from AT&T he did some consulting and teaching at a variety of institutions from the Ford Foundation to the Harvard Business School. In 1970 he wrote a short essay called "The Servant as Leader," which gave the modern name "servant leader" to a set of ideas about leadership. The idea of servant leadership is ancient and has existed in the older literature of the Near and Far East. Greenleaf's idea of a servant leader comes to us via Hermann Hesse's novel *Journey to the East*. (Hesse's novel was probably informed by the ideas of Lao Tzu or other Taoists.) Servant leadership is often used as a model of religious leadership, however, Greenleaf shows us how it can be applied to modern organizations. He says servant leaders should serve people in a way that makes followers grow to be better, more autonomous, wiser, freer people while being served by them.

S ervant and leader—can these two roles be fused in one real person, in all levels of status or calling? If so, can that person live and be productive in the real world of the present? My sense of the present leads me to say yes to both questions. This chapter is an attempt to explain why and to suggest how.

The idea of *The Servant as Leader* came out of reading Hermann Hesse's *Journey to the East*. In this story we see a band of men on a mythical journey, probably also Hesse's own journey. The central figure of the story is Leo who accompanies the party as the *servant* who does their menial chores, but who also sustains them with his spirit and his song. He is a person of extraordinary presence. All goes well until Leo disappears. Then the group falls into disarray and the journey is abandoned. They cannot make it without the servant Leo. The narrator, one of the party, after some years of wandering finds Leo and is taken into the Order that had sponsored the journey. There he discovers that Leo, whom he had known first as *servant*, was in fact the titular head of the Order, its guiding spirit, a great and noble *leader*.

One can muse on what Hesse was trying to say when he wrote this story. We know that most of his fiction was autobiographical, that he led a tortured life, and that *Journey to the East* suggests a turn toward the serenity he achieved in his old age. There has been much speculation by critics on Hesse's life and work, some of it centering on this story which they find the most puzzling. But to me, this story clearly says that *the great leader is seen as servant first,* and that simple fact is the key to his greatness. Leo was actually the leader all of the time, but he was servant first because that was what he was, *deep down inside.* Leadership was bestowed upon a man who was by nature a servant. It was something given, or assumed, that could be taken away. His servant nature was the real man, not bestowed, not assumed, and not to be taken away. He was servant first.

I mention Hesse and *Journey, to the East* for two reasons. First, I want to acknowledge the source of the idea of *The Servant as Leader.* Then I want to use this reference as an introduction to a brief discussion of prophecy.

Fifteen years ago when I first read about Leo, if I had been listening to contemporary prophecy as intently as I do now, the first draft of this piece might have been written then. As it was, the idea lay dormant for eleven years until, four years ago, I concluded that we in this country were in a leadership crisis and that I should do what I could about it. I became painfully aware of how dull my sense of contemporary prophecy had been. And I have reflected much on why we do not hear and heed the prophetic voices in our midst (not a new question in our times, nor more critical than heretofore).

I now embrace the theory of prophecy which holds that prophetic voices of great clarity, and with a quality of insight equal to that of any age, are speaking cogently all of the time. Men and women of a stature equal to the greatest of the past are with us now addressing the problems of the day and pointing to a better way and to a personeity better able to live fully and serenely in these times.

The variable that marks some periods as barren and some as rich in prophetic vision is in the interest, the level of seeking, the responsiveness of the hearers. The variable is not in the presence or absence or the relative quality and force of the prophetic voices. Prophets grow in stature as people respond to their message. If their early attempts are ignored or spurned, their talent may wither away.

It is *seekers*, then, who make prophets, and the initiative of any one of us in searching for and responding to the voice of contemporary prophets may mark the turning point in their growth and service. But since we are the product of our own history, we see current prophecy within the context of past wisdom. We listen to as wide a range of contemporary thought as we can attend to. Then we *choose* those we elect to heed as prophets—*both old and new*—and meld their advice with our own leadings. This we test in real-life experiences to establish our own position.

Some who have difficulty with this theory assert that their faith rest on one or more of the prophets of old having giving the "word" for all time and that the contemporary ones do not speak to their condition as the older ones do. But if one really believes that the "word" has been given for all time, how can one be a seeker? How can one hear the contemporary voice when one has decided not to live in the present and has turned that voice off?

Neither this hypothesis nor its opposite can be proved. But I submit that the one given here is the more hopeful choice, one that offers a significant role in prophecy to every individual. One cannot interact with and build strength in a dead prophet, but one can do it with a living one. "Faith," Dean Inge has said, "is the choice of the nobler hypothesis."

One does not, of course, ignore the great voices of the past. One does not awaken each morning with the compulsion to reinvent the wheel. But if one is *servant*, either leader or follower, one is always searching, listening, expecting that a better wheel for these times is in the making. It may emerge any day. Any one of us may find it out from personal experience. I am hopeful.

I am hopeful for these times, despite the tension and conflict, because more natural servants are trying to see clearly the world as it is and are listening carefully to prophetic voices that are speaking *now*. They are challenging the pervasive injustice with greater force and they are taking sharper issue with the wide disparity between the quality of society they know is reasonable and possible with available resources, and, on the other hand, the actual performance of the whole range of institutions that exist to serve society.

A fresh critical look is being taken at the issues of power and authority, and people are beginning to learn, however haltingly, to relate to one another in less coercive and more creatively supporting ways. A new moral principle is emerging which holds that the only authority deserving one's allegiance is that which is freely and knowingly granted by the led to the leader in response to, and in proportion to, the clearly evident servant stature of the leader. Those who choose to follow this principle will not casually accept the authority of existing institutions. *Rather, they will freely respond only to individuals who are chosen as leaders because they are proven and trusted as servants.* To the extent that this principle prevails in the future, the only truly viable institutions will be those that are predominantly servant-led.

I am mindful of the long road ahead before these trends, which I see so clearly, become a major society-shaping force. We are not there yet. But I see encouraging movement on the horizon.

What direction will the movement take? Much depends on whether those who stir the ferment will come to grips with the age-old problem of how to live in a human society. I say this because so many, having made their awesome decision for autonomy and independence from tradition, and having taken their firm stand against injustice and hypocrisy, find it hard to convert themselves into *affirmative builders* of a better society. How many of them will seek their personal fulfillment by making the hard choices, and by undertaking the rigorous preparation that building a better society requires? It all depends on what kind of leaders emerge and how they—we—respond to them.

My thesis, that more servants should emerge as leaders, or should follow only servant-leaders, is not a popular one. It is much more comfortable to go with a less demanding point of view about what is expected of one now. There are several undemanding, plausibly-argued alternatives to choose. One, since society seems corrupt, is to seek to avoid the center of it by retreating to an idyllic existence that minimizes involvement with the "system" (with the "system" that makes such withdrawal possible). Then there is the assumption that since the effort to reform existing institutions has not brought instant perfection, the remedy is to destroy them completely so that fresh new perfect ones can grow. Not much thought seems to be given to the problem of where the new seed will come from or who the gardener to tend them will be. The concept of the servant-leader stands in sharp contrast to this kind of thinking.

Yet it is understandable that the easier alternatives would be chosen, especially by young people. By extending education for so many so far into the adult normal participation in society is effectively denied when young people are ready for it. With education that is preponderantly abstract and analytical it is no wonder that there is a preoccupation with criticism and that not much thought is given to "What can *I* do about it?"

Criticism has its place, but as a total preoccupation it is sterile. In a time of crisis, like the leadership crisis we are now in, if too many potential builders are taken in by a complete absorption with dissecting the wrong and by a zeal for instant perfection, then the movement so many of us want to see will be set back. The danger, perhaps, is to hear the analyst too much and the artist too little.

Albert Camus stands apart from other great artists of his time, in my view, and deserves the title of *prophet,* because of his unrelenting demand that each of us confront the exacting terms of our own existence, and, like Sisyphus, *accept our rock and find our happiness in dealing with it.* Camus sums up the relevance, of his position to our concern for the servant as leader in the last paragraph of his last published lecture, entitled *Create Dangerously:*

> One may long, as I do, for a gentler flame, a respite, a pause for musing. But perhaps there is no other peace for the artist than what he finds in the heat of combat. "Every wall is a door," Emerson correctly said. Let us not look for the door, and the way out, anywhere but in the wall against which we are living. Instead, let us seek the respite where it is—in the very thick of battle. For in my opinion, and this is where I shall close, it is there. Great ideas, it has been said, come into the world as gently as doves. Perhaps, then, if we listen attentively, we shall hear, amid the uproar of empires and nations, a faint flutter of wings, the gentle stirring of life and hope. Some will say that this hope lies in a nation, others, in a man. I believe rather that it is awakened, revived, nourished by millions of solitary individuals whose deeds and works every day negate frontiers and the crudest implications of history. As a result, there shines forth fleetingly the ever-threatened truth that each and every man, on the foundations of his own sufferings and joys, builds for them all.

One is asked, then, to accept the human condition, its sufferings and its joys, and to work with its imperfections as the foundation upon which the individual will build wholeness through adventurous creative achievement. For the person with creative potential there is no wholeness except in using it. And, as Camus explained, the going is rough and the respite is brief. It is significant that he would title his last university lecture *Create Dangerously.* And, as I ponder the fusing of servant and leader, it seems a dangerous creation: dangerous for the natural servant to become a leader, dangerous for the leader to be servant first, and dangerous for a follower to insist on being led by a servant. There are safer and easier alternatives available to all three. But why take them?

As I respond to the challenge of dealing with this question in the ensuing discourse I am faced with two problems.

First, I did not get the notion of the servant as leader from conscious logic. Rather it came to me as an intuitive insight as I contemplated Leo. And I do not see what is relevant from my own searching and experience in terms of a logical progression from premise to conclusion. Rather I see it as fragments of data to be fed into my internal computer from which intuitive insights come. Serving and leading are still mostly intuition-based concepts in my thinking.

The second problem, and related to the first, is that, just as there may be a real contradiction in the servant as leader, so my perceptual world is full of contradictions. Some examples: I believe in order, and I want creation out of chaos. My good society will have strong individualism amidst community. It will have elitism along with populism. I listen to the old and to the young and find myself baffled and heartened by both. Reason and intuition, each in its own way, both comfort and dismay me. There are many more. Yet, with all of this, I believe that I live with as much serenity as do my contemporaries who ventures into controversy as freely as I do but whose natural bent is to tie up the essentials of life in neat bundles of logic and consistency. But I am deeply grateful to the people who are logical and consistent because some of them, out of their natures, render invaluable services for which I am not capable.

My resolution of these two problems is to offer the relevant gleanings of my experience in the form of a series of unconnected little essays, some developed more fully than others, with the suggestion that they be read and pondered on separately within the context of this opening section.

Who Is the Servant-Leader?

The servant-leader *is* servant first—as Leo was portrayed. It begins with the natural feeling that one wants to serve, to serve *first*. Then conscious choice brings one to aspire to lead. That person is sharply different from one who is *leader* first, perhaps because of the need to assuage an unusual power drive or to acquire material possessions. For such it will be a later choice to serve— after leadership is established. The leader-first and the servant-first are two extreme types. Between them there are shadings and blends that are part of the infinite variety of human nature.

The difference manifests itself in the care taken by the servant-first to make sure that other people's highest priority needs are being served. The best test, and difficult to administer, is: Do those served grow as persons? Do they, *while being served,* become healthier, wiser, freer, more autonomous, more likely themselves to become servants? *and,* what is the effect on the least privileged in society; will they benefit, or, at least, not be further deprived?

As one sets out to serve, how can one know that this will be the result? This is part of the human dilemma; one cannot know for sure. One must, after some study and experience, hypothesize—but leave the hypothesis under a shadow of doubt. Then one acts on the hypothesis and examines the result. One continues to study and learn and periodically one re-examines the hypothesis itself.

Finally, one chooses again. Perhaps one chooses the same hypothesis again and again. But it is always a fresh open choice. And it is always an hypothesis under a shadow of doubt. "Faith is the choice of the nobler hypothesis." Not the *noblest;* one never knows what that is. But the *nobler,* the best one can see when the choice is made. Since the test of results of one's actions is usually long delayed, the faith that sustains the choice of the nobler hypothesis is psychological self-insight. This is the most dependable part of the true servant.

The natural servant, the person who is *servant first,* is more likely to persevere and refine a particular hypothesis on what serves another's highest priority needs than is the person who is *leader first* and who later serves out of promptings of conscience or in conformity with normative expectations.

My hope for the future rests in part on my belief that among the legions of deprived and unsophisticated people are many true servants who will lead, and that most of them can learn to discriminate among those who presume to serve them and identify the true servants whom they will follow.

Everything Begins with the Initiative of an Individual

The forces for good and evil in the world are propelled by the thoughts, attitudes, and actions of individual beings. What happens to our values, and therefore to the quality of our civilization in the future, will be shaped by the conceptions of individuals that are born of inspiration. Perhaps only a few will receive this inspiration (insight) and the rest will learn from them. The very essence of leadership, going out ahead to show the way, derives from more than usual openness to inspiration. Why would anybody accept the leadership of another except that the other sees more clearly where it is best to go? Perhaps this is the current problem: too many who presume to lead do not see more clearly and, in defense of their inadequacy, they all the more strongly argue that the "system" must be preserved—a fatal error in this day of candor.

But the leader needs more than inspiration. A leader ventures to say: "I will go; come with me!" A leader initiates, provides the ideas and the structure, and takes the risk of failure along with the chance of success. A leader says: "I will go; follow me!" while knowing that the path is uncertain, even dangerous. One then trusts those who go with one's leadership.

Paul Goodman, speaking through a character in *Making Do,* has said, "If there is no community for you, young man, young man, make it yourself."

What Are You Trying to Do?

"What are you trying to do?" is one of the easiest to ask and most difficult to answer of questions.

A mark of leaders, an attribute that puts them in a position to show the way for others, is that they are better than most at pointing the direction. As long as one is leading, one always has a goal. It may be a goal arrived at by group consensus, or the leader, acting on inspiration, may simply have said, "Let's go this way." But the leader always knows what it is and can articulate it for any who are unsure. By clearly stating and restating the goal the leader gives certainty and purpose to others who may have difficulty in achieving it for themselves.

The word *goal* is used here in the special sense of the overarching purpose, the big dream, the visionary concept, the ultimate consummation which one approaches but never really achieves. It is something presently out of reach; it is something to strive for, to move toward, or become. It is so stated that it excites the imagination and challenges people to work for something they do not yet know how to do, something they can be proud of as they move toward it.

Every achievement starts with a goal—but not just any goal and not just anybody stating it. The one who states the goal must elicit trust, especially if it is a high risk or visionary goal, because those who follow are asked to accept the risk along with the leader. Leaders do not elicit trust unless one has confidence in their values and competence (including judgment) and unless they have a sustaining spirit (entheos) that will support the tenacious pursuit of a goal.

Not much happens without a dream. And for something great to happen, there must be a great dream. Behind every great achievement is a dreamer of great dreams. Much more than a dreamer is required to bring it to reality; but the dream must be there first.

REVIEW QUESTIONS

1. Why does a leader have to be a servant first?
2. Do you think this notion of leadership is practical?
3. Are most people capable of being a servant leader?
4. Are there any potential moral problems with this kind of leadership?
5. What kind of power does a servant leader have?

The Structure of Moral Leadership

James MacGregor Burns

James MacGregor Burns is a political scientist at Williams College. Burns's book *Leadership* is a multidisciplinary approach to the study of leadership. Like servant leadership, his theory of transforming leadership is a normative theory that describes the leader/follower relationship in terms of shared values. Burns believes that leaders should help followers operate at a higher level of moral development and that followers should do the same for their leaders. This sec-

Pages 36–43 from *Leadership* by James MacGregor Burns. Copyright © 1978 by James MacGregor Burns. Reprinted by permission of HarperCollins Publishers Inc.

220 CHAPTER 5

ond part of the equation is sometimes missing in charismatic leadership. However, according to Burns, one of the essential tasks of a leader is to raise followers' consciousness about what is and ought to be important to them. According to Burns, a transforming leader engages followers in a discussion of values and uses conflict to build consensus and a better understanding of values and common goals. Burns says there are two types of values, *modal* values or values related to the means of doing something, such as due process, and *end* values, such as justice and equality. Transforming leadership elevates people to their values or helps them to become conscious of them. Ideally, a transforming leader, like a servant leader, will make his or her followers into leaders.

In the leadership literature of the 1980s and early 1990s. Burns's theory was almost synonymous with the idea of ethical leadership. This was in part because ethics was rarely mentioned in the literature and most research was on the psychological, social, and political aspects of leadership.

Leadership is a process of morality to the degree that leaders engage with followers on the basis of shared motives and values and goals—on the basis, that is, of the followers' "true" needs as well as those of leaders: psychological, economic, safety, spiritual, sexual, aesthetic, or physical. Friends, relatives, teachers, officials, politicians, ministers, and others will supply a variety of initiatives, but only the followers themselves can ultimately define their own true needs. And they can do so only when they have been exposed to the competing diagnoses, claims, and values of would-be leaders, only when the followers can make an informed choice among competing "prescriptions," only when—in the political arena at least—followers have had full opportunity to perceive, comprehend, evaluate, and finally experience alternatives offered by those professing to be their "true" representatives. Ultimately the moral legitimacy of transformational leadership, and to a lesser degree transactional leadership, is grounded in *conscious choice among real alternatives.* Hence leadership assumes competition and conflict, and brute power denies it.

Conflict has become the stepchild of political thought. Philosophical concern with conflict reaches back to Hobbes and even Heraclitus, and men who spurred revolutions in Western thought—Machiavelli and Hegel, Marx and Freud—recognized the vital role of conflict in the relations among persons or in the ambivalences within them. The seventeenth-century foes of absolute monarchy, the eighteenth-century Scottish moralists, the nineteenth-century Social Darwinists—these and other schools of thought dealt directly with questions of power and conflict, and indirectly at least with the nature of leadership. The theories of Pareto, Durkheim, Weber, and others, while not centrally concerned with problems of social conflict, "contain many concepts, assumptions, and hypotheses which greatly influenced later writers who did attempt to deal with conflict in general." Georg Simmel and others carried theories of conflict into the twentieth century.

It was, curiously, in this same century—an epoch of the bloodiest world wars, mightiest revolutions, and most savage civil wars—that social science, at least in the West, became *most entranced with doctrines of harmony, adjustment, and stability.* Perhaps this was the result of relative affluence, or of the need to unify people to conduct total war or consolidate revolutions, or of the co-option of scholars to advise on mitigating hostility among interest groups such as labor and management or racial groups such as blacks and whites. Whatever the cause, the "static bias" afflicted scholarly research with a tendency to look on conflict as an aberration, if not a perversion, of the agreeable and harmonious interactions that were seen as actually making up organized society. More recently Western scholarship has shown a quickened interest in the role of conflict in establishing boundaries, channeling hostility, counteracting social ossification, invigorating class and group interests, encouraging innovation, and defining and empowering leadership.

The static bias among scholars doubtless encouraged and reflected the pronouncements of political authority. Communist leaders apotheosized conflict as the engine of the process of overthrowing bourgeois regimes and then banned both the profession and the utilization of conflict in the new "classless" societies. Western leaders, especially in the United States, make a virtual fetish of "national unity," "party harmony," and foreign policy bipartisanship even while they indulge in—and virtually live off—contested elections and divisive policy issues. Jefferson proclaimed at his first Inaugural, "We are all Federalists, we are all Republicans." Few American presidents have aroused and inflamed popular attitudes as divisively as Franklin D. Roosevelt with his assaults on conservatives in both parties, his New Deal innovations, and his efforts to pack the Supreme Court and purge the Democratic party, yet few American presidents have devoted so many addresses to sermonlike calls for transcending differences and behaving as one nation and one people.

The potential for conflict permeates the relations of humankind, and that potential is a force for health and growth as well as for destruction and barbarism. No group can be wholly harmonious, as Simmel said, for such a group would be empty of process and structure. The smooth interaction of people is continually threatened by disparate rates of change, technological innovation, mass deprivation, competition for scarce resources, and other ineluctable social forces and by ambivalences, tensions, and conflicts within individuals' personalities. One can imagine a society—in ancient Egypt, perhaps, or in an isolated rural area today—in which the division of labor, the barriers against external influence, the structure of the family, the organization of the value system, the acceptance of authority, and the decision-making by leaders all interact smoothly and amiably with one another. But the vision of such a society would be useful only as an imaginary construct at one end of a continuum from cohesion to conflict. Indeed, the closer, the more intimate the relations within a group, the more hostility as well as harmony may be generated. The smaller the cooperative group—even if united by language and thrown closely together by living arrangements—"the easier it is for them to be mutually irritated and to flare up in anger," Bronislaw Malinowski said. Some conflict over valued goals and objects is almost inevitable. Even small, isolated societies cannot indefinitely dike off the impact of internal changes such as alteration of the birth rate or the disruption caused by various forms of innovation.

The question, then, is not the inevitability of conflict but the function of leadership in expressing, shaping, and curbing it. Leadership as conceptualized here is grounded in the seedbed of conflict. Conflict is intrinsically compelling: it galvanizes, prods, motivates people. Every person, group, and society has latent tension and hostility, forming a variety of psychological and political patterns across social situations. Leadership acts as an inciting and triggering force in the conversion of conflicting demands, values, and goals into significant behavior. Since leaders have an interest of their own, whether opportunistic or ideological or both, in expressing and exploiting followers' wants, needs, and aspirations, they act as catalytic agents in arousing followers' consciousness. They discern signs of dissatisfaction, deprivation, and strain; they take the initiative in making connections with their followers; they plumb the character and intensity of their potential for mobilization; they articulate grievances and wants; and they act for followers in their dealings with other clusters of followers.

Conflicts vary in origin—in and between nations, races, regions, religions, economic enterprises, labor unions, communities, kinship groups, families, and individuals themselves. Conflicts show various degrees and qualities of persistence, direction, intensity, volatility, latency, scope. The last alone may be pivotal; the outcome of every conflict, E. E. Schattschneider wrote, "is determined by the *scope* of its contagion. The number of people involved in any conflict determines what happens; every change in the number of participants . . . affects the results. . . . The moral of this is: If a fight starts, watch the crowd, because the crowd plays the decisive role." But it is leadership that draws the crowd into the incident, that changes the number of participants, that closely affects the manner of the spread of the conflict, that constitutes the main "processes" of relating the wider public to the conflict.

The root causes of conflict are as varied as their origins. No one has described these causes as cogently as James Madison.

> The latent causes of faction are thus sown in the nature of man; and we see them every where brought into different degrees of activity, according to the different circumstances of civil society. A zeal for different opinions concerning religion, concerning government and many other points, as well of speculation as of practice; an attachment to different leaders ambitiously contending for pre-eminence and power; or to persons of other descriptions whose fortunes have been interesting to the human passions, have in turn divided mankind into parties, inflamed them with mutual animosity, and rendered them much more disposed to vex and oppress each other, than to co-operate for their common good. So strong is this propensity of mankind to fall into mutual animosities, that where no substantial occasion presents itself, the most frivolous and fanciful distinctions have been sufficient to kindle their

unfriendly passions, and excite their most violent conflicts. But the most common and durable source of factions, has been the various and unequal distribution of property.

Not only "attachment to different leaders" but all these forces for conflict are expressed and channeled through many different types of leaders "ambitiously contending for pre-eminence and power."

Leaders, whatever their professions of harmony, do not shun conflict; they confront it, exploit it, ultimately embody it. Standing at the points of contact among latent conflict groups, they can take various roles, sometimes acting directly for their followers, sometimes bargaining with others, sometimes overriding certain motives of followers and summoning others into play. The smaller and more homogeneous the group for which they act, the more probable that they will have to deal with the leaders of other groups with opposing needs and values. The larger, more heterogeneous their collection of followers, the more probable that they will have to embrace competing interests and goals within their constituency. At the same time, their marginality supplies them with a double leverage, since in their status as leaders they are expected by their followers and by other leaders to deviate, to innovate, and to mediate between the claims of their groups and those of others.

But leaders shape as well as express and mediate conflict. They do this largely by influencing the intensity and scope of conflict. Within limits they can soften or sharpen the claims and demands of their followers, as they calculate their own political resources in dealing with competing leaders within their own constituencies and outside. They can amplify the voice and pressure of their followers, to the benefit of their bargaining power perhaps, but at the possible price of freedom to maneuver—less freedom to protect themselves against their followers—as they play in games of broader stakes. Similarly, they can narrow or broaden the scope of conflict as they seek to limit or multiply the number of entrants into a specific political arena.

Franklin Roosevelt demonstrated the fine art of controlling entry in the presidential nomination race in 1940. There was widespread uncertainty as to whether he would run for a third term. He himself was following the development of public opinion at the same time that he was influencing it. Leaders in his own party were divided; onetime stalwarts like James A. Farley and Cordell Hull opposed a third term. It was supposed that FDR would discourage Democrats from entering the nomination race. On the contrary, he welcomed them. Secondary figures like Joseph Kennedy, coming to the Oval Office to sound out Roosevelt on his intentions and on their own chances, found themselves flattered and rated as serious and deserving possibilities. The effect was to broaden the field of possible adversaries and hence divide and weaken the opposition. FDR had little trouble winning the nomination.

The essential strategy of leadership in mobilizing power is to recognize the arrays of motives and goals in potential followers, to appeal to those motives by words and action, and to strengthen those motives and goals in order to increase the power of leadership, thereby changing the environment within which both followers and leaders act. Conflict—disagreement over goals within an array of followers, fear of outsiders, competition for scarce resources—immensely invigorates the mobilization of consensus and dissensus. But the fundamental process is a more elusive one; it is, in large part, *to make conscious what lies unconscious among followers.*

The purposeful awakening of persons into a state of political consciousness is a familiar problem for philosophers and psychologists and one that has stimulated thought in other disciplines. For the student of leadership the concept of political consciousness is as primitive as it is fertile. That "conflict produces consciousness" was fundamental in the doctrine of Hegel, Marx, and other nineteenth-century theorists, but they differed over the cardinal question: consciousness of *what?* They recognized the essential human needs but differed as to the nature of those needs. Feuerbach, an intellectual leader of the young Marx, conceived humanity as imbued with real, tangible, solid needs arising from Nature. Marx compared human consciousness with that of animals, which had no consciousness of the world as something objective and real apart from the animal's own existence and needs. But *human* labor, rather than leading to direct satisfaction of need, generates human consciousness and self-consciousness. Thus the early Marx had some understanding of the variety and inexhaustibility of human needs.

It was a marvelous insight, but Marx came to be identified with the doctrine that *true* consciousness, to be achieved through unremitting conflict, was always of *class.* Felt, palpable human needs, however, did not seem to be translated into a rising class consciousness in the capitalist environment of the mid-nineteenth century. Marx and Engels railed at the "false consciousness" of religion and nationalism and the other diversions and superficialities that seemed to engage men who were caught in the iron grip of material deprivation. The progress toward class consciousness was slow, irregular, uneven. The almost automatic movement toward revolution, emerging out of the "spontaneous class-organization of the proletariat," simply did not come about in the great bourgeois societies; ultimately revolution would need to be spurred by militant leadership and iron party discipline.

In the fiery intellectual and political conflict of the nineteenth century both Marxists and their adversaries assumed too much about the central springs of human behavior without knowing enough about motivation or the complex relations between motives and behavior. Few perceived that if people did not behave the way they were supposed to, the fault might lie in the suppositions rather than in the people. One of the suppositions was that ultimately humans would respond rationally and "realistically" to "objective" social conditions. But what was real and rational? If Marx had turned Hegel's dialectic of ideas on its head, Freud turned Marx's Consciousness upside down. Freud was drawn to the function of the unconscious rather than the conscious or the preconscious; for him the unconscious was the "true psychic reality," betrayed by dreams, fantasies, accidents, and curious slips of the tongue. Consciousness and related concepts of alienation and identity have continued to be variously defined and heatedly debated. During the ferment of the 1960s that reached across the Western world, young people were urged to "expand consciousness" and "consciousness-raising" became something of a fad and a profession.

If the first task of leadership is to bring to consciousness the followers' sense of their own needs, values, and purposes, the question remains: consciousness of what? Which of these motives and goals are to be tapped? Leaders, for example, can make followers more conscious of aspects of their *identity* (sexual, communal, ethnic, class, national, ideological). Georges Sorel argued that only through leadership and conflict, including "terrifying violence," could the working class become conscious of its true identity—and hence of its power. But to what extent was Sorel imposing his own values and goals on workers who might have very different, even idiosyncratic, ones? We return to the dilemma: to what degree do leaders, through their command of personal influence, substitute their own motives and goals for those of the followers? Should they whip up chauvinism, feelings of ethnic superiority, regional prejudice, economic rivalry? What must they accept among followers as being durable and valid rather than false and transient? And we return to the surmise here: leaders with relevant motives and goals of their own respond to followers' needs and wants and goals in such a way as to meet those motivations and to bring changes consonant with those of both leaders and followers, and with the values of both.

The Elevating Power of Leadership

Mobilized and shaped by gifted leadership, sharpened and strengthened by conflict, values can be the source of vital change. The question is: at what level of need or stage of morality do leaders operate to elevate their followers? At levels of safety and security, followers tend to conform to group expectations and to support and justify the social order. At a certain stage Kohlberg finds a "law and order" orientation toward authority, fixed rules, and maintenance of the social order for its own sake. At a higher stage Simpson found a significant relation between tendencies toward self-esteem and positive law values (belief that the authority for judgments rests in the laws and norms humans have developed collectively). This is the level of "social contract morality."

At the highest stage of moral development persons are guided by near-universal ethical principles of justice such as equality of human rights and respect for individual dignity. This stage sets the opportunity for rare and creative leadership. Politicians who operate at the lower and middle levels of need and moral development are easily understood, but what kind of leadership reaches into the need and value structures, mobilizing and directing support for such values as justice and empathy?

First, it is the kind of leadership that *operates at need and value levels higher than those of the potential follower* (but not so much higher as to lose contact). This kind of leadership need be neither doctrinaire nor indoctrinative (in the ordinary sense of preaching). In its most effective form it appeals to the higher, more general and comprehensive values that express followers' more fundamental and enduring needs. The appeal may be more potent when a polity faces danger from outside, as from an invasion, or from inside, as in social breakdown, civil war, or natural catastrophe. "If inefficiencies and corruption of governmental and social leadership go beyond 'normal,' if demands are constantly frustrated by incapacities, which can be readily laid at some human door, if all of this is compounded by a rising consciousness of discrimination and sense of justice," according to a four-nation study, "then people can experience great and often very sudden transformation of values, or those values that were subdued can become the basis for vigorous action." No single force, such as economic conditions, predetermines change, this study concluded; other factors—notably the quality of leadership—intervene, so the role of values in social change varies from culture to culture. Among the nations studied (India, Poland, the United States, Yugoslavia) similarities were found in leaders' espousal of innovative change, economic development, and the norms of selflessness (commitment to the general welfare) and honesty.

Second, it is the kind of leadership that *can exploit conflict and tension within persons' value structures.* Contradictions can be expected among competing substantive values, such as liberty and equality, or between those values and moral values like honesty, or between terminal values and instrumental values. "All contemporary theories in social psychology would probably agree that a necessary prerequisite to cognitive change is the presence of some state of imbalance within the system," Rokeach says.

Leaders may simply help a follower see these types of contradictions, or they might actively arouse a sense of dissatisfaction by making the followers aware of contradictions in or inconsistencies between values and behavior. The more contradictions challenge self-conceptions, according to Rokeach, the more dissatisfaction will be aroused. And such dissatisfactions are the source of changes that the leader can influence. There is an implication in Rokeach that the contradictions in themselves cause change, simply on the basis of self-cognition. Typically, however, an outside influence is required in the form of a leader, preferably "one step above." Rokeach bases much of his analysis on experimental situations in which the subjects are exposed to close direction and restraint—certainly a context of manipulation if not of leadership. Autonomous cognition usually is not enough to enable persons to break out of their imprisoning value structures. Experimenters may assume a leadership role.

Given the right conditions of value conflict, leaders hold enhanced influence at the higher levels of the need and value hierarchies. They can appeal to the more widely and deeply held values, such as justice, liberty, and brotherhood. They can expose followers to the broader values that contradict narrower ones or inconsistent behavior. They can redefine aspirations and gratifications to help followers see their stake in new, program-oriented social movements. Most important, they can gratify lower needs so that higher motivations will arise to elevate the conscience of men and women. To be sure, leadership may be frustrated and weakened at the higher levels as well as the lower. Potential support may thin out when immediate parochial needs and values threaten to weaken higher, more general ones. Substantive values, such as liberty or equality, may compete with one another, and, however logically compelling the leader's value priorities may look, they may not co-exist so harmoniously in the political arena. Perhaps the most disruptive force in competitive politics is conflict between *modal values* such as fair play and due process and *end-values* such as equality. Roosevelt's court-packing plan, with its use of dubious means to attain high ends, is a case in point. Some of those believing in equal opportunity today may also believe in certain modes of conduct—endless debate, for example, or elaborate procedures for judicial review—that make the attainment of equal opportunity far less certain.

The potential for influence through leadership is usually immense. The essence of leadership in any polity is the recognition of real need, the uncovering and exploiting of contradictions among values and between values and practice, the realigning of values, the reorganization of institutions where necessary, and the governance of change. Essentially the leader's task is consciousness-raising.

By the same token, Weber's ethic of ultimate ends emphasizes the demands of an overriding, millenarian kind of value system at the expense of the far more typical situation (at least in pluralistic societies) in which choices must be made among a number of compelling end-values, modal values, and instrumental values. And the ethic of responsibility could rather be seen as the day-to-day measured application of the "ethic of ultimate ends" to complex circumstance.

For the study of leadership, the dichotomy is not between Weber's two ethics but between the leader's commitment to a number of overriding, general welfare-oriented values on the one hand and his encouragement of, and entanglement in, a host of lesser values and "responsibilities" on the other. The four-nation study notes the "most important motivational distinction among leaders desiring change—the distinction between those who see progress primarily in terms of political opportunity and those who nurse a feeling of social injustice arising out of the gap between the economically deprived and the privileged," even though no consistent relationship seemed to explain it. The great bulk of leadership activity consists of the day-to-day interaction of leaders and followers characterized by the processes described above. But the ultimate test of moral leadership is its capacity to transcend the claims of the multiplicity of everyday wants and needs and expectations, to respond to the higher levels of moral development, and to relate leadership behavior—its roles, choices, style, commitments—to a set of reasoned, relatively explicit, conscious values.

REVIEW QUESTIONS

1. How is transforming leadership different from servant leadership and charismatic leadership?
2. After reading Burns's description, how would you feel about working for a transforming leader?
3. What does Burns mean when he says the transforming leader operates at a higher need and value level?
4. Where does Burns's distinction between modal values and end values fit in terms of the other ethical theories discussed earlier in the text?

CHAPTER 6

MORAL LEADERSHIP AND CULTURE

INTRODUCTION

Leadership is a social construction shaped by the moral values and the cultural practices and beliefs of a society. Societies have different ideas on leadership and morality. Hence, the idea of a *good* leader may differ from place to place. If every culture has different notions of leadership and morality, then we are left with a number of problems. First, is it possible to understand another culture's values? Second, is it possible to make judgments about another culture's moral values and cultural practices? In an interdependent world where societies and organizations are composed of people from diverse backgrounds, it is important to respect other cultures, but it is also necessary to make choices and judgments about which values and what kinds of leadership are better.

At the beginning of the twentieth century anthropologists were discovering isolated groups of people who had not been exposed to the modern world. Because these people were so radically different from them, many anthropologists were careful not to make moral judgments about their behavior. As Ruth Benedict observes in her article, morality and normality are not fundamental to all human beings. Societies determine who is normal and who is not. The belief that there are no universal human norms and values and all ethical principles are relative to a culture is called cultural relativism. Based on descriptions of cultures, the cultural relativist argues if cultures vary, acculturation processes vary, and most people are ethnocentric, then their moral values will be different. The cultural relativist's position can lead to the moral relativist's position, which is that there are no universal moral values, and because there are no universal moral values, we cannot make judgments about other cultures. Philosopher Mary Midgley disagrees with both the moral and cultural relativists' position. She argues that by accepting the relativist's position, we in effect isolate ourselves from moral discourse with people in other cultures and that this sort of isolation is untenable in today's world.

F. G. Bailey offers a different perspective on ethics and culture. Bailey, who is also an anthropologist, says cultures do not have one set of agreed-upon values. Every culture has contradictory values and beliefs, and leaders pick and choose the ones that serve them best. Because of this, Bailey thinks that most leaders are "skilled manipulators" of the values they think best suit their purposes.

The relativist debate rests on tolerance, respect for cultural traditions, and respect for national sovereignty (even though some believe that the era of the nation-state is over). In recent years leaders from business, politics, and non-governmental organizations increasingly find themselves making moral judgments and intervening on matters that interfere with cultural practices. Controversies over things like female circumcision are debates about the morality of a traditional cultural practice. Those who are against it argue that it violates a universal human right that is more important than a cultural norm or custom.

The case "Diller's Dilemma" presents us with a different cultural issue. In this case the social problems of a country and the way the government wants to solve those problems conflict with the way a foreign company would prefer to solve the problem. Like most cross-cultural ethical problems, the conflict is between local norms and what some believe are universal moral principles.

The United Nations' "Universal Declaration of Human Rights" is arguably the most important international attempt to articulate human values that transcend culture. It was adopted by the general assembly of the United Nations in 1948. The document proclaims the inalienable right of all humans to freedom, justice, and peace. In contrast to Benedict's article, this document asserts that there are universal moral principles that apply to people in all cultures, including the right to cultural identity.

The "Oil Rig" case raises some important questions about the moral obligations that a foreign company has to people with different cultural values and expectations. It is interesting how when people work in other cultures, the golden rule sometimes breaks down. Ethical relativism is not simply the "When in Rome do as the Romans do" question, but would the Romans want to be treated as I would. In his essay, Isaiah Berlin tells us that "by force of imaginative insight" members of different cultures can understand each other and how they would like to be treated. Values between cultures and within cultures may clash, but Berlin argues that there are objective values, such as liberty and equality, that people everywhere value for their own sake.

Our last case study in this text is an interview with Kofi Annan, the General Secretary of the United Nations. Annan is a global leader, who understands his role as a moral leader. The jury of history is still out on how effective Annan is as head of the United Nations, but few today would deny that he possesses moral virtues or qualities of character that are recognizable in any culture. This article is included because sometimes a person helps us understand how a leader practices universal moral values better than all of the theories in leadership and ethics combined.

In an era of globalization and mass immigration, these moral questions are the most basic and difficult questions that leaders from all sectors face. As you read this chapter, keep the following questions in mind. *Are there ways of leading that would be acceptable in other cultures? What criteria would you use to judge the moral quality of leadership in your culture and other cultures? Why is it important to be able to judge the morality of various practices in other cultures?*

Anthropology and the Abnormal

Ruth Fulton Benedict, 1887–1948

Ruth Fulton Benedict was an anthropologist who was born in New York City. She studied at Vassar College and Columbia University. In 1923 she joined the faculty of Columbia University. Benedict did fieldwork on Native American groups between 1922 and 1939. She is considered an authority on the ethnology of Native Americans, but is also well known for her work in cultural anthropology. In this reading Benedict argues that culture determines what is normal and good behavior. Morality is nothing more than what is habitual or conventional. On these grounds, Benedict concludes that culture forms a moral barrier between people.

Modern social anthropology has become more and more a study of the varieties and common elements of cultural environment and the consequences of these in human behavior. For such a study of diverse social orders primitive peoples fortunately provide a laboratory not yet entirely vitiated by the spread of a standardized worldwide civilization. Dyaks and Hopis, Fijians and Yakuts are significant for psychological and sociological study because only among these simpler peoples has there been sufficient isolation to give opportunity for the development of localized social forms. In the higher cultures the standardization of custom and belief over a couple of continents has given a false sense of the inevitability of the particular forms that have gained currency, and we need to turn to a wider survey in order to check the conclusions we hastily base upon this near-universality of familiar customs. Most of the simpler cultures did not gain the wide currency of the one which, out of our experience, we identify with human nature, but this was for various historical reasons, and certainly not for any that gives us as its carriers a monopoly of social good or of social sanity. Modern civilization, from this point

"Anthropology and the Abnormal," by Ruth Benedict in *Journal of General Psychology*, Vol. 10, pp. 59–73, 1934. Published by Heldref Publications, 1319 Eighteenth St., NW, Washington, DC 20036-1802. Copyright 1934.

of view, becomes not a necessary pinnacle of human achievement but one entry in a long series of possible adjustments.

These adjustments, whether they are in mannerisms like the ways of showing anger, or joy, or grief in any society, or in major human drives like those of sex, prove to be far more variable than experience in any one culture would suggest. In certain fields, such as that of religion or of formal marriage arrangements, these wide limits of variability are well known and can be fairly described. In others it is not yet possible to give a generalized account, but that does not absolve us of the task of indicating the significance of the work that has been done and of the problems that have arisen.

One of these problems relates to the customary modern normal-abnormal categories and our conclusions regarding them. In how far are such categories culturally determined, or in how far can we with assurance regard them as absolute? In how far can we regard inability to function socially as diagnostic of abnormality, or in how far is it necessary to regard this as a function of the culture?

As a matter of fact, one of the most striking facts that emerge from a study of widely varying cultures is the ease with which our abnormals function in other cultures. It does not matter what kind of "abnormality" we choose for illustration, those which indicate extreme instability, or those which are more in the nature of character traits like sadism or delusions of grandeur or of persecution, there are well-described cultures in which these abnormals function at ease and with honor, and apparently without danger or difficulty to the society.

The most spectacular illustrations of the extent to which normality may be culturally defined are those cultures where an abnormality of our culture is the cornerstone of their social structure. It is not possible to do justice to these possibilities in a short discussion. A recent study of an island of northwest Melanesia by Fortune (11) describes a society built upon traits which we regard as beyond the border of paranoia. In this tribe the exogamic groups look upon each other as prime manipulators of black magic, so that one marries always into an enemy group which remains for life one's deadly and unappeasable foes. They look upon a good garden crop as a confession of theft, for everyone is engaged in making magic to induce into his garden the productiveness of his neighbors'; therefore no secrecy in the island is so rigidly insisted upon as the secrecy of a man's harvesting of his yams. Their polite phrase at the acceptance of a gift is, "And if you now poison me, how shall I repay you this present?" Their preoccupation with poisoning is constant; no woman ever leaves her cooking pot for a moment untended. Even the great affinal economic exchanges that are characteristic of this Melanesian culture area are quite altered in Dobu since they are incompatible with this fear and distrust that pervades the culture. They go farther and people the whole world outside their own quarters with such malignant spirits that all-night feasts and ceremonials simply do not occur here. They have even rigorous religiously enforced customs that forbid the sharing of seed even in one family group. Anyone else's food is deadly poison to you, so that communality of stores is out of the question. For some months before harvest the whole society is on the verge of starvation, but if one falls to the temptation and eats up one's seed yams, one is an outcast and a beachcomber for life. There is no coming back. It involves, as a matter of course, divorce and the breaking of all social ties.

Now in this society where no one may work with another and no one may share with another, Fortune describes the individual who was regarded by all his fellows as crazy. He was not one of those who periodically ran amok and, beside himself and frothing at the mouth, fell with a knife upon anyone he could reach. Such behavior they did not regard as putting anyone outside the pale. They did not even put the individuals who were known to be liable to these attacks under any kind of control. They merely fled when they saw the attack coming on and kept out of the way. "He would be all right tomorrow." But there was one man of sunny, kindly disposition who liked work and liked to be helpful. The compulsion was too strong for him to repress it in favor of the opposite tendencies of his culture. Men and women never spoke of him without laughing; he was silly and simple and definitely crazy. Nevertheless, to the ethnologist used to a culture that has, in Christianity, made his type the model of all virtue, he seemed a pleasant fellow.

An even more extreme example, because it is of a culture that has built itself upon a more complex abnormality, is that of the North Pacific Coast of North America. The civilization of the Kwakiutl (1–5), at the time when it was first recorded in the last decades of the nineteenth century, was one of the most vigorous in North America. It was built up on an ample economic supply of goods, the fish which furnished their food staple being practically inexhaustible and obtainable with comparatively small labor, and the wood which furnished the material for their houses, their furnishings, and their arts being, with however much labor, always procurable. They lived in coastal villages that compared favorably in size with those of any other American Indians and they kept up constant communication by means of sea-going dug-out canoes.

It was one of the most vigorous and zestful of the aboriginal cultures of North America, with complex crafts and ceremonials, and elaborate and striking arts. It certainly had none of the earmarks of a sick civilization. The tribes of the Northwest Coast had wealth, and exactly in our terms. That is, they had not only a surplus of economic goods, but they made a game of the manipulation of wealth. It was by no means a mere direct transcription of economic needs and the filling of those needs. It involved the idea of capital, of interest, and of conspicuous waste. It was a game with all the binding rules of a game, and a person entered it as a child. His father distributed wealth for him, according to his ability, at a small feast or potlatch, and each gift the receiver was obliged to accept and to return after a short interval with interest that ran to about 100 per cent a year. By the time the child was grown, therefore, he was well launched, a larger potlatch had been given for him on various occasions of exploit or initiation, and he had wealth either out at usury or in his own possession. Nothing in the civilization could be enjoyed without validating it by the distribution of this wealth. Everything that was valued, names and songs as well as material objects, were passed down in family lines, but they were always publicly assumed with accompanying sufficient distributions of property. It was the game of validating and exercising all the privileges one could accumulate from one's various forbears, or by gift, or by marriage, that made the chief interest of the culture. Everyone in his degree took part in it, but many, of course, mainly as spectators. In its highest form it was played out between rival chiefs representing not only themselves and their family lines but their communities, and the object of the contest was to glorify oneself and to humiliate one's opponent. On this level of greatness the property involved was no longer represented by blankets, so many thousand of them to a potlatch, but by higher units of value. These higher units were like our bank notes. They were incised copper tablets, each of them named, and having a value that depended upon their illustrious history. This was as high as ten thousand blankets, and to possess one of them, still more to enhance its value at a great potlatch, was one of the greatest glories within the compass of the chiefs of the Northwest Coast.

The details of this manipulation of wealth are in many ways a parody on our own economic arrangements, but it is with the motivations that were recognized in this contest that we are concerned in this discussion. The drives were those which in our own culture we should call megalomaniac. There was an uncensored self-glorification and ridicule of the opponent that it is hard to equal in other cultures outside of the monologues of the abnormal. Any of the songs and speeches of their chiefs at a potlatch illustrate the usual tenor:

> Wa, out of the way. Wa, out of the way. Turn your faces that I may give way to my anger by striking my fellow chiefs.
>
> Wa, great potlatch, greatest potlatch.[1] The little ones[2] only pretend, the little stubborn ones, they only sell one copper again and again and give it away to the little chiefs of the tribe. Ah, do not ask in vain for mercy. Ah, do not ask in vain for mercy and raise your hands, you with lolling tongues! I shall break,[3] I shall let disappear the great copper that has the name Kentsegum, the property of the great foolish one, the great extravagant one, the great surpassing one, the one farthest ahead, the great Cannibal dancer among the chiefs.[4]
>
> I am the great chief who makes people ashamed.
> I am the great chief who makes people ashamed.
> Our chief brings shame to the faces.
> Our chief brings jealousy to the faces.
> Our chief makes people cover their faces by what he is continually doing in this world, from the beginning to the end of the year,
> Giving again and again oil feasts to the tribes.
> I am the great chief who vanquishes.
> I am the great chief who vanquishes.

Only at those who continue running round and round in this world, working hard, losing their tails,[5] I sneer, at the chiefs below the true chief.[6]

Have mercy on them![7] Put oil on their dry heads with brittle hair, those who do not comb their hair!

I sneer at the chiefs below the true, real chief. I am the great chief who makes people ashamed.

I am the only great tree, I the chief.

I am the only great tree, I the chief.

You are my subordinates, tribes.

You sit in the middle of the rear of the house, tribes.

Bring me your counter of property tribes, that he may in vain try to count what is going to be given away by the great copper-maker, the chief.

Oh, I laugh at them, I sneer at them who empty boxes[8] in their houses, their potlatch houses, their inviting houses that are full only of hunger. They follow along after me like young sawbill ducks, I am the only great tree, I the chief.

I have quoted a number of these hymns of self-glorification because by an association which psychiatrists will recognize as fundamental these delusions of grandeur were essential in the paranoid view of life which was so strikingly developed in this culture. All of existence was seen in terms of insult.[8a] Not only derogatory acts performed by a neighbor or an enemy, but all untoward events, like a cut when one's axe slipped, or a ducking when one's canoe overturned, were insults. All alike threatened first and foremost one's ego security, and the first thought one was allowed was how to get even, how to wipe out the insult. Grief was little institutionalized, but sulking took its place. Until he had resolved upon a course of action by which to save his face after any misfortune, whether it was the slipping of a wedge in felling a tree, or the death of a favorite child, an Indian of the Northwest Coast retired to his pallet with his face to the wall and neither ate nor spoke. He rose from it to follow out some course which according to the traditional rules should reinstate him in his own eyes and those of the community: to distribute property enough to wipe out the stain, or to go headhunting in order that somebody else should be made to mourn. His activities in neither case were specific responses to the bereavement he had just passed through, but were elaborately directed toward getting even. If he had not the money to distribute and did not succeed in killing someone to humiliate another, he might take his own life. He had staked everything, in his view of life, upon a certain picture of the self, and, when the bubble of his self-esteem was pricked, he had no interest, no occupation to fall back on, and the collapse of his inflated ego left him prostrate.

Every contingency of life was dealt with in these two traditional ways. To them the two were equivalent. Whether one fought with weapons or "fought with property," as they say, the same idea was at the bottom of both. In the olden times, they say, they fought with spears, but now they fight with property. One overcomes one's opponents in equivalent fashion in both, matching forces and seeing that one comes out ahead, and one can thumb one's nose at the vanquished rather more satisfactorily at a potlatch than on a battle field. Every occasion in life was noticed, not in its own terms, as a stage in the sex life of the individual or as a climax of joy or of grief, but as furthering this drama of consolidating one's own prestige and bringing shame to one's guests. Whether it was the occasion of the birth of a child, or a daughter's adolescence, or of the marriage of one's son, they were all equivalent raw material for the culture to use for this one traditionally selected end. They were all to raise one's own personal status and to entrench oneself by the humiliation of one's fellows. A girl's adolescence among the Nootka (16) was an event for which her father gathered property from the time she was first able to run about. When she was adolescent he would demonstrate his greatness by an unheard of distribution of these goods, and put down all his rivals. It was not as a fact of the girl's sex life that it figured in their culture, but as the occasion for a major move in the great game of vindicating one's own greatness and humiliating one's associates.

In their behavior at great bereavements this set of the culture comes out most strongly. Among the Kwakiutl it did not matter whether a relative had died in bed of disease, or by the hand of an enemy, in either case death was an affront to be wiped out by the death of another person. The fact that one had been caused to mourn was proof that one had been put upon. A chief's sister and her daughter had gone up to Victoria, and either because they drank bad whiskey or because their boat capsized they never came back. The chief called together his warriors. "Now I ask you, tribes, who shall wail? Shall I do it or shall another?" The spokesman answered, of course, "Not you, Chief. Let some other of the tribes." Immediately they set up the war pole to announce their intention of wiping out the injury, and gathered a war party. They set out, and found seven men and two children asleep and killed them. "Then they felt good when they arrived at Sebaa in the evening."

The point which is of interest to us is that in our society those who on that occasion would feel good when they arrived at Sebaa that evening would be the definitely abnormal. There would be some, even in our society, but it is not a recognized and approved mood under the circumstances. On the Northwest Coast those are favored and fortunate to whom that mood under those circumstances is congenial, and those to whom it is repugnant are unlucky. This latter minority can register in their own culture only by doing violence to their congenial responses and acquiring others that are difficult for them. The person, for instance, who, like a Plains Indian whose wife has been taken from him, is too proud to fight, can deal with the Northwest Coast civilization only by ignoring its strongest bents. If he cannot achieve it, he is the deviant in that culture, their instance of abnormality.

This head-hunting that takes place on the Northwest Coast after a death is no matter of blood revenge or of organized vengeance. There is no effort to tie up the subsequent killing with any responsibility on the part of the victim for the death of the person who is being mourned. A chief whose son has died goes visiting wherever his fancy dictates, and he says to his host, "My prince has died today, and you go with him." Then he kills him. In this, according to their interpretation, he acts nobly because he has not been downed. He has thrust back in return. The whole procedure is meaningless without the fundamental paranoid reading of bereavement. Death, like all the other untoward accidents of existence, confounds man's pride and can only be handled in the category of insults.

Behavior honored upon the Northwest Coast is one which is recognized as abnormal in our civilization, and yet it is sufficiently close to the attitudes of our own culture to be intelligible to us and to have a definite vocabulary with which we may discuss it. The megalomaniac paranoid trend is a definite danger in our society. It is encouraged by some of our major preoccupations, and it confronts us with a choice of two possible attitudes. One is to brand it as abnormal and reprehensible, and is the attitude we have chosen in our civilization. The other is to make it an essential attribute of ideal man, and this is the solution in the culture of the Northwest Coast.

These illustrations, which it has been possible to indicate only in the briefest manner, force upon us the fact that normality is culturally defined. An adult shaped to the drives and standards of either of these cultures, if he were transported into our civilization, would fall into our categories of abnormality. He would be faced with the psychic dilemmas of the socially unavailable. In his own culture, however, he is the pillar of society, the end result of socially inculcated mores, and the problem of personal instability in his case simply does not arise.

No one civilization can possibly utilize in its mores the whole potential range of human behavior. Just as there are great numbers of possible phonetic articulations, and the possibility of language depends on a selection and standardization of a few of these in order that speech communication may be possible at all, so the possibility of organized behavior of every sort, from the fashions of local dress and houses to the dicta of a people's ethics and religion, depends upon a similar selection among the possible behavior traits. In the field of recognized economic obligations or sex tabus this selection is as nonrational and subconscious a process as it is in the field of phonetics. It is a process which goes on in the group for long periods of time and is historically conditioned by innumerable accidents of isolation or of contact of peoples. In any comprehensive study of psychology, the selection that different cultures have made in the course of history within the great circumference of potential behavior is of great significance.

Every society,[9] beginning with some slight inclination in one direction or another, carries its preference farther and farther, integrating itself more and more completely upon its chosen basis, and discarding those types of behavior that are uncongenial. Most of those organizations of personality that seem to us most incontrovertibly abnormal have been used by different civilizations in the very foundations of their institutional life. Conversely the most valued traits of our normal individuals have been looked on in differently organized cultures as aberrant. Normality, in short, within a very wide range, is culturally defined. It is primarily a term for the socially elaborated segment of human behavior in any culture; and abnormality, a term for the segment that that particular civilization does not use. The very eyes with which we see the problem are conditioned by the long traditional habits of our own society.

It is a point that has been made more often in relation to ethics than in relation to psychiatry. We do not any longer make the mistake of deriving the morality of our own locality and decade directly from the inevitable constitution of human nature. We do not elevate it to the dignity of a first principle. We recognize that morality differs in every society, and is a convenient term for socially approved habits. Mankind has always preferred to say, "It is a morally good," rather than "It is habitual," and the fact of this preference is matter enough for a critical science of ethics. But historically the two phrases are synonymous.

The concept of the normal is properly a variant of the concept of the good. It is that which society has approved. A normal action is one which falls well within the limits of expected behavior for a particular society. Its variability among different peoples is essentially a function of the variability of the behavior patterns that different societies have created for themselves, and can never be wholly divorced from a consideration of culturally institutionalized types of behavior.

NOTES

1. The feast he is now engaged in giving.
2. His opponents.
3. To break a copper, showing in this way how far one rose above even the most superlatively valuable thinks, was the final mark of greatness.
4. Himself.
5. As salmon do.
6. Himself.
7. Irony, of course.
8. Of treasure.
8a. Insult is used here in reference to the intense susceptibility to shame that is conspicuous in this culture. All possible contingencies were interpreted as rivalry situations, and the gamut of emotions swung between triumph and shame.

9. This phrasing of the process is deliberately animistic. It is used with no reference to a group mind or a superorganic, but in the same sense in which it is customary to say, "Every art has its own canons."

REVIEW QUESTIONS

1. Do you think the leaders described in Benedict's article are good for the people in their culture? What might those leaders do different or better?
2. Do you agree with Benedict that all normal and abnormal behavior is culturally determined?
3. Would you be comfortable making a moral judgment about the values and behavior of the people that Benedict studied?

Trying Out One's New Sword

Mary Midgley

Mary Midgley is a philosopher at the University of Newcastle-Upon Tyne in the United Kingdom. In this article she argues that the ethical relativist's position, which she also calls moral isolationism, is impractical because it not only prevents us from making moral judgments about other cultures, but it inhibits our ability to make moral judgments about our own. Furthermore, Midgley reminds us that if we can't make negative judgments about other cultures, we can't make positive ones either. In today's world leaders do not have the option of refusing to make moral judgments about practices in other cultures because it is almost impossible to isolate ourselves from them.

All of us are, more or less, in trouble today about trying to understand cultures strange to us. We hear constantly of alien customs. We see changes in our lifetime which would have astonished our parents. I want to discuss here one very short way of dealing with this difficulty, a drastic way which many people now theoretically favour. It consists in simply denying that we can ever understand any culture except our own well enough to make judgements about it. Those who recommend this hold that the world is sharply divided into separate societies, sealed units, each with its own system of thought. They feel that the respect and tolerance due from one system to another forbids us ever to take up a critical position to any other culture. Moral judgement, they suggest, is a kind of coinage valid only in its country of origin.

I shall call this position "moral isolationism." I shall suggest that it is certainly not forced upon us, and indeed that it makes no sense at all. People usually take it up because they think it is a respectful attitude to other cultures. In fact, however, it is not respectful. Nobody can respect what is entirely unintelligible to them. To respect someone, we have to know enough about him to make a *favourable* judgement, however general and tentative. And we do understand people in other cultures to this extent. Otherwise a great mass of our most valuable thinking would be paralysed.

To show this, I shall take a remote example, because we shall probably find it easier to think calmly about it than we should with a contemporary one, such as female circumcision in Africa or the Chinese Cultural Revolution. The principles involved will still be the same. My example is this. There is, it seems, a verb in classical Japanese which means "to try out one's new sword on a chance wayfarer." (The word is *tsujigiri,* literally "crossroads-cut.") A samurai sword had to be tried out because, if it was to work properly, it had to slice through someone at a single blow, from the shoulder to the opposite flank. Otherwise, the warrior bungled his stroke. This could injure his honour, offend his ancestors, and even let down his emperor. So tests were needed, and wayfarers had to be expended. Any wayfarer would do—provided, of course, that he was not another Samurai. Scientists will recognize a familiar problem about the rights of experimental subjects.

Now when we hear of a custom like this, we may well reflect that we simply do not understand it and therefore are not qualified to criticize it at all, because we are not members of that culture. But we are not members of any other culture either, except our own. So we extend the principle to cover all extraneous cultures, and we seem therefore to be moral isolationists. But this is, as we shall see, an impossible position. Let us ask what it would involve.

We must ask first: Does the isolating barrier work both ways? Are people in other cultures equally unable to criticize *us?* This question struck me sharply when I read a remark in *The Guardian* by an anthropologist about a South American Indian who had been taken into a Brazilian town for an operation, which saved his life. When he came back to his village, he made several highly critical remarks about the white Brazilians' way of life. They may very well have been justified. But the interesting point was that the anthropologist called these remarks "a damning indictment of Western civilization." Now the Indian had been in that town about two weeks. Was he in a position to deliver a damning indictment? Would we ourselves be qualified to deliver such an indictment on the Samurai, provided we could spend two weeks in ancient Japan? What do we really think about this?

My own impression is that we believe that outsiders can, in principle, deliver perfectly good indictments—only, it usually takes more than two weeks to make them damning. Understanding has degrees. It is not a slapdash yes-or-no matter. Intelligent outsiders can progress in it, and in some ways will be at an advantage over the locals. But if this is so, it must clearly apply to ourselves as much as anybody else.

Our next question is this: Does the isolating barrier between cultures block praise as well as blame? If I want to say that the Samurai culture has many virtues, or to praise the South American Indians, am I prevented from doing *that* by my outside status? Now, we certainly do need to praise other societies in this way. But it is hardly possible that we could praise them effectively if we could not, in principle, criticize them. Our praise would be worthless if it rested on no definite grounds, if it did not flow from some understanding. Certainly we may need to praise things which we do not *fully* understand. We say "there's something very good here, but I can't quite make out what it is yet." This happens when we want to learn from strangers. And we can learn from strangers. But to do this we have to distinguish between those strangers who are worth learning from and those who are not. Can we then judge which is which?

This brings us to our third question: What is involved in judging? Now plainly there is no question here of sitting on a bench in a red robe and sentencing people. Judging simply means forming an opinion, and expressing it if it is called for. Is there anything wrong about this? Naturally, we ought to avoid forming—and expressing—*crude* opinions, like that of a simple-minded missionary, who might dismiss the whole Samurai culture as entirely bad, because non-Christian. But this is a different objection. The trouble with crude opinions is that they are crude, whoever forms them, not that they are formed by the wrong people. Anthropologists, after all, are outsiders quite as much as missionaries. Moral isolationism forbids us to form *any* opinions on these matters. Its ground for doing so is that we don't understand them. But there is much that we don't understand in our own culture too. This brings us to our last question: If we can't judge other cultures, can we really judge our own? Our efforts to do so will be much damaged if we are really deprived of our opinions about other societies, because these provide the range of comparison, the spectrum of alternatives against which we set what we want to understand. We would have to stop using the mirror which anthropology so helpfully holds up to us.

In short, moral isolationism would lay down a general ban on moral reasoning. Essentially, this is the programme of immoralism, and it carries a distressing logical difficulty. Immoralists like Nietzsche are actually just a rather specialized sect of moralists. They can no more afford to put moralizing out of business than smugglers can afford to abolish customs regulations. The power of moral judgement is, in fact, not a luxury, not a perverse indulgence of the self-righteous. It is a necessity. When we judge something to be bad or good, better or worse than something else, we are taking it as an example to aim at or avoid. Without opinions of this sort, we would have no framework of comparison for our own policy, no chance of profiting by other people's insights or mistakes. In this vacuum, we could form no judgements on our own actions.

Now it would be odd if Homo sapiens had really got himself into a position as bad as this—a position where his main evolutionary asset, his brain, was so little use to him. None of us is going to accept this sceptical diagnosis. We cannot do so, because our involvement in moral isolationism does not flow from apathy, but from a rather acute concern about human hypocrisy and other forms of wickedness. But we polarize that concern around a few selected moral truths. We are rightly angry with those who despise, oppress or steamroll other cultures. We think that doing these things is actually *wrong*. But this is itself a moral judgement. We could not condemn oppression and insolence if we thought that all our condemnations were just a trivial local quirk of our own culture. We could still less do it if we tried to stop judging altogether.

Real moral scepticism, in fact, could lead only to inaction, to our losing all interest in moral questions, most of all in those which concern other societies. When we discuss these things, it becomes instantly clear how far we are from doing this. Suppose, for instance, that I criticize the bisecting Samurai, that I say his behaviour is brutal. What will usually happen next is that someone will protest, will say that I have no right to make criticisms like that of another culture. But it is most unlikely that he will use this move to end the discussion of the subject. Instead, he will justify the Samurai. He will try to fill in the background, to make me understand the custom, by explaining the exalted ideals of discipline and devotion which produced it. He will probably talk of the lower value which the ancient Japanese placed on individual life generally. He may well suggest that this is a healthier attitude than our own obsession with security. He may add, too, that the wayfarers did not seriously mind being bisected, that in principle they accepted the whole arrangement.

Now an objector who talks like this is implying that it *is* possible to understand alien customs. That is just what he is trying to make me do. And he implies, too, that if I do succeed in understanding them, I shall do something better than giving up judging them. He expects me to change my present judgement to a truer one—namely, one that is favourable. And the standards I must use to do this cannot just be Samurai standards. They have to be ones current in my own culture. Ideals like discipline and devotion will not move anybody unless he himself accepts them. As it happens, neither discipline nor devotion is very popular in the West at present. Anyone who appeals to them may well have to do some more arguing to make *them* acceptable, before he can use them to explain the Samurai. But if he does succeed here, he will have persuaded us, not just that there was something to be said for them in ancient Japan, but that there would be here as well.

Isolating barriers simply cannot arise here. If we accept something as a serious moral truth about one culture, we can't refuse to apply it—in however different an outward form—to other cultures as well, wherever circumstance admit it. If we refuse to do this, we just are not taking the other culture seriously. This becomes clear if we look at the last argument used by my objector—that of justification by consent of the victim. It is suggested that sudden bisection is quite in order, *provided* that it takes place between consenting adults. I cannot now discuss how conclusive this justification is. What I am pointing out is simply that it can only work if we believe that c*onsent* can make such a transaction respectable—and this is a thoroughly modern and Western idea. It would probably never occur to a Samurai; if it did, it would surprise him very much. It is *our* standard. In applying it, too, we are likely to make another typically Western demand. We shall ask for good factual evidence that the wayfarers actually do have this rather surprising taste—that they are really willing to be bisected. In applying Western standards in this way, we are not being confused or irrelevant. We are asking the questions which arise *from where we stand,* questions which we can see the sense of. We do this because asking questions which you can't see the sense of is humbug. Certainly we can extend our questioning by imaginative effort. We can come to understand other societies better. By doing so, we may make their questions our own, or we may see that they are really forms of the questions which we are asking already. This is not impossible. It is just very hard work. The obstacles which often prevent it are simply those of ordinary ignorance, laziness and prejudice.

If there were really an isolating barrier, of course, our own culture could never have been formed. It is no sealed box, but a fertile jungle of different influences—Greek, Jewish, Roman, Norse, Celtic and so forth, into which further influences are still pouring—American, Indian, Japanese, Jamaican, you name it. The moral isolationist's picture of separate, unmixable cultures is quite unreal. People who talk about British history usually stress the value of this fertilizing mix, no doubt rightly. But this is not just an odd fact about Britain. Except for the very smallest and most remote, all cultures are formed out of many streams. All have the problem of digesting and assimilating things which, at the start, they do not understand. All have the choice of learning something from this challenge, or, alternatively, of refusing to learn, and fighting it mindlessly instead.

This universal predicament has been obscured by the fact that anthropologists used to concentrate largely on very small and remote cultures, which did not seem to have this problem. These tiny societies, which had often forgotten their own history, made neat, self-contained subjects for study. No doubt it was valuable to emphasize their remoteness, their extreme strangeness, their independence of our cultural tradition. This emphasis was, I think, the root of moral isolationism. But, as the tribal studies themselves showed, even there the anthropologists were able to interpret what they saw and make judgements—often favourable—about the tribesmen. And the tribesmen, too, were quite equal to making judgements about the anthropologists—and about the tourists and Coca-Cola salesmen who followed them. Both sets of judgements, no doubt, were somewhat hasty, both have been refined in the light of further experience. A similar transaction between us and the Samurai might take even longer. But that is no reason at all for deeming it impossible. Morally as well as physically, there is only one world, and we all have to live in it.

REVIEW QUESTIONS

1. What would you want to ask the Samurai about the method he uses to test his sword? What moral justification might the Samurai give for it?
2. Where is the moral problem here? Is it in the reasons for trying out the sword, the method of testing it or both?
3. Does the answer to these questions about the sword matter to the ethical relativist?
4. Would it be possible for you to have a meaningful discussion about the morality of the practice?

Values, Beliefs, and Leadership
F. G. Bailey

F. G. Bailey is an anthropologist at the University of California, San Diego. In this essay he asks, "If values and beliefs determine which leadership styles are effective, what freedom do leaders have to transcend those values and beliefs?" Are they stuck having to play into the values and beliefs of their culture, or may they use others as well? Bailey is far less reverent about the unity of cultural values than Benedict. He agrees with Midgley that most cultures, when looked at over a long history, are a conglomeration of other cultures and their values. Like James MacGregor Burns, he maintains that the currency of leadership is values. However, his studies in India and other places have led him to conclude that leadership is not only the art of shaping values, but it is also the art of "exploiting" the values and beliefs of a culture or several cultures.

Societies vary widely in their views on leadership. In some (Nazi Germany, Mussolini's Italy, the United States during a presidential campaign) leadership itself is elevated; in others it is belittled (the legendary frontier societies of Australia and North America). Furthermore, attitudes change as the context changes: in wartime Coriolanus is a hero, in peacetime an embarrassment. That, less starkly, was also Churchill's fate. If the styles of leadership that are valued vary, then people's expectations constitute part of the context that explains why one style rather than another is effective. The expectations are themselves a function of values (how the world should be), beliefs (how the world is), and customs (how one conducts oneself under the guidance of a particular set of values and beliefs). Values, beliefs, and customs together constitute culture.

How comprehensive is an explanation of leadership styles that is drawn only from culture? Or, to transform the question, if values and beliefs determine what leadership styles are effective, what freedom do leaders have to transcend those values and beliefs? How much room do they have for maneuver?

My answer will be that every leader does have such room because cultures are not unitary things. One might say that every culture contains contradictory values or—as I prefer to see the matter—that individuals have at their disposal a variety of cultures among which they may choose (Bailey 1960). These cultures have varying degrees of moral saliency: some are respectable to the point of being officially dominant, while others, the least respectable, are "underground." In fact, a leader's necessary "malefactions," described earlier, consist of ventures into one or another of those underground cultures.

It is in the interest of a leader, while himself requiring to be aware of the wide plurality of values, to restrict this awareness in the mass of his followers and so to define the situation for them that they see only those alternatives that are to his strategic advantage.

Is Culture King?

Members of the British ruling class in the days of empire conceived a vast admiration for those of their subject peoples whom they saw to be like themselves. Specifically, they found in the tribal peoples of India and in its "martial races" (Sikhs, Jats, Rajputs, the northern hill peoples, and above all their Gurkha soldiers) those virtues that are supposed to characterize the product of British public schools: physical hardiness, a curious combination of individual self-respect with an unswerving mindless devotion to the herd (people like themselves) and an equally unswerving contempt for those on the outside, and, third but not least, a marked disdain for "clever" people. Brains took second place to character. You could rely on simple people: they were men of honor, men of their word, men of the sword.

Here is Sam MacPherson, a soldier in the East India Company's armies charged with suppressing human sacrifice (called *meriah*) and female infanticide among the Konds of highland Orissa in India, writing probably about 1840:

> The distinguishing qualities of the character of the Khonds appear to be these: a passionate love of liberty, devotion to chiefs, and unconquerable resolution. They are beside faithful to friends, brave, hospitable, and laborious. Their vices, on the other hand, are the indulgence of revenge and occasionally brutal passion. Drunkenness is universal; the habit of plunder exists in one or two small districts alone.
>
> Among savage tribes the state of war is universal. At a more advanced stage, such as that which the Khonds have reached, hostility is limited or modified by special compacts; but war is still the rule, peace the exception. [MacPherson 1865:81]

Helped by the incompetence, irresolution, and factiousness of the British and by endemic cerebral malaria (fatal in those days), the Konds held out in their hills for more than twenty-five years. Kond society was of a form not known to Europeans at that time, for it had no "chiefs." Those to whom MacPherson refers were probably Oriyas from the plains, settled for several generations in the hills. The "devotion" he mentions poses a problem that will be considered later. The Oriyas (because their language was understood by the British and that of the Konds was not) were MacPherson's chief interlocutors, and in fact Oriyas came to dominate the region and exploit the Konds only after the British inadvertently made it possible for them to do so. I have no doubt, however, that before the Meriah Wars the disposition of the Konds as followers of anyone would have been best described as autarkic.

Another example, well known to anthropologists, is the Nuer of southern Sudan, described by E. E. Evans-Pritchard as he saw them between 1930 and 1936:

> That every Nuer considers himself as good as his neighbor is evident in their every movement. They strut about like lords of the earth, which, indeed, they consider themselves to be. There is no master and no servant in their society, but only equals who regard themselves as God's noblest creation. Their respect for one another contrasts with their contempt for all other peoples. Among themselves even the suspicion of an order riles a man and he either does not carry it out or he carries it out in a casual and dilatory manner that is more insulting than a refusal. [Evans-Pritchard 1940:182]

There are no rulers. "Leadership in a local community consists of an influential man deciding to do something and the people of other hamlets following suit at their convenience" (1940:181). In larger groups leadership is even more attenuated. Certain ritual figures are respected and feared, but even of the most powerful (the prophet Gwek) it is said only that he "came nearest to exercising political functions" (1940:188).

It seems reasonable to say of both the Konds and the Nuer that their values (and the accompanying segmentary social structure) leave little room for leadership. Those two cultures constitute the normal disposition as anarchic, valuing equality and disvaluing authority.

Other peoples go in the opposite direction and seem to value authority, or at least to rejoice in the presence of powerful people. Most Hindu traditions assume a "natural" (that is, divinely ordained) inequality between human beings and assume that without leaders life becomes insupportable. A state of nature in which life is "solitary, poor, nasty, brutish and short" is described, in anticipation of Hobbes, in ancient India:

> According to most Hindu traditions, in the period of anarchy before government was instituted men had become so evil that the strong destroyed the weak and all creatures "in fear scattered in all directions" [Manu, VII, III], until kingship was instituted by divine decree. . . . Nearly all Hindu legends on the origin of kinship depict men in a state of anarchy as praying to the gods to save them. [Basham 1963:14–15]

The divine origin of kings is consistent with natural inequality. Hindus of each caste are constituted in their own unique fashion, and those of higher rank are closer to the divinity and therefore are endowed with truer worth than those of lower rank. Ranking does not coincide exactly with the exercise of power, since those who are most pure (the Brahmans) do not govern. But those who do govern and do possess authority, the kings, are not unhallowed, as the legend of their origin indicates.

Hinduism, of course, is not alone in its assumption of natural inequality, but perhaps exceptional in the degree to which the concept is elaborated, both in theology and in action. In daily life the notion seems to pervade every transaction and every anticipated transaction. The humble person can do nothing in the face of a superior without the help of a patron, a personal Leviathan, so to speak. The ordinary policeman, the clerk in a government office, minor functionaries at railway stations or in the post office assume toward their inferiors an attitude at best of indifference, more often of contempt, always stiffened by a firm display of their own effortless superiority.

The same sort of thing goes on at higher levels, and even people who are aware of other ways and perhaps would like to behave differently find themselves imprisoned in the system. I had a friend, a high official, a decent man and one who, it so happened, had already attained in an American university the doctorate in social science for which I was then working. One day in his office he was reading a large ledger-like book, running his finger down the columns. As he neared the bottom of the page, he stretched out his left hand and banged a bell on the desk. The door from the veranda burst open and a peon (servant) flung himself across the room, turned the page, and then backed out. As he went, the official said, curtly, "Next time, faster!"

I said nothing to him but on my return to the village where I lived I described the scene to some men. The story made no impression and I found myself explaining that I thought the official could have turned his own pages. Then they were puzzled, even shocked. "But he's the collector!" they said. "It's Naika's *privilege* to do that. He's the peon."

Inherited ideas, whether about equality or inequality, are not easily dislodged. October 2 is the anniversary of Gandhi's birth. In 1952 I attended a celebration, riding in a cavalcade of cars carrying a government minister and his retinue of politicians and officials to inaugurate development projects in certain villages and to inspect those already under way elsewhere. Most of these sites lay within the boundaries of what had been a small kingdom, the raja of which had been deposed (like all the other rajas) five years earlier, when India gained her independence. That raja was part of the cavalcade, somewhere near the back.

It was a good day to observe leadership in action: lots of humbuggery and some unintended comedy. Like any pageant, this one had a theme, both acted out and enunciated again and again in the speeches. At the principal site, after lunch, every politician and official on the platform made a speech. There were sixteen of them. They said that the days of the British autocrats had ended, democracy had come, the people ruled themselves, and when the people worked on development projects, they were working not for the government (as in British days) but for themselves. Equality had come to India.

Those on the platform sat on chairs under an awning that shielded them from the high sun. The villagers squatted in the dirt, down below and without protection from the sun. The minister sat in the middle of the platform, and rank descended on each side of him, the tail-enders being myself and the deposed raja. Speeches were made in order of seniority, and longwindedness shortened as rank diminished. Neither I nor the ex-raja spoke.

When the speeches stopped, the villagers put on their entertainment. It consisted of two men extemporizing short satirical rhythmical songs, to the music of small, bell-like cymbals. The idiomatic Oriya was beyond my comprehension but it was evident that, unfortunately as early as the third stanza, they had come too near the bone. The ex-raja and the official who had brought me guffawed, and hastily checked themselves. The minister frowned his displeasure, and the officials put a peremptory stop to the performance.

At that point a petitioner came forward. Evidently his mind was in the past, because he approached the one white face on the platform, which was mine. The officials hastily shooed him away and the unfortunate man turned to the one face he knew among the notables, the dethroned raja. That provoked another outcry and this time they led him to the minister, before whom he knelt and began to make his plea. The minister listened to a few sentences and ended the affair by telling a local official to do "the necessary."

Finally we set off to act democracy by building a road for the villagers. For ten frantic minutes, while the village band played and the bemused villagers looked on, we reversed roles with them, taking off our shirts and shoveling earth into baskets and dumping it on the road. When the time was up, we washed our hands (the villagers bringing water for all of us and a towel as well for the minister), got into the cars, and drove away. My last memory is of the village bandsmen dropping their instruments in indignant pursuit of the minister's car, because he had not tipped them.

Most of all from that day I recall the speech of a Public Relations Department official, a one-time freedom fighter. He set out to explain clearly and directly what independence meant. It meant, he said, that those on the platform were not the government. They, the villagers, were the government: the people on the platform were their servants. Some of the men down in the dust and the heat were listening, and when they heard these words their expressions signaled uneasiness that such an important man should be saying something so obviously absurd.

Minds fixed in the habit of subordination are evidently not easily changed, and, one would think, these people must be as amenable to strong leadership as the Konds and the Nuer are hostile even to weak leadership. If this is correct, it would follow that a display of authority among the Nuer would excite immediate insubordination and that anything stronger than the mildest persuasion would be ineffective. That is, in fact, what Evans-Pritchard says: "When a Nuer wants his fellows to do something he asks it as a favor to a kinsman, saying 'Son of my mother, do so-and-so', or he includes himself in the command and says: 'Let us depart', 'Let the people return home', and so forth" (1940:182).

Conversely, it should also follow that in the extravagantly hierarchical world of the Hindu villager, the man in authority must be remote, aloof, and somewhat awesome if his communications are to be understood and his legitimacy maintained. An attempt (by him) at familiarity should invite contempt or suspicion. Several speakers in the October 2 tamasha ("entertainment" such as a fair or a festival) began their addresses in good democratic style with "Brothers and sisters . . .," thus doubling the confusion, as women were not part of the public life of such places at that time. How it is in rural India now I do not know, but at that period the fraternal form of appeal to voters, standard in a democracy, was viewed with suspicion, especially since, as the vignette shows, notables found it hard to conduct themselves with anything less than their accustomed self-importance. Certainly the considerable number of deposed rajas who stood as candidates for the legislature fared well by presenting themselves to the electorate in the manner of kings, not as supplicants.

Is it then to be concluded that "culture is king"? Knowing the values and beliefs, can we then predict what styles leaders must follow? The matter is not so simple, and the proposition could be maintained only if one ignored the historical evidence.

Consider, first, what was happening to the Nuer. There is no reason to doubt their readiness, man to man, to down anyone pretending to superiority. But there are also pointers in another direction. They respect elders and, not surprisingly, men "of character and ability" (1940:179). But Evans-Pritchard found it "the more remarkable [given their sentiments about authority] that they so easily submit to persons who claim certain supernatural powers" (1940:184). These persons were the owners of fetishes, having prestige but, Evans-Pritchard hastens to add, without political authority. A third category of superior person, the prophets, did have wide influence, however, and were able to coordinate tribes and tribal segments for raids against the Dinka and for "opposition to Arab and European aggression" (1940:188). Evans-Pritchard insists that government reports had "exaggerated" the power of these prophets and that they were in any case a recent phenomenon, a response to Arab and European incursions. But one general conclusion is beyond dispute: the prophets existed, they had great influence and prestige, and they had sufficient authority to coordinate warlike activities despite the fact that every Nuer insisted that he was as good as his neighbor. In other words, values and beliefs may yield to circumstances and new styles of leadership may become customary. To this extent a leader is not a prisoner of his culture (although constrained by it), first because he may exploit possibilities hitherto latent in that culture, and second, because changing circumstances may invalidate existing beliefs and values.

I have presented only a fragment of Nuer history, the beginning of a trend arrested by the actions of the colonial power. The Kond story is complete. The "ordered anarchy" of tribal life vanished, replaced formally by the regimented order of an authoritarian bureaucracy, helped out by the regimented hierarchy of the Hindu social system. Clan areas were placed under the jurisdiction of chiefs, most of whom belonged to the dominant Hindu caste of Warriors. In this way the Oriya settlers in the Kond hills became an intermediate "ruling race" (as colonial dominators once were described).

The office of chief—they were called sirdars—has now been abolished, being replaced by local government institutions and elected officials. That system was in its infancy when I lived there, and I was still able to see the sirdars in action and to observe their style of leadership and the behavior of their followers.

The sirdar where I lived was a Hindu and an Oriya. His subjects in his own village were Oriyas like himself, about 700 of them out of the 2,000 people in his jurisdiction. The rest were Konds scattered in villages up to ten miles away.

Legally the sirdar was a government servant, paid by grant of land. He had certain bureaucratic duties (mainly collecting taxes and reporting violent deaths and civil disorders) and was generally charged with maintaining peace and order and with assisting officials who came to his area in the course of their duties. His style, however, was not in the least that of a bureaucrat. It was personal (in a particular way that will be described shortly). Nor did he restrict himself to certain functions in the manner of an official: no aspect of his subjects' lives was beyond his concern or his interference. In a word, he conducted himself like a feudal chieftain. Alternatively, in case the word "feudal" suggests Camelot, King Arthur, and Mark Twain's boneheaded aristocrats, he was a patriarch. Somewhat better off than most of his subjects, the sirdar was nevertheless still a peasant like them. He dressed like them, ate like them, and worked in the fields and the forest like them.

Oriya and Kond, they came to him for advice and to ask protection from each other and from bullying or exploiting outsiders. They came to him to air their grievances and to have disputes settled and quarrels mended. These affairs were conducted in panchayats, councils of senior men, over which the sirdar presided. He did so in a way that at first seemed to me extremely self-effacing. In the course of the discussion, and in the questioning of the parties concerned, he rarely had anything to say: other people did the talking. Only at the conclusion of the meeting did he speak, when he appeared to be announcing a consensus reached without his participation.

Later I had a different interpretation. He was not self-effacing. What his detached behavior and his silent aloofness signaled was that he was above it all. He was not trying to impose his will on anyone; emphatically he was not part of any competition. But neither was this remote and effortless superiority that of a judge charged with seeing that the law was observed. The aim was not in the least to identify applicable law and enforce it, but rather to restore harmony to relationships that had been disrupted.

From where, then, did his authority come? Certainly there was never any notion that it was delegated to him by the people, as is supposed to be the case for elected leaders. No word or symbolic action ever indicated anything of the sort. Nor did it come from his government appointment, from a rational fear that he could enforce his will through the administration's police or courts. There was a hint in that direction, on some occasions, but if it had been of much significance, he would surely have justified some of his decisions by reference to his official position, and he never did so. Nor, finally, did his authority come from charisma. He had a touch of that, mostly a lingering reputation for effectiveness and vigor, now much diminished by democratic institutions and the antipathy with which the Congress government was known to hold sirdars as a "remnant of colonial feudalism." But he had in himself nothing of the spellbinder.

The authority lay in the role, which descends in a straight line from that of the Hindu king, the guardian of the social order. The king is like the patriarch, placed where he is not by anyone's consent or by election but rather by the divinity: he is part of the natural order. It is this given authority that seems to me to lie behind the studied and detached superiority with which the sirdar presided over meetings. He stood above the competition and descended in the end to announce a verdict that was not his but had come from a divine source. A panchayat in fact is supposed to find a consensus, and that consensus is the voice of God.

The mystique involved in this kind of leadership is not that of the charismatic leader. The veneration attaches to the office first, and only secondarily to the person. At the same time the remoteness and the awe are modified because the incumbent of the office is seen, symbolically, as an older kinsman. Conventional rhetoric in the panchayat called for an invocation of the sirdar as a "father" or *mabap* (mother-father). He addressed people by kinship titles. The familial idiom was also evident in feudalistic paternalism. When the sirdar's son married, the Konds of his domain arrived in hundreds to pay willing homage and to be feasted generously for several days.

These are the same Konds who, a little more than a century before that time, were turbulent and warlike and had a "passionate love of liberty." Can one pay willing homage to a feudal leader and at the same time love liberty? If this is a paradox, there are several ways to resolve it. First, the homage may have been unwilling. But I saw it, both at the wedding and on other occasions, and it seemed natural, unforced, and ungrudging. Second, perhaps more than a century of often vicious domination and exploitation had broken the nerve of the Konds. To some extent it had; but it was not loss of nerve that was symbolized in the way they conducted themselves in the presence of the sirdar, at least on those occasions. Moreover, in nonceremonial and nonjudicial situations, the idiom of interaction was as with a kinsman, markedly more egalitarian than the sirdar's interactions with his lower-caste Oriya subjects.

There is a simple way out of these apparent contradictions. It is to assume that while there is a Kond culture that can be conceived as an internally consistent set of beliefs and values and their corresponding customary rules and institutions, the Kond people had access also to other cultures that in some respects were not consistent with Kond culture but contradicted it. In other words, the range of cultures available to the Kond people (their social universe) was more extensive than Kond culture alone.

This explanation would allow one to accept with equanimity MacPherson's description of them as devoted to their chiefs. Presumably the display of homage that I saw at that wedding in the 1950s was not something that had emerged from the pacification of the region but was a spectacle that could have been seen before the Konds were subjugated. They had access then, as they did in the 1950s, to Hindu political culture, which, being hierarchical, was in marked contradiction with the egalitarian values of Kond culture. Indeed, as I have argued elsewhere (Bailey 1960), Konds nowadays have access not only to their own culture and to Hindu culture but also to the cultures that go with a bureaucratic administration and with a representative democracy (and they sometimes made use of these values and beliefs to round on and harass those sirdars who failed in their patriarchal duties).

What does this say about leadership and culture? Cultures that appeared strongly to favor anarchy did not apparently deter people from subordinating themselves to leaders. The Konds, for example, entertained contradictory values and in fact made active use of the diversity of customs at their disposal to gain whatever ends they had in view. Evidently, even if some cultures in certain circumstances seemed to be dominant, no particular culture could be called king. Certainly cultures put constraints on leadership styles, but flexibility was retained (and uncertainty introduced) insofar as the leader had a variety of cultures among which to choose. His problem was less to escape from the cultural straitjacket than the reverse: to narrow down a complicated variety of possible courses of action. The investigator's task then is to comprehend not only the cultures that constitute a leader's strategic environment but also the rules that guide his choices among alternatives.

Having freed the leader from perpetual bondage in a monolithic directive culture, I will now put back some of the shackles. In doing so I will be guided by a broad axiom for the study of power in any form: leadership and other forms of domination are to be understood as (among other things) the art of using values and beliefs and their accompanying institutions as a resource, while at the same time avoiding, when necessary, their constraints. From this viewpoint leadership is the art of exploiting cultures.

REVIEW QUESTIONS

1. Is there anything wrong with leaders acting on the values that best suit their strategic purposes?
2. If all cultures carry conflicting values, what moral principles should a leader use to decide which values are the best?
3. Do you think that leadership is the art of manipulating values?

machavelli

Case: Fuller's Dilemma: Street Children and Substance Abuse
Adapted by Karen Marquis and Joanne Ciulla

Walter Fuller, Chief Executive Officer of H. B. Fuller, Inc., faced a formidable problem. Could the company continue production of its most profitable adhesive product, Endurol, and at the same time manage to maintain its impeccable image for social responsibility?

The executives at H. B. Fuller, Inc., first became aware of the substance abuse problem back in 1986 when Honduran newspapers carried articles about police arrests of street children who drugged themselves by sniffing glue. Most of the orphaned or runaway children lived in the poorest slums of the big cities where they scratched out a minimal existence as beggars and illegal squatters. The commonly available adhesive known as Endurol emerged as the substance of choice among these young junkies due to its low price and hallucinogenic qualities. The highly-addictive glue induced immediate feelings of elation, grandeur and power, but it also initiated irreversible liver and brain damage when used over a long period of time. Although the street children abused other substances in addition to Endurol, they soon became tagged as "Enduroleros," a name that eventually became synonymous with all street children, whether they used the drug or not.

Malena Chemical Industries, S.A., one of H. B. Fuller's wholly-owned subsidiaries, first introduced Endurol to the Central American market in the early 1980s. Malena manufactured and distributed more than a dozen different adhesives under the Endurol brand name in several countries. In Honduras, where Endurol was manufactured, the products had a strong market position. The adhesives were intended primarily for use in shoe manufacturing and repair, leather work, and carpentry. The most common forms of Endurol had properties similar to those of airplane glue or rubber cement and were readily available at household goods stores throughout the country. Malena maintained tight control over the wholesale distribution of Endurol. Nearly all glue products that reached the Enduroleros came from retail outlets; either directly or through street pushers.

From "H. B. Fuller in Honduras" by Karen Marquis and Joanne B. Ciulla in *Ethics of Business in a Global Economy* edited by Paul Minus, pp. 148–150. Copyright © 1993. Reprinted by permission of Kluwer Academic/Plenum Publishers and the author.

In spite of the competitive challenge of operating under unstable political and economic conditions in Central America, Malena managers stressed the objective of going beyond the bottom line in their annual report:

> Malena carries out business with the utmost respect for ethical and legal principles. Its orientation is not solely directed to the customer, who has the highest priority, but also to the shareholders, to employees, and to the communities where it operates.

Fuller's founder and Chairman of the Board, J. Grant Fuller, had become a legendary figure in the local area. He had served several terms in local government and remained active in civic affairs. Fuller saw the company through four decades of financial success as President and Chief Executive Officer before handing over the managerial reigns to his son Walter in January 1989.

Three months into Walter's term as President, angry letters began to trickle in from the stockholders. Some of these individuals heard of the Endurol problem through international press releases, while others had witnessed the problem first-hand in Central America. On November 2, 1989, Fuller received an irate call from a shareholder whose daughter worked with an international aid group in Honduras. The man demanded, "How can a company like H. B. Fuller claim to have a social conscience and continue to sell Endurol which is 'practically burning out the brains' of children in Latin America?" The letter's timing was uncanny. Walter was about to meet with a national group of socially responsible investors who were considering H. B. Fuller's stock for inclusion in their portfolio.

Meanwhile, Walter learned that Malena management had failed to dissuade the Honduran government from regulating Endurol. As a solution to the glue sniffing problem, the legislature mandated that oil of mustard, allyl isothiocyanate, be added to Endurol to prevent its abuse. They argued that a person attempting to sniff glue with oil of mustard included would find it too powerful to tolerate; like getting an "overdose of horseradish." However, independent toxicology reports revealed that the oil of mustard had some acute side effects. The material could prove fatal if inhaled, swallowed or absorbed through the skin, caused severe irritation or burns, and could destroy tissues of the mucous membranes, upper respiratory tract, eyes and skin. In addition, the Endurol with the oil of mustard included had a shelf life of only six months.

Given H. B. Fuller's high visibility as a socially responsible corporation, the glue sniffing problem had the potential for becoming a public relations nightmare. Fuller's staff suggested a number of options including withdrawal of the product from the market or altering the formula to make Endurol a water-based product. Both would solve the glue-sniffing problem. However, any formula alteration would also affect the strength and durability of the glue, its most valuable properties.

Case continued

Finally, Fuller decided to go to Honduras and see what was going on. Upon his return, he realized that the situation involved more than product misuse and the company's image; it had social and community ramifications as well. The issue was substance abuse by children, regardless of who manufactured the product.

The depth of poverty in Honduras exacerbated the problem. In 1989, 65 percent of all households in Honduras lived in poverty, making it one of the poorest countries in Latin America. The government remained highly unstable with a large turnover rate. Officials usually settled for a quick fix. They seldom stayed in office long enough to manage a long term policy. By the time of Fuller's trip, the oil-of-mustard law had been on the books for several months. However, officials had yet to implement the rule, and the country had scheduled national elections in three months.

Fuller wondered if his company could do much to solve this complicated social problem.

Questions

1. What are the long-term ethical ramifications of either pulling your product off the market or keeping it there and doing nothing? What will this decision say about your leadership?
2. Is a company responsible for the misuse of its product in another culture?
3. How much of an obligation do companies, countries, NGO or individuals have to address serious social problems in developing countries? If so how does one determine this obligation?
4. Do companies, countries, NGO, or individuals have the right to interfere with the way other countries deal or fail to deal with their social problems?

Universal Declaration of Human Rights

United Nations Commission on Human Rights

The Universal Declaration of Human Rights was created in 1946 by the United Nations Commission on Human Rights, which was composed of eighteen member states. Eleanor Roosevelt chaired the commission in its early years and was dedicated to the task of getting the statement written and ratified. Roosevelt believed that human rights began "in small places, close to home." It was there,

---

"Universal Declaration of Human Rights," reprinted by permision of United Nations.

she said, where people needed to live according to the fundamental rights of human dignity, equality, and justice without discrimination.

The drafting committee consisted of members from Australia, Chile, China, France, Lebanon, the Union of Socialist Republics, the United Kingdom, and the United States. It took two years to draft the document. Although the declaration is not legally binding, it has inspired more than sixty other international documents on human rights that constitute an emerging standard of human rights. The document is considered one of the greatest achievements of the United Nations. Of the fifty-eight members, forty-eight adopted the declaration; six nations from the Soviet block countries, South Africa, and Saudi Arabia abstained from voting; and two countries were absent for the vote.

This document demonstrates that people from other cultures can agree on a set of universal values. However, as we know, many of the countries that wrote and signed the document do not adhere to all of its values.

On December 10, 1948 the General Assembly of the United Nations adopted and proclaimed the Universal Declaration of Human Rights. Following this historic act the Assembly called upon all Member countries to publicize the text of the Declaration and "to cause it to be disseminated, displayed, read and expounded principally in schools and other educational institutions, without distinction based on the political status of countries or territories."

Preamble

Whereas recognition of the inherent dignity and of the equal and inalienable rights of all members of the human family is the foundation of freedom, justice and peace in the world,

Whereas disregard and contempt for human rights have resulted in barbarous acts which have outraged the conscience of mankind, and the advent of a world in which human beings shall enjoy freedom of speech and belief and freedom from fear and want has been proclaimed as the highest aspiration of the common people,

Whereas it is essential, if man is not to be compelled to have recourse, as a last resort, to rebellion against tyranny and oppression, that human rights should be protected by the rule of law,

Whereas it is essential to promote the development of friendly relations between nations,

Whereas the peoples of the United Nations have in the Charter reaffirmed their faith in fundamental human rights, in the dignity and worth of the human person and in the equal rights of men and women and have determined to promote social progress and better standards of life in larger freedom,

Whereas Member States have pledged themselves to achieve, in cooperation with the United Nations, the promotion of universal respect for and observance of human rights and fundamental freedoms,

Whereas a common understanding of these rights and freedoms is of the greatest importance for the full realization of this pledge,

Now, Therefore THE GENERAL ASSEMBLY proclaims THIS UNIVERSAL DECLARATION OF HUMAN RIGHTS as a common standard of achievement for all peoples and all nations, to the end that every individual and every organ of society, keeping this Declaration constantly in mind, shall strive by teaching and education to promote respect for these rights and freedoms and by progressive measures, national and international, to secure their universal and effective recognition and observance, both among the peoples of Member States themselves and among the peoples of territories under their jurisdiction.

Article 1.

All human beings are born free and equal in dignity and rights. They are endowed with reason and conscience and should act towards one another in a spirit of brotherhood.

Article 2.

Everyone is entitled to all the rights and freedoms set forth in this Declaration, without distinction of any kind, such as race, color, sex, language, religion, political or other opinion, national or social origin, property, birth or other status. Furthermore, no distinction shall be made on the basis of the political, jurisdictional or international status of the country or territory to which a person belongs, whether it be independent, trust, non-self-governing or under any other limitation of sovereignty.

Article 3.

Everyone has the right to life, liberty and security of person.

Article 4.

No one shall be held in slavery or servitude; slavery and the slave trade shall be prohibited in all their forms.

Article 5.

No one shall be subjected to torture or to cruel, inhuman or degrading treatment or punishment.

Article 6.

Everyone has the right to recognition everywhere as a person before the law.

Article 7.

All are equal before the law and are entitled without any discrimination to equal protection of the law. All are entitled to equal protection against any discrimination in violation of this Declaration and against any incitement to such discrimination.

Article 8.

Everyone has the right to an effective remedy by the competent national tribunals for acts violating the fundamental rights granted him by the constitution or by law.

Article 9.

No one shall be subjected to arbitrary arrest, detention or exile.

Article 10.

Everyone is entitled in full equality to a fair and public hearing by an independent and impartial tribunal, in the determination of his rights and obligations and of any criminal charge against him.

Article 11.

(1) Everyone charged with a penal offence has the right to be presumed innocent until proved guilty according to law in a public trial at which he has had all the guarantees necessary for his defense.
(2) No one shall be held guilty of any penal offence on account of any act or omission which did not constitute a penal offence, under national or international law, at the time when it was committed. Nor shall a heavier penalty be imposed than the one that was applicable at the time the penal offence was committed.

Article 12.

No one shall be subjected to arbitrary interference with his privacy, family, home or correspondence, nor to attacks upon his honor and reputation. Everyone has the right to the protection of the law against such interference or attacks.

Article 13.

(1) Everyone has the right to freedom of movement and residence within the borders of each state.

(2) Everyone has the right to leave any country, including his own, and to return to his country.

Article 14.

(1) Everyone has the right to seek and to enjoy in other countries asylum from persecution.
(2) This right may not be invoked in the case of prosecutions genuinely arising from non-political crimes or from acts contrary to the purposes and principles of the United Nations.

Article 15.

(1) Everyone has the right to a nationality.
(2) No one shall be arbitrarily deprived of his nationality nor denied the right to change his nationality.

Article 16.

(1) Men and women of full age, without any limitation due to race, nationality or religion, have the right to marry and to found a family. They are entitled to equal rights as to marriage, during marriage and at its dissolution.
(2) Marriage shall be entered into only with the free and full consent of the intending spouses.
(3) The family is the natural and fundamental group unit of society and is entitled to protection by society and the State.

Article 17.

(1) Everyone has the right to own property alone as well as in association with others.
(2) No one shall be arbitrarily deprived of his property.

Article 18.

Everyone has the right to freedom of thought, conscience and religion; this right includes freedom to change his religion or belief, and freedom, either alone or in community with others and in public or private, to manifest his religion or belief in teaching, practice, worship and observance.

Article 19.

Everyone has the right to freedom of opinion and expression; this right includes freedom to hold opinions without interference and to seek, receive and impart information and ideas through any media and regardless of frontiers.

Article 20.

(1) Everyone has the right to freedom of peaceful assembly and association.
(2) No one may be compelled to belong to an association.

Article 21.

(1) Everyone has the right to take part in the government of his country, directly or through freely chosen representatives.
(2) Everyone has the right of equal access to public service in his country.
(3) The will of the people shall be the basis of the authority of government; this will shall be expressed in periodic and genuine elections which shall be by universal and equal suffrage and shall be held by secret vote or by equivalent free voting procedures.

Article 22.

Everyone, as a member of society, has the right to social security and is entitled to realization, through national effort and international co-operation and in accordance with the organization and resources of each State, of the economic, social and cultural rights indispensable for his dignity and the free development of his personality.

Article 23.

(1) Everyone has the right to work, to free choice of employment, to just and favorable conditions of work and to protection against unemployment.
(2) Everyone, without any discrimination, has the right to equal pay for equal work.
(3) Everyone who works has the right to just and favorable remuneration ensuring for himself and his family an existence worthy of human dignity, and supplemented, if necessary, by other means of social protection.
(4) Everyone has the right to form and to join trade unions for the protection of his interests.

Article 24.

Everyone has the right to rest and leisure, including reasonable limitation of working hours and periodic holidays with pay.

Article 25.

(1) Everyone has the right to a standard of living adequate for the health and well-being of himself and of his family, including food, clothing,

housing and medical care and necessary social services, and the right to security in the event of unemployment, sickness, disability, widowhood, old age or other lack of livelihood in circumstances beyond his control.

(2) Motherhood and childhood are entitled to special care and assistance. All children, whether born in or out of wedlock, shall enjoy the same social protection.

Article 26.

(1) Everyone has the right to education. Education shall be free, at least in the elementary and fundamental stages. Elementary education shall be compulsory. Technical and professional education shall be made generally available and higher education shall be equally accessible to all on the basis of merit.

(2) Education shall be directed to the full development of the human personality and to the strengthening of respect for human rights and fundamental freedoms. It shall promote understanding, tolerance and friendship among all nations, racial or religious groups, and shall further the activities of the United Nations for the maintenance of peace.

(3) Parents have a prior right to choose the kind of education that shall be given to their children.

Article 27.

(1) Everyone has the right freely to participate in the cultural life of the community, to enjoy the arts and to share in scientific advancement and its benefits.

(2) Everyone has the right to the protection of the moral and material interests resulting from any scientific, literary or artistic production of which he is the author.

Article 28.

Everyone is entitled to a social and international order in which the rights and freedoms set forth in this Declaration can be fully realized.

Article 29.

(1) Everyone has duties to the community in which alone the free and full development of his personality is possible.

(2) In the exercise of his rights and freedoms, everyone shall be subject only to such limitations as are determined by law solely for the purpose of securing due recognition and respect for the rights and freedoms of

others and of meeting the just requirements of morality, public order and the general welfare in a democratic society.
(3) These rights and freedoms may in no case be exercised contrary to the purposes and principles of the United Nations.

Article 30.

Nothing in this Declaration may be interpreted as implying for any State, group or person any right to engage in any activity or to perform any act aimed at the destruction of any of the rights and freedoms set forth herein.

REVIEW QUESTIONS

1. Which principles does your own country fail to practice?
2. What does it mean for world leaders to adopt such a statement?
3. Would the statement have been stronger if it were written in terms of duties and responsibilities rather than rights?
4. Which principles in this statement do you think are universal? Which are not?

Case: The Oil Rig
Joanne B. Ciulla

You have just taken over as the new chief executive officer of Stratton Oil Company, an exploration and drilling firm under contract to a major multinational oil company. Your enterprise has experienced ups and downs over the last few years because of the fluctuation in international oil prices and complications with overseas operations.

Many of the operational problems stem from difficulties with Stratton's offshore oil drilling rigs. Maintenance and equipment costs have skyrocketed. You have received several reports of strained labor relations on the platforms. One incident caused such an uproar that the rig manager halted operations for more than a week. In addition, there have been a number of complaints from conscientious shareholders concerned with the environmental impact of these rigs.

In an attempt to address these issues, you decide to get a first-hand look at the offshore drilling operations. On your first excursion, you visit a rig off the coast of Africa, dubbed the "Voyager 7." You discover that an oil rig is really a small society, separate and distinct from the rest of the world.

From Joanne B. Ciulla.

Case continued

Stratton's *Voyager 7* is a relatively small "jack-up"[1] with dimensions of about 200 feet by 100 feet. The platform houses a crew of 150 men, made up of skilled laborers, "roustabouts" or unskilled laborers, maintenance staff, and 30 expatriates. The expatriates work as roughnecks, drillers, technicians, or administrators. The top administrator on the *Voyager 7* is the "tool pusher," an expatriate who wields almost absolute authority over matters pertaining to life on the rig.

Stratton engineers modified the crew quarters on the *Voyager 7* for operations in Africa. They installed a second galley on the lower level and enlarged the cabins to permit a dormitory-style arrangement of 16 persons per room. This lower level of the rig makes up the "African section" of the rig, where the 120 local workers eat, sleep, and socialize during their twenty-eight-day "hitch."

The upper level of the platform houses the 30 expatriates in an area equal in square footage to that of the African section. The "expatriate section" contains semiprivate quarters with baths and boasts its own galley, game room, and movie room. Although not explicitly written, a tacit regulation prohibits African workers from entering the expatriate section of the rig except in emergencies. The only Africans exempt from this regulation are those assigned to the highly valued positions of cleaning or galley staff in the expatriate section. The Africans hold these positions in high esteem because of the potential for receiving gifts or recovering discarded razors and other items from the expatriates.

Several other rig policies separate the African workers from the expatriates. African laborers travel to and from the rig by boat (an eighteen-hour trip) whereas expatriates receive helicopter transportation. An expatriate registered nurse dispenses medical attention to the expatriates throughout the day, but Africans have access to treatment only during shift changes or in an emergency. The two groups also receive disparate treatment when serious injuries arise. For instance, if a finger is severed, expatriates are rushed to the mainland for reconstructive surgery. However, because of the high cost of helicopter transportation, African workers must have an amputation operation performed on the rig by the medic.

The company issues gray coveralls to the Africans whereas the expatriates receive red coveralls. Meals in the two galleys are vastly different: the expatriate galley serves fine cuisine that approaches gourmet quality, whereas the Africans dine on a more proletarian fare. Despite the gross disparity in numbers served, the catering budgets for the two galleys are nearly equal.

---

[1] A platform with legs.

Communication between the expatriates and the Africans is notably absent on the Voyager 7, because none of the expatriates speaks the native language and none of the Africans speaks more than a few words of the expatriate's language. Only the chef of the catering company knows both languages. Consequently, he acts as an interpreter in all emergency situations. In the everyday working environment, management must rely on sign language or repetition of example to train and coordinate efforts.

From time to time an entourage of African government officials visits the Voyager 7. These visits normally last only for an hour or so. Invariably, the officials dine with the expatriates, take a brief tour of the equipment, and return to shore by helicopter. No entourage has ever expressed concern about the disparity in living conditions on the rig, nor have officials ever bothered to speak with the African workers. Observers comment that the officials seem disinterested in the situation of the African workers, most of whom come from outside the capital city.

The presence of an expatriate black worker has little effect on the rig's segregated environment. The expatriate black is assigned to the expatriate section and partakes in all expatriate privileges. However, few expatriate blacks participate in the international drilling business and the few who do are frequently not completely welcomed into the rig's social activities.

You leave the oil rig feeling uneasy. You know that there has always been a disparity in living conditions on the drilling platforms. However, you want to make Stratton a socially responsible and profitable company. You wonder how you can best accomplish your dual goals.

Questions

1. What do you think is bothering the workers? What do you think is wrong with the set up of the oil rig?
2. What kinds of inequalities are intolerable in organization? Are any of the workers' human rights being violated?
3. Whose standards of treatment and behavior should a company use in a developing country—theirs or the host country's?
4. Does an organization have an obligation to treat employees in other countries the same or better than they expect to be treated?

The Pursuit of the Ideal

Isaiah Berlin, 1909–1997

Sir Isaiah Berlin was born in Riga, Latvia. In 1921 his family moved to England and Berlin was educated at Corpus Christi College, Oxford University. He went on to join the Oxford faculty as a professor of social and political theory. At Oxford he was the founding president of Wolfson College and president of the British Academy. He wrote extensively on the history of ideas and was a lifelong defender of civil liberties. In 1988 Berlin wrote this essay, "In Pursuit of the Ideal," and read it when he received the Senator Giovanni Agnelli International prize for his work on "the ethical dimension in advanced societies."

At a certain stage in my reading, I naturally met with the principal works of Machiavelli. They made a deep and lasting impression upon me, and shook my earlier faith. I derived from them not the most obvious teachings—on how to acquire and retain political power, or by what force or guile rulers must act if they are to regenerate their societies, or protect themselves and their states from enemies within or without, or what the principal qualities of rulers on the one hand, and of citizens on the other, must be, if their states are to flourish—but something else. Machiavelli was not a historicist: he thought it possible to restore something like the Roman Republic or Rome of the early Principate. He believed that to do this one needed a ruling class of brave, resourceful, intelligent, gifted men who know what they mean. If they are human, they are not beings with whom I can communicate—there is a real barrier. They are not human for me. I cannot even call their values subjective if I cannot conceive what it would be like to pursue such a life.

What is clear is that values can clash—that is why civilisations are incompatible. They can be incompatible between cultures, or groups in the same culture, or between you and me. You believe in always telling the truth, no matter what; I do not, because I believe that it can sometimes be too painful and too destructive. We can discuss each other's point of view, we can try to reach common ground, but in the end what you pursue may not be reconcilable with the ends to which I find that I have dedicated my life. Values may easily clash within the breast of a single individual; and it does not follow that, if they do, some must be true and others false. Justice, rigorous justice, is for some people an absolute value, but it is not compatible with what may be no less ultimate values for them—mercy, compassion—as arises in concrete cases.

Both liberty and equality are among the primary goals pursued by human beings through many centuries; but total liberty for wolves is death to the lambs, total liberty of the powerful, the gifted, is not compatible with the rights to a decent existence of the weak and the less gifted. An artist, in order to create a masterpiece, may lead a life which plunges his family into misery and squalor to which he is indifferent. We may condemn him and declare that the masterpiece should be sacrificed to human needs, or we may take his side—but both attitudes embody values which for some men or women are ultimate, and which are intelligible to us all if we have any sympathy or imagination or understanding of human beings. Equality may demand the restraint of the liberty of those who wish to dominate; liberty—without some modicum of which there is no choice and therefore no possibility of remaining human as we understand the word—may have to be curtailed in order to make room for social welfare, to feed the hungry, to clothe the naked, to shelter the homeless, to leave room for the liberty of others, to allow justice or fairness to be exercised.

Antigone is faced with a dilemma to which Sophocles implies one solution, Sartre offers the opposite, while Hegel proposes "sublimation" on to some higher level—poor comfort to those who are agonised by dilemmas of this kind. Spontaneity, a marvellous human quality, is not compatible with capacity for organised planning, for the nice calculation of what and how much and where—on which the welfare of society may largely depend. We are all aware of the agonising alternatives in the recent past. Should a man resist a monstrous tyranny at all costs, at the expense of the lives of his parents or his children? Should children be tortured to extract information about dangerous traitors or criminals?

These collisions of values are of the essence of what they are and what we are. If we are told that these contradictions will be solved in some perfect world in which all good things can be harmonised in principle, then we must answer, to those who say this, that the meanings they attach to the names which for us denote the conflicting values are not ours. We must say that the world in which what we see as incompatible values are not in conflict is a world altogether beyond our ken; that principles which are harmonised in this other world are not the principles with which, in our daily lives, we are acquainted; if they are transformed, it is into conceptions not known to us on earth. But it is on earth that we live, and it is here that we must believe and act.

The notion of the perfect whole, the ultimate solution, in which all good things coexist, seems to me to be not merely unattainable—that is a truism—but conceptually incoherent; I do not know what is meant by a harmony of this kind. Some among the Great Goods cannot live together. That is a conceptual truth. We are doomed to choose, and every choice may entail an irreparable loss. Happy are those who live under a discipline which they accept without question, who freely obey the orders of leaders, spiritual or temporal, whose word is fully accepted as unbreakable law; or those who have, by their own methods, arrived at clear and unshakeable convictions about what to do and what to be that brook no possible doubt. I can only say that those who rest on such comfortable beds of dogma are victims of forms of self-induced myopia, blinkers that may make for contentment, but not for understanding of what it is to be human.

REVIEW QUESTIONS

1. Unlike Bailey, Berlin argues that there are objective values that all people pursue for their own sake. If this is true, what objective values should all leaders pursue in their work?
2. Are the rights listed in the U.N. Universal Declaration of Human Rights pursued for their own sake?

Case: The Five Virtues of Kofi Annan
Joshua Cooper Ramo

Time Magazine reporter Joshua Ramo frames his interview of United Nations General Secretary Kofi Annan around the five virtues from a Fante proverb. As you read this interview, reflect on the virtues named in this article and Annan as a man and as a leader.

> Se eye ndzeye pa enum yi a, na eye barima (*Gather the five virtues, then you are a man*).
>
> —*Fante tribal proverb*

I. Enyimnyam (Dignity)

"Once my father did something that quite shocked me," Kofi Annan is talking. He is nestled in the back of a royal-blue Mercedes, part of a six-car motorcade flying along the streets of Accra, Ghana. Air conditioning purrs inside the car. Outside, motorcycle outriders scream past, inches from the doors, sirens singing as they race ahead. Annan shakes his head and gives the tiniest of sighs. "I asked them to skip the outriders. I asked for a nice, low-key day out." A grin. The streets are lined with men and women who become ecstatic as the cars breeze by. Their heads flop back, their eyes sparkle and their arms shoot up into the air. Libyan leader Muammar Gaddafi is also in

From Joshua Cooper Ramo, "The Five Virtues of Kofi Annan," *Time Magazine*, September 14, 2000, 35–42.

town this weekend. Local gossips say he has driven across the desert in a motorcade of 420 cars—a romantic, incredible tale in this poor country. Perhaps, Annan wonders, the crowds think this motorcade is Gaddafi's? "Father," they shout as the cars pass. "Father!" They recognize Annan. A nice, low-key day out.

"I was a kid," Annan continues in his quiet voice.

What Annan proposes is nothing less than a world filled with dignified people. A world where Sierra Leonean rebels would have enough innate dignity to not chop off the arms of infant girls. A planet where India and Pakistan would be dignified enough not to blow up each other, where the indignities of chemical weapons would be a thing of the past, where the world's rich would be, yes, dignified enough to worry about the millions of Africans who will die of AIDS in the next two decades. This is the kind of world Annan imagines. It is the sort of world his very presence—serene, quiet, intent—suggests.

Next week, when 159 heads of state convene in New York City for the U.N. Millennium Summit—the largest such gathering ever (and doubtless a traffic nightmare that the city will not forget soon)—Annan will press this idea further. In the past few years, he has been refining a policy that calls on the states of the world to step in wherever and whenever human lives are being consumed in conflagrations of hate, disease or poverty. He has not always succeeded. On his watch, in places like Rwanda and Bosnia, he has seen thousands die as they awaited help. He is haunted by their faces—and determined to perfect his organization so those mistakes never occur again.

He is also determined to plug the rest of the world into these horrors, to make leaders aware of their responsibility not just for their own citizens but also for the health of the global soul. Annan believes that nothing—particularly not state borders—should stand in the way of intervention. He believes that the old orthodoxy that states can do as they please behind their borders is nonsense in a world of borderless information and travel and communication. He has boiled down his thinking to a simple idea—call it the Kofi Doctrine—which has a chance of becoming as elemental to this century as the Truman Doctrine was to the last: Sovereignty is not a shield.

The idea terrifies the Chinese, who think of Tibet when they hear it. It unnerves the Russians. "When we say Kosovo," Annan says by way of picking an example of how the world should step into emergent disasters, "they hear Chechnya." And it bothers the U.S. because, in Annan's view, the doctrine works both ways. Seeing a crime and failing to prevent it are as bad as committing the crime. But who in the U.S. wants to send troops parachuting into every flaming country on earth?

Annan's critics find his outlook naive. His aides even joke about his world view, calling it "Star Trek Planet," after the show on which Russians and Scots worked merrily on dilithium-crystal drives as their ship shot through space at warp speed. That world is as remote as transporter beams. Annan's critics also lash him for his willingness to "do business" with anyone. When he returned from negotiations in Baghdad in 1998 and mildly said he had "a good human rapport" with Saddam Hussein, the White House shrieked. Others said he sounded like Neville Chamberlain praising Hitler. Annan's very decency, some believe, stands in the way of his preventing the indecent acts he so badly wants to stop.

Is Annan's dignity really a disadvantage? Observe, for a moment, Annan in Ghana. His motorcade arrives at a local market, and he discovers, much to his delight, that the Ghanaian national soccer team is practicing nearby. So he strolls over to where a crowd has gathered, hoping to catch a few minutes of the scrimmage. It is not possible. The mob erupts when they see him, shouting and dancing. Annan's security guards quickly press him back into his car. They try to drive away, but the thick, gleeful crowd has the cars glued in place. The Ghanaians risk trampling one another in their eagerness to get close to Annan. "Hey, father!" they shout. "Father!"

When it is clear the motorcade is stuck and the scene outside is growing dangerous, Annan cracks open his door, steps into the mosh pit around him and begins to speak. He is not a man with a loud voice. In the noise of the crowd it is impossible to hear what he says, even from 4 feet away. He stands outside the car for 10 seconds, moving his mouth like a character in a silent film. And having seen him speak—not having heard a word he said—the rabid crowd calms and parts.

II. Awerehyemu (Confidence)

Madeleine Albright was yelling. Aides could hear her from several yards away as she berated Annan over the telephone. It sounded like a jackhammer crossbred with an opera singer. It went roughly like this: "THERE IS NO WAY THAT YOU ARE GOING TO DO THIS. NO WAY." Albright is a savvy diplomat, and the screaming was more of a debate tactic than anything else. (She says she never yelled at Annan. Their aides have a different recollection.) But though she was doing her best to stop him, Annan was going to negotiate with Saddam Hussein.

One of the problems of Annan's job is that everyone has an idea of what he should do. Annan listens eagerly to all of them (perhaps less eagerly when they are screaming) and does what he feels he must. In 1998, as Albright raged at him, the White House had wanted to send Saddam a message: he could choose between arms inspectors or bombs. Annan thought the choice absurd. "I worry about our Iraq policy," he said recently, using the our to reflect the international community. "We don't have one." What Annan did know was that innocent Iraqis were suffering as ineffectual U.N. sanctions hurt all the wrong people. And having seen Saddam face to face, Annan had a sense that bombs weren't the answer. Albright blasted him and told him not to forget how he got his job—a blunt reference to the fact that the U.S. had eased Annan in after despairing of working with his predecessor, Boutros-Ghali. But Annan wasn't playing that game. He did what he felt he had to. Says Albright today: "He feels his responsibility is to make sure always that there's peace, that you can work things out. We want peace too, but we have our national interests."

Annan was bred for such moments. His elder sister Essie recalls how their father, after dinner, would hold mock court sessions in which he would "try" his children for their misdeeds. Henry Reginald Annan was less interested in their excuses than in their comportment. Did they change their story? Were there holes in their logic? Did they pause and stutter and shuffle while they spoke? Kofi, his sister recalls, never hesitated. Often he would collapse the proceedings with a well-timed joke.

Awerehyemu. When Annan, age 21, went to America in 1959 to study economics at Macalester College in St. Paul, Minn., he was wrapped in the stuff. A picture from the period shows a couple of delighted girls fingering a kente *cloth draped around Annan's shoulders. His history has always been for him like that* kente *cloth—protection against the elements, a cloak of awerehyemu. His presence at Macalester was a sign that the world was shrinking—an economic, technological and even, in his eyes, moral event. It would be decades before* kente-cloth *fashions appeared at the Gap, but Annan's arrival in the U.S. evoked a closer global community. He was instantly comfortable. "When he came back [from America]," his sister recalls, "he had a certain serenity. He looked very calm, very cool . . . He knew what he was about."*

What Annan was about was a little bit subversive by Eisenhower-era standards. In a world buzzing with the polarizing chatter of mutually assured destruction, Annan was a committed globalist. Something about America—perhaps the striking disparity between the nation and the rest of the world—set Annan to noodling about the obligations of the powerful to the powerless. The problems of that disparity had been brewing inside his skull for some time—an obvious legacy of an African childhood of plenty in a land with little. America had a searing, sealing effect on Annan's thinking. In the long winter nights, he and his friends would cram into a beat-up old car and shoot out onto the Midwestern highways, driving through snow and ice to debating contests around the state. Annan's speech was almost always the same, a reasoned and moving pitch for global community. To the debate geeks who listened, the young man with the quiet voice was unforgettable.

Everyone on campus knew who Annan was. It was not simply that he was a handsome black man in the middle of the lily-white Midwest. It was that he carried himself with complete assurance. Today his appearance is as much an element of his ethos as his velvet voice or his poetic words. "Such elegance," a French journalist exclaimed after meeting him. "The ideas, the politics, the clothes!"

Annan is 5 ft. 9 in. tall and stands perfectly straight, but with an easy bearing, not a soldier's forced rigidity. He has an athlete's muscular build— left over from his college running days—and a trim weight that can drop as much as 10 lbs. when he is worried, or overworked, or sad—as when his twin sister died a rapid death from a still unknown disease in 1991. And he is always perfectly dressed. When journalist William Shawcross refers to him as a "secular pope," the observation is almost as much sartorial as moral. But Annan's assurance rests mostly in his eyes. Flip this magazine back to the cover, and look into them for a moment. It was often said of Gandhi that he had eyes that reflected the world's sorrows. Annan's seem to hold the world's hopes. He relies on them in negotiations and grumbles when his interlocutors look away from him to take notes or read talking points. He likes to go eye to eye. "He is captivating in the best sense of the word," says former German Chancellor Helmut Kohl, whom Annan has supported as a friend through difficult times. "When he approaches you," Kohl explains, "it is not possible to keep up any barriers."

III. Akokodur (Courage)

In dangerous situations—the kind that would have most of us tingling with a little bit of healthy fear—Annan becomes calmer, aides say. His jokes get funnier; his voice is quieter. People who worked with him in the field when he was running the U.N.'s peacekeeping division say no weather was ever too bad, no road too dangerous, no campsite too open to sniper fire for Annan. He regularly put himself in harm's way to negotiate access for medical supplies, food aid and humanitarian personnel in the world's hellholes. An aide recalls one night last year sitting with him on a Macedonian balcony overlooking Kosovo as U.S. air strikes reverberated nearby. Annan calmly chatted up world leaders by cell phone for two straight hours. He wears a thick U.N. flak jacket with as much dignity and ease as a kente cloth.

The end of the cold war brought murderous burdens that the U.N. has been unable to handle. U.N. troops are routinely asked to plunge into chaos—Sierra Leone, the Democratic Republic of Congo, East Timor. Annan isn't opposed to these missions. He has the courage to order the U.N. in wherever it is needed. But he has nightmares about trying to contain some of the world's most evil men with the resources of a local sheriff's department. He has tried that before: Rwanda, where 800,000 Tutsi were slaughtered by rival Hutu tribesmen; Srebrenica, Bosnia, where 8,000 Muslims were killed by Serbs. It wasn't only the U.N. that walked away from these tragedies. In both cases the Security Council—led, at times, by the U.S.—cowered. But the U.N.'s peacekeeping division, under Annan's leadership during these *conflicts, bungled its attempts to implement the doctrine he would later preach. Annan now wants to ensure that his legacy isn't only a doctrine but also an institution that is capable enough—and courageous enough—to enforce it.*

Last week the U.N. issued a report that reflects the heart of Annan's new vision for peacekeeping. The idea is that the U.N. would call on ready battalions from armies around the world to step into emerging hot spots. These "surge" troops would be trained to work together and deploy quickly. Tactical units from Sweden, say, would be trained to work side by side with Pakistani logistics officers. Lego blocks for international order—but Legos with teeth. While the U.N. would hold to the rules that permit peacekeepers to fire only in self-defense, the definition of self-defense would be stretched. If troops on the ground saw a left hook coming in, they would be free to do much more than duck.

Annan's goal is to formalize peace-keeping, to banish the deadly ad hocery that so often cripples good intentions. He envisions a time when countries will be eager to have their troops serve. His sales pitch is simple: U.N. operations are the best preview of the kinds of battles countries are likely to face in the future, conflicts that are less state vs. state and more state vs. maniac. "During the cold war, conflicts were neater," he explains. "You had client states [that] could be controlled. Here you are dealing with warlords who don't understand the outside world and don't care. Unless we are prepared to counter force with force, there is very little we can do. The problem is that you have countries like the U.S. that will not accept a single casualty. And that philosophy is spreading."

But how do you persuade Americans to grind up their children in a world that seems filled with endless hate? Annan believes it is all about leadership, about explaining how seeing a crime obligates us to prevent others if we can. He won't bash Clinton directly, but he suggests much of the killing that has gone on in the past decade could have been prevented by stronger U.S. leadership. "Bush had no problem in the Gulf—a vital national interest was at stake there—but he had no problem in Somalia either," Annan says. Courage, he believes, will always trump cowardice.

IV. Ehumbobor (Compassion)

During a visit to East Timor last year, a man rushed up to Annan, burst into tears and began recounting everything that was happening. Annan— already overbooked and running late—stayed with him for more than an hour. In Kosovo he sat with a 100-year-old woman who could only say over and over again, "How could this happen to me at my age?" Annan is not a physically expansive man, but he held the woman's hand and listened without moving.

Nane Annan—a slim, strikingly beautiful Swede—had been in love with Annan for a few months when the following happened: "We were walking along on Roosevelt Island [in New York City] one night, and Kofi saw a figure hunched over in a telephone booth. It was off to the side, maybe the kind of thing other people wouldn't notice. There was a young man sobbing in the booth. So Kofi went and talked to him and listened to his problem, something about his father. And for some time after that, we had this young man coming to visit us once, twice a week, to come by and talk to Kofi."

Nane calls his compassion "part of his core. In Swedish we have a word—'cast whole.' That is him." The two met in Geneva. It was, she says, a thunderbolt when she saw him at a friend's party.

Their marriage—16 years now—was a second marriage for both. He has two children, a son and a daughter, from his first. It is impossible if you are standing nearby to miss their deep affection. Stories of their romance charm New York's social world. Annan's friend Richard Holbrooke, the U.S. ambassador to the U.N., recalls a gala where, long after most guests had gone home, Kofi and Nane stayed out on the dance floor, dancing by themselves.

Nane is the niece of Swedish diplomat Raoul Wallenberg, who saved thousands of Jews during World War II and then disappeared after being captured by the Soviet army in 1945. "When you think of what he did, you ask yourself, 'But how come there were so few Raoul Wallenbergs?'" Annan says. "When you talk to his sister—my mother-in-law—she says he was not a daredevil but a very calm, gentle man. Yet he had a kind of inner strength that let him do what he needed to do to save people. But you ask yourself, 'There were all these other, more powerful people—where were they?'"

It is easy—even popular in some circles—to attack Annan's compassion. The argument is that his warm heart, while praiseworthy on an individual level, would be a disastrous global paradigm. As Shawcross argues in Deliver Us from Evil, *his study of U.N. peacekeeping, pure implementation of the Kofi Doctrine would lead to a world with never-ending humanitarian wars. It is an awful paradox that compassion should come at so steep a price. This is why Annan doesn't insist on universal application of his doctrine. What he believes is that the world needs to create a climate in which brutality is the exception rather than the rule. It means using other weapons—sanctions, for instance—to slow killing. And it means giving nations trapped in cycles of violence the tools they need to join the world community. It means, in short, being compassionate.*

V. Gyedzi (Faith)

Many mornings, Annan wakes early. The light is just beginning to creep into the bedroom of his town house overlooking the East River. And as he lies in bed, he begins to pray. "Sometimes," he says, "I ask questions in my prayers.

The world is so cruel. How can people be so cruel? What can one do?" Annan pauses for a moment and closes his eyes. *"I'm still struggling with evil. I still don't understand how there can be so much evil, and I'm not sure that I will ever understand. Perhaps we all tend to project, and if we are not made that way, we cannot understand. But the degradation of the soul that we see with the evil in the world . . . You look at the impacts, you see young people who have no hope. They are destroyed.*

"I think I have always been quite strong and determined," he continues. "People miss that because I am quite soft spoken. But this job placed me on another level. But it is interesting, if someone knew me when I was young, they say, 'We should have known that you were a leader.' But perhaps once you are really challenged, you find something in yourself. Man doesn't know what he is capable of until he is asked.

"But you see Karadzic and Mladic and Milosevic," he says, rattling off the names of three indicted Balkan war criminals. Then an aside: "Once when I went to see Milosevic, I was stuck in the elevator for 15 minutes! After that I would always take the stairs." He laughs and continues, "But when you see these guys, it is hard to understand. Milosevic will talk about his days when he was a banker here in New York City. He speaks English, sounds like a rational, reasonable person, and yet he is capable of all sorts of acts. How do they do it? How does someone behave like such a normal human being and suddenly turn so evil?

"So I ask questions when I pray. What can one do? Recently I saw Paul Kagame, the President of Rwanda. The Organization of African Unity had just brought out a report on [the genocide in] Rwanda that went after Albright, that demanded compensation from the Americans. And I said to Kagame, 'Don't let them tie you up on this. It's nice to hear that you think people should pay compensation, but you need to move beyond it. You have other problems.' The Rwandans said to me before, 'But without compensation, what will happen next time?' And I was just stunned. What do you mean, 'next time'?" Annan raises his voice slightly, the first time I have ever heard him do this. "How can you even think of a next time? You have to ask, What is it in our society that makes it possible? It's absolutely frightening." He pauses.

"And it may happen again. And if it does, I cannot ensure that the world will stop it."

What you discover in Annan's job fairly quickly is that a moral compass is not enough for you to find your way. You are moving too fast, in what he has called "the race to stop the killing." The job requires more than a sense of right and wrong; it also demands a special kind of diplomatic telemetry. It requires faith. You are sitting across from Milosevic. He is prattling on in his wonderful English and recalling his days as a banker in New York, asking whether certain restaurants are still open. He has just finished meeting with *his generals. Surely they have discussed the killing that is under way. What should you do now? Suddenly the moral instinct alone does not answer. You are on your own, trying to find a direction in a world in which there are no marked paths. You are sitting across from pure evil. What do you do now?*

Questions

1. Do you think Annan's "virtues" would be respected everywhere?
2. Would he be considered a good leader in every culture, regardless of his position in the U.N.?
3. What can we learn from Annan about ethical values and leadership in an era of globalization?